W9-DIM-710

# SEMITIC WRITING

## *FROM PICTOGRAPH TO ALPHABET*

BY

G. R. DRIVER, M.A., F.B.A.

FELLOW OF MAGDALEN COLLEGE
AND
PROFESSOR OF SEMITIC PHILOLOGY, OXFORD

THE SCHWEICH LECTURES
OF THE BRITISH ACADEMY
1944

*NEWLY REVISED EDITION 1976*

EDITED BY
S. A. HOPKINS

LONDON
PUBLISHED FOR THE BRITISH ACADEMY
by OXFORD UNIVERSITY PRESS

*Oxford University Press, Walton Street, Oxford,* OX2 6DP

OXFORD LONDON GLASGOW NEW YORK
TORONTO MELBOURNE WELLINGTON CAPE TOWN
IBADAN NAIROBI DAR ES SALAAM LUSAKA ADDIS ABABA
KUALA LUMPUR SINGAPORE JAKARTA HONG KONG TOKYO
DELHI BOMBAY CALCUTTA MADRAS KARACHI

*First Edition 1948*
*Revised Edition 1954*
*Newly Revised Edition 1976*

*Printed in Great Britain*
*at the University Press, Oxford*
*by Vivian Ridler*
*Printer to the University*

PJ3019
.D78
1976
SWTS



# PREFACE

THE origin and development of the alphabet is a subject of perennial interest, even though the axiom of the historian Gibbon, a former member of my own college, that the use of letters is the principal characteristic which distinguishes a civilized people from a herd of savages, reflects rather the outlook of his own than of our age, which has done so much to disprove it. There is therefore no need to make excuses for my choice of a subject for this course of lectures on the Schweich Foundation.

The composition of these lectures has been a matter of considerable difficulty in consequence of the war and its aftermath of trouble. I had been out of England for the two years preceding the invitation to give the lectures and was fully engaged in London for the first six of the twelve months allowed for their preparation; during this period my lodgings were set on fire by incendiary bombs and I was compelled thereafter to sleep and work in my office, where I had only one table for official and private papers. Even after my return to Oxford I had little leisure for research in view of the numerous other claims on my time after several years of absence. Finally, the lectures themselves were given in the winter, while the war still raged, in a room of which the heating system eventually failed, and I can but express my admiration of those hearers who stayed the whole course.

Other difficulties were equally serious. Scarcely a single museum was open and most were closed for some time after the cessation of hostilities; I have therefore been unable to obtain fresh photographs of old objects or any photographs of new exhibits and I have been forced to take all my illustrations at second hand from published works. Here therefore I take the opportunity of thanking all those authors and publishers (notably the Presses of the Universities of Cambridge and Chicago, the Trustees of the British Museum, the Royal Asiatic Society, the Committee of the Palestine Exploration Fund and the Egypt Exploration Society, the Wellcome Trustees, the *Librairie Orientaliste* of M. Paul Geuthner (acting on behalf of Professors M. Dunand, R. Dussaud and C. Virolleaud), Professor S. H. Hooke, Dr. C. F. A. Schaeffer and Dr. D. Diringer) and the *Pontificio Istituto Biblico*, whose illustrations are used; a list is given hereafter. Further, since the outbreak of war there has been continuous difficulty and delay in obtaining books from abroad, and copies of many important works have reached me only after the printing of the whole text. Much, therefore, that ought to have found a place there has perforce been squeezed into the notes, and I can only hope that such patchwork may not have too often obscured the argument.

The lecturer is required to give three lectures, and this number has dictated the plan of the present course and will explain why no lecture is devoted to the Egyptian script, important as it is for the study of the alphabet; for, being compelled to leave something out, I chose to omit that of which I had no knowledge at first hand. I am therefore indebted for anything that I say on this matter to others, especially to Professor B. Gunn, to whom I offer my heartfelt thanks for all the help that he has so ungrudgingly given me, and to Dr. Gardiner for the loan of several important pamphlets; at the same time I cannot refrain from expressing the hope that some future lecturer will fill the gap thus left in my story.

Two points may here be mentioned. First, I have given unusually full references both to ancient, especially Accadian, and to modern literature; the reason is for the former that Accadian words and phrases can be traced and verified only with the greatest difficulty since the current dictionaries are already antiquated and totally inadequate, and for the latter that modern, especially periodical, literature on Semitic and Biblical studies is still an unindexed wilderness. Second, I have followed the chronology of Langdon and Fotheringham (1928) for Sumerian and early Accadian history, although their dates are too high, possibly by as much as two centuries, for the first dynasty of Babylon; but, as the effect of the reduced chronology on other periods has not yet been fully worked out, I have preferred the old and consistent system to a hotch-potch of systems in which this and the new may here and there conflict with one another.

In conclusion, I wish to thank the Trustees for the honour that they have done me in asking me to give these lectures on the Schweich Foundation, on which my father delivered the first course nearly forty years ago.

כבוד איש כבוד אביו

MAGDALEN COLLEGE
OXFORD
31 *May* 1948

# PREFACE TO THE REVISED EDITION

THIS revised edition of my Schweich Lectures contains such small corrections as can be made in the sheets and also a number of ' Additions and Corrections ', in which all the fresh matter which has come to my notice (marked with an asterisk in the text to warn the reader to consult the end of the book) in the last three years is collected.

I am especially indebted to the *Pontificio Istituto Biblico* at Rome for permission to reproduce the illustration of the important new tablet giving the order of the Ugaritic alphabet and to Miss L. H. Jeffery (D.Phil., Oxon.) for several acute suggestions (indicated by the addition of her name after them) regarding the transmission of the Phoenician alphabet to Greece.

MAGDALEN COLLEGE
OXFORD
14 *July* 1951

# PREFACE TO THIRD EDITION

I GREATLY regret the delay, due to ill health, in the publication of this, the third, edition of my Schweich Lectures delivered in 1944, and published originally in 1948 and republished with additions and corrections, bringing it more or less up to date, in 1954. The present edition has the same text with a few verbal alterations but considerably expanded additions and corrections; but little that is new has been introduced since 1967, when regular work on it became impossible. Consequently much new matter, which ought to have been considered, has inevitably been passed over or indeed missed.

I must, however, express my grateful thanks to those who have from time to time helped by sending me off-prints, photographs, and drawings, and granting me permission to use them; both authors and editors have been equally generous. Such are my recently deceased friend the Rev. Roland de Vaux (1962), Dr. H. J. Franken and the Rev. Prof. H. Cazelles (1965), Professor C. Virolleaud (1965), Dr. M. Fitz-Maurice Moor (1966), Professor D. J. Wiseman and the Very Rev. M. Black (1966); and similarly the Keeper of Western Asiatic Antiquities at the British Museum (1960), the Curator of the Archaeological Museum at Amman (1963), the Manager of the *Illustrated London News* (1965), the Editor of *Vetus Testamentum* (1966), the Editor of *Iraq* (1966), the Director of the *Scuola Orientale* of the University of Rome (1966).

In conclusion, I am happy to acknowledge a courteous letter from Mr. Chandler writing from Gothenburg in Sweden (1961), to criticize some points in the previous edition of these lectures and to bring forward two or three fresh suggestions for my consideration for any future edition; I have accepted almost all that he says and have inserted it, wherever possible, at the appropriate place. I am also most grateful to Prof. W. D. McHardy for much welcome help in reading the proofs.

G. R. D.

*12 May 1972*

# EDITOR'S PREFACE

THE manuscript notes and annotated proof-sheets which form the basis of this the third edition of the late Sir Godfrey Driver's *Semitic Writing* were entrusted to the undersigned by the British Academy in March 1975 shortly before the author's death. The preparation of this material for the press has on the whole been restricted to the correction of a number of evident slips and the identification of some of the more cryptic references. I have, in addition, introduced several bibliographical references in places where it was thought that these would be found useful, but in no case has any opinion been included that does not come from the author himself.

Had Sir Godfrey Driver been alive today I feel sure he would have wished to add to or to modify what appears here. In the circumstances, however, I fervently hope that the book in its present form is a faithful reflection of his intentions. זכר צדיק לברכה.

*Cambridge, July 1975* S. A. HOPKINS

# CONTENTS

## I. CUNEIFORM SCRIPTS



## II. ALPHABETIC WRITING



## III. THE ORIGIN OF THE ALPHABET

# ILLUSTRATIONS

## I. DRAWINGS AND FIGURES IN THE TEXT

## II. PHOTOGRAPHIC PLATES

(*at end of volume*)

# I

# CUNEIFORM SCRIPTS

*NAM.DUB.SAR^{RA} AMA GÙ.DÉ-KE$_4$.E.NE A.A UM.ME.A-KE$_4$.EŠ*

'Writing is the mother of speakers, the father of scholars'*

## 1. Historical Background

BABYLONIA has for many years been regarded as the home at any rate of one form of writing, once widely diffused over the Semitic world; and it has been a part of this belief that the credit of inventing that form of writing which lies behind the cuneiform script belongs to the Sumerians, a non-Semitic people whose origin is disputed but who are known to have occupied the southern part of the country by the time of, if not before, the coming of the Semites into that part of the Middle East. The problem, however, is not now so easily settled in view of recent discoveries.[1] For, while a script that was clearly a prototype of the later cuneiform script was used under the first dynasty of Ur (*c.* 2575–2400 B.C.), the earlier systems at Jamdat Nasr, like the contemporary and later systems in Elam, were quite different and far closer to their pictographic archetypes. Possibly then two distinct traditions of writing were current: abstract signs at Ur and Lagash, pictographic signs at Kish (*c.* 2700–2400 B.C.) and in Elam (*c.* 2370–2225 B.C.). As the two systems were practically contemporary, the one could not have been developed out of the other; if that were so, the presumption would be that the Sumerian writing, which was evolved from a system of pictography, owed its origin to the people of Jamdat Nasr[2] and the proto-Elamites.[3] The only plausible conclusion in the present

[1] Cp. Speiser 'Mesop. Orig.' $74^{45}$, whose statement of the problem is here summarized.

[2] S. pp. 4–8.*

[3] A proto-Elamite or Elamite or perhaps some related people apparently constituted an important element in the original pre-Sumerian population of Babylonia, which possibly remained bilingual for some time until the Sumerian speech prevailed. The Sumerians remained in the country side by side with the Semites and held the dominant position in the south (Shumer or Sumer) until the Semites from the north (Accad) checked

state of knowledge is that these two types of script are derived from a common source. It must also be remembered in this connexion that the Indus Valley has recently yielded seals inscribed with a semi-pictographic script showing certain general resemblances with the Sumerian system.[1] Two explanations of these facts are possible: either the resemblances between these various systems of writing are accidental and each is derived from a distinct source, or the resemblances indicate some inner connexion and all go back to a common source; and, if that is so, the question of the locality of that source demands an answer. As yet, however, no evidence throwing any light on this problem has been discovered, and it must for the time being remain an unsolved riddle. However this may be, the subject of the present work is not so much the invention of writing as the evolution of the Semitic systems of writing with especial reference to the origin of the alphabet. The Sumerian system is only of importance for this inquiry in so far as one branch of the Semites, namely the Accadians,[2] borrowed the Sumerian script and adapted it to the needs of their own language; and it is therefore studied here only for the light which it throws, and the effect which it has had, on the Accadian script and language. If, too, the credit of having invented writing may not be given to the Sumerians, it is at any rate their merit to have introduced the art to one branch of the Semitic race, which has exerted so powerful an influence on the whole civilized world; and for this reason, if for no other, their part in the story of writing deserves some consideration.

The reasons for the invention of writing are tolerably clear. The development of the cuneiform script was due to economic necessity, and the form that it took was conditioned by the means afforded by the Mesopotamian river-country. The earliest Elamite and Sumerian records, so far as they can be deciphered, are mere lists of objects pictorially jotted down on clay-tablets with the numbers of each beside them, indicated by a simple system of strokes, circles and semicircles. All such col-

their expansion and finally destroyed their power; meanwhile the Elamites continued to harry the Mesopotamian plains and even re-established their power in some parts of the country, thus helping to overthrow the Sumerians, until they in their turn were driven out by the brilliant first (Amorite) dynasty of Babylon, when the Babylonian language won the day (Speiser 'Mesop. Orig.' 46–7, 68, 152–3).

[1] Cp. Langdon 'Pict. Inscr.' vi.

[2] This term is conventionally used for Babylonians and Assyrians when there is no need to distinguish them.

lections of texts come from ancient centres of cult or court and refer to the property and accounts of the temples, which seem to have resembled medieval monasteries or modern colleges in their far-flung interests, or of the households of the king and other high officers of state as centres of government; for their contents at this time are purely economic or administrative, never religious or historical. Writing in fact seems to have existed for over 500 years before being put to such other uses; the only exceptions are scholastic texts, as yet mere lists of signs and words, required for the training of scribes.[1] The same or a similar phenomenon appeared in Egypt, where writing was invented and developed at approximately the same time, possibly under Sumerian influence. The motive again was economic, but of a different kind: it was the need to keep a trustworthy calendar for calculating the annual flood of the Nile and to give permanent form to the spells and prayers necessary to ensure a plentiful harvest year after year and to transmit them in the correct form to future generations. In both countries a large priestly class devoted itself to the leisurely exploitation of a complicated and esoteric if artistic system of writing. Syria and Palestine could afford nothing of this sort; but the commercial genius of their peoples went to the very heart of the problem, borrowed what was essential in the Sumero-Accadian or Egyptian systems, and adapted it to their own urgent needs.

## 2. Source and Date of the Earliest Inscribed Tablets

The earliest documents, if indeed they can be called documents, hitherto found on Babylonian soil, are small tablets from Uruk of burnt gypsum mixed with sand; in shape they are roughly square with the surface slightly convex and the corners rounded off. They carry the imprint of a cylinder-seal and one or several roundish depressions which are possibly intended to indicate numbers (s. pl. 1, 1).[2] These tablets are as old as the inscribed clay-tablets from the same place and belong to that remote period when the seal must have been serving its most ancient function as a mark, presumably of ownership, of an individual person and perhaps also of a corporation.[3] Such

[1] S. pp. 67–8. [2] Jordan *Dritter vorläufiger Bericht über Uruk* 29.

[3] Such a 'clay-seal' indicating ownership was the Sum. *IM-É-ŠÀ-DUB*$^{BA}$ = Acc. *šá-an-da-ba-ku*, which is explained as *kangu šâ nikkassi* 'sealed, of accounts' (Rawlinson 'C.I.W.A.' v 32 a-c 18; cp. Langdon in *R.A.* XXVIII 120–1 O. iv. 4–17), attached to stores; hence the overseer of the royal stores was called $^{LU}$*šandabak(k)u* (s. Landsberger in *Z.A.* XLI 189[1]).

tablets or documents seem to embody a type of marking very widely spread before the development of writing, but it has not yet been possible to fix their date with any accuracy. Even, too, if they were the precursors of written documents in the strict sense, as their rapid disappearance after the emergence of true writing suggests, it would be difficult to discover any direct transition from the one to the other; possibly the great achievement of the invention of writing lies between them. Yet the idea of writing may well have come from these primitive methods of indicating identity and ownership.

The earliest tablets which can be called written documents belong to collections of considerable size from four sites in southern Babylonia, namely Warkah and Jamdat Nasr, Tell-elMuqaiyar and Fârah; they may be assigned to a period of approximately six hundred years between *c.* 3500 and *c.* 2900 B.C. A few other tablets from the same or not far distant sites belong to the same period,[1] but these four collections alone are of importance for the study of the origin of the cuneiform script.[2]

One of the earliest texts from the Semitic world is a tablet from Kish[3] (s. pl. 1, 2); unfortunately the nature of its contents can be hardly even guessed as it cannot be read. Roughly contemporaneous with this tablet is a large collection of some 570 tablets which the fourth and lowest stratum at Uruk[4] has yielded (s. pls. 1, 3; 2), a tablet supposed to have been found at Umma, and another, known as the Walters-tablet (p. 40, fig. 16) of unknown origin and of the same date*. The third and second strata at Uruk also yielded a small collection of 34 tablets (s. pl. 3, 1). A few isolated tablets from other, in several cases unknown, sites belong to this period, of which the best-known representatives are the so-called Blau-monuments and the Hoffmann-tablet (s. pl. 3, 2). These texts are overlapped by another considerable collection of 194 tablets from Jamdat Nasr (s. pl. 4),[5] which is a small mound situated about 17 miles to the north-east of Kish.[6] All the tablets so far mentioned are in-

[1] Barton 'Babylonian Writing' I xiv–xv, Contenau *Man. d'Arch. Or.* i 207–10, Falkenstein *Uruk* 67–8, and Deimel *Farah* II 73–5 (illustrations).

[2] Cp. Contenau op. cit. IV 1822–4, where the difficulty of fixing the order of these early texts is emphasized.

[3] Arab. تلّ الأحيمر (*Tall-al'Uḥaimir*) 'the reddish mound'.

[4] Hebr. *'Ereḵ* (Gen. x 10) and Arab. وركة (*Warkah*).

[5] Arab. جمدة نصر (*Jamdat Naṣr*).

[6] The considerable collection of proto-Elamite texts from Susa, the capital city of Elam, are assigned to the same period as those from Jamdat Nasr.

scribed with pictographic writing of which the meaning can often be more or less roughly guessed, although they can hardly be read in the strict sense.

The next group calling for consideration consists of several hundred tablets from the famous royal cemetery at Ur (s. pl. 5);[1] a few of these overlap those from Jamdat Nasr or the following lot from Shuruppak,[2] but the bulk falls squarely between those two periods. The last group comprises the very large collection of something like 1,000 tablets from the ancient Shuruppak, of which only 250 have been published (s. pl. 6). A solitary tablet of the same period belongs to Enḫegal, king of Lagash.[3] The writing on the tablets of these last two classes is passing, if it has not already passed, out of the pictographic stage, and the signs can for the most part be identified with their counterparts in subsequent periods; consequently interpretation or decipherment in the true sense begins to become possible.

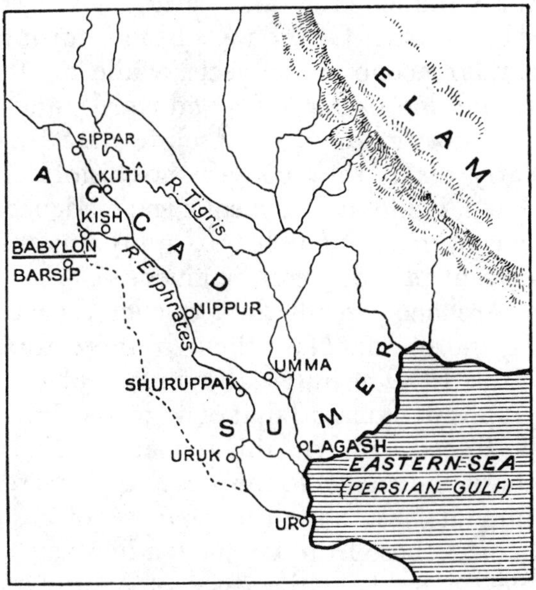


FIG. 1. Sumer and Accad.

All these places lie within the oblong strip of country whose limits are approximately Babylon in the north and the Persian Gulf on the south, and the two rivers, the Euphrates and the Tigris, with their tributary or subsidiary streams on respectively its western and eastern sides. This was the ancient Sumer (or rather Shumer) and Accad, which at this time was under Sumerian hegemony.

[1] Hebr. אוּר כַּשְׂדִּים 'Ur of the Chaldees' (Gen. xi 28, Nehem. ix 7); modern Arab. تلّ المقيّر (*Tall-alMuqaiyar*) 'the asphalted hill' or 'mound' (Delitzsch *Paradies* 226–7).

[2] Modern Arab. فارة (*Fârah*), already described as old in the Babylonian story of the Deluge (Thompson 'Gilgamish' 60 xi 11–13).

[3] Modern Arab. تلّ اللوح (*Täll-alLôḥ*) 'the mound of tablets' together with the mounds of Surĝul and alḤibbah (King 'Sumer and Akkad' 16–21).

The subjects with which the first two main groups deal are economic, as the texts consist almost exclusively of numbers followed by depicted objects. The tablets from Ur deal also with economic matters such as land and its products, agricultural implements, and cattle; amongst them are also a few school-texts. Of the texts from Shuruppak some 170 deal with similar economic subjects, while another 80 are school-texts containing lists of signs and words, and so on.

Unfortunately, no absolute dates can be assigned to these early texts; they contain no historical allusions that can be dated, while the archaeological evidence speaks not in years but in centuries. Nonetheless, approximate dates, sufficient for the present purpose, can be given.

Archaeologically the sequence is clear: Uruk IV, Uruk III–II, and Jamdat Nasr, then Ur, thereafter Shuruppak, and finally Uruk I.[1] The internal evidence of the transition from pictographs to signs and that of linguistic development, so far as it can be traced, confirm this sequence. Thus Uruk IV has writing consisting solely of numbers and pictured objects; the texts from Jamdat Nasr have the first use of a sign with determinative value;[2] those from Ur show a few signs sparingly used as syllables to indicate the cases of nouns and verbal inflexions; at Shuruppak signs representing syllables begin to be used not only for indicating inflexions but also for the phonetic spelling of difficult words.[3] In texts from Uruk I signs are further employed as syllables in the so-called phonetic complement[4] and for the plural ending; and those from Ur use them, though sparingly, to indicate both the genitival and datival relationship and also verbal inflexions. At Lagash the texts of Ur-Nanshe have reached approximately the same stage of linguistic development, while those of Eannatum commonly employ all such devices to aid reading.[5] Again, in the economic texts from Shuruppak the signs are still not arranged in the order required by the sense but are distributed arbitrarily within compartments; this freedom of arrangement is still the rule in Ur-Nanshe's texts, whereas those of Eannatum have the signs arranged in logical order. The texts from Shuruppak, then, may be put one or two centuries before Ur-Nanshe, while those

[1] The strata at Uruk are known as Uruk IV, Uruk III, Uruk II, Uruk I; Uruk IV, which was excavated fourth and last, was the lowest and most ancient, while Uruk I excavated first was the most recent and uppermost.

[2] S. pp. 60–1. [3] Falkenstein *Uruk* 37[2] 38[6]. [4] S. p. 61.

[5] Cp. Rutten in *R.É.S.B.* I 14.

from Jamdat Nasr must be put somewhat before this date. The other collections must be ranged round these dates approximately at the following dates:

| | |
|---|---|
| Uruk IV | *c.* 3500 B.C. |
| Uruk III–II | *c.* 3300 B.C. |
| Jamdat Nasr | *c.* (?)–2900 B.C. |
| Uruk I | *c.* 2650–2400 B.C. |
| Shuruppak | *c.* 2600–2500 B.C. |
| Ur | *c.* 2575–2475 B.C. |
| Lagash | *c.* 2575–2400 B.C. |
| Agade | *c.* 2370–2200 B.C. |

At the same time it must be remembered that, while individual dates may be too low, most before the Cassite period are very probably still too high and may have to be further reduced*.

The writing on the tablets from Uruk and Jamdat Nasr is indisputably an early form of the Sumero-Accadian script, but whether the language which it expresses is Sumerian has been called in question. The chief grounds for this doubt relate to the texts from Jamdat Nasr; for the archaeological remains from that site show Elamite affinities, and the numerical system used by the writers there has been thought to be decimal like that of the Elamites, whereas the Sumerians are known to have preferred the sexagesimal system. Such arguments have been held to support a view that the population of Jamdat Nasr was a non-Sumerian people culturally related to the Elamites but using a type of Sumerian language and script borrowed from an unknown source, or a branch of the Sumerians strongly influenced by some foreign people, whether Gutians or Elamites, but using a form of their own Sumerian language.[1] These arguments are not very strong nor convincing. The original editor indeed of the texts from Jamdat Nasr, in claiming that the language is Sumerian, does not adduce any convincing reasons to support his opinion;[2] but a recent analysis of these texts leave little doubt that it must have been Sumerian. The sporadic use of phonetic complements, the presence of the Sumerian plural sign, the spelling and composition of certain proper names, and other small points cumulatively are irresistible, and the discovery that the decimal system is reserved for use with grain and that the sexagesimal system is employed in

[1] Speiser 'Mesop. Orig.' 72–6. The proto-Elamite tablets are approximately contemporary with those from Jamdat Nasr (Falkenstein *Uruk* 42).

[2] Langdon 'Pict. Inscr.' v–vi.

all other cases deprives the numerical argument of its value. These and similar arguments are applicable, though less strongly, to the language of the tablets of every period from Uruk as also to that of those from Shuruppak. The only reasonable conclusion, then, is that the language of Uruk IV is in all probability, and that of Jamdat Nasr is quite certainly, Sumerian.[1]

## 3. Clay-tablets

The earliest material for writing in Babylonia and Assyria, although plaster and gypsum were occasionally used, was clay of a particularly fine but coherent kind; of this an abundance was found in the alluvial soil of these two countries, while it was scarce elsewhere. Consequently, although the 'clay-tablet'[2] obtained some currency also amongst neighbouring peoples, Elamites and Persians, Vannians and Hittites, Syrians and Palestinians, as well as Egyptians and even Cretans, its use was sporadic and short-lived amongst all but the Babylonians and Assyrians, with whom it persisted for nearly four thousand years.

This clay for the purpose of writing had to be moist and soft enough to take the impression of the stylus, but not so soft that it clung to it or adhered to the writer's hand and hindered him as he worked. At Uruk lumps of clay were found which had been prepared for use, as they bore the imprint of the fingers of the person who had kneaded them into shape, but which had not actually been used; and indeed the impression of the writer's fingers was often left on the edges of the tablet, showing how he had grasped it as he made the signs (s. pl. 13, 1). At the same time the clay must take enough time in drying to allow the whole surface to be covered with writing before hardening. Large tablets, which would require some considerable time for writing, were kept soft by being wrapped in damp cloths which have often kept the mark of their pattern stamped in the clay (s. pl. 20, 1).[3] The clay was not much cleansed or purified, as extraneous objects, such as stones and even date-stones, might be left in it. While moist the clay was kneaded to the required shape between the palms of the hands and was then polished with the smooth

[1] Falkenstein *Uruk* 37–43.

[2] Sum. *IM-DUB* = Acc. *dubbu* or *ṭuppu* (Muss-Arnolt 'C.D.A.L.' 262–3) and *tuppu* (Eilers in *O.Lz.* xxxiv 931) 'clay-tablet'. What exactly *ṣi'pu* 'letter' (Ungnad *B.B.* 364) really denotes is not clear (s. Landsberger in *Z.D.M.G.* lxix 527 and *O.Lz.* xxvi 73, and Albright in *Z.A.* xxxvii 140)*.

[3] Cp. Legrain 'Ur' iii 22 (where a stopper of clay showing cloth-marks is described).

end of the stylus, lumps flattened out, angles rounded off, and so on. If the tablet required was too large to be held in the hand, as indeed tablets soon became and often were, it was laid on a support, as though on a board, and so pressed into shape with the hands.[1] Thus, while in the smaller tablets both surfaces might be more or less convex, in the larger the upper tended to be convex while the lower was more or less flat. Further, if both sides were flat, a large tablet would be likely to be broken across, so that the centre was often thickened and so strengthened with an additional lump of clay which was worked into it, giving it a fully convex surface. Finally, a hollowed mould was drawn along the sides of the tablet, rounding off the upper edges; the lower edges against the support usually remained fairly sharp as they were not affected by this process.

The scribe normally began by writing on the flat under-surface and then turned the tablet over to continue writing on the convex upper surface; for the writing on the flat surface when turned over on a board or similar support was not spoiled as the pressure was equally distributed over the whole of it. If, however, the convex surface, after being covered with writing, had been turned over while the flat side was used, the whole weight of the writer's hand would have pressed the centre of the convex surface hard on to the support and obliterated the writing.

The early tablets, and indeed many of every epoch, were not artificially hardened beyond being dried in the sun. Such sun-dried bricks were hard enough for most purposes, especially if the text was of an ephemeral nature, but it made alteration, whether honest or dishonest, possible by 'moistening' the clay anew and 'rubbing' it[2] when the original writing could be erased and fresh signs or words written over the erasure; such legitimate correction made at the time of writing is attested by many extant examples, and Hammurabi's Code of Laws refers to it.[3] Indeed, early contracts often contain a clause to the effect that, if any other document turns up, it is 'forged' and must be 'broken' or 'destroyed';[4] for 'breaking' or 'destroying' a tablet was a normal safeguard when an agreement expired.[5] Forgery,

[1] S. pp. 34–6.

[2] Bab. *ruṭṭubu*$^{m}$ 'to moisten' (s. n. 3) and Ass. *marāqu* 'to rub' (Ebeling *K.A.R.I.* I 143 R. 19); s. p. 28 n. 1.

[3] In § 48 col. xiv a ll. 13–14; s. p. 12 n. 3.

[4] Bab. *sar* and *ḫibi* (Schorr *Urkunden* 293 28; cp. 238 B 10). Also *napālu ša ṭuppi* is given in a native vocabulary (s. Meissner in *G.G.A.* CXVI 756). *.

[5] C. H. § 37 col. xii a 15–16 (s. San Nicolò & Ungnad *Neubab. Urk.* I 741).

too, was not uncommon*, and one punishment inflicted on the forger was 'the branding of his (forged) tablet on his forehead'.[1] Another consequence of using only sun-baked clay was that tablets might be in very bad condition when wanted for the recopying of ancient texts; the scribe then said in the colophon that he was copying a tablet 'which was damaged in the text' or inserted a note, which was generally written in very small script, in the text that the original tablet was 'broken' or that there was an 'old break' or a 'new break'[2] at that point so that it could not be reproduced.[3] Consequently tablets came, especially if they were important, to be baked in the fire,[4] whereby their durability was increased and the possibility of falsification eliminated. They were apparently laid on a tripod of clay, of which many examples (though not proved to have been used for this specific purpose) are known, and covered with a dome-shaped lid during the baking[5] to prevent blackening of the surface and disfigurement of the text; if large, they were also often pierced that the baking might not burst them open and injure the written surface*.

The earliest tablets so far recovered are mostly rectangular, whether square or oblong, measuring 4–5 cm. in length and 2·5–3 cm. in breadth; the edges are also sharply rectangular and the sides flat enough to take writing, even though never perhaps so used, while the corners are somewhat rounded (s. pl. 1, 3). The form of the surface varies considerably, being now almost flat and now moderately convex; very rarely the uninscribed reverse is quite flat while the inscribed obverse bulges. In this period, too, oval tablets occasionally occur; both obverse and reverse bulge considerably, the edges are fairly sharp and the sides unsuitable for writing. As time goes on, the size of the tablets increases until one from Uruk measures 11·3 × 10·6 cm. (s. pls. 1, 3; 2; 3, 1); the surfaces become flatter and the edges more rounded, while a few with flat under-surfaces are found at Uruk, as often at Jamdat Nasr (s. pl. 4). The

1 Acc. *kanīkšu ina pûtišu ṣarāpu* (Landsberger *ana ittišu* $87_{15}$–$88_{27}$).

2 Acc. *ḫibi*, or *ḫibi labīru* or *ḫibi eššu* (Oppenheim 'Ass. Dict.' VI 196). An 'old break' was one in the archetype.

3 S. pp. 69–70.

4 A cylinder of baked clay of Samsu-iluna (*c.* 2024–1987 B.C.) is known (Speiser in 'B.A.S.O.R.' LXX 9–10).

5 De Morgan in *R. d. Tr.* XXVII (*N.S.* XI) 246; cp. Hilprecht 'Explorations' 487–91. If the 'baking oven' is called *liginnu* (Langdon in *R.A.* XXXI 112–3), what is *ligin(n)u* in letters of the Sargonid epoch (Harper 'A.B.L.' V 447 O. 4, VI 604 R. 9, VII 722 R. 2, IX 878 O. 6)*?

tablets from Shuruppak show other peculiarities, notably those of which the breadth exceeds the length; these were used for the special purpose of drawing up long lists and inventories of property and were therefore also divided into numerous columns,[1] which were unusual at any rate on tablets from Uruk (s. pl. 6, 1).[2] Large and occasionally also quite small tablets of this shape reappear in the latest periods, from the sixth century B.C. onwards (s. pl. 15, 1).

Under the first dynasty of Agade (*c.* 2751–2568 B.C.) the oblong form of tablet became usual with the obverse flat and the reverse convex; but towards the end of this period the obverse began to show some degree of convexity, the edges were flattened and the sides were made slightly concave and adapted to take writing, and rounded gave place to squared corners. This form remained standard in the case of ordinary tablets till approximately the seventh century B.C. Then in the Neo-Babylonian and Persian periods both surfaces of the small tablets used for daily business were bulged and the edges convexed, while the oblong shape still predominated; but old types also still lingered on in occasional use.[3]

In the Old-Babylonian period, especially under the first dynasty (*c.* 2169–1870 B.C.), which was an age of great commercial and legal activity, an 'envelope'[4] was devised for the protection of important documents. This was a case of clay of the same oblong shape as, but larger than, the tablet which it was designed to hold (s. pl. 12); it was moulded round the written tablet when it had been dried, or this was slipped into it, whereupon the end was closed with fresh clay, and a duplicate copy or summary of the text was inscribed on the outer surface.[5]

[1] Sum. *DUB-DAGAL* 'broad tablet' (Deimel *Sum. Lex.* II 341 138 55).

[2] S. pp. 39–44.

[3] The Sum. *IM-GÍD*$^{DA}$ = Acc. *giṭṭu*, whence the Hebr. גֵּט 'bill' perhaps comes, may be derived from the Sum. *GÍD* 'long' on account of its shape (Reisner *Sum.-Bab. Hymn.* xii; s. Muss-Arnolt 'C.D.A.L.' 215); but this is not proved (Deimel *Sum. Lex.* II 787–8 399 184; s. Eilers in *O.Lz.* XXXIV 930)*.

[4] O.-Bab. *irmum* (Schorr *Urkunden* 317 22) or O.-Ass. *ṭuppum ḫarmum* or *armum* (Eisser & Lewy *Aa.Ru.K.* I 270$^b$; s. Meissner in *A.Of.* II 268 and Eilers in *O.Lz.* XXXIV 929$^3$). The verbs are *ḫarāmu*$^m$ or *ḫarrumu*$^m$ 'to encase' (Eisser & Lewy ibid. 270$^b$; s. Christian in *W.Z.K.M.* XXXVI 13–17 against this explanation of these words) and *pitû*$^m$ 'to open' (Eisser & Lewy op. cit. 326 33–4)*.

[5] Other, not clearly distinguished, words for 'case' or 'case-tablet' are *imgurru*, *erimtu* (Deimel op. cit. 782 399 89) and *garṭuppu* (s. p. 74 n. 10), *sûtu*, *širmu* (Hallock 'Ass. St.' VII 66–7; s. Jensen in *K.B.* VI i 268–9 O. 4)*.

The 'enclosed tablet',[1] however, unfortunately often stuck to the case, so that the text of both tablet and envelope was apt to be damaged if not destroyed in opening it. Not a few legal tablets of this period, however, are slightly concave on both upper- and under-surfaces, being so shaped to prevent the inner tablet adhering to the outer case and having its text made illegible; and the surfaces of the inner tablet may perhaps have been sometimes sprinkled with dry powdered-clay to prevent their adhering to the envelope.[2] Thus the envelope had considerable value in protecting the main text inscribed on the tablet both from 'forgery'[3] and from accidental injury; and so the judges in one extant case found that the envelope was injured so that the copy of the text of one of the parties was unreadable and 'they broke his case-tablet open' in order to discover its contents.[4] Any number of tablets might be similarly packed in a special 'sealed case' or 'container'[5] of large size, to which Old-Assyrian texts occasionally refer, for safety in transport. In course of time these cases went out of use, as fire-baked tablets[6] had little or no need of such protection.

The normal tablet was quite small, but occasionally very large ones were required, such as that on which the Middle-Assyrian Laws are inscribed; this tablet measures 315 × 206 × 32 mm., and the text contains 828 lines of writing arranged in eight columns, four on the obverse and four on the reverse side.[7] So large a tablet of clay, however, was exceptional.

Many other shapes were developed in the course of time, mostly for the particular purposes to which they were thought appropriate. The earliest were circular tablets, which were commonly used for school-texts and for those dealing with landed property (s. pl. 6, 2); these were employed in every period. There were also small tablets shaped like eggs or three-sided cones bearing the impress of the owner's seal and bored for a string (s. pl. 10), probably intended for tying on to objects as a mark of ownership. Somewhat similar were lumps of clay shaped like slates or olives bearing usually a religious name, sometimes bored

[1] Ass. *ṭuppu ṣapîtu* (Ebeling *K.A.J.I.* 104 7 122 4–5) or Bab. *ṣipû* (Thompson 'C.T.' XII 33 K. 2034 R. i–ii 2).

[2] King 'L.I.H.' III xxii–xxiii; s. Clay 'B.E.U.P.' XIV 9.

[3] Bab. *šunnû* 'to alter' the text on a tablet (Clay 'YBT.' III 106 34–7))*.

[4] Bab. *ṭuppašu išrumu* (Schorr *Urkunden* 317 22–3).

[5] Ass. *tamalaku$^m$* (Eisser & Lewy *Aa.Ru.K.* II 78$^c$; cp. 298 9–16, 29–31, for a number of tablets in one such 'container' and for the sealing of it).

[6] S. p. 10.

[7] Schroeder *K.A.V.I.* 1–14 1 (V.A.T. 10,000).

and sometimes not bored; the purpose of these olives was often perhaps to serve as amulets (s. pl. 11, 1 and 2). A nail- or wedge-shaped tablet[1] was common in every period. The earliest, on which the inscription was vertical, were very thick and had no dome or head; but *c.* 2600 B.C. the shape was improved and the dome appeared, giving them a definitely nail-like appearance, and *c.* 2300 B.C. the figure of a mannikin took the place of the dome. Then *c.* 2000 B.C. the Babylonians ceased to use this type and the Assyrians took it over from them. By *c.* 1700 B.C. it had been broadened and hollowed, and the text was written transversely across the nail and sometimes even concentrically round the dome; and by *c.* 1300 B.C. the broadening became even more marked and mushroom-like, while the dome became bullet-shaped with a hole at the top, and this form persisted to the end. The Babylonians inserted these objects as a type of foundation-deed in the walls of their temples, while the Assyrians similarly put them into the walls of their fortifications. Prisms, already used by Lugalushumgal king of Agade,[2] with six, eight, or ten sides, became very common during the Assyrian empire, when they were used for the purpose of historical records. Inscribed cylinders,[3] found already in the Sumerian period, lasted into Seleucid times, when they were generally thickened round the waist like barrels; they were favoured by the Babylonians, who often built them in a casing of brick into the angles of temple-walls. Finally, there were tablets of various shapes, such as the four-sided block of clay forming a kind of elongated cube whose height was $9\frac{1}{2}$ in. and whose sides measure $3\frac{3}{4}$ in., dated *c.* 2000 B.C., containing lexicographical information. Others were designed to meet special needs, for example paw-shaped brackets and arm-shaped ledges, door-sockets,[4] circular tablets for drawings, plans, and maps (s. pl. 16), liver-shaped tablets for hepatoscopical information[5] (s. pl. 11, 3 and 4), and so on; some were mere freaks of imagination, such as a tablet shaped like an ox-hoof for a collection of omens.[6]

[1] Acc. *sikkatu*(*m*) or *zigatu* (s. Unger *Bab. Schr.* 7–8).

[2] Schileico in *Z.A.* XXIX 78–84.

[3] Bab. $^{NA_4}$*a-su-mi-ni-e-ti* ... *šá ga-la-la šá-aṭ-ri-e-ti* (Clay 'Y.O.S.' III 4 6–8)*.

[4] Schroeder *K.A.H.I.* II 44, 46.

[5] Cp. Rutten in *R.A.* XXXV 36–70.

[6] Handcock 'Mesop. Archaeol.' 115–16.

## 4. Stone and Metal, Wood and Ivory, Papyrus and Leather

Stone was rare in Babylonia and indeed also in Assyria, though not so much so,[1] and kings had no scruples about 'altering'[2] or erasing their predecessor's inscriptions in order to re-use the stone on which they were engraved;[3] the method was 'to destroy' the text 'with a stone'.[4] Not only soft stone like limestone and marble but also the hardest volcanic rock, such as basalt and dacite, dolerite and diorite, were chosen for inscriptions. The softer stones were used in considerable quantities for tablets with pictographic inscriptions and especially for those carrying inscriptions, notably royal inscriptions, for which some degree of permanency was required (s. pl. 7); for clay-tablets, even when baked in the fire, could not be expected to last indefinitely like a *stele* or 'inscribed stone'.[5] Further, the texts on clay-tablets recording grants of land by Babylonian kings to loyal servants were copied on to boundary-stones erected as visible monuments perpetuating the memory of the gift.[6] Soft stone, too, especially alabaster and marble,[7] and occasionally also onyx and lapis lazuli, was used for encomiastic inscriptions glorifying important persons, votive or dedicatory and historical

[1] The Babylonians used mostly hard stone imported from the hills while the Assyrians found soft stone to hand in their own country. Occasionally *abnu* 'stone' is used for 'inscribed monument' (s. Steinmetzer *Grenzsteine* 100).

[2] Acc. *nukkuru*, which may refer to turning the stone round so as to use the back for a fresh inscription (Haupt *ap.* Muss-Arnolt 'C.D.A.L.' 675). Another method was 'to cover with earth' or 'paste' (Acc. *ina epri* or *piššati katāmu*) the text in order merely to make it illegible (ibid. 457–8).

[3] So a gate-socket of Lugal-kigub-nidudu was re-used by Shar-gali-sharrī and a stone of Shulgi by Kurigalzu (Hilprecht 'B.E.U.P.' 1/i 31, ii 45–6). Many inscriptions include curses against anyone who shall re-use a stone or destroy it (s. Budge & King 'A.K.A.' 1 106–8 viii 63–88).

[4] Bab. *ina abnim ubbutum* (Gadd & Legrain 'Ur' 1 165 ii 15–16); cp. *ša* . . . $^{ZA}$*nārûa* . . . *ina abni ubbasu* (which is an error for *ubbatu*) 'who destroys my inscription with a stone' (Scheil *D. P.*, *Mém.* VI 36 iv 29–v 2) and *matî-ma* . . . *ina abnim uab*[*ba*]*tu* 'when . . . he destroys (it) with a stone' (King 'B.B.-S.' 21–2 4 iii 12–iv 4)*.

[5] Sum. $^{ZA}$*NA.RÚ.A* = Acc. *nārû*$^{m}$ 'engraved stele' and *asumê/îtu* or rather *asumittu* (Muss-Arnolt 'C.D.A.L.' 76, 724–5; s. Meissner in *M.Va.G.* x iv 6 and Ebeling *Nb.B.U.* 4 6), *s(z)umîtu* (Koschaker in *O.Lz.* xxxv 321) or *sumûtu* (Scheil *N.V.B.* 45$^{53}$) 'ornamental stele'*, identical with the Aram. סותא and אשיתא and the Palm. וסמיתא (Nöldeke *ap.* Jensen *Kosm. d. Bab.* 349$^{1}$); also *šiknu* 'monument' and *kudurru* 'boundary-stone' (s. Steinmetzer op. cit. 100–18).

[6] King 'Boundary-Stones' xii–xiii.

[7] Cp. Ebeling in *Altor. Bibl.* I 50–1 xix 3 6.

texts. The lions and bulls and other *colossi* erected at the gates and mythical figures carved in relief and set up along the walls of Assyrian palaces were of stone; they bore highly laudatory inscriptions commemorating the exploits of their authors, and the cuneiform wedges often attained a length of 2 in., while the texts ran over uncarved stone and sculptured figure alike (s. pl. 8, 2)*. Fairly hard and semi-precious stones of many kinds were cut for seals. The 'seal'[1] might be conical in the early period, but the vast majority of them were cylindrical in shape,[2] and these last normally bore brief inscriptions identifying their owners, with the text, which was reversed, most often running downwards[3] (s. pl. 9) as it did on other monuments of stone till the Cassite period (s. pl. 8, 1). Such seals have been found in very large numbers, since every Babylonian gentleman of rank is said to have possessed a seal,[4] and even slaves are known to have had them.[5] Finally, the hardest rock was reserved either for objects in whose case hardness was essential, such as inscribed maces and door-sockets, or for the most important texts; for example, the famous Code of Hammurabi (*c.* 2067–2025 B.C.)*, which ran to 4,000 lines (albeit short lines) or thereabouts,[6] was carved on a solid block of diorite 2·25 m. high and measuring 1·65 m. round the top and 1·90 m. round the bottom.[7]

Inscribed tablets were sometimes of ivory or of more or less precious metals; and several specimens have been found of antimony, copper and bronze, silver and gold.[8] The metals were naturally used mostly for weapons and objects of art, such as lance-heads of copper, swords and door-plates of bronze, bowls of silver, plaques of gold (s. pl. 15, 2) and so on, which were generally inscribed with brief texts giving the name of the person who owned them or of the deity to whom they were dedicated or similar information in the cuneiform script. Bronze

[1] Acc. *unqu* 'seal-ring' and *kunukku* 'cylinder-seal' (Muss-Arnolt 'C.D.A.L.' 71–2 and 919–20). The seal was bored with a hole through which a cord was passed to hang it round the owner's neck (Harper 'A.B.L.' x 1042 O 5–6; s. Oppenheim in 'J.A.O.S.' LXIV 195).

[2] Ward 'Seal-Cylinders' 5–9, and Frankfort 'Cylinder-Seals' 4–5.

[3] S. pp. 38–9. [4] Herodotus *Hist.* i 195. [5] Boyer in *S.D.* II 209[4].

[6] Actually 3,637 lines are preserved, but some five to seven columns, containing about 75 lines each, are missing from the middle, whence they have been erased. [7] Scheil *D.P.*, *Mém.* IV 12.

[8] Wiseman in *Iraq* XVII 3–13.

[9] Place *Ninive et l'Assyrie* III 77; s. Lie *Sargon II* 76–7 v 14–5. Hittite texts have been found also on lead (s. p. 84, n. 11) and are mentioned on bronze (Andrae *Assur* 19; s. Hrozný *K. Bo.* v 6 R. iv 17).

was used also for inscribed duck-weights and lion-weights[1] fixing the standards current in the country*.

Wood seems occasionally to have been employed for writing tablets, since words denoting them may take the determinative sign for wood not only in syllabaries but also in ordinary literature of various periods, both Old-Babylonian and Neo-Assyrian, if this point may be pressed.[2] So tablets made of tamarisk, cypress and cedar are occasionally mentioned in extant texts, and some on walnut have been found.[3] Further, some of the tablets depicted in the hands of the scribes on Assyrian monuments have the appearance of being double or hinged; indeed, hinged tablets of ivory have now been found (s. pls. 25, 26)*.

Finally, both papyrus and leather are known from literary allusions to have come into use at a late period. The word by which 'papyrus' is known, which is of Egyptian origin,[4] seems to be first mentioned in a text of the Assyrian king Sargon (721–705 B.C.),[5] that for 'leather'[6] is not apparently found before the Persian period, while the 'writer on parchment'[7] does not certainly occur before the early years of the Seleucid

[1] Meissner *Bab. u. Ass.* I 360–1; cp. Barrois in *R.A.* XXV 51–2 (Nêrab) and Handcock 'Mesop. Archaeol.' 26, where duck-weights of stone and marble are described.

[2] Sum. $^{GIŠ}$*LI.U$_5$.UM* = Acc. $^{iṣ}$*lê'u$^m$* (s. Steinmetzer *Grenzsteine* 113–14, 236) and $^{iṣ}$*zû* (Streck *Assurb.* II 318$^b$ 332$^m$ 364$^i$); cp. *akî ša ina* $^{iṣ}$*lê'i šaṭiruni* 'as it has been written on a wooden tablet' (Harper 'A.B.L.' I 53 R. 11–12)*.

[3] Lie *Sargon II* 76–7 V 14–15 and Craig 'A.-A.T.' 13 (K. 3044) 5, 32 (K. 5822) 8, 73 (K. 3163) R. 11 (s. Schott in *Z.A.* XLII 207 and Güterbock in *S.D.* II 33–5; s. pp. 72–3).

[4] Acc. *ni'āru* or *niyāru* = Hebr. נִיָּר 'paper' from Eg. **n-ỉ(t)r(w)* = Copt. *ⲡ-ⲉⲓⲟⲟⲣ 'the (stuff) from the river' (Eilers *Ken. Weihinschr.* 40 after Bondi in *Z.Ä.S.* XXXIII 67), like Gk. *πάπυρος* (= Aram. פִּיפְיוֹרָא 'papyrus', whence Engl. 'paper') from Eg. **pꜣ-p-ỉ(t)r(w)* = Copt. *ⲡⲁ-ⲡ-ⲉⲓⲟⲟⲣ 'the growth of the river' (Bondi l.c. 64–7); also Acc. $^{iṣ}$ or $^{šam}$*urbānu* 'papyrus = Aram. אוּרְבָּנָא 'rushes' (Klauber *P.-R.T.* xxvii–xxviii). A curse invoked on those who violate treaties is that their clothing may be *ni'āru* (Weidner in *A. Of.* VIII 20–1 R. iv 15–16). Another synonym is *nibzu* 'written document' (Boissier in *Bab.* IV 92–3), of which the root is uncertain (s. Zimmern *A.Fw.*$^2$ 19, Schiffer in *Oriens* I 34$^{43}$ and Albright in *Z.A.* XXXVII 140). In late texts *u'iltu* (s. p. 222) 'bond' is used for 'tablet' (San Nicolò & Ungnad *Neubab. Urk.* I 752)*.

[5] Dougherty in 'J.A.O.S.' XLVIII 131–3.

[6] Bab. $^{KUŠ}$*šipirtum* or *šipištum*, meaning literally 'missive of leather' (Augapfel *Bab. Rechtsurk.* 118; s. Dougherty in 'J.A.O.S.' XLVIII 125$^{103}$).*

[7] Sum. *LÚ-KUŠ.ŠAR* from *KUŠ* 'hide' and *ŠAR* 'to write'. An Acc. **kuššarru* (Schroeder in *Z.A.* XXX 91–2) or **kuššarû* 'writer on parchment' (Meissner *Beitr. z. Ass. Wörterb.* I 51) has not been established beyond doubt

period (311–95 B.C.), although parchment has a very ancient history in Egypt and some history also in Persia.[1]* Dougherty[2] indeed has sought to prove from the Assyrian reliefs depicting two scribes the one writing on a clay-tablet and the other on a soft material falling from his hands (s. p. 22, fig. 4, pls. 23, 2 and 24)[3] that leather was in use already in the Neo-Assyrian empire, but Eilers[4] has rightly objected to this suggestion that these reliefs do not show clearly whether papyrus or leather is intended. The problem can hardly be solved on this somewhat unsatisfactory evidence, as no such documents have been recovered from Assyrian or Babylonian soil, mainly because it was unsuitable to the conservation of such perishable stuff as papyrus and leather, but also probably because neither was so extensively used as in Egypt and elsewhere.[5]

## 5. Writing Implements

Writing on soft stone or on stone of ordinary hardness was presumably engraved with a chisel of metal, if the stone was soft enough, or otherwise with a flint, and that on metal and ivory was presumably executed with similar graving tools. How hard stone like diorite was engraved is not known; for there is no evidence to show that the Babylonian, like the Egyptian, engravers practised the Egyptian method of boring a number of minute holes and then breaking down the walls between them. Seals of shell and soft stone could easily be cut with flint, which was in common use in chips and flakes, knives and saws. When

(s. San Nicolò & Ungnad *Neubab. Urk.* I 798 on Ungad *Va. Sd.* VI 192 7). That *sipīru* or *sipirru* denotes a 'writer on leather, parchment' (Dougherty in 'J.A.O.S.' XLVIII 110–30) has been doubted as there is no evidence that the word describes any kind of scribe, and neither the Acc. *KUŠšipirtu* or *šipištu* 'missive' (s. p. 16 n. 6) nor the Hebr. סֹפֵר 'scribe' (s. pp. 88–9) is connected with it (Eilers in *O.Lz.* XXXIV 931–3)*. There is, too, no real evidence that *LÚA.BA* = *ṭupsarru* 'scribe' (Genouillac in *R.A.* X 75₆; cp. Howardy *C.C.* 837 549/86) denotes a 'writer on leather' at Nineveh except in the late Assyrian period. The *LÚA.BA* (s. p. 65 n. 1, p. 72 n. 4) is of Assyrian or Aramaean or even Egyptian race, while an Aramaean woman is described as *SALA.BA*, so that they may have been as much translators as scribes (Dougherty ibid. 128–30; cp. Klauber *A.B.* 38³).
*A.B.* 38³).

[1] S. pp. 81–2.

[2] In 'J.A.O.S.' XLVIII 109–35.

[3] S. pp. 20–3.

[4] In *O.Lz.* XXXIV 931–3.

[5] S. pp. 81–3, where both leather and papyrus are shown to have been in common use in Egypt and elsewhere in the ancient East.

they were of hard stone, e.g. quartzite, some harder substance would be required; this was probably corundum or emery, of which Armenia produced the best kind known in antiquity, whether in chipped points or in powder, since crude corundum was in use at an early date in Egypt. All the earlier seals were thus cut with the free hand. Revolving tools of metal for engraving design and legend were introduced from Egypt. Syria learnt their use at the time of the Egyptian invasion of the XVIII Dynasty (*c.* 1580–1350 B.C.), and the Babylonians got them thence in the Cassite age. Three types of such tools have been recognized: a burr, large or small, to make round holes; a disk, of which the edge was applied to the stone, very thin for mere lines and quite thick for bodies of men or beasts; and a tube for cutting circles or, held at an angle, to make crescents and so on. In earlier times the tool would be of copper, in later times of iron, with a flake of corundum attached to or fixed in it. Such a tool seems to have been revolved generally with a bow-string, but may conceivably in the latest period have been revolved by attachment to a wheel which, like the potter's wheel, will have been worked by the foot; but there is no certain evidence of such a device.[1]

The text was not engraved directly on to the stone, but a preliminary 'copy' was made on clay[2] for the guidance of the engraver. Thus the preparatory sketch on clay of a sculptured relief of Ashurbanipal spearing a lion[3] and the rough drafts on clay of two epigraphs inscribed on bas-reliefs of the same king[4] are still extant (s. pl. 16, 3). Further, the text was traced in colouring matter[5] on the actual stone, of which the surface had already been prepared, so that the engraver had only to follow the lines laid down for him by the draughtsman. This practice is well attested in Egypt;[6] and there is a Middle-Babylonian boundary-stone on which the sculpture has already been executed, the surface of the stone dressed and faint lines traced on it in readiness for the text, which however was never finished*.[7]

Writing on clay required a special instrument, which has received much study. This was a peculiar stylus called a 'tablet-

[1] Ward 'Seal Cylinders' 9–10.

[2] Bab. *nis(i)ḫu ša ṭîṭi* (s. p. 70 n. 12) and also $^{is}$*lê'u*; a subsequently made duplicate copy is called *gab(a)rî* $^{is}$*lê'i* (Steinmetzer *Grenzsteine* 107–11; s. Reisner *Sum.-Bab. Hymn.* xi–xii).

[3] Handcock 'Mesop. Archaeol.' 118 (BM. 93001).

[4] Ibid. (Sm. 1350 and K. 4453+K. 4515).

[5] S. pp. 30–1.

[6] Williams 'Tomb of Per-Nēb' 3–15.

[7] Contenau *Man. d'Arch. Or.* II 901.

reed',[1] and it produced a wedge-shaped or cuneiform[2] stroke which was called a 'finger'.[3] This stylus was made neither of flint nor of bone nor generally of wood, but normally of reed; for this is what the name clearly implies, while marks of reed-fibre have been detected under the microscope in signs on actual tablets, and suitable reeds with a hard sheath and a tough fibre grow in profusion in both Babylonia and Assyria*. This hard sheath prevents the absorption of moisture from the damp clay, which has been shown by experiment to cling to wood and so to clog the writing and mar the clearness of the signs. At the same time the wooden stylus was perhaps not unknown; for a note was occasionally appended to a tablet to say that it was written 'with the wood'[4] of such and such a scribe, whose name followed. In any case, the material of which the stylus was made could not stand up to long use without its losing its edge, and a 'reed-stone',[5] probably a pumice-stone, was kept for sharpening it.

No object which can be certainly identified as a stylus has yet been recovered by excavation from the soil for the obvious reason that the reed, of which it is supposed to have been usually made, must in most cases long ago have perished.[6] The claim has, however, been put forward on behalf of several objects superficially resembling one. Thus Langdon has argued that a stylus-like object of bone found by him at Kish is in fact a stylus for writing cuneiform signs, and that a similar instrument found with it is a tracer for ruling lines on a tablet (s. pl. 20, 2);[7] but this claim is disputed chiefly because the

[1] Sum. *GI-DUB*$^{BA(\grave{A}M)}$ = Acc. *qan-ṭuppi*$^{m}$ or *ṭuppāni* (Rawlinson 'C.I.W.A.' II 44 e–f 63 and Langdon in *R.A.* XIV 79 K. 152 O. 12; s. Muss-Arnolt 'C.D.A.L.' 263a, 917a). What is *kîpu* or *kipû ša qan-ṭuppi* (Thompson 'C.T.' XII 46 K. 40 ii O. 37–9b)? The *malṭāru* 'writing instrument' of wood or bronze (s. Meissner in *G.G.A.* CXVI 753) served perhaps for other forms of writing than on clay (s. p. 70 n. 12).

[2] Cp. Hyde *Hist. Rel. Vet. Pers.* (*Oxon.*, *MDCC*) 526–7, where the Old-Persian signs (s. pp. 131–2) are described as *ductuli pyramidales seu cuneiformes*, which appears to be the source of the adjective 'cuneiform', at any rate in this sense.

[3] Ass. *ubânu* (Harper 'A.B.L.' VII 688 R. 11).

[4] Acc. *ina iṣi* (Reisner *Sum.-Bab. Hymn.* xii–xiii).

[5] Acc. *ZÁ-qa-nu-*[*ú*] or *za-qa-nu* (Campbell Thompson 'D.A.C.G.' 169, 191).

[6] Cp. De Morgan in *R. d. Tr.* XXVII (*N.S.* XI) 240², who remarks that no instrument found up to that date (1905) has a point adapted for making wedge-shaped signs on clay, such as the true stylus must have had.

[7] In 'Kish' I 95–8.

signs made with it do not resemble normal cuneiform wedges of any period,[1] and it is by no means certain that the supposed stylus is not in fact a simple form of comb ![2]

The stylus, however, is represented, or thought to be represented, in art on a number of monuments.[3]* First, it is clearly depicted on sculptures of the Neo-Assyrian empire, of which nearly thirty have been found in the palaces chiefly of Tiglath-pileser III (745–727 B.C.), Sargon (721–705 B.C.), and Sennacherib (704–681 B.C.),[4] depicting two scribes writing down lists of booty; one of them holds a stylus in the right and a tablet in the left hand, while the other holds a reed-pen in the right and a roll of papyrus or leather in the left hand (s. pls. 23, 2 and 24).[5] Second, the stylus is apparently represented on a number of boundary-stones (s. pl. 21, 2)[6] and a few seals;[7] it thus appears now single (s. p. 21 fig. 3 A and B) and now double (s. p. 21 fig. 3 C and D) on the boundary-stones but only double on the seals, often in a conventionalized form (s. pl. 22).

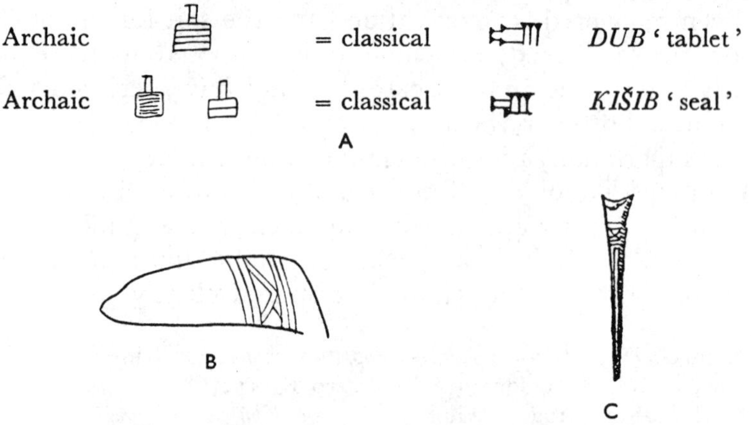


FIG. 2. The stylus in script and sculpture.

The single stylus, here represented lying flat, is very probably rightly identified (s. fig. 2 B); for the same object forms a part of the primitive sign for a clay-tablet (s. fig. 2 A). The same bands

[1] Falkenstein *Uruk* 6[2]. [2] Messerschmidt in *O. Lz.* IX 372–3.

[3] A stylus was often branded on slaves and beasts as the mark of their owner (Clay 'B.E.U.P.' VIII 106 9–10, Ungnad *Va. Sd.* V 94 2, where such a mark is described as *šarḫu* 'fine and large'). [4] Unger *Bab. Schr.* 8–9.

[5] Bonomi 'Nineveh and its Palaces' 277; Botta & Flandin *Monument de Ninive* II 141, 146; Layard 'Monuments of Nineveh' I 58 II 26, 29, 35–7, 42, 50 (s. p. 22).

[6] King 'Boundary-Stones' xiv–xv; s. Steinmetzer *Grenzsteine* 145–6, 166–7, 183. [7] Ward 'Seal-Cylinders' 401–2.

appear on both representations; they may be intended to represent bandages to prevent the splitting of the reed, or, if not, they must be regarded as mere ornamentation.[1] The doubled stylus has been doubted; but the identification is made probable by a comparison with that, now single and now double (s. fig. 3),[2]

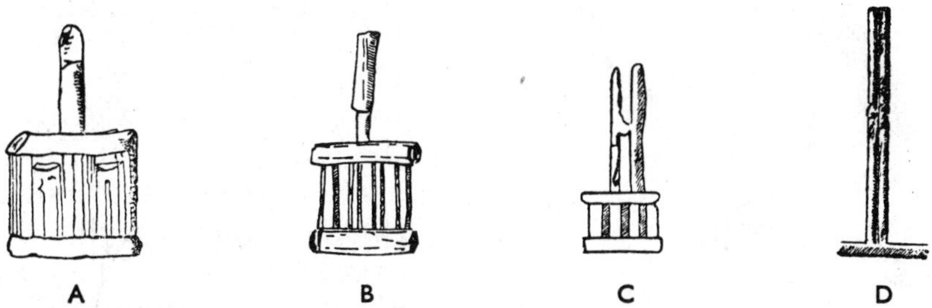


FIG. 3. Single and double stylus on a base or throne on Middle-Babylonian boundary-stones.

amongst the emblems of Nabû (the Biblical Nebo), god of writing, on a number of Middle-Babylonian boundary-stones.[3] If the doubled stylus is thus rightly identified with these objects,[4] it symbolizes Nabû, whose other emblem is two cuneiform wedges one above another,[5] and the base on which it stands represents his seat or throne.[6] Third, it has been suggested that two objects carved on the monument of the Sumerian Gudea priest-king of Lagash (*c.* 2425 B.C.) in connexion with a plan[7] may be a tracer and measuring rod (s. pl. 21, 1);[8] of these identifications the former, if not correct, must come very near the truth, as some instrument used by a surveyor must be intended, while the second may be confidently accepted. In all these representations, however, the stylus is so small or the stone has been so badly worn that only a very general impression of its form can

[1] Unger *Bab. Schr.* 9, who speaks of them as decorated with cross-strokes.

[2] Cp. Steinmetzer *Grenzsteine* 159–60, who suggests a bundle of reeds; but the stylus was of reed (s. pp. 18–9). A similar doubling of an object may be seen in the double baton carried by certain officers in the left hand on Assyrian reliefs (Botta & Flandin *Monument de Ninive* I 40 [hindmost figure], II 82 [foremost figure]).

[3] S. p. 64.

[4] It has been thought to be an engraver's chisel (Contenau *Man. d'Arch. Or.* I 162), but the Roman reed-pen is thus occasionally represented on monuments tied up in bundles (Nettleship & Sandys 'Dict. of Class. Antiq.' 100).

[5] Cp. Ward 'Seal-Cylinders' 401/1302.

[6] Another view is that the two sticks or columns, here taken as a doubled stylus, are two peaks over which the sun-god rises, and that the base, here taken as Nabû's seat or throne, is his temple from which he emerges at dawn (Weber in *Altor. Stud. Hommel gewidm.* II 375–82).

[7] De Sarzec & Heuzey *Découvertes en Chaldée* II pl. XV nos. 1–2.

[8] S. p. 32.

be obtained; no details of its shape, such as the angle of its sides, can be made out. These can only be worked out by experiment after careful examination of the script on actual tablets.

The earliest picture in which the stylus is depicted, if indeed it is correctly interpreted as representing a scribe writing on a tablet, since the stone is badly damaged, is on a plaque of limestone tentatively assigned to the age of the third dynasty of Ur[1] (*c.* 2408–2282 B.C.), but nothing can be learned from it owing to its condition. There are also several sculptures of the late Assyrian period in which scribes are shown in the act of writing on tablets; of these the earliest comes from a palace probably of Tiglath-pileser III (745–727 B.C.) at Til-Barsip on the Euphrates in northern Syria (s. fig. 4), while the rest come from the royal palace at Nimrud of various kings from the same Tiglath-pileser III onwards (s. pls. 23 and 24). The stylus is variously held. In the first it is pressed on the thumb with the four fingers closed over it in such a way that the top protrudes between the first finger and the thumb which projects awkwardly under it (s. fig. 4 B); in the others it is clasped like a dagger in the palm of the hand with the four fingers closed over it to grasp it[2] and the thumb pressed down on it from the other side when in use (s. pl. 24, lower figure) or with four fingers open above it when not in actual use (s. pls. 23, 2 and 24, upper

FIG. 4. Reed-pen and stylus as held by scribes*.

[1] Opitz in *A. Of.* VI 63–4 (*Taf.* iii/1).

[2] The stylus might thus be said almost to be held 'in the closed fist' (Breasted in 'A.J.S.L.' XXXII 242–4 and Unger *Bronzetor von Balawat* 51–2), and not in a loose grip between the finger-tips (Deimel *Sumer. Gramm.* 12–13) or between the thumb on the one side and the fingers on the other side (Falkenstein *Uruk* 6[2]). The sculptures do not support the last views, but the difficulty of using the instrument satisfactorily on the first view, however great, may possibly have been overcome by constant practice*. The modern method of holding a pen is equally difficult for a child and an uneducated person and is but laboriously acquired.

figure).[1] The method in which the stylus is held in all these pictures seems very awkward, and the suspicion that the execution of his intention has proved itself something beyond the skill of the artist can hardly be resisted. The reed-pen for use with ink is held like a modern pen when the scribe is writing with it.

The stylus is clearly not carved accurately enough in any of these sculptures to put the details of its form beyond doubt; for example, it is not possible from them to settle the vexed question whether its writing end was rectangular or triangular. Accordingly various scholars have devoted considerable pains to a detailed study of the strokes and wedges, often extremely fine and minute, as impressed on actual tablets of varying date, with a view to inferring its shape; amongst these scholars Zehnpfund[2] and Clay[3] argue for a rectangular, De Morgan[4] and Messerschmidt,[5] and most recently Falkenstein,[6] plead for a triangular tip, and all have designed and reproduced models of the instrument which they prefer.

The stylus, as plausibly suggested by Messerschmidt, was apparently cut out of a reed in such a way that one piece might yield several instruments (s. p. 25 fig. 6 A adc, a–d–c, b–d–c). It had as one side the curved outer edge, which made a concave imprint in the clay but was so hard and smooth as to leave no mark of fibre in it (s. p. 25 fig. 6 B a–c, C and D c–b), and as the other two sides the inner edges, which were cut flat and left the marks of the fibrous core in the clay (s. p. 25 fig. 6 C and D a–e–b, a–e–c); and it had the end with which the signs were imprinted in the clay cut in the shape of a triangle whose apex or tip resembled the knicked off point of a blunted knife. Already at a quite early date the head at the point of impression was slightly bevelled (s. p. 24 fig. 5 B2 and 3 f–e, E2), as shown by the imprint of strokes on actual tablets, so that the edge came out vertical in the clay. This bevelling remained the rule for all time. Again, as shown by its imprint, the stylus had one side of its tip slightly rounded (s. p. 24 fig. 5 B 1–3 e, and p. 25 fig. 6 B c), possibly to prevent the sharp point from catching in the clay and tearing pieces out with the result that

[1] There seems no reason to suppose that the tablet was held in the right and the stylus in the left hand by the Old-Assyrian scribes because their signs lean forward (Smith 'C.T.C.T.' I 5).

[2] In *Actes du 8me Congrès International des Orientalistes* I B 267–72.

[3] In B.E.U.P. XIV 17–20.

[4] In *R. d. Tr.* XXVII (*N.S.* XI) 234–49.

[5] In *O. Lz.* IX 185–96, 304–12, 372–80.

[6] In *Uruk* 5–7.

the forms of the signs might be spoiled. Originally the stylus was held upright over the tablet and the lines or strokes were made as though with a vertically held blunt needle; but it was quite soon turned over in order to shift the main pressure on

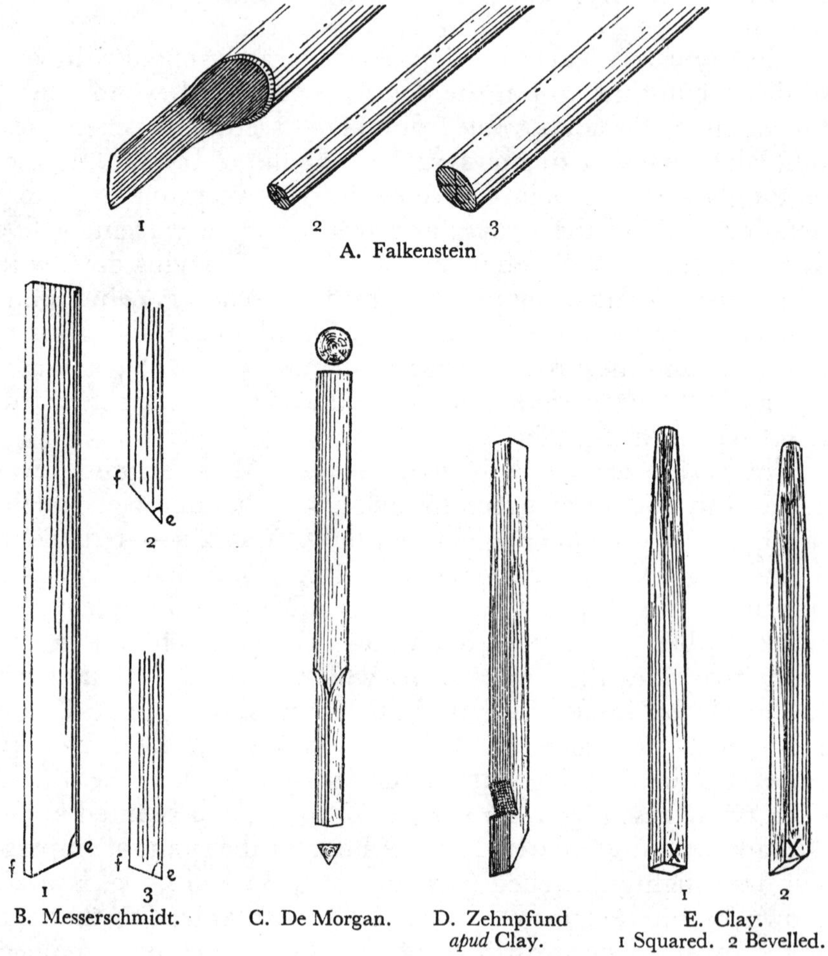


FIG. 5. Stylus as reconstructed.

to one side. This was mainly the curved outer side which, being harder, was better suited to constant use and pressure.[1] The result was that fine hair-like strokes became rare and eventually ceased to be made, and the normal line or stroke acquired the appearance of a wedge very long in comparison with its breadth and deeper at its head than at its tip. In the archaic period

[1] Possibly the horizontal and sloping strokes as well as the angular hook were made with the left side and the vertical strokes with the right side (Unger *Bab. Schr.* 9).

the angle at the point or tip, as Falkenstein's stylus shows it (s. p. 24 fig. 5 A 1), was extremely fine and capable on occasional tablets of producing exceptionally fine lines or strokes (s. fig. 7). This angle was soon broadened, perhaps for the reason that the

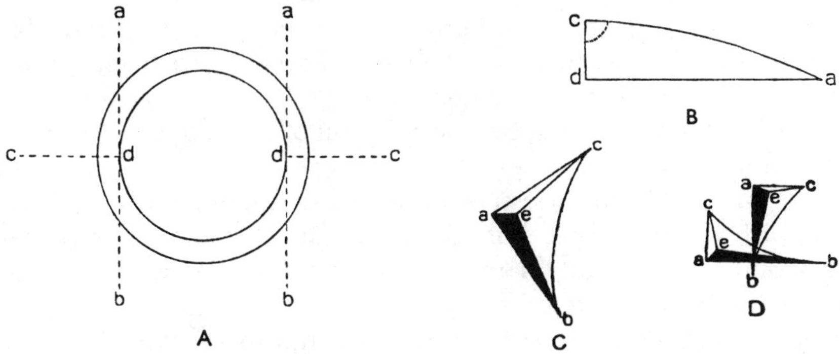


FIG. 6. Sections of reed and angles of wedges.

clear but delicate lines of the earliest tablets did not stand out enough, and they gained added clearness from the broader impression. Thus the angle varied very considerably with the period and locality. In the earliest period the apex of the triangle was so acute that its angle was one of only about 10° at Uruk III and Jamdat Nasr, but gradually rose to 45° at Shuruppak and

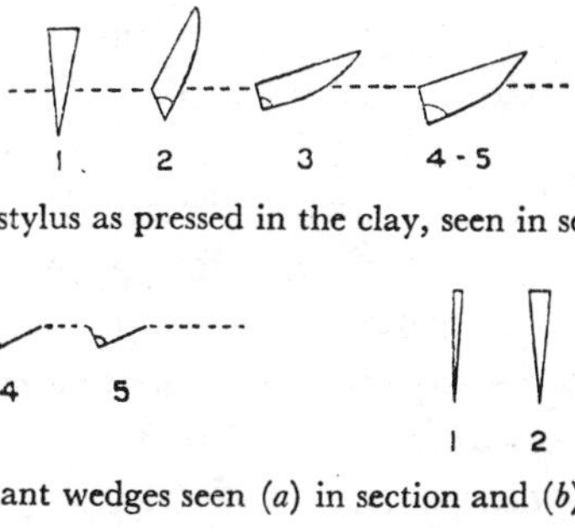


A. The stylus as pressed in the clay, seen in section

B. The resultant wedges seen (*a*) in section and (*b*) from above

FIG. 7. The angles varying with the periods.

ranged from 45° to 60° on tablets of Urukagina, until it reached 90° under the third dynasty of Ur (*c.* 2408–2301 B.C.) and even 95° on the tablets from Tell-elAmarna (*c.* 1411–1358 B.C.), which however lay outside the main stream of development; the angle remained at approximately 90° for many centuries until it was reduced to 80° or thereabouts in the Neo-Babylonian period (s. fig. 7 A 1–5). Correspondingly, the wedges in the clay show an ever-increasing angle as seen on (1) the archaic pictographic tablets, (2) the square tablets with rounded edges of the Old-Sumerian and Old-Babylonian period, (3) the tablets from Telloh, (4) those of Hammurabi, and (5) those of the Neo-Assyrian empire (s. p. 25 fig. 7 B 1–5), only decreasing slightly in the Neo-Babylonian scripts. Further, the length of the wedges naturally varied with the size of the script, but the average for the time of Hammurabi was about 6–7 mm. for the outer edge (s. p. 25 fig. 6 B a–c) and ranged from 4 mm. to 2·5 mm. for the upper end or head (s. p. 25 fig. 6 B c–d); these figures suffice to show the relation of the edge to the base, if nothing else.

De Morgan's and Messerschmidt's instruments both had triangular writing ends, but the angle at the point or tip was broadened[1] to fit the script of the later periods, when the stylus came to be cut out of a thicker reed, resulting in an angle which reached 95° in some texts. Zehnpfund's stylus had one end cut into an exact square which was then shaved away obliquely so that two of the corners of the end formed somewhat acute angles; it was held in the same way as a pen, and pressure was applied chiefly to the upper end in the direction of the point with a slight inclination leftwards. In using this instrument, however, he gave an excessively rectangular appearance to all the signs, as in 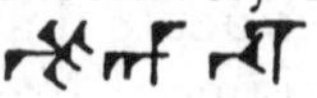 for  (*MU-AN.NA*), which was most unusual; but such a stylus could be used with a little ingenuity if and when 90° was the measure of the angular hook. Clay's stylus, which was similar, was simply a stick with a square corner with an angle of 90°; by holding this instrument beneath the palm of the hand between the thumb and the middle finger with the forefinger on the top and by pressing the angular corner into the clay he obtained the impression of an almost perfect wedge. If such a stylus was laid over on its side with the handle inclining rightwards and turned some 45° outwards and so pressed into the clay, this side and the angle marked X on the figures of his models (s. p. 25 fig. 5 E 1–2) made the angular hook; if the stylus was not turned far enough, the impression thus made resembled the oblique wedge, so that every variation from such a wedge to a perfect hook could be produced with it. In most periods, especially from the time of the first Babylonian dynasty onwards, the stylus apparently had its head not squared (s. p. 25 fig. 5 E 1) but sloped to one side (s. p. 25 fig. 5 E 2): when the top of the perpendicular wedge did not slope (), the hook had a perfect

[1] The head ought perhaps to be cut away slantwise or bevelled not only from the left but also from the right edge (Unger *Bab. Schr.* 9).

right angle (); but when it was sloped () the stylus would be so cut that the angle of the hook might be less than a right angle () since, when the top was perfectly square, the end of the hook was apt to spread more than the scribe might like. The angle of the hook varied according to this slope: the greater the bevel at the top of the stylus, the smaller the angle of the hook in the clay. To prolong the horizontal wedges for the purpose of filling out partly unwritten lines,[1] since the scribes abhorred a vacuum, the handle of the stylus was lowered on to the clay so that a wedge or stroke of the same length as the stylus itself could be produced. Similarly, the stylus was simply laid lengthwise across the tablet, especially small tablets, for ruling long lines across it; there would therefore be no need of a special tracer for this purpose.

On the earliest tablets the scribe proceeded down the tablet as he wrote the text, with his hand gradually advancing towards himself; he had then to hold the stylus with the upper end inclined towards himself in order that he might look over and down it and so keep the point of impression in view. When he came subsequently to write the signs across the tablet from left to right, he held the stylus slanting for the same reason. This slant is shown by the fact that, while the wedge-shaped head is equally poised in signs engraved on stone (), it reaches farther on the under-side than on the upper-side when imprinted in clay ( or ).

Further, each row or 'line of writing'[2] on a clay-tablet may be separated from the next by a line drawn across it from left to right; this line is simply an ordinary wedge-shaped sign prolonged and tapering to a point. It has been thought that the instrument used for drawing it was not the usual stylus but a spatula or tracer,[3] but there seem to be no sufficient grounds for supposing that the same stylus could not be used for these lines as for the strokes in the signs; it was necessary only to set its tip or point in the clay as a pivot and then to let down the handle so that its sharp edge came down on to the clay and could be pressed into it to produce a straight line like a furrow across the surface of the tablet. Obviously, too, the stylus could be roughly drawn, e.g. cross-wise or in a triangle, across the tablet to make the coarse lines with which a text was cancelled[4]

[1] Like the *litterae dilatabiles* in Hebrew Bibles.

[2] Possibly Acc. *tikip* or *tiqip santakkī* or *sattakkī* (Muss-Arnolt 'C.D.A.L.' 787b, 1158b, s. Streck *Assurbanipal* II 422)*.

[3] S. pp. 21, 32.

[4] Reisner *Sum.-Bab. Hymn.* xiv–xv; s. Weidner in *A. Of.* XII 50 on Schroeder *K.A.V.I.* 14 I R. viii *ad finem* where twenty-one lines of text have

(s. pl. 18, 4); and it could be used also for the erasure[1] of single incorrect signs by rubbing them out with its hard and smooth outer surface[2] or with the rounded head which was especially suitable for this purpose.[3]

At the same time such a stylus as one or other of these just described was probably not the sole implement in the hands

FIG. 8. Archaic numerical signs.

of the scribes. First, several signs which the ordinary stylus, an instrument designed properly for a linear script, cannot have made appear in many early texts. Thus in the earliest Sumerian and Elamite texts numbers are represented and continue till the third dynasty of Ur (*c.* 2408–2301 B.C.) to be represented by circular and semicircular marks in the clay (s. fig. 8) which generally show no imprint of fibre, although its marks can be traced occasionally in such signs on tablets from Uruk I. Similar circular and semi-circular marks appear as check-marks in accounts and lists of property on tablets of subsequent periods.[4] At Uruk a stylus having a rounded end with a diameter of about 4 mm. for the units and tens and another with one of 8–11 mm. for the sixties and hundreds and other high numbers seem indeed to have been necessary;[5] in subsequent periods, so long as the numbers continue to be represented by circles and the like, one other stylus with a suitably blunted or rounded end[6] or the wrong end of the ordinary instrument similarly rounded[7] may have served the scribe's purpose. The stylus was pressed perpendicularly in making the

been cancelled, and Jean *T. C.*, *Louvre* XI 222 for a completely cancelled tablet.

[1] Acc. *pussusu ša qan-ṭuppi* (Deimel *Sum. Lex.* II 340 138 22) or *marāqu* (s. p. 9 n. 1). Presumably *puṣṣû ša qan-ṭuppi* 'to whiten, of a stylus' is to wipe it clean when clogged (Thompson, 'C.T.' XII 14 a 8, 49 d 35).

[2] Messerschmidt in *O. Lz.* IX 311; cp. De Morgan in *R. d. Tr.* XXVII (*N.S.* XI) 242.

[3] S. pp. 9–10. That 'he will not erase (his) written name' (Ass. *šuma šaṭra lâ ipašiṭ*) is a prayer commonly addressed by the scribe to the user of a tablet (s. Meissner in *Ao.T.U.* II/i 72 R. iv 4; cp. C. H. xxvi b 33–4).

[4] Clay 'B.E.U.P.' XIV 16–7.

[5] Falkenstein *Uruk* 7.

[6] De Morgan in *R. d. Tr.* XXVII (*N.S.* XI) 245 and Messerschmidt in *O. Lz.* IX 309–11.

[7] The Lat. *vertere stilum* similarly means 'to make an erasure', as in *saepe stilum vertas, iterum quae digna legi sint scripturus* (Horace *Sat.* I x 72–3).

circles and leaning lengthwise when making the semi-elliptical signs into the clay. Second, archaic tablets from Uruk show writing with thin wedges of different thicknesses; one tablet from Uruk III seems to have been written with two distinct instruments, a fine on the obverse and a coarse on the reverse side.[1] Obviously, too, the ordinary stylus was not suited to any kind of drawing, a sketch in the middle of a tablet,[2] a plan,[3] or a map (s. pl. 16),[4] or other work requiring fine or curved lines*, even if it could be roughly adapted to such purposes, and an instrument shaped like a blunt needle was more probably employed for them.[5] It may also be added that the signs on many Neo-Babylonian tablets do not show the usual sharp or clear-cut lines characteristic of most cuneiform texts; this bluntness may be due to the fact that the stylus was not properly sharpened or that some less suitable instrument was substituted for it.[6]

Clearly, therefore, a single stylus cannot have served all purposes in the archaic period and, even though one type may have sufficed for ordinary writing in subsequent periods, it must have varied in shape as much as the wedges themselves according to the period and the custom of the individual scribe or the school to which he may have belonged; and a special stylus must almost certainly have been necessary for particular purposes. Indeed, the double stylus on seals and boundary-stones[7] suggests that such functionaries may often have provided themselves with varying types for use according to need, as the Egyptian scribes seem to have kept several reed-pens at hand in their writing outfits. The stylus also without doubt easily became worn and lost its edge, so that an addional one would always be useful. Further, both rectangular and triangular

[1] Falkenstein *Uruk* 6[3].

[2] Such as a sketch of a palm-tree in the middle of a contract for work on an orchard (Krückmann *Rechts- und Verwaltungsurkunden* 135).

[3] Such as cadastral plans (Scheil *Sippar* 125–6).

[4] Sum. ${}^{GI\check{S}}$*ḪAR* = Acc. *uṣurtu*$^{m}$ (Handcock 'C.T.' XXXI 14 K. $2089_5$) or *iṣirtu*$^{m}$ (Schorr *Urkunden* 275 8); cp. C. H. xxiv b 91 xxv b 73 xxvi b 9, 31 where *uṣurātu* are 'reliefs' engraved on a monument (s. Steinmetzer *Grenzsteine* 118).

[5] Such a tablet was called ${}^{IM}$*DUB ša ṣalmānu* 'clay-tablet with pictures' (Ungnad *Va. Sd.* VI 120 10, 12) for which *GI-MEŠ ša ṣalmānu* 'reeds for pictures' (ibid. 5), presumably styluses shaped for drawing fine lines, were required (s. San Nicolò *Rechtsquellen* 121[1]).

[6] Cp. Messerschmidt in *O. Lz.* IX *Abb.* 12, De Morgan in *R. d. Tr.* XXVII (*N.S.* XI) 248/39, Clay in 'B.E.U.P.' XIV 19, and Chiera & Cameron 'They Wrote On Clay' 70 for examples of writing on clay imitated by modern scholars from ancient texts.

[7] S. p. 20.

instruments may have been used at the whim of the writer; for, if the modern scholar can produce copies that are perfect so far as they can be studied in photographs with either type (s. pl. 27), there is no reason to doubt the ancient scribe's ability to use either with equal skill.

Again, Aramaic sentences are added to the cuneiform texts of a certain number of commercial tablets of the Neo-Assyrian and Neo-Babylonian periods (s. pl. 17); and there are also a few unbaked clay-tablets of the latest period, dated *c.* 140–80 B.C., with Accadian words on one side and Greek uncial transliterations of them on the other side (s. pl. 18, 1).[1] The Aramaic notes are sometimes written in ink and sometimes scratched, as the Greek words always are, on the clay. The strokes then show no trace of fibre, so that they were probably made with a needle or similar instrument; and, as the coarse lines show, this must have been blunt. Moreover, they are very lightly impressed and probably made therefore after the clay had hardened; this suggestion agrees with the fact that a needle, unlike a stylus, works ill in moist and therefore soft clay. Further, the Aramaic endorsements are generally upside down in relation to the cuneiform text;[2] and this fact too suggests that they were added some time after it, possibly by a different scribe, in the dry hard clay. For, if they had been written simultaneously with the cuneiform text, they would surely have been put right way up on the tablet.[3]

The writing of cuneiform signs on clay-tablets in ink with a reed-pen[4] was extremely rare; but both Assyrians[5] and Hittites[6]

FIG. 9. Cuneiform inscription painted on glazed earthenware.

occasionally used ink for brief notes. In the Assyrian form the wedge becomes T-shaped, as in  for , after the fashion of signs as painted on pottery (s. fig. 9); in the Hittite forms

[1] Pinches in 'P.S.B.A.' XXIV 108–19 (s. p. 46); cp. Sayce ibid. 120–5 and Van der Meer in *A.Of.* XIII 125–6.

[2] These endorsements were usually added towards the end of the text and so near the bottom of the tablet; possibly therefore the scribe grasped the upper half as larger and easier to hold while he scratched the new text on the lower half, now become the top of the tablet.

[3] S. p. 122.

[4] S. pp. 85–6.

[5] Schroeder *K.A.V.I.* 77 and Ungnad *Va. Sd.* I 64; s. Bezold 'Catalogue' III 1064 (K. 10100) and IV 1565 (D.T. 273).

[6] Forrer in *Z.D.M.G.* LXXVI 180.

the wedge shows three inner edges which come together in a central point and three outer edges forming a triangle ( ▽ ); the modern scholar, reproducing such a sign in ink on paper, represents middle lines between the two (Y), but the Assyrian scribes drew the inner lines (Y) and the Hittite scribes drew the outer lines (▽). Ink, too, would have been employed on wooden tablets.[1] Cuneiform inscriptions are also occasionally painted on coloured glazed pottery, in very dark brown or black ink[2] or else dull blue-grey tints or in white paint on colour[3] (s. p. 30 fig. 9). Pieces of earthenware thus inscribed have been found at Asshur[4] and bear the names of various Assyrian kings from Adad-nirāri I (*c.* 1306–1290 B.C.) to Ashur-nāṣir-apli (*c.* 884–859 B.C.). Here the heads of the wedges of the cuneiform script have become for the most part almost mere strokes (⊢ for ➤— and ≺ for ❬), so that it acquires an ugly spidery appearance, not unlike that occasionally found on Assyrian inscriptions when the material is lapis lazuli, alabaster or onyx.[5] In all cases of ink or paint some sort of reed-pen must have been used.[6]

Whether the stylus was fixed in a holder is uncertain; for the identification of an hollowed object of polished shell from Uruk as such is quite uncertain (s. pl. 20, 3).[7] When not in use, however, the writing implements were kept in a 'case',[8] which was carried 'in the sash' or 'waistband'[9] as the Hebrew scribe carried his 'by his side',[10] to ensure that its edges and point suffered no damage. This case was usually of leather, if the determinative *KUŠ* 'leather' prefixed to the Sumerian word denoting it may be trusted, and this is indeed the obvious material for it; but none have been recovered by excavation, so that the point cannot yet be settled.

[1] S. p. 16. For smearing with clay or wax like Greek and Roman tablets see p. 80 n. 1 and additions to p. 16.

[2] The brown colour may be that of black ink changed by the firing or as seen through the glaze.

[3] Smith 'Ass. Disc.'[2] 79, Andrae 'Coloured Ceramics' pp. 22–3 (pl. 6), and Thompson in 'A.A.A.' XVIII pls. xxix–xxx, xxxii. The Ass. *šiṭir burummê* is not 'coloured writing' (Smith 'Sennacherib' $70–1_{64}$) but 'the writing of the firmament' where the plan of Nineveh, to which the phrase refers, was laid up from the beginning of the world (cp. Meissner *Bab. u. Ass.* II 110)*.

[4] Andrae op. cit. p. 9 (fig. 1), p. 27 (pl. 8), p. 70 (pls. 31–2).

[5] Messerschmidt *K.A.H.I.* I 31–3, 35–6, 53–4.

[6] S. pp. 85–6.

[7] Nies & Keiser 'B.I.N.' II 56.

[8] Sum. $^{KUŠ}$*TÙN-GI-DUB*$^{BA.A}$ = Acc. *ta*(?)-*kal*-[*ti ṭup-pi*] (Rawlinson 'C.I.W.A.' v 27 c–d 8) and Sum. $^{KUŠ}$*DÙG.GAN-DUB*$^{BA.A}$ = Acc. *tuk-kan qa-an ṭup-pi* (?) (ibid. II 44 e–f 63).

[9] Acc. *ina rikis qabli* (Jensen in *KB* VI i 268–9 O. 5).

[10] S. pp. 86–7.

Two instruments of precision, namely the calculating 'board'[1] and the 'measuring rod',[2] which too, at any rate originally, was of reed[3] (s. pl. 21, 1), may perhaps be mentioned, even though they do not properly enter into the present discussion.

Late copies of early inscriptions are very common (s. pl. 18, 2 and 3). Many bricks recovered from the foundations of buildings and carrying brief records of the construction or repair of the edifice in or under which they have lain embedded, however, are remarkable for the numerous copies of them, each so close a replica of the others that the conclusion that many have

FIG. 10. Text set up with movable signs.

come from a single die is irresistible.[4] In fact, so exact are the duplicate copies that they exhibit over and over again the peculiarities of the script and even the very mistakes of the original text. The probability is that the lettering was first cut in wood and then imprinted on a die or stamp of clay while this was still moist enough to take the impression, in which the text was of course reversed; and the suggestion that such dies were used is proved not only by the fact that the marks of the die can still be traced on the hard-baked brick[5] but also by the discovery of actual dies made of clay (s. pl. 19) of Sargon (*c.* 2751–2696 B.C.), Narâm-Sin (*c.* 2671–2634 B.C.), and Shar-gali-sharrī (*c.* 2633–2610 B.C.) kings of Agade.[6] On the earliest of these bricks so far recovered, those of Urgur, ruler of Ur (whose date is uncertain),[7] and of Irishum I, king of Assyria

[1] Acc. *šukâmu* and *šukammu* (Bezold *Glossar* 269; s. p. 21). The word has also been translated 'intelligence' (Dhorme in *R.A.* XI 109–15 i 10) and 'written sign' (Landsberger in *Z.A.* XLIII 60–1 xix 205) and 'stylus' (Pinckert *Nebo* 27–8 5 4).

[2] S. p. 21. Sum. *$^{GI}$MAŠ.GAR* and *$^{GI}$NINDÁ.GÁN* (Deimel *Sum. Lex.* II 85/171, 273) = Acc. *$^{GI}$ni(n)danaku* (Pinckert ibid. 25 iv 8) or *$^{GI}$nindanaqqu* (Deimel; s. Ungnad in *Z.A.* XXXI 257) and Sum. *GI–GUB.GUB$^{BA}$* = Acc. *qan mindati* (Reisner *Sum.-Bab. Hymn.* 6 R. 17–18); but *ni(n)danaku* is 'surveyor' in texts from Elam (Scheil *A.J.S.* 115 3), while *$^{is}$mindatu* and *$^{is}$taiyāru* are 'measuring rod' in those from Nuzi (Koschaker *N.K.Ru.* $73^{1}$).

[3] Rawlinson 'C.I.W.A.' IV$^{2}$ 14 3 8.

[4] Schroeder in *Z.A.* XXXIV 157–61.

[5] Schroeder *K.A.H.I.* II 39 (Ass. 17877b).

[6] Hilprecht 'B.E.U.P.' I i 15 and Lloyd 'Twin Rivers' 33–4.

[7] King 'C.T.' XXI 2–6.

(*c.* 2150 B.C.),[1] the signs consist of lines with little or no heads, as in 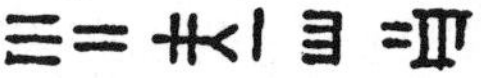 for  *I-ri-šu-um*; these closely resemble those written in ink or painted on pottery.[2] Occasionally block-letters, like movable type, seem to have been used in making the dies;[3] for the alinement is uneven and the spacing irregular and, most important of all, letters occasionally appear askew (like  for 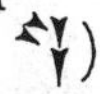) or upside down (like  for  and  for ).[4] The Assyrians therefore came very near to the printing art but failed to exploit the possibilities of their own invention.

Occasionally, too, an impression or 'squeeze'[5] of an ancient inscription was taken on the principle of the seal, with which the Babylonians were thoroughly familiar. So a Neo-Babylonian scribe of the sixth century B.C. made a copy of an archaic text of Shar-gali-sharrī which he had found in the palace of Narâm-Sin at Agade, adding a note on the back of his squeeze to say what he had done (s. pl. 18, 3).[6] On this squeeze the characters are raised in relief and the text is reversed, as on stamps and seals, so that it must be read backwards.

## 6. The Formation of Pictographic and Cuneiform Signs

The earliest pictographic signs were made by drawing a pointed instrument or perhaps the pointed tip of the stylus through the clay like a pen running over paper; but, as this pushed its way forward, the clay tended to be heaped up in front of the tip and so to blur the lines. It was also liable to be torn out where the lines crossed one another, so that the shape of the signs was further obscured. The scribes therefore began to impress the head of the stylus like a die or stamp, though sideways, into the clay; and this development was hastened by

[1] Schroeder *K.A.H.I.* II 9. [2] S. pp. 30–1.

[3] The signs were perhaps stamped individually by hand and not fixed in a holder and stamped altogether on the die, as crooked signs would hardly have kept their place in any such instrument.

[4] Schroeder *K.A.H.I.* II 149; cp. ibid. II $159_2$ (which has one sign not only erroneously written but also standing on its head). The second sign, which appears upside down, is seen when turned rightway up to be reversed; the reason for this incomplete inversion was perhaps the engraver's subconscious feeling that the two horizontal strokes had to come at the front of the sign. It must surely therefore have been cut separately from the others; these too then presumably were all separately made.

[5] Acc. *zi'pu* or *zîpu* 'mould' (Rawlinson 'C.I.W.A.' III 13 4 24 = King 'C.T.' XXVI 27 vii 16) and 'squeeze' (s. Landsberger in *O.Lz.* XXVI 73).

[6] Hilprecht 'Explorations' 516–17.

the speed and simplicity of the operation. Thereby the original picture ceased to be recognizable as the signs degenerated into mere clusters of wedges set at various angles to one another*.

The customs or caprices of the scribes in developing the cuneiform script have been laid bare by the examination of numerous tablets of differing epochs and districts.[1] If the scribe made the stroke with the head of the stylus, the resulting impression was wedge-shaped; if he made it with its side or edge, it was almost rectangular. In tablets of the third dynasty of Ur (*c.* 2408–2301 B.C.) the mark of the reed-fibre is always on the left, the smooth impression always on the right side of the wedge. As the scribe wrote more with the flat surface, the right angle of the horizontal stroke faced downwards ( , rarely if ever ) and to the right side of vertical strokes ( and , never or ). It may also be noticed that the scribes so late as the time of Urukagina had not yet developed the angular head so characteristic of classical signs; they wrote for *IGI* 'eye'. Further, tablets of the first Babylonian dynasty (*c.* 2169–1870 B.C.) occasionally show a peculiar wedge with elongated lines projecting at either side of the head ( for ), made apparently by lightly scratching the clay with the sharp tip of the stylus.

Theoretically strokes pointing in every direction were possible, but in practice those pointing from right to left were avoided because they gave the scribe the trouble of reversing the direction of the stylus which he normally held in such a way as to make strokes pointing only from left to right. Thus some eight types of cuneiform stroke were available (s. fig. 11); of these *a* and *b* survived only in a couple of signs in the time of Urukagina; by the period of Ur *b* had fallen into disuse and *a* had been replaced by *h* or *g* in consequence of the turning of the tablet 90° backwards. Soon afterwards *h* became obsolete, so that only *c d e f g* remained in use.

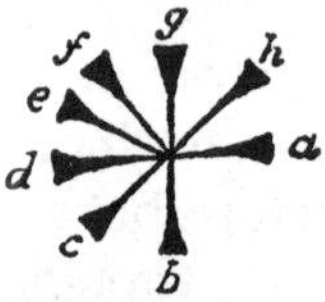


FIG. 11. Possible strokes.

Another important alteration was the angle at which the tablet was held while being inscribed, and it requires careful explanation, as it is vital for understanding the changed direction of the strokes or wedges effected during the transition from pictographs to signs.[2] The earliest tablet was small enough to be held in the palm of the left hand where it rested

[1] Cp. Deimel *Sumer. Gramm.* 11–12. [2] Cp. Hooke in 'Antiquity' XI 274–6.

at an angle of 45° to the body, while the signs were impressed on it as though it was more or less vertical (s. fig. 12 A). When

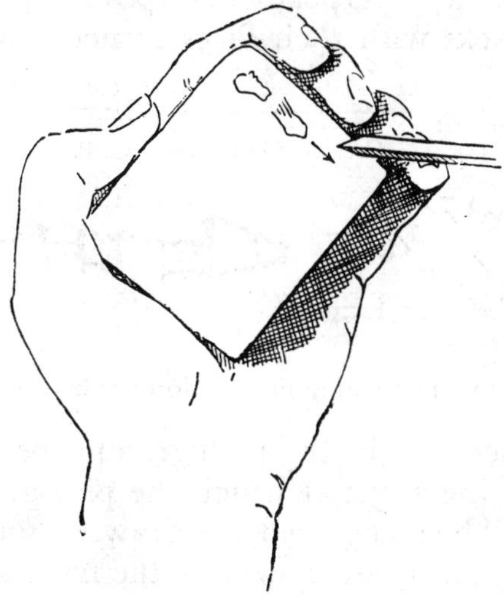

A. Signs written from top to bottom but columns running from right to left.

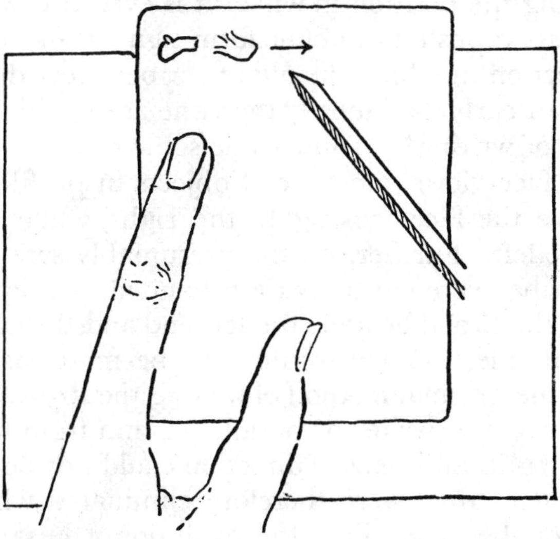

B. Signs written horizontally from left to right and columns running from top to bottom.

FIG. 12. The position of the tablet in writing.

the tablet increased in size it could not be so held; it was then laid on something serving as a desk or table at right angles to the body (s. fig. 12 B).[1] Thus the tablet was, as it were, revolved widdershins until it came to rest at right angles to the

[1] S. pp. 10–11.

body; but, although it was turned back through an angle of 45°, the signs were still written as before so that, when the text was read in the new perpendicular position, they appeared to lie on their backs with their faces turned upwards. As this

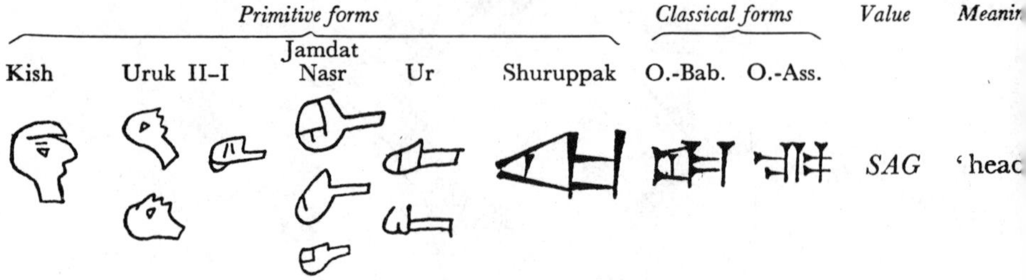


FIG. 13. The changing position angle of the signs.

change took place within the pictographic period, it can be traced clearly in the angle at which the pictographs, of which the origin can still be recognized, are drawn. For example, that depicting the human head shows it in the natural upright position on the primitive tablet from Kish, while on the tablets of Uruk II–I it now leans back and now lies back (s. p. 35 fig. 12), thus reaching the position in which it is ever afterwards drawn both in pictographs and in cuneiform signs (s. fig. 13).

The direction in which the oldest scribes drew the signs was already at an early date mostly the same as that followed in the latest form of writing*. Thus, while some of the earliest pictographs are face-views, most are of objects in profile, and these always have the face looking to the right, while the back is towards the left. Further, on the presumably safe assumption that the scribes were normally right-handed, the signs would be made with the broad head at the left end and the narrow point at the right side, as they would thus be most easily written. Since, too, the original method of writing the strokes ran downwards towards the writer or parallel to him from left to right, signs pointing in an opposite direction could not be made with equal firmness; they were therefore eliminated whether accidentally or deliberately. First, the revolution of the tablet resulted

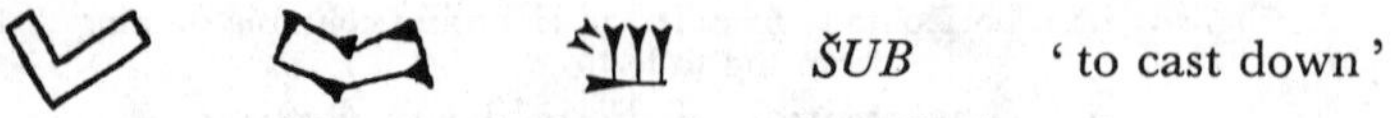


FIG. 14. Awkward strokes eliminated.

in many cases in their automatic disappearance (s. fig. 14). Second, the scribes consciously got rid of them; for example, when they converted the pictographic  '(rising) sun' into a sign composed of cuneiform strokes, they wrote it not as  but as 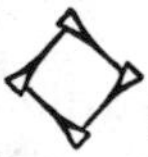, thus avoiding most of the strokes which they disliked.[1] Alternatively, in the few cases in which signs containing such strokes survived after the period of pictography, the scribes deliberately reversed them (s. fig. 15). When once this had happened, all the signs could be made with equal ease.

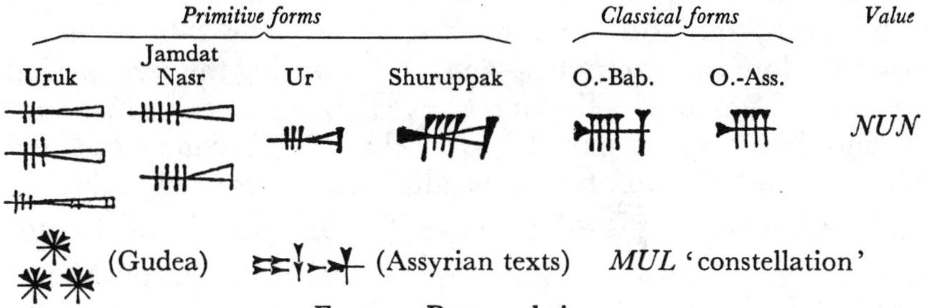
Primitive forms
Classical forms
Value
Uruk
Jamdat Nasr
Ur
Shuruppak
O.-Bab.
O.-Ass.
NUN
(Gudea)
(Assyrian texts)
MUL 'constellation'

FIG. 15. Reversed signs.

The result of these processes was that the scribes of the classical periods were limited to strokes of four main types ( , , , ), with an additional stroke not so frequently employed ( ). These were set at various angles to one another and drawn in such a way that, if two strokes intersected one another, the horizontal stroke was generally made before the vertical stroke which cut it but was not cut by it. The signs were thus formed into groups of diverse patterns; and each group, composed of anything from one to twenty-seven such wedges in the classical script, constituted a single symbol or 'sign'[2] reproducing an object or representing a sound in a purely conventional form. In drawing such a group the horizontal strokes were generally made before the vertical strokes, which cut them and were not cut by them.[3]

During the long period for which the cuneiform script remained in use, the signs naturally underwent considerable transformation, to which early and late copies of the same text recovered at different depths in buildings by excavation bear primary witness (s. pl. 18, 2) but which can be traced through every stage in the development of the individual signs.[4] Thus there were the peculiarities of certain individual scribes or schools of scribes, such as the sloping forward as seen in  for  *a*, which is characteristic especially of the so-called 'Cappadocian' texts.[5]

[1] Cp. Deimel *Sumer. Gramm.* 13.

[2] Ass. *ittu* (Ebeling *K.A.R.I.* 1 111 O. ii 7; s. p. 65).

[3] De Morgan in *R. d. Tr.* XXVII (*N.S.* XI) 245 (where the reference is actually to signs on proto-Elamite tablets).

[4] Cp. Deimel op. cit. 15.

[5] Smith 'C.T.C.T.' 1 5.

The tendency, too, towards a cursive script, first noticeable in the smaller signs of the first Babylonian dynasty (*c.* 2169–1870 B.C.), was another important factor in modifying the appearance of the signs. Henceforth two tendencies showed themselves, the one towards a Neo-Assyrian style as seen especially on the tablets from the great library of Ashurbanipal (668–626 B.C.) at Nineveh, and the other toward that of the tablets of the Neo-Babylonian empire (604–538 B.C.). During this long period five main lines of development reveal themselves. First, converging lines become parallel, whereby becomes *AB* cow'; second, the number of parallel lines is reduced and fairly stabilized, whereby becomes *GAL* 'great'; third, component groups of strokes within a sign are assimilated in appearance to other signs with which they have no inner connexion, whereby becomes *SAG* 'head' through assimilation to *si* and *pa*, *ḫat*; fourth, similar signs fall together, as when *SAR* '3600; abundance' and *DUG* 'good' are merged in or *ŠAR* '3600; abundance' and *DUG* 'good'; fifth, one sign is developed into two signs, as when *a'*, *aḫ* is differentiated into *aḫ* and *a'*. Occasionally, too, the scribes in certain centres, for example at Nuzi, showed a tendency to use a sign of simple pattern to avoid the complex types, such as *ti* for *di* or *qa* for *ga* and *ka*, although the values were not exact;[1] but this practice had no wide currency.

These and similar principles, visible at work modifying the forms of signs as the centuries passed, did not of course operate uniformly or to an equal extent in every period or locality where the cuneiform script was in use; and the Neo-Babylonian form, although it had several centuries more of life, was less affected by them than the Neo-Assyrian type.

On monuments of stone old methods of writing lingered far into the historical period and on seals it persisted almost to the end. Archaic forms of signs were retained, and even in the epoch of the first Babylonian dynasty the signs were written from above to below and the columns ran from right to left. The reader therefore continued to be able to read the signs without regard to the angle at which they lay to him.[2] It was

[1] Steele 'Nuzi' 45–6.

[2] S. p. 15. The scribes without doubt recognized the signs equally well whether they ran down or across the field and would not have had to put

only after the old traditions had been forgotten during the two centuries or so of Hittite rule that in the Cassite period the new methods were adopted also in inscriptions on stone. The script, however, remained for some time stiff and crude, and a cursive style only gradually made its way on official monuments. At the same time a consciously archaizing script was not uncommon and was much used right down into Neo-Babylonian and even Seleucid[1] times. A peculiarly Assyrian script was developed *c.* 2000 B.C.; this was more regularly and symmetrically written and generally of a less cursive type than the Babylonian. Vertical writing, however, seems to have remained the rule on seals of every period and locality with the exception that a few late Cassite and Middle-Assyrian seals have horizontal legends (s. pl. 9); the script on all seals is archaistic and stiff or stylized.

## 7. The Arrangement of the Text

On the earliest tablets no attempt was made to break up the text into lines or columns or to arrange the words in logical order.[2] Thus the small rectangular and oval tablets from Uruk IV and other primitive tablets from elsewhere for the most part had no division of the surface by horizontal or vertical lines to guide the reader in making out the sense, and the signs were more or less uniformly distributed over the available space without regard to the sense (s. pls. 1, 3 and 2).

So soon, however, as the tablets increased in size, a rudimentary division of the text into compartments was attempted (s. p. 40 fig. 16). Thus tablets from Kish and Uruk IV already occasionally had horizontal lines dividing the text into two or three compartments running from above to below (s. pls. 1, 2 and 2); and a very few from Jamdat Nasr had the text divided by vertical lines into columns (s. p. 40 fig. 17), while within such bands or columns the signs were still arranged without regard to

themselves in impossible positions to read a text which ran in a different direction to that usually current, as sometimes supposed (s. Winckler *Ges. Hamm.* vii–viii).

[1] Antiochus Soter (280–262/1 B.C.) had a text recording his restoration of Esagila and Ezida, temples in Babylon and Borsippa, in 270 B.C., written in an archaic form of the Babylonian script (Rawlinson ‘C.I.W.A.’ v 66).

[2] Cp. Thureau-Dangin *Écrit. Cunéif.* xi–xii and Falkenstein *Uruk* 11–12.

[3] The text on some of the earliest proto-Elamite tablets, dated *c.* 3000 B.C., is inscribed in vertical columns, but it is sometimes necessary to set the columns horizontally with the beginning at the right side in order to make the groups of signs easily intelligible (De Morgan in *R. d. Tr.* XXVII [*N.S.* XI] 237).

order.[3] The next stage, made necessary by the introduction of still larger tablets, while already visible in Uruk IV and fairly common in Uruk III–II, was fully developed in Jamdat Nasr; the surface was not divided into regular columns but had one or

Sum. *ḪE-GI-UL-EN-DU* | *600 BUR KI-*(?) | *DINGIREN-SAR-NUN*
Engl. 'Ḫegiulendu (the priest of) the god Ensarnun : 600 BUR of (?) land.'[1]

FIG. 16. Archaic tablet (Walters) with rudimentary arrangement of text.

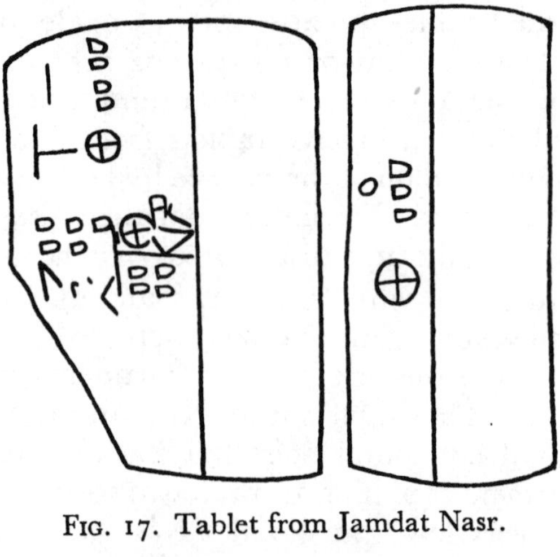

FIG. 17. Tablet from Jamdat Nasr.

more vertical lines dividing the signs or groups of signs into cases or compartments, or else it was divided by vertical lines running down the whole length of the tablet and gathering the cases together one to a column (s. p. 41 fig. 18). Some unusually large tablets from Uruk III and Jamdat Nasr had the text divided into columns wide enough to hold several cases or groups of signs which are separated from one another by vertical lines (s. p. 42 fig. 19). These vertical lines were very rarely curved or bent in such a way as to take in single signs or groups of signs written out of alinement; straight lines were the rule. The columns thus ruled followed each other from right to left. By the

[1] Deimel *Sumer. Gramm.* 93–4.

time of the tablets from Ur the signs were regularly arranged in horizontal bands across, often also with columns down, the tablets; but the horizontal line was not always drawn (s. p. 43 fig. 20), as the scribe acquired skill in keeping the signs in line

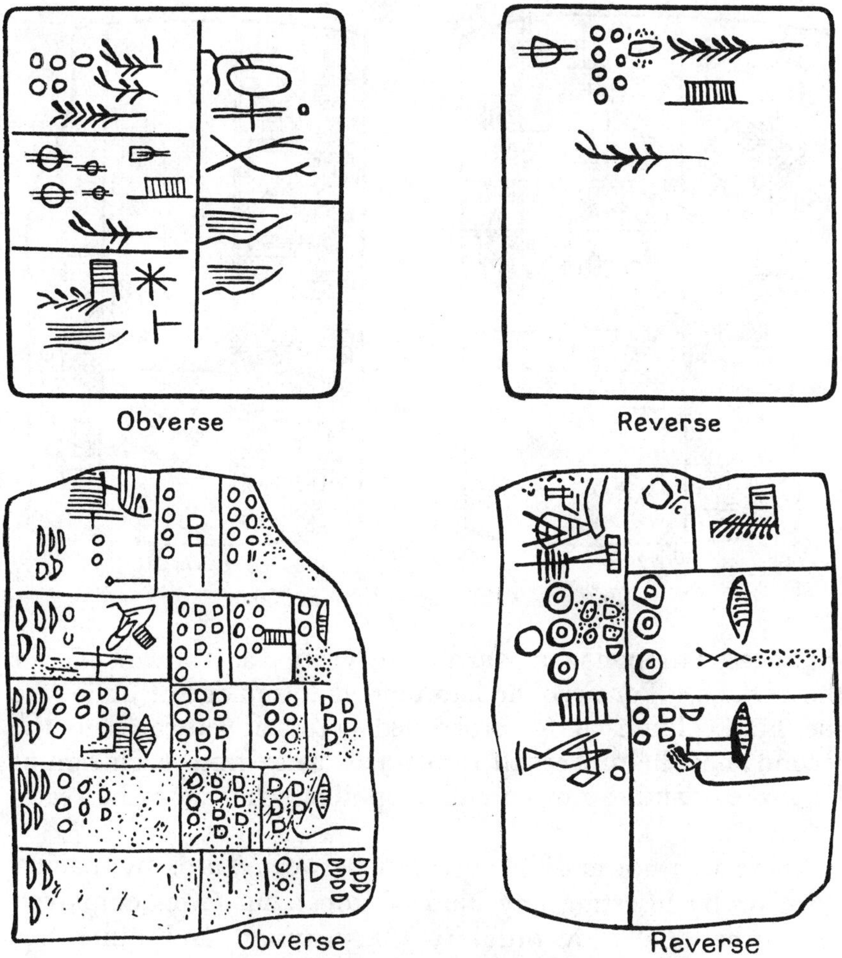


FIG. 18. Tablets from Jamdat Nasr.

as he worked his way across the surface. Thus the practice which was destined to be followed to the end was fully established by, if not before, the time of these early tablets from Ur.

As already said, the earliest scribes began the text at the upper right corner of the tablet, namely that nearest to the tip of the stylus which was normally held in the right hand, since this was the obvious and easiest point of beginning; and they thence wrote the columns running from right to left while the signs in them ran downwards from above to below. When, however, the tablet was swung round through an angle of 45° backwards,[1] what had been written from above to below came to be written from left to right, and the columns necessarily followed suit. This method finally prevailed largely because the scribe's hand

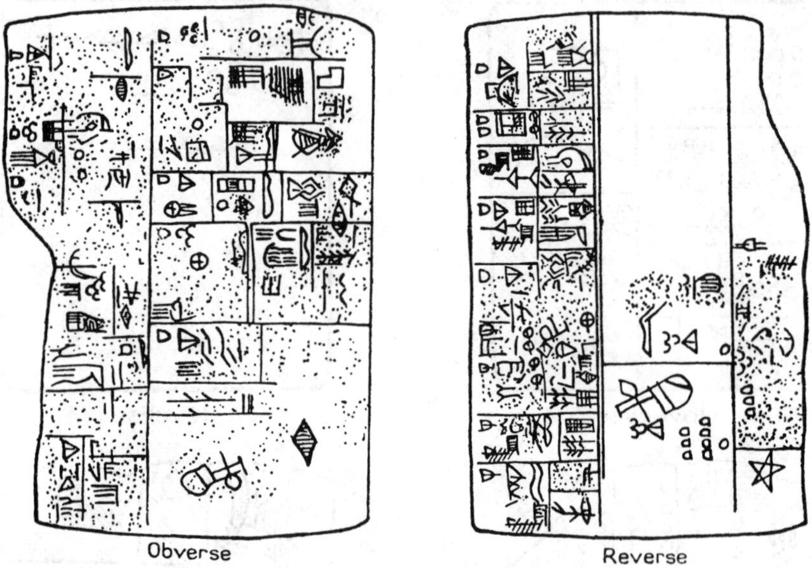


FIG. 19. Tablet from Jamdat Nasr.

thus ceased to spoil what was already written as it advanced over the surface.[2] Formerly he had tended to smudge or obliterate the first column as he proceeded across it leftwards to the second; now he proceeded rightwards away from each sign as he wrote it and so ran no risk of spoiling what he had already written*.

There was normally no division between words by spacing them or by inserting any kind of stops; but 𒁹 was employed very occasionally by ordinary Old-Assyrian and quite frequently on the so-called 'Cappadocian' tablets[3] and 〈 regularly in the Persian text at Bisutûn as word-dividers.[4] The division of a word between two lines was generally avoided. The scribes usually preferred, when writing on clay-tablets, to run on over the edge of the tablet, whether straight on if it was a matter

[1] S. pp. 34–6.

[2] Already in the Old-Babylonian period a tablet in which the columns on the obverse side are read from right to left is a freak (De Genouillac in *R.A.* XXV 124–6, where a syllabary with the Sumerian text in the right and the Babylonian text in the left column is published).

[3] Gelb in 'J.N.E.S.' I 221 and Smith 'C.T.C.T.' I 6.

[4] S. p. 186 n. 2.

of a very few signs or obliquely upwards if several remained to be written, in order to finish the word before proceeding to the next line. If, however, the text was divided into columns, especially when it was carved on a fine monument of stone

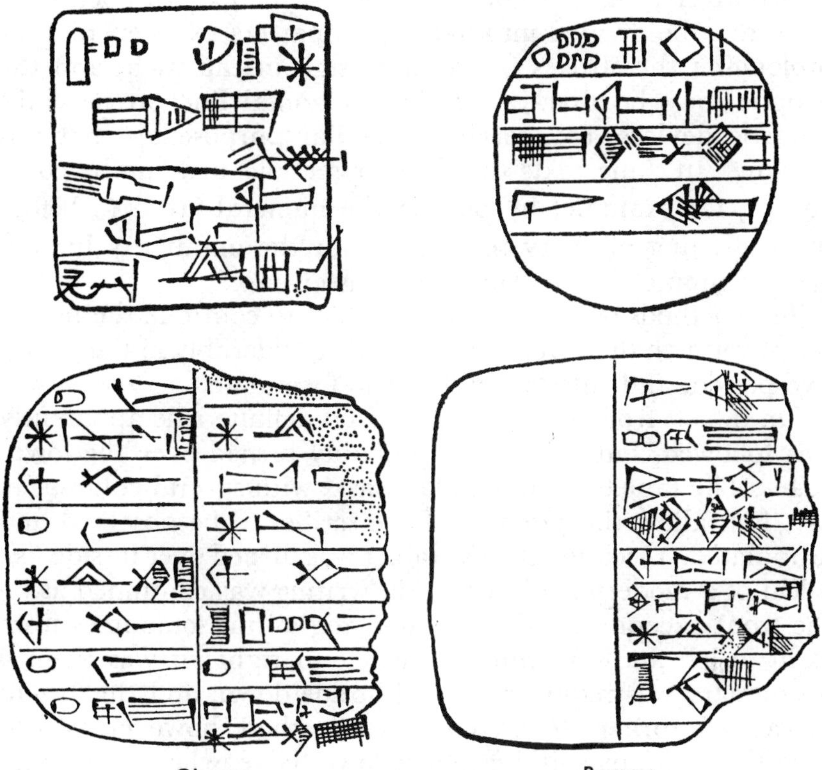


FIG. 20. Tablets from Ur.

such as was the Code of Hammurabi, the scribe or carver did not generally run over the line of the column but divided the word, finishing it on the next line, when he usually put the overflowing signs not at the beginning but at the end of this line;[1] he rarely divided a word between two lines but went straight on to the next line.[2] Exceptions, however, to these rules are not uncommon. If the signs were too few to fill the available space, they might be spaced widely for the purpose, but there was no rule governing the practice of the scribes on this point*.

In important texts the sentence or 'section'[3] was often marked off by a line or lines drawn across the tablet: for example,

[1] Cp. C. H. i a 26. [2] C. H. xxv b (xlix) 103–4.

[3] Acc. *sadīru* or *sadru* 'section marked off by lines' (Von Soden in *Z.A.* XLIII 26 and Landsberger *ana ittišu* ix–x, citing an instance where the sections or

the sections on copies of the Code of Hammurabi on clay-tablets and on the original tablet containing the Middle-Assyrian laws. Further, in these laws the first sign of each section is slightly set back so as to stand out of alinement with the rest of the text. Alternatively, the space of a line was left blank. In poetry the verse may be divided into halves or quarters by deepening or prolonging the strokes of the final sign in the stich, and the strophe may be marked off by horizontal lines at its end.[1] Acrostic devices, too, serving a similar purpose are not unknown.[2] In some texts the lines or sections are numbered in groups, for example, by putting the numeral '10' (<) before the beginning of every tenth line;[3] or the number of lines in each column or in the whole tablet is given.[4]

The methods of turning over a tablet to continue the text of the obverse on the reverse side varied considerably in the primitive period, and rules are difficult to formulate.[5]

On tablets from Uruk IV–III/II no definite rule apparently was followed, but most were probably turned over the lower edge. The tablets from Jamdat Nasr[6] with several columns of text first allow the practice of the scribes to be observed and formulated. Occasionally the tablet was turned over its side like a leaf of a modern book, when the writing was continued as on the front except that the columns might run sometimes from right to left and sometimes from left to right; it was then, if a summary was required, turned upside down, and this began at the left corner. The commonest method, however, was to turn the tablet over its bottom or lower edge, when the writing was continued at the right or the left upper corner; it began with almost equal frequency at either point in the early period. There are a few variations from these rules, chiefly on tablets from Uruk and Jamdat Nasr; of these, which are of slight importance, the most remarkable is the habit of continuing the

lines are wrongly counted) and hence 'register' on sculptured work (Weidner in *A. Of.* VIII 178–9 i 13); further Sum. *DUR*=Ass. *turru* 'band, paragraph' (Thompson 'A.M.T.' 66 4 i 2, 4; s. Meier in *O.Lz.* XLIII 25), as well as *kibsu* or *kibšu* 'passage, paragraph' (Thureau-Dangin in *R.A.* XXXII 27–8) and *pirsu* 'chapter; portion occupying a whole tablet' (Thureau-Dangin *ibid.* 99; cp. Landsberger & Bauer in *Z.A.* XXXVII 62[1] and Schuster *ibid.* XLIV 246).

[1] King 'Creation' I cxiv–v; s. Zimmern in *Z.A.* VIII 121–4.

[2] S. p. 208.

[3] Langdon in *R.A.* XIV 79 (K. 152).

[4] Clay 'Y.B.T.' I 19.

[5] Langdon 'Pict. Inscr.' iii–iv and Falkenstein *Uruk* 12.

[6] At Jamdat Nasr the convex side of the tablet was the obverse and the flat side the reverse, contrary to the usual Sumerian practice.

text of the obverse for a few columns on the reverse, then turning the tablet completely over and finishing the text from the left corner of the remaining space on the reverse in such a way that it was upside down to the columns which had just been written. At Shuruppak[1] the custom was, when the tablet held several columns of text, to turn it over the lower edge and begin again at the right upper corner and continue thence by columns to the left upper corner, namely in the opposite direction to that followed on the front (s. fig. 21); and this practice became thenceforth the rule with all large tablets with few exceptions.[2] The reason for this custom was that the writer thus continued, running over the bottom, in the same column as it were as that in which the previous text had been written, even though he did so at the risk of damaging what he was writing as he proceeded by columns from the right to the left instead of from the left to the right side of the tablet*.

In thus continuing the text over the bottom, which became the rule with tablets of every size, the scribe did not usually leave the bottom or lower edge blank but continued the text over it before proceeding on to the reverse, so that he lost no available writing-space, since the edges were generally wide enough, owing to the thickness of the tablets, to take several lines of text. Similarly, when writing on the reverse side overran the surface, it was continued for a line or so on the upper edge until it came of necessity to an end. If space for writing was still required, the scribe might use the left edge of the obverse, starting at the point from which he had commenced writing the text; but the opposite right edge was never used except very rarely when the ends of the lines of the obverse overflowed on to it. This fact serves to show which is the obverse and which the reverse of the tablet, the beginning and end of the text.

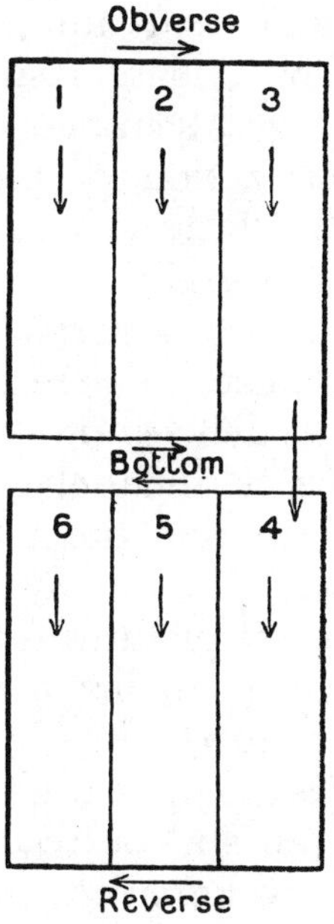


FIG. 21. Turning over the page.

[1] At Shuruppak the obverse and reverse sides are not distinguished by being flat or convex.

[2] Such as the longer tablets of the period of Urukagina, on which the writing began in the left upper corner on the reverse as on the obverse side (Deimel *Sumer. Gramm.* 14).

The curious tablets described above[1] containing Accadian words on one side in the cuneiform script and on the other side the words transliterated into Greek letters (s. pl. 18, 1) were turned over from right to left; if they are turned over from top to bottom, the writing on the reverse side is found to be upside down.[2] This peculiarity cannot be explained as a harking back to ancient custom; it must rather be due to Greek influence.[3]

## 8. From Picture to Symbol

In the tablets from Kish there is a mere handful of signs of a very simple form, and nothing can be said of the development of the script there at this very early epoch. The next collection from this centre hardly falls within the primitive period.

In Uruk IV the forms of the signs are remarkably free from variation compared with those of Uruk III–II or Shuruppak, and their number is considerably below those of those other collections. It is not that pictography was being forced into a greater uniformity of style; for in the first place the characterization of the signs as pictorial is already true of only a relatively small number of them and, secondly, it is just the pictorial signs which show the most marked variations in the following periods of their development. It is rather that these tablets are so near the first beginnings of writing that the diverse tendencies productive of variation have not yet had time to work themselves out. Whether these tablets from Uruk IV represent the actual first essays at writing is disputed; but the fact that many signs have already ceased to be in any true sense pictures of the objects which they are intented to represent suggests that a stage in which all the signs in use were fully pictorial already lay far behind them. At the same time, uniform as the signs at Uruk IV may be, the peculiarities of various scribes can still be recognized; and this, too, suggests some previous development. A completely standardized style of impression is hardly reached before Shuruppak, where individual signs still continue to exhibit variations. The reasons for this lingering lack of uniformity are probably that the stylus had not yet been standardized, and that the practice of distributing the signs over the surface of the tablet, and often in small compartments without regard to order, compelled a certain amount of adaptation to the space available for them.

[1] S. p. 30. [2] Pinches in 'P.S.B.A.' XXIV 109.

[3] For δέλτοι πολύπτυχοι are mentioned already by the second century A.D. (Lucian *Am.* 44).

In the earlier texts from Uruk, although the forms of the signs are fixed, the manner of drawing them varies with the whim of the scribe. For example, the same sign may consist of four strokes meeting at haphazard or of two intersecting strokes, and the number of these may vary considerably; but in the later texts the complex tend to give place to the simple forms.

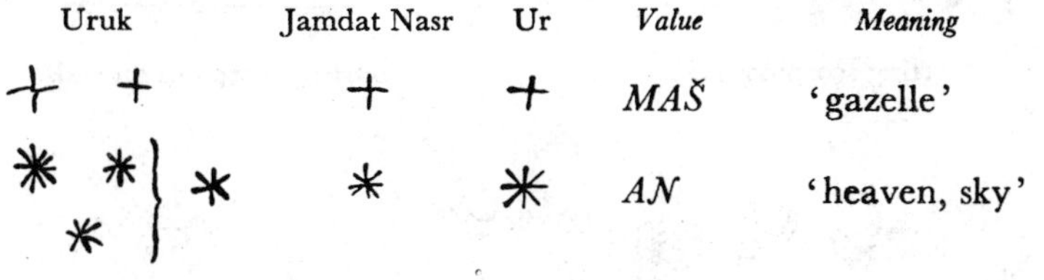
Uruk
Jamdat Nasr
Ur
*Value*
*Meaning*
*MAŠ*
'gazelle'
*AN*
'heaven, sky'

FIG. 22. Early cuneiform signs.

The same tendencies are at work also at Jamdat Nasr and Ur (s. fig. 22). This fact also contributed not a little to the degeneration of the original pictographs, for varieties of handwriting were not checked by the growing conventionalization of the script.

The character of every sign was originally pictographic, and the picture remained recognizable for a varying period of time. Sometimes nature as well as art must be invoked in identifying the source of this or that sign when its form has become obscured and so ceases to strike the eye or catch the imagination. For example, the origin of the sign for a scorpion (s. p. 48 fig. 23 A), a ship (s. p. 48 fig. 23 B) and a fold or pen (s. p. 49 fig. 23 C), becomes obvious when their latest forms have been traced back to their source and the earliest forms, thus revealed, are compared with the representation of that object in art.

Already, however, in the earliest texts there are many pictographs or signs representing objects of which the identity is not immediately apparent, while others have been so far conventionalized that the objects depicted cannot be identified at all. Thus in Uruk IV the picture of the aurochs is clear, at Jamdat Nasr it is hardly to be recognized, and at Shuruppak it is quite unrecognizable; but the ox, seen in profile, can hardly be identified even in Uruk IV and is quite unidentifiable at Jamdat Nasr*. The sign for a sheep, obviously a head depicted full face with eyes, nose and mouth, roughly represented by cross-lines, is already completely conventionalized in Uruk IV (s. p. 49 fig. 24). The reason for this distinction between pictographs whose subjects are obvious and those whose subjects are not easily or cannot be recognized is that those signs that represented objects

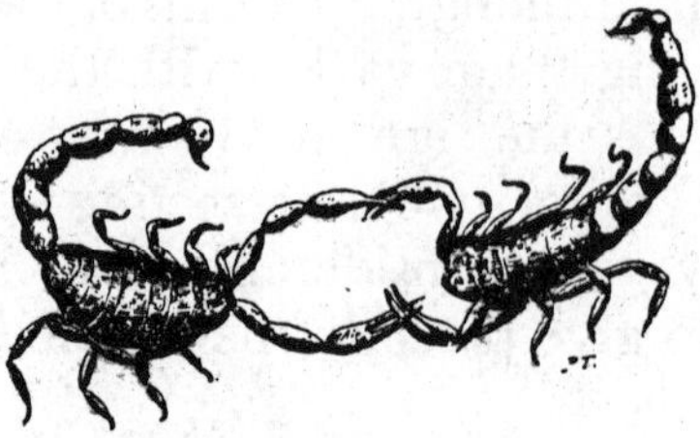

Courting scorpions from nature.

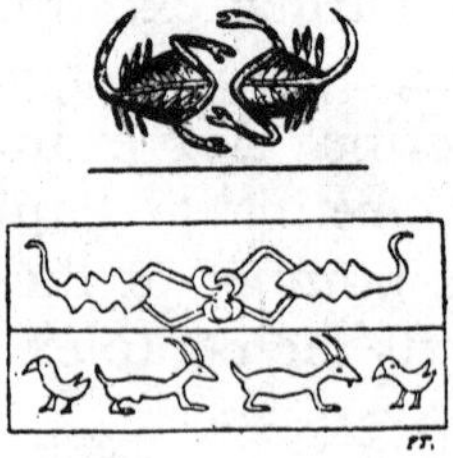

Courting scorpions on seals.

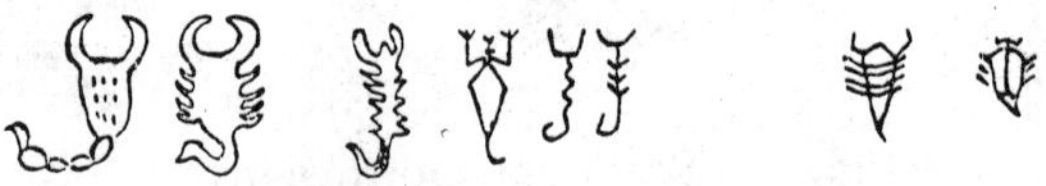

Scorpions engraved on seals and in sculpture.

Scorpions painted on bowls.

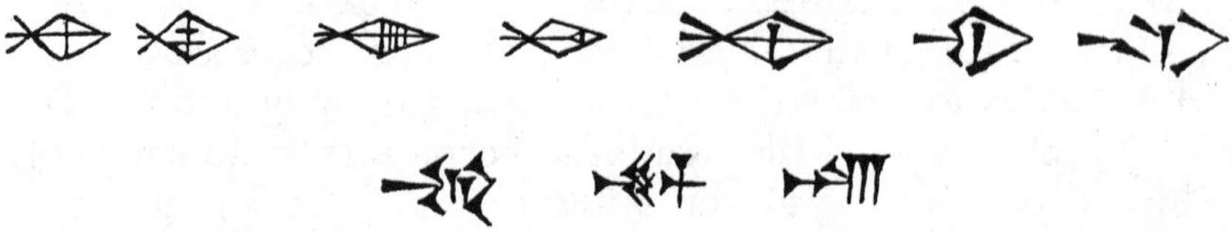

A. Cuneiform signs for a scorpion.

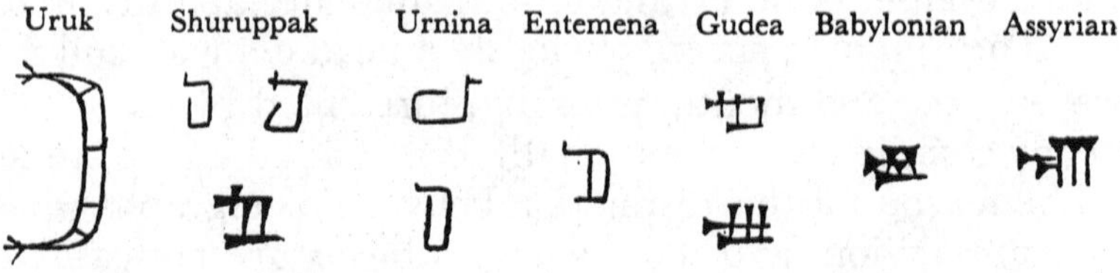


B. A ship on a Sumerian seal *c.* 3200 B.C. and the cuneiform sign for 'ship'.

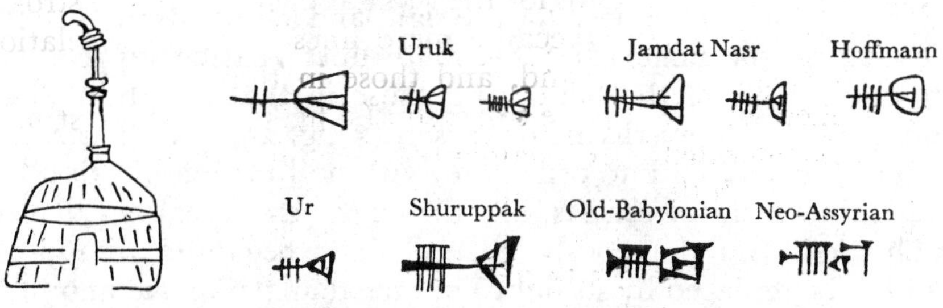


C. A fold or pen in sculpture and the cuneiform sign for 'pen, fold'.

FIG. 23. The origin of signs in nature and in art.

rarely seen remained truly pictorial, while common objects came to be hastily scrawled as the scribes ceased to bestow pains on them; thus they rapidly deteriorated and became mere conventional representations of actual objects. Occasionally, too, the original object presented difficulties of drawing which the primitive scribes never overcame. There were also signs devised to represent abstractions, for which the scribes used symbols whose origins were easily forgotten and which were therefore readily conventionalized.

Again, in Uruk III–II, and especially at Ur, a noticeable change in the script is the greater thickness of the lines, which increases for some time to come; the causes of this change are

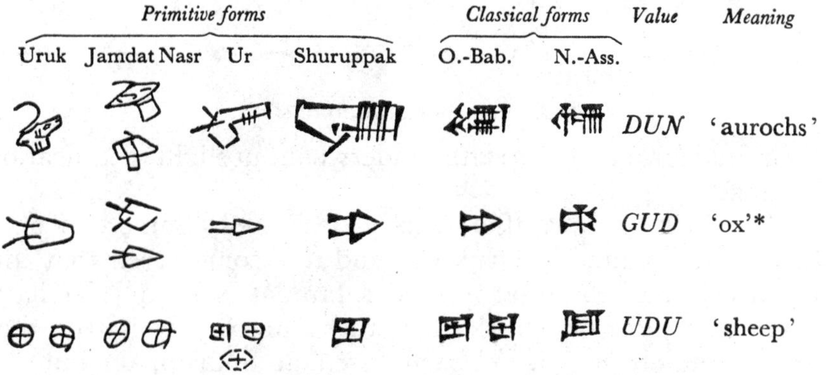
Primitive forms
Classical forms
Value
Meaning
Uruk
Jamdat Nasr
Ur
Shuruppak
O.-Bab.
N.-Ass.
DUN
'aurochs'
GUD
'ox'*
UDU
'sheep'

FIG. 24. Recognizable and unrecognizable pictographs.

the transition from drawing to imprinting the sign and the coarser stylus which was required for this method and which came to be preferred as increasing the legibility of the signs, together with a striving after cursive forms consequent on the growing use of and carelessness in writing. The pictograph thus underwent marked transformation and even deterioration, and the majority lost all resemblance to the object originally depicted, becoming in the end nothing but unrecognizable symbols.

For example, in the signs for the right and left hands the strokes indicating the fingers became mere lines bearing no relation to the fingers of the hand, and those in that for grain were multiplied without rhyme or reason (s. fig. 25). So the strokes often degenerated into ornament with no function but to fill a vacuum which the scribes, like the engravers of seals, evidently abhorred. Simultaneously curved lines began to disappear and to be replaced by straight lines set at angles to one another. This conversion of the strokes into wedges finally obscured the identity of the pictograph and, except in the rarest cases, it became normally impossible to recognize what the picture once had been; and, by the time of the Old-Babylonian texts, the signs had reached what was to all intents and purposes

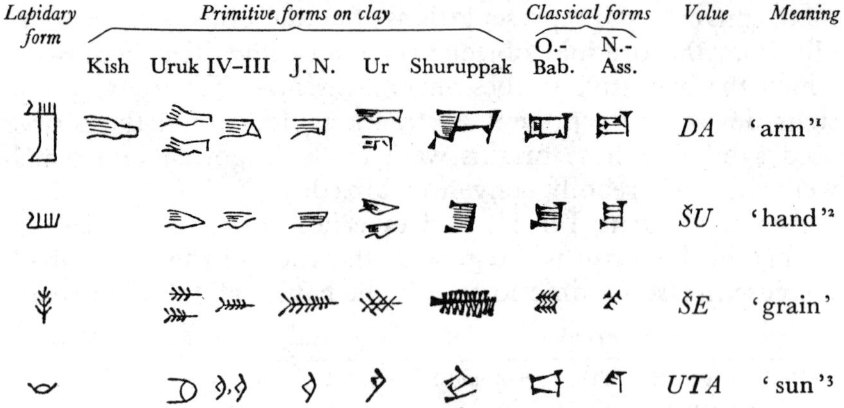


FIG. 25. Deterioration of signs.

their final form and thereafter underwent but slight modification in detail.

The stock of signs also steadily decreased. Some 900 signs have been counted in Uruk IV, and it is conjectured that this is scarcely half the total number; Jamdat Nasr and Ur have about 400 signs or a little over that number. It is true that approximately 800 have been listed at Shuruppak, but the range of subjects here is greatly extended. This reduction on the one hand in the number of signs is due to a simplification whereby, for example, the thirty-one forms of the signs for *UDU* 'sheep' in Uruk IV become only three in Uruk III and two in

[1] Originally the left fore-arm.

[2] Originally the inner side of the left hand.

[3] Originally the sun rising between the peaks of two mountains (s. Contenau *Man. d'Arch. Or.* IV 2014). Such signs prove the Sumerians to have been originally a people dwelling in mountainous country, not in the flat Babylonian plain.

Uruk I; these diverse signs, intended perhaps to some extent to denote distinct breeds or qualities, have been replaced by one or two generic terms, which may be accompanied by qualifying terms. As such qualifying terms, for example adjectives of colour, can be applied also to oxen and other objects of every sort and kind, the number of signs required is greatly diminished by their introduction. Another, though uncommon, cause of reduction was the merging of two or so similar archaic signs into a single modern sign. This process, however, was not an unmixed blessing; for although the number of signs was reduced, the variety of values or meanings which a single sign could have was augmented to the confusion of the reader *.

Any reduction, however, in the number of the signs was to a considerable extent if not wholly offset by two opposite tendencies to increase the number of the signs. These were the development of a single sign into two distinct signs in order clearly to express the various concepts expressed by the original simple sign and the formation of compound signs, whether by the modification of a single sign into two signs by means of additional strokes or by the union of two originally distinct signs into a single sign.

The first process was not very common, and a single example of its operation will suffice. The primitive  *UŠ* 'male organ; to stand up' was differentiated into 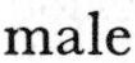 *UŠ* 'male organ; man' and  'slave; slave girl'. The second process was originated at a very early period. The first step was the formation of a new sign and of an old sign by some internal modification of it, such as the addition of a few strokes, or by joining another sign

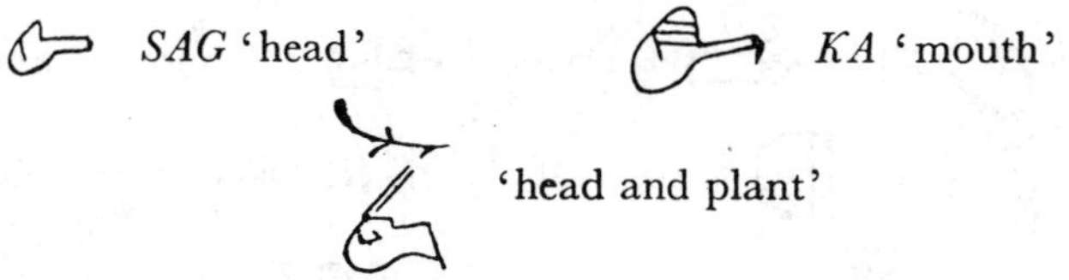


FIG. 26. Formation of compound pictographs.

to it by means of a ligature. Thus the sign for *SAG* 'head' was converted by the addition of a few strokes, probably representing the teeth, into that for *KA* 'mouth'; or a plant was linked to the human head so as to constitute a composite or double sign, of which the meaning is unfortunately unknown (s. fig. 26). The use of ligatures, however, was not developed, and examples are few. The second and usual method was to set the component signs side by side and eventually to fuse them into a single sign; so signs for *GAL* 'great' and *LÚ* 'man' were formed into *LUGAL* 'king' and those for *SAL* 'woman' and *KUR* 'mountain; foreign country' were similarly combined into a single sign representing *GEME* 'slave-girl'; for slave-girls were mostly captives taken in war in the hilly foreign lands lying to the east of the Babylonian plain. In this example the component signs are

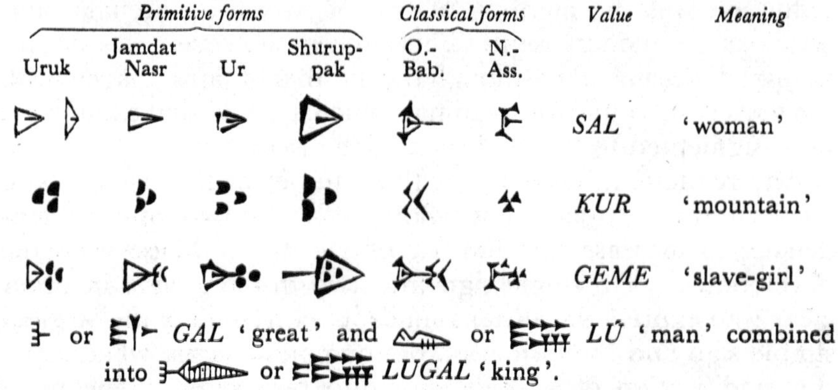


FIG. 27. Fusion of simple into compound signs.

still separate in Uruk IV, connected at Jamdat Nasr, and fused at Shuruppak as in the late classical form (s. fig. 27).

This method of forming compound signs, originally devised in the earliest period for the expression of quite simple concepts which could not be easily represented by ordinary single signs, was increasingly used as time went on for the creation of new signs expressive of verbal notions. In the archaic texts tolerably simple, but in the latest texts the most complex or abstract ideas, both nominal and verbal, are thus expressed (s. fig. 28):

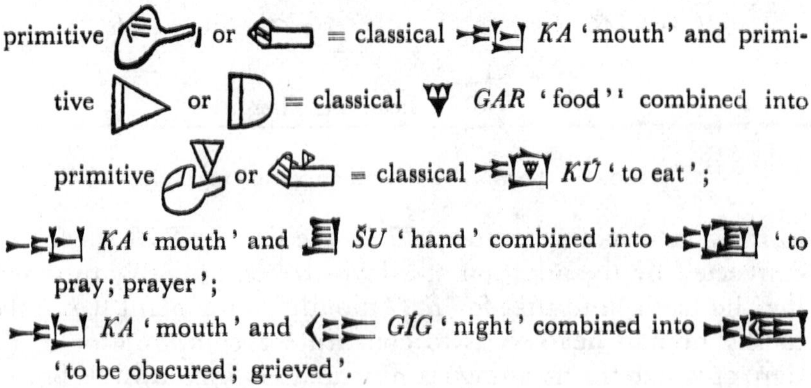
primitive or = classical KA 'mouth' and primi-
tive or = classical GAR 'food'[1] combined into
primitive or = classical KÚ 'to eat';
KA 'mouth' and ŠU 'hand' combined into 'to
pray; prayer';
KA 'mouth' and GÍG 'night' combined into
'to be obscured; grieved'.

FIG. 28. Verbal notions represented by compound signs.

[1] Possibly in origin a picture of a loaf of bread.

The composition of all such compound signs is not of course always so self-evident as that of those here depicted (s. fig. 29) and cannot always be unravelled, but the same or similar principles must have underlain them all *.

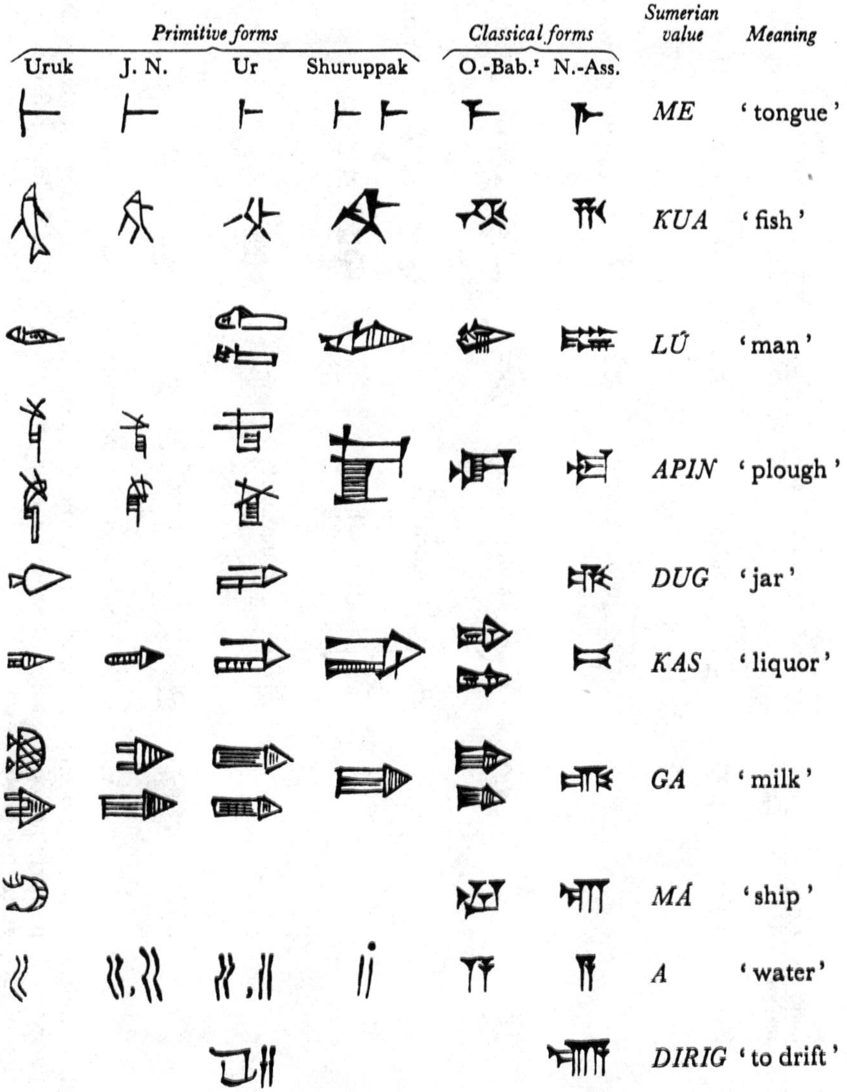
Primitive forms
Classical forms
Sumerian value
Meaning
Uruk
J. N.
Ur
Shuruppak
O.-Bab.[1]
N.-Ass.
ME 'tongue'
KUA 'fish'
LÛ 'man'
APIN 'plough'
DUG 'jar'
KAS 'liquor'
GA 'milk'
MÁ 'ship'
A 'water'
DIRIG 'to drift'

FIG. 29. Types of simple and compound pictographs.

Some of the principles of Sumerian pictography have now been laid bare, and others remain to be mentioned; and all the main principles of this system may be conveniently brought

[1] Only such forms as occur in the Code of Hammurabi are given, for uniformity of comparison.

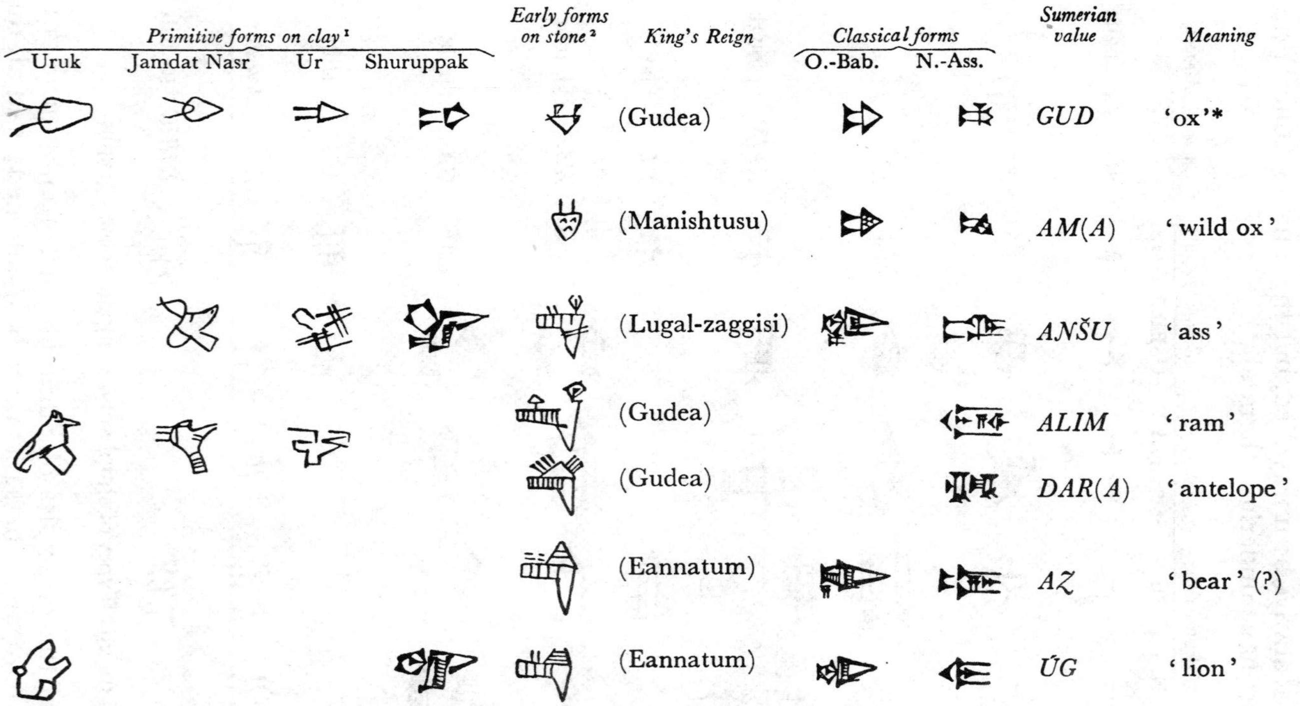


Fig. 30. Differentiation of pictographs.

[1] Not all the primitive forms have been found or identified, and the identification of them is not always certain.

[2] Writing on stone in the early period runs downwards and thus, even when itself often late, reflects the original upright position of the sign (s. pp. 38–9, 41–2).

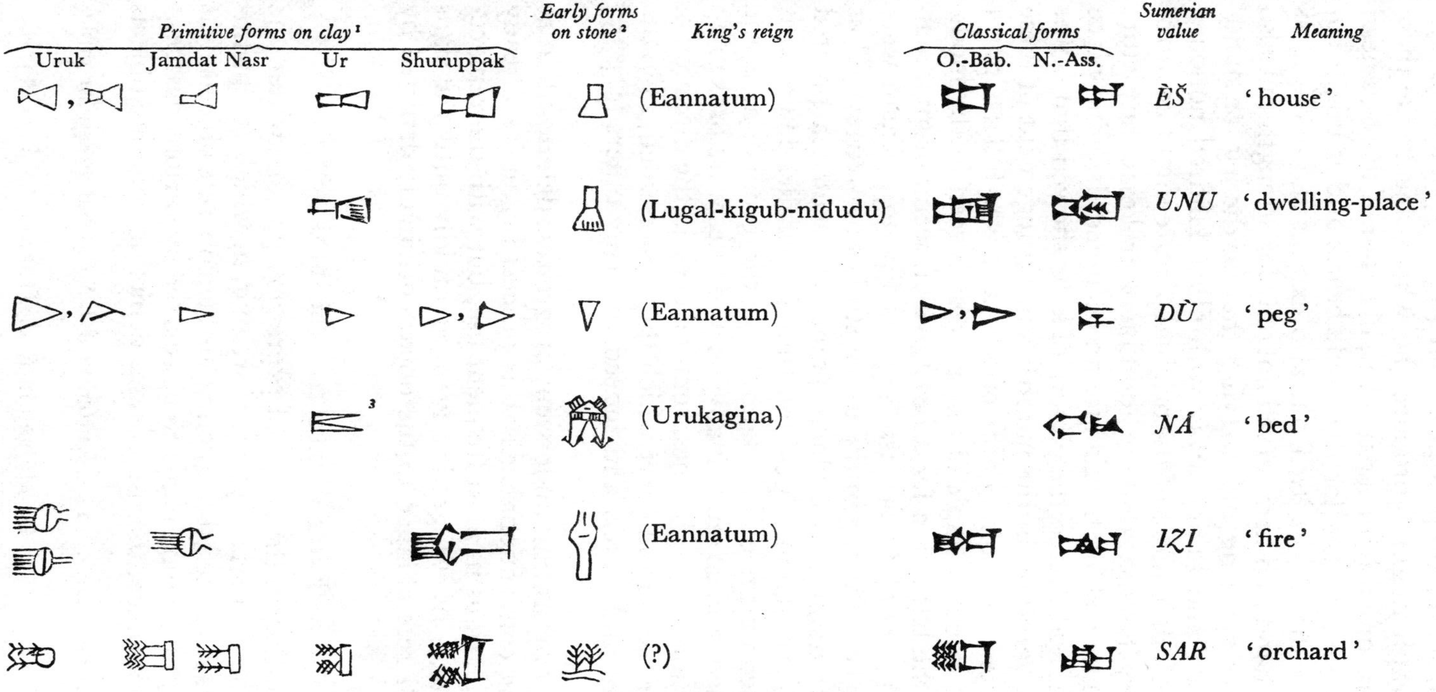
Primitive forms on clay[1]
Uruk
Jamdat Nasr
Ur
Shuruppak
Early forms on stone[2]
King's reign
Classical forms
O.-Bab.
N.-Ass.
Sumerian value
Meaning
(Eannatum)
ÈŠ
'house'
(Lugal-kigub-nidudu)
UNU
'dwelling-place'
(Eannatum)
DÙ
'peg'
3
(Urukagina)
NÁ
'bed'
(Eannatum)
IZI
'fire'
(?)
SAR
'orchard'

FIG. 31. Transition from pictographs to symbols.

[1] Not all the primitive forms have been found or identified, and the identification of them is not always certain.

[2] Writing on stone in the early period runs downwards and thus, even when itself late, reflects the original upright position of the sign (s. pp. 38–9, 41–2).

[3] Imperfectly preserved.

together and summed up at this point (s. pp. 54–5 figs. 30–1).[1] The pictograph might reproduce the whole object, like those for the tongue or a fish, or a part of it, like that of the ox's head which stood *pars pro toto* for the whole beast; and it might not only indicate the object itself but also express its function, as that for the hand and arm served not only for strength but also for, respectively, giving and carrying, that for the leg for standing and going and taking away with other kindred notions,[2] and so on. Modifications of the original picture might be introduced to vary its sense; thus the addition of strokes to the picture of a bare house yielded the sign for an occupied dwelling-place and a similar addition to the picture of a jar showed that it was full, while a variation in the number and arrangement of these signs indicated the commodity of which it was full (s. p. 53 fig. 29).[3] A good example of this process is seen in the modifications of the basic sign for a beast, which seems originally to have been intended for an ass (s. p. 54 fig. 30). There were also regular conventions in the use of strokes or wedges. Thus two wedges running to a single point represented a pointed object, as in the sign for a peg, but running parallel downwards they represented an object standing on the ground, as in the sign for a bed, and so on. Finally, curved lines were broken up into two or more straight lines, running each in the direction of one or other part of the curve which they represented, as in the signs for fire and water, and indeed in many others (s. p. 55 fig. 31).

The pictographs thus underwent progressive deterioration as they became conventionalized; this process began, as already said, with the signs in most frequent use, but with the replacement of strokes by wedges it advanced rapidly until the signs soon lost all resemblance to the objects originally depicted by them.

## 9. From Words to Syllables

The limitation to the range of expression possible within the bounds of the Sumerian system of writing, in which the primitive sign was restricted to depicting visible concrete objects, was very severe; but it soon came to be relaxed by various devices.[4]

In the first place, the use of signs depicting concrete objects

[1] Cp. Unger *Bab. Schr.* 9–12; s. Rutten in *R.É.S.B.* 1940 33–49 for tables of signs.

[2] S. p. 61. [3] Cp. De Morgan in *R. d. Tr.* xxvii (*N.S.* xi) 237–8.

[4] Cp. Falkenstein *Uruk* 29–43.

was extended to express similar concrete concepts and analogous abstract conceptions. Thus the pictograph consisting originally of four crossed strokes terminating in eight points and so depicting a star became the ordinary sign for *AN* 'sky, heaven' and the symbol for *DINGIR* 'god'; it came to serve also for the adjective 'high' and a number of other conceptions. Again, the pictograph for *DU* 'leg' did duty at the same time for several verbs including *GUB* 'to stand' and *GIN* 'to go' and *TŬM* 'to carry off',[1] and so on. This principle was seriously strained when the use of a sign was stretched to make it serve for something with which it had no semantic or logical connexion but of which the name had a similar sound. The earliest example of this abusive employment of a sign occurs in the writing of a proper name occurring on several tablets from Jamdat Nasr, whereby  *TI* 'arrow' is improperly used for  *TI*(*L*) 'life; to live' in *EN.LÍL-TI* '(may the god) Enlil (grant) life'.[2] The defects of such a system of writing are obvious: ambiguity is unavoidable and the range of expression gravely restricted. The earliest texts, however, were inventories or lists of objects, receipts, and so on, and such a system was more or less sufficient for their needs. It was only when the desire to write down connected, for example religious or historical, texts arose that such a purely pictographic method of expression revealed its inadequacy.

In the second place, a momentous development in the use of the script was inaugurated: many signs[3] were taken also to represent syllables. For example, the sign cited above for *TI* 'arrow', which had already been stretched to do duty for *TI*(*L*) 'life', came to be used also for *ti* and *tìl* as mere syllables in the phonetic spelling of other words. In other words, a sign that had originally only a word-value acquired also a syllable-value which could be used in writing any word which consisted of that syllable or of which that syllable was a component element. This practice was apparently initiated at Jamdat Nasr, where a phonetic *ME* was added to nouns to indicate the plural number, as in *AB-ME* 'elders' and *EN-ME* 'masters'. Soon other grammatical inflexions came to be so written; thus the texts from Ur used a few phonetically written verbal inflexions and comple-

[1] S. p. 61.

[2] Falkenstein *Uruk* 37–8. The final *L* of *TIL* 'life' was commonly dropped in pronunciation, which aided the confusion.

[3] This development was greatly facilitated by the fact that the vast majority of Sumerian roots were monosyllables.

ments indicating cases. The first phonetically written words were *MA.NA* 'maneh' a very common measure of weight, and *TÁM.KÀR* 'merchant' in texts from Shuruppak.[1] Neither concept could be easily or lucidly represented in pictorial form, and both terms were probably foreign, namely Accadian, loan-words, which would enhance the need of writing them out in phonetic form.

The origin of this device, then, must be sought in the need to indicate grammatical relations so soon as words began to be strung together in sentences; for these were indicated in the Sumerian language by, largely monosyllabic, prefixes and affixes attached to the basic root which remained unchanged. It was also required for foreign words, for referring to persons and places 'whose names were not easy to write',[2] and for indicating the pronunciation of ideograms and of dialectical forms in syllabaries for the use of students. At the same time the practice of syllabic writing was kept strictly within bounds, and common terms such as *UDU* 'sheep' and *SIBA* 'shepherd' were for the most part never spelled out at any period, except in school-texts and similar works.

This transition, whereby symbols representing objects or words came to denote sounds or syllables,[3] in other words, whereby the ideogram[4] became a phonogram,[5] did not take place without difficulty; and this was increased when the need arose of adapting signs designed originally for the agglutinative[6] Sumerian speech to the inflective[7] Accadian language. An example of forced adaptation may be seen in the use of the ideogram or word-sign for *KUA* 'fish' to serve for *ḫa* as a mere syllable in both languages. The signs as thus used represented

[1] Falkenstein *Uruk* $37^2$ $38^6$.

[2] Ass. *ša nibît šumīšunu ana šaṭāri lâ ṭâbu* (Thureau-Dangin *Sargon* $56–7_{364}$).

[3] As though a row of pictures for 'eye, can, knot, meat, hymn' did duty for and could be read as meaning 'I cannot meet him'.

[4] A character or figure symbolizing the notion of a thing without expressing its name, like the Chinese characters, and pronounced according to the reader's whim, as the sign '+' may be read *plus* or 'more' or 'in addition to' according to the context.

[5] A symbol or character representing a spoken sound or phoneme.

[6] Adding qualifying words in the form of prefixes or suffixes to the root and so building up longer or shorter compound words round the unchanged root with a view to expressing modifications of its meaning.

[7] Indicating the relation of the inflected word to others in the same sentence or some aspect of the conception which it expresses by internal modification of the root or by the addition of prefixes and suffixes which have no independent existence or meaning.

four of the five vowels*, namely *u*, *a*, *i*, *e*,[1] and a large number of syllables beginning and ending with a consonant or consisting of a vowel + consonant or a consonant + vowel;[2] for neither people succeeded in isolating the consonants from the vowels and representing them by their own signs. Consequently an inordinately large number of such signs was required to represent every possible combination of consonant and vowel.[3]

Thus the possibility of making the cuneiform system of writing syllabic or phonetic lay near to hand, but the Sumerians took only the first halting steps in this direction; the Babylonians succeeded only in developing the syllabic system, thereby gaining much in simplicity and intelligibility. The reasons for this distinction are clear. On the one hand the Sumerians had little need for signs representing syllables, not only because those which they were using had been designed to represent their own names of common objects in daily use, but also because their own words were largely monosyllabic and underwent no internal alteration through inflexion, which was indicated mostly by simple prefixed and suffixed syllables, and comparatively few signs with syllabic values sufficed for this purpose and to eke out the phonetic representation of awkward words that could not be pictorially represented. On the other hand the Babylonians, except when they used the old signs as ideograms, which were foreign to their language, as a kind of shorthand, were compelled to spell out every single word by syllables. Hence the great development of the syllabic use of these signs was their work. In other words, the basis of the Sumerian system of writing was word-values, while that of the Accadian method was syllable-values *.

This application of a single script to a dual purpose, namely to ideographic and syllabic writing and to two totally different languages, had the result that almost every sign ultimately became a polyphone,[4] to the great confusion of the reader. Thus the sign which originally depicted the rising sun came

[1] In their Accadian order (Thureau-Dangin in *R.A.* XXXII 100); s. pp. 179–8*.

[2] A form with one or two consonants was called *ḫamṭu* 'swift' and one with three consonants + vowel + consonant *marû* 'fat' (Haupt in *Z.A.* XXXIII 66–7), one for vowel + consonant was called *malû* 'full' and one for a vowel alone *rîqu* 'empty' (Thureau-Dangin in *R.A.* XXXII 100–2)*.

[3] For example, distinct signs were required for *i*, *'i*, *ib*, *id*, *ig*, *iḫ*, *il*, *im*, *in*, *ir*, *is*, *iš*, *bi*, *di*, *gi*, *ḫi*, *ki*, *li*, *mi*, *ni*, *pi*, *qi*, *ri*, *si*, *ṣi*, *ši*, *zi*, *ti*, *ṭi*, *bid*, *bil*, *bir*; only nineteen instead of thirty-two signs would be necessary to represent all these sounds on the principle of the alphabet.

[4] A sign representing many sounds.

to represent over 70 other words (nouns, particles, adjectives, verbs) and to serve for some dozen separate syllables;[1] it was also the first element in another 170 or so compound ideograms,[2] and a component element in many others. At the same time, as most signs represented a number of different words each differently pronounced, there were many signs for many syllables.[3]

That an ideogram might represent many objects or concepts and therefore be read in a number of ways introduced much ambiguity and confusion if not actual error into the interpretation of written texts, and two important devices were invented to help the reader in his task, the use of ideographic signs with determinative value and of syllabic signs as phonetic complements.

The determinative sign was one put before or after an ideogram to indicate the general class to which the object denoted by it belonged; such classes were those comprising deities, men and women, beasts and birds and fishes, plants and trees, objects of wood or leather, stones, rivers, towns and countries, and so on. The place of the determinative sign, though originally variable, was already fixed at Shuruppak, where *URU* 'city' preceded and *KI* 'place' followed the term qualified, as they continued to do ever afterwards. Thus 𒀳 might by itself be read, as said above, either *APIN* 'plough' or *ENGAR* 'ploughman'; in the former case the sign for *GIŠ* 'wood', in the latter that for *LÚ* 'man' was commonly prefixed to it to show how it was to be read. So, too, Babylon was called *KÁ–DINGIR (RA)*$^{KI}$ 'the gate of god (place)', where *KI* showed that a place on earth was intended. In Uruk IV the determinative *DINGIR* 'god' perhaps occurs, while *KI* 'place' is first attested at Jamdat Nasr and *LU* 'man' in a text from Kish contemporary with those from Shuruppak. The chief part played by this device in this early period was in the scholastic texts from Shuruppak, which contain a long list of signs and words, for

[1] Namely *u, ud/t, d/tu, ta, d/tam, bir, pa(i)ur, la/iḫ, maḫ, ḫiš*, of which however all are not employed with equal frequency.

[2] Such as that written *UD + KA + BAR* but read *ZABAR* 'copper'.

[3] For example, the sign for *ME* 'oracle' and *IŠIB* 'augur', whence *ŠIB* 'to practise augury' was derived, might be used for *me* and *šib* as mere syllables in the writing of other words; this principle was carried so far that some syllables could be represented by several different signs. Inversely, as mere syllables *du* and *gur* could be represented by respectively thirteen and eleven different signs; each sign, of course, had originally stood for a distinct word or words (s. p. 66 n. 1).

example of divine names or fishes or the like, classified according to their nature by determinative signs; the general use of it was a subsequent development.

The phonetic complement, found already in texts from Jamdat Nasr, was a simple sign representing a syllable beginning with a consonant and ending with a vowel, usually *a*, which was put after a polyphone to indicate the intended value; that was the one ending with the same consonant as that with which the complementary sign began. Thus *DU* 'leg' stood also for *GUB* 'to stand' and *GIN* 'to go' and *TŪM* 'to bring'; which was meant was indicated by writing -*NA* for *GIN* and -*BA* for *GUB* and -*MA* for *TŪM*. These additional signs were not read or pronounced but merely showed visually which of the various values borne by the sign was intended by the writer.[1]

The final complication was the invention of 'secret writing'[2] for the purpose of cipher or code and possibly musical notation; few examples of this device are known, and the decipherment of such examples as have been recovered is a matter of the greatest difficulty.[3]

Ultimately then the Sumerians succeeded in isolating the vowels and representing them by distinct signs, but they failed to isolate the consonants and so to represent them by distinct signs*. The reason for their success with the vowels was that these four sounds represented actual words in their language,[4] so that the signs for the vowels as it were fell ready made into their hands; the reason for their failure with the consonants was that these, unlike the vowels, could not have any existence as separate words, so that there were no signs at hand to serve

[1] Hence written *GIN*(*NA*) or $GIN^{NA}$, *GUB*(*BA*) or $GUB^{BA}$, *TŪM*(*MA*) or $T\hat{U}M^{MA}$ in modern transliterations (s. p. 57). The accents, such as that on *TŪM*, are also a modern device to indicate which of the five signs for *TUM* (conventionally written *TUM*, *TŪM*, *TÙM*, $TUM_4$, $TUM_5$) stands in the cuneiform text.

[2] Acc. *niṣirtu* and *piristu* or *pirištu* (Ebeling in *Z.D.M.G.* LXX 535[5]; s. Zimmern ibid. LXXIV 434–5) and *lišānu aḫītu*, meaning literally a 'strange tongue' (Landsberger in *Oppenheim* 177–80).

[3] E.g. Frank *Str. Kt.* 49, 50. One such text (Ebeling *K.A.R.I.* 1 4) is perhaps an example of musical notation (Galpin 'Music of the Sumerians' 42–50). Another, dated about the 17th. century B.C., in which the manufacture of glass is described in a script using all the rarest values of the signs (Gadd & Thompson in 'Iraq' III 87–96), is obviously designed to preserve a trade-secret.

[4] Such as *A* 'water' and *E* 'trench'. Conventionally the ideographic value may be written in capital letters and the syllabic value in small letters, for the convenience of the modern reader.

for them. Contrariwise the Egyptians, owing to the nature of their language, succeeded with the consonants but failed with the vowels, and thus enormously reduced the number of signs required for the phonetic representation of a word.[1]

In this elaborate system the form of the script and the use of the signs were to all intents and purposes fully developed by the time of Uruk I (*c.* 2900 B.C.), and the direction of the writing and the arrangement of the words according to their logical position in the sentence were fixed by the time of Eannatum, priest-king of Lagash (*c.* 2850–2825 B.C.), and neither was substantially modified during a period of nearly three thousand years.[2]

### 10. Scholars and Scribes

The complex system of writing invented by the Sumerians and developed by the Accadians was a 'secret treasure' or 'mystery'[3] which the layman could not be expected to understand and which was therefore the peculiar possession of a professional class of clerks or scribes.[4]

Although in most periods or at any rate in the most enlightened periods of Accadian history a fair number of laymen could read if not write the cuneiform script, the bulk of the population had recourse to professional scribes to write what they wanted for them, as elsewhere in the ancient and modern East;[5] for scribes often added their names after those of the witnesses on legal documents which they had drawn up. The party to the contract did not sign his name but had simply 'to seal' the tablet while the clay was still moist with his 'seal' (s. pl. 13, 2);[6] if he

[1] S. pp. 133–6.

[2] The latest tablet that can be dated refers to the retrogression of Jupiter and Saturn in Virgo on 24 November 7 B.C. (Schaumberger in *Anal. Or.* XII 279–87)*.

[3] Ass. *niṣirtu katimtu* (Streck *Assurbanipal* II 254–5 i 13) or *piris/štu*, of which Nabû was the inventor (Rawlinson 'C.I.W.A.' V 43 d 32).

[4] That *DUB.SAR* and *šāṭir ilki* 'administrator of taxes' are equated in a native syllabary (De Genouillac in R.A. XXV 124 i 28) shows how varied the scribe's duties must have been. Already under the 3rd dynasty of Ur (*c.* 2408–2301 B.C.) scribes were important administrative officers (s. Schneider in *Orient.* XV 64–88); but their continued connection with the priesthood is reflected by the use of the same ideogram for priest and scribe even in Neo-Babylonian texts (San Nicolò *Rechtsquellen* 142).

[5] S. pp. 88–90.

[6] Acc. *barāmu* and *kanāku* (Muss-Arnolt 'C.D.A.L.' 192, 919–20; s. San Nicolò *Rechtsquellen* 135–40); also *garāru* 'to be rolled' and *šugruru* 'to roll' in reference to cylinder-seals (Pfeiffer 'EN.' II 108 6 Chiera 'JEN.' IV 321 15, 47 330 13; Lewy in *Orient.* XI 331[1], quoting an unpublished tablet for the causative theme), and *ina šiṭir šumāti barāmu* 'to seal with the writing of the names' (Landsberger *ana ittišu* $88_{30-6}$)*.

had none, he pressed the 'nail',[1] usually of his thumb (s. pl. 14, 1), or the 'fringe'[2] or 'corner'[3] of his garment (s. pl. 14, 2) on the clay[4] so that it left its imprint on it as a permanent record*. The seal, which was usually engraved with its owner's name, served not only in place of a signature but also as a mark of assent to a contract. The mark, however, neither of the nail, in the days before the science of finger-prints, nor of the fringe could serve such a purpose; the former, therefore, was simply the mark of an illiterate person's assent to a contract which was attested by witnesses, whereas the latter proved symbolically by its contact

A. Two vertical wedges on an Accadian cylinder-seal.

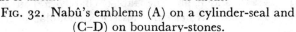

B. Two horizontal wedges on a tablet resting on a base or throne.

C–D. Single wedge or stylus on a base or throne.

FIG. 32. Nabû's emblems (A) on a cylinder-seal and (C–D) on boundary-stones.

with the tablet that the wearer of the garment bound his person to fulfil the obligation into which he was entering.[5]

[1] Acc. *ṣupru*$^{m}$ (s. San Nicolò *Rechtsquellen* 139[1], 140–1), especially in *kûm kunukkišu ṣupuršu iškun* 'he has put his nail instead of his seal' (Johns 'A.D.D.' I 365 1 +).

[2] Acc. *sis(s)iktu*$^{m}$ (s. ibid. 140–1), especially in *sisiktašu kîma* $^{ZA}$*kunukkišu* 'his fringe in place of his (stone) seal' (Clay in 'B.E.U.P.' XV 55 10–11; s. Ungnad in *O.Lz.* IX 163–4 and XII 479).

[3] Bab. *qarnu* or *qannu* (s. Lewy in *Orient.* XI 313[2]).

[4] Occasionally one party impresses his nail and another his fringe on the same document (Clay in 'B.E.U.P.' XIV 86 case 17–18).

[5] Cp. Koschaker in *N.K.Ru.* 20, 24 and *G.Ru.* 111–7, Boyer in *S.D.* II 208–18. So, when a husband divorced his wife, *sissiktaša ibtuq* 'he cut her fringe' or, in other words, severed her connexion with himself (Landsberger *ana ittišu* 99 ii 50); similarly Jesus, when the woman with an issue

The needs therefore of the temples and the government as well as of the civil population brought a large professional class of scribes into being, and these formed a powerful guild whose patron deity was the god Nabû, the Biblical Nebo;[1] his emblems were the tablet and wedge or the wedge without the tablet and the stylus (s. p. 63 fig. 32),[2] and he was described as 'the inventor of the writing of the scribes',[3] 'the unrivalled scribe',[4] and 'the scribe of the gods, wielder of the reed-pen'*.[5] The goddess Nidaba or Nisaba,[6] who was called the 'universal scribe'[7] or secretary general and the 'great scribe of heaven',[8] and a god called Ḫani or Ḫaya, her consort, described as 'lord of the seal' or 'sealed tablet' and the 'god of scribes',[9] are occasionally mentioned as patrons of learning,[10] while the goddess Bêlitṣîri, whose stylus was said to be lapis lazuli and cornelian,[11] is known as secretary to the queen of the underworld.[12]

The art of writing was studied in a school called a 'tablet-house',[13] of which one was attached to each of the most important temples,[14] and in these schools not only boys but presumably

of blood ἥψατο τοῦ κρασπέδου τοῦ ἱματίου αὐτοῦ (Matt. ix 21), remarked τὴν ἐξ αὐτοῦ δύναμιν ἐξελθοῦσαν (Mk. v. 30). The garment represented the person who wore it.

[1] Hebr. נְבוֹ (Isa. xlvi 1). [2] Cp. Steinmetzer *Grenzsteine* 165–6.

[3] Acc. *bānû šiṭri ṭupsarrūti* (Rawlinson 'C.I.W.A.' v 43 d 33).

[4] Ass. *ṭupsar lâ šanān* (Ebeling *K.A.R.I.* 104 15).

[5] Ass. *ṭupsar ilāni ṣābit qan-ṭuppi* (Schrader *K.B.* IV 102–3 l 3), and *bêl qan-ṭuppi* (Zimmern *B.K.B.R.* 156–7 45 vi 2)*.

[6] The 'reed-pen' or 'stylus' (Sum. *GI-DUB*$^{BA}$) is mentioned in a text of Gudea of Lagash (*c.* 2425 B.C.) as the emblem of Nisaba (Thureau-Dangin *S. A. Ki.* 94–5 4 25), and it and the 'tablet' (Bab. *lê'u*$^{m}$) in one of Lipit-Ištar of Isin (*c.* 2250 B.C.) as her emblems (De Genouillac in *R.A.* XXV 150 ii 21, 25).

[7] Ass. *ṭupsar kali* (Peiser in *K.B.* II 48–9 2 59).

[8] Sum. *DUB.ŠAR-MAḪ* (Scheil in *O. Lz.* VII 254–5$_{10\text{-}11}$).

[9] Bab. *bêlum kunuk* (Langdon 'S. B. P.' 156$^{11}$; s. 'Bab. Lit.' 141–2) and Ass. *ilu ša ṭupsarrī* (Luckenbill 'Sennacherib' 147 2 19; Tallqvist *Akkad. Götterepith.* 320–1).

[10] Clay 'Y.B.T.' I 28 vi 2–3.

[11] Ebeling *Tod und Leben* I 147–8 30 F 15–6.

[12] Jensen in *K.B.* VI i 190–1 v 47, where she is called *ṭupsarrat irṣitim* 'female scribe of the (under)world' (s. Deimel *Panth. Bab.* 200/2455–6); here *irṣitum* means the underworld as she is kneeling before Ereshkigal, queen of the underworld (s. Von Soden in *Z.A.* XLI 233–6). She is also called *šas(s)ukkatu* 'female secretary' (Muss-Arnolt 'C.D.A.L.' 1078; s. Dhorme *R.A.B.* 137). The *šassuk(k)u* was perhaps properly a 'registrar of land' (Von Soden).

[13] Ass. *bît ṭuppāte* (Ebeling *K.A.R.I.* 111 ii 6, 122 O. 10).

[14] E.g. at Nippur (Hilprecht 'Explorations' 512–25) and Sippar (Scheil *Sippar* 30–4).

girls[1] might learn to read and write; but such a place was, as its name suggests, nothing but a writing school,[2] and another type of school called the 'house of wisdom'[3] gave what higher education was required*. The patrons of these institutions, too, were naturally Nabû and Nidaba or Nisaba. To proceed to such a place was 'to enter the house of wisdom',[4] where 'the wise men who dwell in the house of wisdom'[5] were to be found guarding the mysteries. There presumably the youthful aspirant for a learned career, seated on benches of stone without backs (s. pl. 29),[6] studied mathematics and astronomy, medicine, magic arts and theology, and all the varied branches of 'the learning and the tongue of the Chaldaeans'.[7] The motto therefore of the school at Sippar was not inappropriately the prayer

'May he who sits in the place of clerkly lore shine like the sun!'[8]

and he certainly deserved to shine and be held in honour; for the course in 'the learning and tongue of the Chaldaeans' did not last for three years, as Daniel thought,[9] but from childhood to manhood, as the master declared in the charge quoted below to his pupil.

The method of instruction can be studied in a tablet containing a dialogue in which the 'master'[10] converses with his pupil, saying:

'Come in to the college of scholars, the courtyard [of the school];

[1] The 'woman scribe' (Sum. $^{SAL}$*DUB.ŠAR*$^{tu}$ = Bab. *ṭupsarratu*$^{m}$), usually a priestess, is not uncommon in Old-Babylonian texts (Pinches 'C.T.' VI 24 b 18, 35 a 18, Ranke 'B.E.U.P.' VI i 7 22–3); and an Aramaean woman is described as $^{SAL}$*A.BA* 'female scribe' (s. p. 16). Further a document 'which a woman has written' (Ass. *ša sinništu tašṭuru*) is mentioned in two Assyrian letters (Harper 'A.B.L.' XIII 1367 R. 4, 1368 R. 6)*.

[2] What does the Sum. *É-DUB*$^{BA}$=Acc. *šubat ṭupserti* (De Genouillac in *R.A.* xxv 124) precisely denote?

[3] Ass. *bît mumme* (Ebeling *K.A.R.I.* I 122 9).

[4] Ass. *erīb* (*bît*) *mumme* (Meissner & Rost in *B.A.S.S.* III 234–7$_{21, 24}$).

[5] Bab. *enqūtu* for *emqūtu āšib bît mummu* for *mumme* (Langdon *Neubab. Königsinschr.* 256–7 i 33, where the nom. *mummu* stands for the gen. *mumme*).

[6] Cp. Hilprecht 'Explorations' 510–25. Two school-rooms with remarkably well preserved benches, dated *c.* 2000 B.C., have been excavated at Mâri (Burrows 'What mean the Stones?' 183).

[7] Dan. i 4.

[8] Sum.-Acc. *šâ MU.UN-TIL* | *KI-NAM.DUB.SAR*$^{RA}$*-KA* | *BABBAR-DÍM ḪÉ-È* (Scheil *Sippar* 33).

[9] Dan. i 5.

[10] Ass. *ummânu*. This term originally denoted any skilled worker or master workman, whatever craft or trade he followed, and was applied especially to clerks of various grades. Here the *ummânu* is a schoolmaster, and he often appears as head of the school and library attached to a temple (Weidner *K.A.* 10¹), acting as librarian and archivist (s. pp. 74–5; cp. Scheil

come in, my son, (and) sit at [my feet]. Come, let me speak to thee (and) open thou [thine] ears.

'From thy childhood to [thy] manhood thou hast sat at school; hast thou learnt the writing art and knowest not the signs thereof?

'What is there that I know not?'

'What dost thou [know]? Come, let me ask thee, and [answer thou me]! Come, let me speak to thee, and answer thou me!

'Ask me, that I may tell thee; tell me that . . .

'If thou answerest [me] not, [I will say to thee]: why [answerest thou me not]?'[1]

Instruction therefore was by question and answer and presumably also by repetition, as all the world over*.

The study of writing[2] involved a knowledge of the old Sumerian language as well as of the native Accadian speech to make the aspirant not merely 'a school-scribe'[3] but also a 'master of language'.[4] For not only were many of the old texts, especially those dealing with religious, liturgical, and magical subjects, entirely Sumerian, but Sumerian phrases lingered, like Latin formulae in English legal documents, in Semitic documents, especially in those concerned with the law; further, numerous

in *R.A.* xv 143 A) and choosing and excerpting texts to be copied by the scribes (Ebeling *K.A.R.I.* II 177 O. iv 26–30), serving on a commission to collect important tablets for the royal library (s. pp. 76–7) or as the secretary who reads the king's correspondence to him (s. p. 72); and so Ashurbanipal speaks of himself as copying texts *ina tapḫarti ummânī* (s. p. 76 n. 5). Finally, the word is applied to an ox trained for irrigating work (Hilprecht & Clay 'B.E.U.P.' IX 49 2, 6). So Jewish scribes called themselves כותבנים אומנים 'master writers', i.e. 'artist-scribes, calligraphers' (Leveen 'Hebrew Bible in Art' 6–7).

[1] Bab. *ina pu-ḫur um-ma-ni ki-sal* [*É ṭup-pi*] | *al-ka ma-ri ti-šab ina pa-*[*ni GIR-2-ya*] | *GA.NA lu-uq-bi-ḳúm-ma pi-te uz-*[*ne-ka*] | *ul-tu UD*^um^ *ṣi-ḫi-ri-ka a-di meṭ-lu-ti-*[*ka*] | *ina É ṭup-pi ǎs-*[*ba-ta*] | *ṭup-sar-ru-ta ta-ḫu-su i-da-as-sa* (s. p. 37) *ul ti-*[*di*] | *me-nu-ú šá la i-du-u* | *me-na-a ti-*[*di-e*] | *GÁ.NA lu-šal-ka-ma* . . . | *GÁ.NA lu-uq-bi-kam-ma ap-la-an* (?)-[*ni*] | *šá-la-an-ni-ma lu-uq-bi-ka qí-ba-am-ma lu-* . . . | *ul tap-pal* . . . | *am-me-ni la tap-*[*pal*] (Ebeling *K.A.R.I.* I 111 O. ii 2–14)*. The text is transliterated syllabically, Sumerian ideograms or words in capital and Assyrian words in small italic letters; words in square brackets are conjecturally inserted where the tablet is illegible, those in round brackets are added to adapt Semitic to English idiom. The use of two different signs for the same syllable namely (𒂵 *GA* and 𒂷 *GÁ*) will be noticed (s. p. 60 n. 3).

[2] Tablets occur with simple signs or compound groups endlessly repeated for learners (Hilprecht 'Explorations' 525–6; cp. Scheil 'Sippar' 34–40).

[3] Ass. *ṭupsar mumme* (Ebeling *K.A.J.I.* 79 25).

[4] Ass. *bêl lišāni* (Harper 'A.B.L.' IV 342 O. 18, where the expression seems to refer to one acquainted with a foreign language); cp. Bab. ^LÚ^*lišānu*^m^ 'interpreter' (Schroeder *Va. Sd.* XVI 82 6; s. Kraus *Ab. B.* I 86).

Sumerian ideograms were retained in the written language, even in Accadian texts, as a kind of abbreviated script or shorthand*.

In some classes of texts Sumerian, in others Accadian, prevailed, and, although there was a progressive tendency in ordinary texts for Sumerian to give place to Accadian, the result was often more or less of a hotchpotch; and the difficulty of reading them must have been enhanced by the fact that the reader read the Sumerian signs as Accadian words, being thus engaged in a mixture of reading and translating. Further, as Sumerian became an ever less known language, it came to be ever more incorrectly written, to the increasing bewilderment of the reader. The Accadians at the same time were continually raising the number of signs which might be read syllabically as well as the number of syllabic values that any individual sign might have, until eventually nearly 300 of the 550 or so known ideograms came to be employed also to represent syllables.

Such a system of writing was immensely complicated and therefore difficult to use, and a considerable literature grew up for teaching and learning it. The 'text'[1] itself might be interlinear in two languages, the one explaining the other, or it might be furnished with glosses; it might take the form of a 'commentary'[2] on another difficult text or it might be lexical or philological. Already the tablets from Shuruppak reveal the beginning of this work, and scholars before the age of Sargon of Agade (*c.* 2751–2568 B.C.) were busy on lists of signs and words which were systematically drawn up and which were recopied by subsequent generations of scribes. The period of the third dynasty of Ur (*c.* 2408–2282 B.C.) saw the compilation of an increasing number of such lists which again in their turn were recopied when the Sumerian terms were explained by Babylonian translations in subsequent ages. This same period saw also the collection of much matter that went afterwards to the making of school-texts; of these the most famous are the two series known respectively as *ḪAR.RA* = *ḫubullû* and *ana ittišu*, containing explanations of words and phrases, especially of legal import, in parallel columns in the two languages. The bulk, however, of these texts took

[1] Acc. *šiṭru* (Ebeling in *B.B.Kf.* I/iii 4).

[2] Sum. (*UD.*)*UL.DÙ.A* = Acc. *ṣâtu* 'tradition; archaism; list of archaic words; philological commentary', put in the left column and *šût* or *ša pî* 'oral interpretation; pronunciation' put in the right column; also Sum. *NÍG.PÀD*[DA] = Acc. *mukallimtu* 'exposition of subject-matter' and *egirtu* 'commentary' (s. Kraus in *M.Va.Ä.G.* XLI/ii 33–4, Oppenheim in 'J.A.O.S.' LXIV 190, Bauer in *Z.A.* XLIII 313, Meier in *A.Of.* XII 237–40 and Weidner ibid. XIV 179)*.

shape under the first Babylonian dynasty (*c.* 2169–1870 B.C.), when Sumerian was receding before Accadian, and continued to be copied throughout the Cassite epoch (*c.* 1642–1176 B.C.); but most extant copies were made under the Neo-Assyrian (*c.* 726–609 B.C.) and Neo-Babylonian (*c.* 604–538 B.C.) kingdoms.

These lexical tablets are of various types and classes. Some of them give signs or ideograms with their names and pronunciation or with their Sumerian and Accadian word-values or meanings in three columns, while others combine this information in four columns; both simple and compound ideograms are thus explained. Others set correct and dialectal Sumerian words beside one another and add Accadian explanations after them; or they explain Sumerian ideograms by equivalent Accadian words which are further glossed by Accadian synonyms or paraphrases. There are lists of gods with their names in both languages, their titles or functions or temples, lists of countries and towns with their names in both languages, and so on. Other series contain lists of purely Accadian synonyms in two columns or glossaries of Hittite, Cassite, and even Hurrian or 'Horite', words and phrases. Phrase-books, too, have been recovered containing Sumerian and Accadian words with nominal and verbal inflexions and expressions in which they may occur.[1] Historical texts do not come within the sphere of the present study, but passing mention may be made of the lists of kings and archons and of the synchronous tables of dynasties and rulers and important events as not the least valuable part of the labours of these ancient scholars. The exact sciences, too, were not neglected, and many tablets contain long and often quite elaborate mathematical,[2] astronomical or astrological tables, magical and medical prescriptions, and so on.

Much therefore that has been preserved of Sumerian and Accadian literature, especially of a literary and religious or technical nature, rests solely on the evidence of school-texts drawn up for the use of or copied by students; but these often perpetuate the very mistakes which their youthful copyists have made. Chiera,[3] in commenting on this class of texts, has made

[1] There are, however, extant tablets containing texts in languages which still defy decipherment because of their brevity or the absence of lexical assistance from ancient scholars (e.g. Knudtzon *A-T.* I 32, Frank *St.Kt.* 49, 50, Böhl in *A.Of.* VIII 169–74).

[2] A 'list of numbers' or 'mathematical table' was called *arû* (Bauer in *Z.A.* XLIII 313²)*.

[3] In 'They wrote on Clay' 169–72.

several interesting points. First, numerous duplicate copies reveal frequent variations of spelling, to which indeed the cuneiform syllabary readily lent itself; this fact suggests that such scholastic texts were not always copied by eye from the archetype but were often taken down from dictation.[1] Second, the story or matter on many of them has neither beginning nor end, which points to excerpts taken at random for the purpose of exercises. Third, when long classical texts are in question, the copies of the opening chapters are often numerous but diminish in number as the work proceeds, until only fragments of the concluding sections are found; the reason seems to be that the students, before working their way through a whole text, have gone on to other works in order to gain experience in the widest possible field of literature.[2]

The 'copy',[3] in spite of mistakes, commonly carried a colophon that 'it has been written according to its archetype and collated',[4] or similar words, together with a note stating whence it was taken, and it was normally guaranteed by the addition of the name of the scribe who made it. The colophon might also contain not only the title of the work and the catch-line connecting the tablet with the preceding and following tablets of the same work,[5] but also its serial number in the work and

[1] The same cause accounts for the use of the wrong homonym in Sumerian texts, such as *SÙ.SÙ* for *SU.SU* 'to make good' (Lutz 'P.B.S.' I/ii 100 ii 15 = 101 O. ii 13). Such errors are aural and so distinct from those found in texts copied from clay on to stone or *vice versa*, which are commonly ocular.

[2] Hence 'incomplete' (Sum. *NU AL-TIL*) was often put at the end of such texts (Clay 'B.R.L.M.' IV 12 81 13 78; cp. Reisner *Sum.-Bab. Hymn.* xii). Occasionally tablets have gaps for filling in, e.g. names (Dougherty 'Y.B.T.' VI 10 3, 6–7)*.

[3] Sum. *GAB.RI* = Acc. *gabrû* (Streck *Assurbanipal* II $333^{6}$; cp. 354–5 b 4–5 where *ṭuppu* ^iš^*lê'u gabrû* occur together) or *gabbirû* (Oppenheim in 'J.A.O.S.' LXIV 193), from which *me/iḫru* (King 'C.T.' XXIX $39_{17}$ and Ungnad *B.B.* 268 17; s. Kraus *Ab. B.* II 170) or *me/iḫirtu* (Eilers in *O. Lz.* XXXIV $928^{1}$) 'duplicate text', chiefly of a private document, must be distinguished (s. San Nicolò *Rechtsquellen* $164^{2}$)*.

[4] Acc. *ana pî ṭupgallî labīri* (King 'C.T.' XXIV 36 R. xii 8; s. Reisner op. cit. xi–xii), *kîma labīrišu šaṭir-ma bari* (Rawlinson 'C.I.W.A.' II 10 a 25 v 25 a–b 29) or the like*.

[5] Sum. *KU.KÀR* = Acc. *iškāru* 'series' (Deimel *Sum. Lex.* II 981 536 207; s. Langdon in *Bab.* VII 94 and Ebeling *B.B.Kf.* I/iii 2), called 'strange' i.e. 'uncanonical' (Acc. *aḫû*) if not belonging to the canon, as when a text is *ša lâ KU.KÀR-ma ša pî ummâni* (s. p. 71 n. 3) 'not from the series but from the mouth of a master' (Harper 'A.B.L.' v 519 R. 1; cp. IV 447 R. 20); also *rikis girri* 'serial arrangement' (s. Bauer in *Z.A.* XLIII 313–14 and Weidner in *A.Of.* XIV 179–80)*; s. p. 81 n. 1.

even the number of lines on the tablet as well as the date not only of the original tablet but also of the copy itself*. Occasionally a copyist records that the text is 'divided into hemistichs like the archetype';[1] or he may declare that 'he has not made any mistake, he has not added a word to it'.[2] Further, if the archetype was imperfect, he might add a note that 'the copy . . . is incomplete, requiring to be made good',[3] and even a blank space in it was noted by adding 'there is nothing'[4] at that point in the copy. Finally, he may declare that he cannot rightly understand[5] a text, or that he will not divulge or publish[6] or arbitrarily withhold[7] one from such use*.

The pupil's teacher 'caused him to acquire tablet-writing',[8] as the phrase means literally, and learning was called 'acquisition'[9] from the instruction which he received from him. The first steps were reading, which was called 'hearing from' or most often 'seeing (on) a tablet',[10] and 'writing'[11] out texts; and the scholar continued these exercises until he was

[1] Ass. *ša ana pî šaṭāri ṣullupu* (Langdon 'Creation' 148–9 col. 2; s. Lambert 'Babylonian Wisdom' 66[1]). This verb perhaps means also 'to cancel' (Oppenheim 'A. D:' XVI 71, 240); cp. Syr. *ṣlap̱* 'tore apart' (Brockelmann *Lex. Syr.*[2] 630).

[2] Gössmann *Era-Epos* 36–7 v 43–4 (Bab. *šumu* 'name' = 'word'; cp. Syr. *šmâ* 'name' = 'noun').

[3] Bab. *nisḫi . . . lâ gamru ana ṭûb nisḫi* (Reisner *Sum.-Bab. Hymn.* 24 R. 28); the meaning of *ana zamar gimri* (ibid. xii–xiii) is not clear.*

[4] Ass. *la-šú* (King 'C.T.' XV 49 ii 31). Once a copyist notes that 'his case is not complete and not written' (Bab. *dînšu ûl qati u ûl šaṭir*), meaning that he cannot find the required section of the law as the following tablet is lost (Peiser in *Sb. K.P.A.W.* 1889 xxxviii 825).

[5] Bab. *uštêšir*. This verb is also used of translating a text into another language (Langdon 'P.B.S.' x iv 329 R. 25; cp. Lehmann *Šamaššumukîn* XXXV 13 i 17). [6] Bab. *ušâpi*. [7] Bab. *ikalli*.

[8] Ass. *ṭupsarrūta ušâḫisu* (Rawlinson 'C.I.W.A.' II 9 c–d 66).*

[9] Ass. *iḫzu* (Streck *Assurbanipal* II 4–5 i 33, 210–11 ll O. 8, 254–5 9 O. i 11), whence *ana iḫzi ašābu* 'to sit down to a lesson' (Waschow in *M.Ao.G.* x/i 30–1 iv l 10) is derived; cp. Hebr. לֶקַח 'taking' for 'instruction'*.

[10] As in Bab. *ṭuppī ina šemêm* 'on hearing my tablet' (Alexander in 'Y.B.T.' VII 58 4; cp. 57 8), with which the Hebr. שמע (s. p. 89 n. 4) and the Gk. ἀκούειν 'to hear; to read' may be compared, and Bab. *ṭuppī anniām ina amārim* 'on seeing this my tablet' (Driver 'Letters' A 6 4–5); also *ina ṭuppi amāru* 'to see on a tablet' (Macmillan in *B.A.S.S.* v $558_{19}$)*.

[11] Acc. *nasāḫu* 'to take an extract' (s. p. 18 n. 2; cp. Muss-Arnolt 'C.D.A.L.' 699–701), whence the Arab. *nusḫatu*[n] 'copy' of a manuscript is derived, and Acc. *šaṭāru* 'to write' and *šiṭru* or *šaṭ(ṭ)āru* 'writing, written document' and perhaps 'scroll' (Schroeder in *Z.A.* XXXIV 158[1]) as well as *mašṭāru* or *malṭāru* 'written document' (Muss-Arnolt op. cit. 602 and 1023–5; s. p. 19 n. 1), from whose root the Hebr. שֹׁטֵר 'officer' is derived (cp. LXX at Exod. v 6+)*; also Ass. *dannitu* 'confirmed document' for 'tablet, text' (ibid. 262–3) = Aram. דנת 'deed' (Delaporte *Ép. Aram.* 14–15).

proficient in them or was forced to say 'I know not' or 'I cannot',[1] and so to give up his studies. For, as his employer had 'to dictate (the text of) the document'[2] which he wished to have taken down, the scribe had to be able 'to write at the dictation of'[3] his employer. Such a scholar was called in the first days of his novitiate a 'young apprentice' or 'student'[4] or a 'young scribe'[5] whom his master employed in copying texts 'for the salvation of his soul';[6] he might then become, when fully qualified, a 'penman'[7] or 'writer of clay-tablets',[8] and perhaps a 'chief scribe'.[9] Native syllabaries, too, give lists of clerkly titles, of which not all are entirely understood; but they show that the scribe or clerk might aspire to employment in civil or military administration, in temples[10] or in law-courts;[11] and separate mention is made of 'a scribe of Sumerian'[12] who must have been useful both in the temple and in the law-court. Mention is made, too, of a 'mathematical scholar' and also, in a text from Hittite territory, of a 'physician's clerk.'[13] Thus a varied career lay open before the young scribe, who might become

[1] Acc. *ûl îdi* (Rawlinson 'C.I.W.A.' v 31 d 11).

[2] Acc. *giṭṭa qabû* (Harper 'A.B.L.' III 308 O. 4); this phrase means also 'to read a document' (ibid. XII 1245 O. 6–8)*.

[3] Ass. *ištu pî . . . šaṭāru* 'to write at the mouth of . . .' (ibid. IV 434 R. 8–12). Hence texts are described as *ša pî ummâni* or *ummâni šanê* 'from the mouth of a master' or 'of another master' (s. p. 69 n. 9) according to the source of the tradition (s. Weidner in *A.Of.* XIV 182–4).*

[4] Sum. *ŠAGAN-LÁ TUR* = Acc. *šamallû*[m] *ṣiḫru*[m] (Delitzsch *Ass. Lesest.*[3] 90 v), whence the Aram. *šᵉwalyâ* 'apprentice' is derived.

[5] Sum. *DUB-SAR TUR* = Acc. *ṭupsarru*[m] *ṣiḫru*[m] (Meissner *Ass. Stud.* VI 71 vi 83).

[6] Ass. *ana balāṭ napšātišu* (Scheil *Nouv. Voc. Bab.* $16–18_{212–14}$).

[7] Sum. *EN-GI* 'master of the reed' (Rawlinson 'C.I.W.A'. IV[2] 9 b 45) or *EN-GI-DUB* 'master of the tablet-reed' (Smith 'Bab. Hist. Texts' 85 iv 6).

[8] Sum. *IM-DUB.SAR* or *DUB.SAR* (from *IM* 'clay' and *DUB* 'tablet' and *SAR* 'to write') = Acc. *ṭupsarru*, whence the Hebr. טִפְסָר or טַפְסֵר 'marshal' is derived (Muss-Arnolt 'C.D.A.L.' 264–5), and occasionally *LÚ-KIŠIB* from *LÚ* 'man' and *KIŠIB* 'seal, sealed tablet' (Krückmann *Rechts- und Verwaltungstexte* 49[2])*.

[9] Sum. [LÚ]*GAL-DUB.SAR* (Bezold 'Catalogue' IV 1734 on 80–7–19, 56) or *DUB.SAR-MAḪ* (Scheil in *R. d. Tr.* XXXVI [*N.S.* XX] 184–6 R. 5), and Acc. [LÚ]*rab-ṭupsarrī* (Rawlinson 'C.I.W.A.' IV[2] 9b 43)*.

[10] Scheil ibid. R. 7–12; cp. San Nicolò & Ungnad *Neubab. Urk.* I *Gl.* 166–7. The *ṭupsar bîti* was the third officer in a Neo-Babylonian temple (San Nicolò in *Bayern* 1941 ii/2, 28–9, 37)*.

[11] Walther *Ab. Gw.* 179–80.

[12] Sum. [*DUB.SAR*] *EME.KU* = Acc. *ṭupsar šumē*[*ri*] (Scheil ibid. R. 13)*.

[13] Acc. *ṭupsar minâti* (Zimmern in *Z.D.M.G.* LXXIV 433) and Sum. *DUB.SAR A.ZU* (Weidner *ap.* Scheil ibid. 186)*; cp. Hilprecht 'Explorations' 531 for a mathematical school-tablet.

'the scribe of the city' or 'the secretary of the country',[1] 'the scribe of the palace',[2] 'the scribe of the palace-harem' or 'of the lady of the palace',[3] 'the king's scribe' or even 'the king's chief scribe'.[4] The myth of Ira, the god of pestilence and plague, recognized the importance of the scribe in a prayer that the singer who chants it might not fall into the clutches of the law and meet with punishment, and that the scribe who studied it might escape from his enemies and enjoy his meed of honour,[5] while a scribe who accepted a bribe was a rarity, at any rate in literature.[6] For in public esteem 'the cuneiform script, the beginning of kingship',[7] as it was called, was regarded as a high road to the highest positions in the State*.

Royal personages did not usually learn to read and write but relied on a secretary to take charge of their correspondence. Thus a correspondent writing to Ashurbanipal tells the king that 'the chief clerk' must read (this letter) twice or thrice to him,[8] naturally expecting that the king would be unable to read his report. He was wrong; for Ashurbanipal (668–626 B.C.) while crown-prince had tablets copied for his use, as the colophon of one now in the British Museum declares,[9] and the vanity with which he set his scholarly achievements on record is pardonable. He was perhaps the first king to read the cuneiform script. Thus he tells how he mastered 'the choicest of clerkly skill'[10] such as none of his predecessors had acquired, and how 'I wrote the marks of cuneiform signs, as many as have been devised, arranged in columns upon tablets, and collated

[1] Sum. *DUB.SAR URU* (Ebeling *K.A.J.I.* 244 15 248 17) or *A.BA KUR* (Waterman 'R.C.A.E.' IV 145).

[2] Acc. *ṭupsar êkallim* (Strassmaier *B.T.*, *Dar.* 393 17; cp. Ebeling *Nb.B.U.* 318 13 323 4 332 11).

[3] Sum. $^{\text{LÚ}}$*DUB.SÀR ša SAL-É.GAL* (Johns 'A.D.D.' II 1141 45); cp. Unger *Liste* iv 6.

[4] Sum. $^{\text{LÚ}}$*DUB.SAR LUGAL* (Scheil in *R. d. Tr.* XXXVI [*N.S.* XX] 184–6 R. 6 and Meissner *Ass. Stud.* VI 71 vi 85) = $^{\text{LÚ}}$*ṭupsar šarri* (Delitzsch *Ass. Lesest.*[3] 90 col. vi), who might be found in a remote city-state such as Nuzi (Chiera 'J.E.N.' III 324 34), where the scribe is called $^{\text{LÚ}}$*A.BA* (s. p. 16 n. 7).

[5] Jensen in *KB* VI i $72\text{–}3_{18\text{–}20}$.

[6] Von Soden in *Z.A.* XLIII 19 = 25 R. 73–5.

[7] Ass. *rêš šarrūti santakku* (Ebeling *K.A.R.I.* I 111 O. ii 15).

[8] Ass. *2-šu 3-šu-ma um-ma-[nu] ina pa-an šarri lil-su* (Harper 'A.B.L.' x 1006 R. 14–15; s. Oppenheim in 'J.A.O.S.' LXIV 195). The Acc. *šasû* 'to cry out' p. 73 n. 2 means also 'to read aloud' (s. p. 89 n. 4; cp. C.H. xxv b 9–11).

[9] Delitzsch *Ass. Lesest.*[3] p. 90 col. v.

[10] Ass. *nišiq ṭupsarrūti* (Streck *Assurbanipal* II 356–7c 4).

(them)',[1] and 'I read the cunning tablets of Sumer (and) the dark Accadian (language which is) difficult rightly to use; I took my pleasure in reading tablets (written) before the deluge',[2] taking his texts 'according to tablets of clay and wood[3] and copies from Assyria, Sumer and Accad',[4] and so proving himself a master of the old Sumerian language as well as of the Babylonian and Assyrian dialects[5] of the Semitic speech currently used in his own days. Yet within a century the taunt is levelled at Cyrus (538–529 B.C.) that 'he knows not the stroke of the stylus';[6] but this does not imply so much that he was expected to be a master of the cuneiform script, since such an accomplishment was obviously rare outside the class of professional scribes, as that he was a foreigner totally ignorant of the Babylonian language*.

## 11. Archives and Libraries*

Babylonian libraries were mostly temple-libraries, and every considerable temple needed one to hold the archives of the house, the title-deeds of its property, its collections of liturgical and religious texts, and other literary treasures (s. pl. 26, 1). Thus the oldest scholastic texts from Shuruppak belonged to the temple-library; the library of Nippur contained a large and varied collection of texts going back to the epoch of the king of Isin (*c.* 2301–2076 B.C.), vocabularies, legal texts, myths and other documents of the Cassite period (*c.* 1642–1176 B.C.), and that of Uruk lasted from the earliest times well into the Seleucid era, a period of some 3,000 years. The treasures of Babylon, Borsippa and Sippar did not reach so far back. The largest library, however, which archaeologists have so far uncovered is the famous royal library which Ashurbanipal 'set up in his palace'[7] beside that of Nabû's temple[8] in his capital city of Nineveh.

[1] Ass. *tikip santakkī mala bašmu ina ṭuppāni aštur asniq abrê* (Streck *Assurbanipal* 7–8; s. Schott in *Z.A.* XLIV 198[2] and Böhl in *M.Ao.G.* XI/iii 21). A considerable number of such colophons have been recovered (Streck ibid. 356–75); cp. *sanāqu ša ṭupsarrūti* (Rawlinson 'C.I.W.A.' v 41 a–b 46).

[2] Ass. *aštasi* (s. p. 72 n. 8) *kammu naklu ša šumêri ṣullulu akkadû ana šutêšuri aštu* | *ḫadâku šitassê* (?) *abnē ša lâm abūbi* (Streck op. cit. 256–7 17–18)*.

[3] S. p. 16.

[4] Ass. *kî pî ṭuppāni lê'ē gabrī* $^{māt}$*Aššur*$^{KI}$ $^{māt}$*Šumēri u Akkadî*$^{KI}$ (Streck op. cit. 354–5 b 4–5).

[5] S. pp. 88–9.

[6] Bab. *miḫiṣ GI-DUB*$^{bu}$ *ûl îdi* (Smith 'Bab. Hist. Texts' 86/90 v 10)*.

[7] Streck op. cit. II 354–5 b 4–8. Ashurbanipal's library seems, like any modern library, to have been adorned with statues (Gadd 'C.T.' XXXV 39 l R. 1–3).

[8] Streck op. cit. 364–5 n 15, 369–79 o 17.

Such importance was then attached to written records that, as Berosus[1] and Abydenus[2] report, Atrahasīs or Xisuthros (the Babylonian Noah) buried all documents before the Deluge that they might be preserved for the use of men after the disaster. Consequently the chief secretary as 'archivist'[3] was a high officer of state, and an important part of a scribe's work was 'to enter' and 'to take out'[4] tablets and 'to store them in perpetuity'[5] in the library.

A particularly valuable tablet might have a case specially made to protect it, like that which the Babylonian king Nabopolassar (604–562 B.C.) had made for the preservation of one relating to his predecessor Nabû-apal-iddin (*c.* 879–855 B.C.).[6] Usually, however, tablets were stored in a basket of reed-work, a chest of wood or a jar of earthenware;[7] and such cases of clay have been recovered from Babylon[8] (s. pl. 28, 2) and Nippur[9] and other places. Hence the archives were called by a term which means, literally translated, a 'pot of tablets',[10] and the archivist enjoyed the title of 'a son of a pot of tablets'.[11] Such a pot with increasing skill in craftsmanship gave place to a chest with a lid and an inscription describing its contents (s. pl. 28, 3); it was perhaps a 'book-case' or 'book-chest' of this sort that was called a 'clay-tablet-holding wooden container',[12] which was in charge of a 'scholar-

[1] Müller *Fragm. Hist. Graec.* II 501–2 vii 2, 7.

[2] Ibid. IV 280 i 38b (cp. Eusebius *Evang. Praep.* [414d] ix 12).

[3] Acc. *ummânu* (s. p. 65 n. 10).

[4] Bab. *šûrubu* and *šûlû* (Harper 'A.B.L.' III 334 R. 6–10).

[5] Bab. *ana ûmē ṣâti šakānu* ( ibid. R. 12–13).

[6] King 'Boundary-Stones' c–ci; s. King *Tukulti-Ninib I* 15–40.

[7] Sum.*$^{GI}$GÁ* or *GI.MAL* = Acc. *pisannu$^{m}$* (Ranke 'B.E.U.P.' VI i 103 41; s. Ungnad in *Z.A.* XXXVIII 78) where the determinative *GI* 'reed' shows the material of which such receptacles must originally or usually have been made (cp. Böhl *M.K.A.W.*, *A.L.* LXXVIII B 55–6, where the transfer of such a basket of tablets is discussed in an O.-Bab. text); also Bab. *pisan kunukkī* (Ungnad *Va. Sd.* IX 221 20–1) and Ass. *quppātu ša ṭuppāte* (Ebeling *K.A.J.I.* 310 38).

[8] Koldewey *Babylon*[4] 239–41.

[9] Hilprecht 'Explorations' 512–13, 516–19.

[10] Sum. *GÁ-DUB$^{BA.(A)}$* (Howardy *C. C.* 400–1 241 24; s. Kraus *Ab.B.* I 64) or *GÁ-DU.UB** = *gar-ṭup-pu* (s. p. 11 n. 5; cp. Ungnad ibid. 78, who doubts this equation)*.

[11] Sum. *DUMU-GÁ-DUB$^{BA.(A)}$* (Alexander 'B.I.N.' VII 50 13+)*.

[12] Sum. *IM.GÚ-LÁ-GIŠ-TUK* = Acc. *girginakku* (King 'Supplement' to Bezold's 'Catalogue' xiv–xv; s. Deimel *Sum. Lex.* II 781–2 399 79, 84–5)*; also simply *IM-LÁ* or *IM-GÚ* or *IM-GÚ-LÁ* (s. Streck *Assurbanipal* II 365[9], Zimmern in *Z.A.* XXXVI 204[7] and Scheil in *R.A.* XV 143). What is *DUB-LÁ(-MAḪ)* exactly (Legrain 'Ur' II 22)?

librarian'[1] called 'the chief of the tablet-chest'.[2] The largest collections required a whole library, called a 'house of tablet(s)' or 'of seals'[3] for their storage, like 'the house of the archives' to which Ezra refers.[4] In the various rooms in such a library, jars or chests containing the tablets, which often bore the mark of the library to which they belonged,[5] were ranged on shelves of clay or wooden ledges on the walls, as in the temple libraries unearthed at Nippur[6] and Kish.[7] The contents of the jars were presumably indicated by some kind of note or label, such as have been found at Quyunjik.[8] Thus the excavators at Kish[9] found jars, unfortunately all broken, arranged round the sides of certain rooms which had obviously served as library apartments; these contained or had contained tablets, of which many lay around mixed up with the fragments of the jars. Whole rooms were assigned to tablets of the same class, for example those dealing with grammatical and philological or religious subjects, and jars never held tablets of different contents. Such orderly arrangement was probably the rule in all libraries. Further, even private documents were generally preserved in archives attached to a temple or a palace where they might be thought to be safe; thus Hammurabi, king of Babylon, when instructing Sin-idinnam, a governor of Larsa, in a case regarding a plot of land of which the ownership is in dispute, tells him that 'a tablet has been inspected in the palace' and will be useful to settle the question.[10] Catalogues have been found at Asshur,[11] and labels, indicating the ownership of such collections of tablets, have been recovered from the archives in the palace at Mâri, unfortunately separated from the jars to

[1] Acc. *ummânu* (s. p. 65 n. 10).

[2] Sum.-Acc. *[LÚ]rab IM-GÚ* or *rab girginakki* (Langdon in *Bab.* VII vi R. 19a).

[3] Sum. *É-DUB* (Meissner *Bab. u. Ass.* I 120; cp. Böhl in *M.K.A.W.*, *A.L.* LXXVIII B 55–6 R. 8) or *É-KIŠIB* (Reisner *Sum.-Bab. Hymn.* 4 2 32, 86 48 O. 45).

[4] Aram. בֵּית סִפְרַיָּא (Ezra vi 1).

[5] Unger *Bab. Schr.* 13/14, where a tablet with the mark of Ashurbanipal's library at Nineveh is reproduced.

[6] Hilprecht 'Explorations' 342–3, 513–14.

[7] Langdon 'Kish' I 90–1.

[8] Meissner *Bab. u. Ass.* II 335. Such must have been the purpose of two small labels of clay giving the titles of two sets of tablets dealing respectively with astrology and omens (Bezold 'Catalogue' I 282/K. 1400, 305/K. 1539).

[9] Langdon 'Kish' I 90–1.

[10] King 'L.I.H.' III 23–4 9 12 (Bab. *ṭuppum ina êkallim in[namir]*).

[11] For example, catalogues of hymns (Ebeling *K.A.R.I.* I 158) and astronomical texts (Weidner in *A.Of.* XIV 184–9)*.

which they must have once been attached.[1] Finally, commercial houses in the Persian period kept their archives in 'a house of documents', of which 'a keeper of the documents' had charge.[2]

In spite of all this care expended on the libraries by the clerks, tablets frequently went astray; for there was no little borrowing (in the literal and also in the euphemistic sense of this word) of the literary treasures of these libraries. Thus a tablet of the time of Sargon, king of Assyria (*c.* 621–612 B.C.), in the library at Uruk has a note stating that it was a copy of one lent by 'the palace of Assyria'[3] and then presumably returned; another borrowed from Uruk by Nabopolassar, king of Babylon (626–604 B.C.), but not restored by him is noted as a tablet 'which he had purloined'[4] and which a priest from Uruk found in Elam and brought back to its proper home at some time in the reigns of Seleucus (311–281/0 B.C.) or Antiochus (280–262/1 B.C.). It was, however, Ashurbanipal (668–626 B.C.) who availed himself most freely and in royal manner of the privilege of borrowing books from both public and private libraries. In this manner he collected tablets from all over Assyria and Babylonia and copied them 'in a college of scholars'[5] and deposited them in his palace 'for the reading of my majesty'.[6] Apparently he incorporated whole private libraries in the royal collections, since many of the tablets from Quyunjik were inscribed with their previous owners' names. He also had copies made of large numbers of tablets in public libraries (s. pl. 18, 2), notably in those attached to temples at Babylon, Kûta and Nippur, as shown by colophons inscribed on many of them.[7]

This acquisitive spirit is reflected in several royal letters of the Neo-Assyrian empire, of which it is generally impossible to identify the king; several, however, probably come from or relate to Esarharddon (680–669 B.C.) or his successor Ashurbanipal (668–626 B.C.). Thus the writer of one letter, referring to the king's instruction 'in regard to the Sumerian

[1] Thureau-Dangin in *S.D.* II 119–20.

[2] Bab. *É-SAR*$^{RI}$ = *bît šaṭāri* and $^{LÚ}$*URÙ* (= *nāṣir*) *šaṭāri* (Clay 'B.I.M.' I 98 7 and II 33 4 56 19). What are the Sum. *É-DUP*$^{PA\cdot A}$ = Acc. *šandabakku* (Muss-Arnolt 'C.D.A.L.' 1072–3) and the Sum. *É-GA*$_4$.*-DUB* = Acc. *šaddabakku* (Meissner *B.A.Wb.* I 81 ii 60) as well as the Ass. *LÚ šandabakki* (Klauber *A.B.* 26–7)? [3] Ass. *êkalli* $^{māt}$*Ašur*$^{KI}$ (Clay 'Y.B.T.' I 38 ii 40).

[4] Bab. *ša . . . išlulu* (Thureau-Dangin in *R.A.* XI 141–2$_{3-6}$).

[5] Ass. *ina tapḫarti ummânī* (Streck *Assurbanipal* II 354–5 b 6); s. p. 65 n. 10.

[6] Ass. *ana tâmarti šarrūtiya* (ibid. 354–5 b 8).

[7] Meissner *Bab. u. Ass.* II 332–3; s. Weidner in *A.Of.* XIV 178–9.

tablets',[1] says that he is taking steps to send them to the king, and the writer of another says that he is bringing 'an original tablet which king Ammu-rapi made'[2] from Babylon as the copy on which the king is engaged is imperfect. There is another letter still extant in which the king instructs one of his officers to proceed with certain named 'specialists'[3] to Borsippa and bring thence the tablets specified in the text, even 'all the tablets that are in their houses and all the tablets that are stored in Ezida',[4] the temple of Nabû in that city; these tablets include those which refer to war and exploration, ritual and liturgical texts, inscriptions and 'what is good for kingship',[5] texts for the purification of the city and for averting the evil eye, and 'whatever is needed for the palace',[6] and finally any 'precious tablets which are not known (?) to you in the land of Assyria'.[7] Finally, in the Persian period many scholastic tablets, especially those carrying the highly valued syllabaries, contain a prayer that 'the scholar who does not alter' or perhaps 'remove the inscription but puts (it back intact) in the library' may prosper[8] or a request that 'he will not change (its text) wilfully', that 'he will not take (it) away wilfully (?)' and that 'he will not detain (it) wilfully'*.[9] Such methods of collecting, while highly injurious to the libraries thus despoiled of their treasures, have however been instrumental in preserving much that must otherwise have inevitably perished for the information of future generations of scholars; for Ashurbanipal's principal residuary legatee has been the British Museum.

[1] Ass. *ina muḫḫi šumērāni* (Harper 'A.B.L.' I 18 R. 1).

[2] Bab. *ṭuppi [la]bēru* (for *ṭuppa [la]bēra*) *ša Ammu-rapi šarru [î]pušu* (Harper ibid. III 255 O. 8–9), where *Ammu-rapi* stands for *Ḫammu-rabi* king of Babylon (*c.* 2067–2025 B.C.).

[3] Bab. *ummânū* (s. p. 65 n. 10).

[4] Bab. *ṭuppānu mala ina bîtātišunu ibaššû u ṭuppānu mala ina E-ZI.DA šaknu* (Thompson 'C.T.' XXII 1 8–9).

[5] Bab. *ša ana šarrūti ṭâbi* (Thompson 'C.T.' XXII 1 25).

[6] Bab. *mimma ḫišiḫti ana êkalli mala bašû* (ibid. 27–8).

[7] Bab. *ṭuppānu atrūtu ša mîdakkunūšimma* (?) *ina*$^{\text{māt}}$ *Ašur*$^{\text{KI}}$ *ya'nu* (ibid. 28–30).

[8] Bab. *ummânu ša MU.⟨ŠAR⟩ NU GI.GI* (= *lâ ušannû* or perhaps *ikkimu*) *u IM-LÁ(.A) BA-GAR* (Scheil in *R.A.* XV 143).

[9] Bab. *ina mêrištišu lâ ušamkir* (for *ušankir*) and *ina SAR*$^{\text{tum}}$ (for *SAR*$^{\text{tim}}$) *lâ itabal*, if *ina SAR*$^{\text{tim}}$ is taken as standing not for *ina šiṭirtim* (Scheil) but abusively for *ina mîrišti* (s. Howardy *C.C.* 307 177 35), and *ina mêrešti lâ ikalli* (Scheil ibid. 144; cp. C.H. XXVI b 9–10, 31–2).

# II
# ALPHABETIC WRITING

*ante alpha et beta*
'before the alphabet'
(Juvenal *Satire* XIV 209)

## 1. Means and Manner of Writing

THE earliest writing yet discovered in the West was on stone, carved in the living rock, incised on roughly dressed blocks or scratched on small pieces of stone; this remained one of the commonest if not the most common of the materials used from *c.* 2000 B.C. for many centuries. So the Sinaitic inscriptions in the temple at Sarâbîṭ-alḪâdim and the earliest Phoenician and Aramaic inscriptions were all carved on rock or stone. The use of fragments of pottery, commonly called 'ostraca',[1] was equally early; the oldest fragment from Gezer, also dated in the Sinaitic period, was an inscribed potsherd, and these too continued to be used right down to the Hellenistic period and indeed afterwards for unimportant notes or the like. Objects of metal, too, were often inscribed with brief texts, such as an inscribed dagger of bronze from Palestine dated *c.* 1700–1555 B.C. and a Phoenician arrow-head of the same metal from the Lebanon assigned to the tenth century B.C.

Clay was employed for writing, but to an almost insignificant extent compared with the lavish use of it in the East. The only considerable collection of clay-tablets are such of the 360 or so from Tell-elAmarna[2] in Egypt, belonging to the fifteenth and fourteenth centuries B.C., as were written in Syria or Palestine (s. pl. 44, 1); and these are the majority of them. A very few clay-tablets have also been recovered by excavation at various sites in Palestine[3] (s. pl. 44, 2). These were all inscribed with texts in the Babylonian cuneiform script and language. Another important and growing collection is from Ugarit, the modern Râs-ashShamrah[4] in Syria, containing texts in a simplified cuneiform script and a new Semitic dialect (s. pl. 45); and a few tablets with texts in this dialect have recently been found

[1] Gk. ὄστρακον 'earthen vessel; potsherd' (s. pp. 80–1).

[2] Arab. تلّ الآمرنا (Bezold & Budge 'Tell el-Amarna Tablets' ix) or ʿAmârna (Knudtzon *A.-T.* I 1–2); s. pp. 103–4.

[3] Such as Eglon, Gezer, Lachish, Taanach, and Tell-elḤesy.

[4] Arab. رأس الشمّرة 'the head (promontory) of fennel'.

at Beisân (Beth-Shean) and 'Ain-Shems (Beth-Shemesh) in Palestine*. The reason for both clay-tablets and cuneiform script in the case of these two considerable collections of documents was not that the North-Semitic alphabet did not exist at that time but that the method of writing a linear script with ink on potsherds was probably not yet sufficiently developed for the purpose of a long correspondence, nor durable enough for the preservation of documents in frequent use or of important records. The reasons for the rarity of clay-tablets and the early disuse of them in the West were the difficulty of obtaining suitable clay in Syria and Palestine and the development of a linear script including curved strokes and so unsuitable for use on it.[1]

Few texts of this early period contain any description of the means nor indeed any reference to the art of writing, and what information can be gleaned during many ensuing centuries comes almost exclusively from the Old Testament*.

Job,[2] living in the southern parts of the region now being considered, speaks of words 'graven in the rock'.[3] There is, too, unambiguous reference to writing on stone in the description of the 'stones'[4] on which Joshua[5] inscribed a copy of the law of Moses, as also of those which the Hebrew people[6] were bidden to set up and cover with plaster in the Egyptian fashion that they might have a surface capable of taking a legible text of the laws. There is therefore no reason to doubt that the 'tablets'[7] on which Moses received and afterwards rewrote the Law on Sinai were slabs of stone[8] and not cuneiform tablets,[9] to which there is no clear allusion in the Old Testament; the script on these was 'the writing of God',[10] fine work as of a god in contrast with the scratchings of a mere man on a potsherd.[11] Elsewhere the 'tablet'[12] mentioned by Isaiah[13] and Habakkuk[14] is as likely

[1] S. pp. 28–9. [2] Jb. xix 24. [3] Hebr. בַּצּוּר יֵחָצְבוּן.

[4] Hebr. אֲבָנִים. If these stones were the same as the unhewn stones of which the altar was made, they would have been plastered to take the inscription. [5] Josh. viii 32 (JER).

[6] Deut. xxvii 2–3 (D). This must have been a common practice in Palestine, where the stone is bad; this will explain why so few inscriptions have been recovered, since such inscriptions cannot have survived long in the climate of that country.

[7] Hebr. לֻחֹת. [8] Exod. xxxiv 1, 4 (JE); cp. xxxi 18 (P).*

[9] Naville 'The Text of the Old Testament' 36–45, whose theory is disproved by numerous modern discoveries (s. p. 196 n. 2).

[10] Hebr. מִכְתַּב אֱלֹהִים (Exod. xxxii 16; cp. xxxi 18)*. [11] S. pp. 84–5.

[12] Hebr. לוּחַ. The cognate Acc. *lê'u* 'tablet' was possibly of wood, as the determinative *GIŠ* 'wood' was intended to show (s. p. 16).

[13] Is. xxx 8. [14] Hab. ii 2.

to have been of wood as of clay.[1] The nearest approach to a clay-tablet is the 'brick'[2] on which Ezekiel[3] in the Babylonian captivity was bidden to make a plan of Jerusalem; such a plan might resemble those of Babylon and Nineveh on clay-tablets, but any flat brick or tile would equally have served the prophet's purpose. The great 'tablet'[4] upon which Isaiah[5] was commanded to write with 'the pen of a man' may not have been a tablet*, and the Hebrew word thus translated has been thought to denote a 'blank surface' or unwritten space[6]* on material suitable for writing, here perhaps wood in view of the kind of pen used,[7] or even a 'sheet' as distinct from a roll of writing material.[8] Whether there were also double or hinged writing tablets,[9] like those of the Romans, in Biblical times is uncertain.[10]

Potsherds or ostraca[11] occasionally written on both sides,[12] were very commonly used, being often recovered in the course of excavation; the space available was naturally limited, and their chief purpose was for taking a name, when they served as a mark of ownership, brief memoranda, lists or letters; the political letter found at Asshur[13] was unusually long for a potsherd. Possibly therefore ostraca were used for writing down or taking notes of the 'oracles' of the prophets, of proverbs and gnomic sayings, for their immediate preservation until there were enough of them or there was an opportunity to collect them into a book.[14] So Mohammed's followers were said to have collected his utterances and other *obiter dicta*, which had been hastily jotted down on leaves and such-like objects at the time of their delivery, into book-form after his death. Such a method

[1] Whatever the case may be in Accadian literature (s. pp. 16, 31), tablets of wood are mentioned in the earliest Greek literature (Homer *Il.* vi 169), waxed (Herodotus *Hist.* vii 239) as with the Romans. At Athens tablets white-washed for ink served for official notices in the fourth century B.C. (Aristotle *Ath. Pol.* xlvii 2). The Egyptians used wooden tablets smeared with stucco (Wiedemann *A. Äg.* 82). Cp. p. 31 n. 1.

[2] Hebr. לְבֵנָה. The cognate Acc. *libittu* 'brick' was not generally applied to an inscribed clay-tablet.

[3] Ezek. iv. 1; cp. xxxvii 16–20, where the 'stick' (Hebr. עֵץ 'wood') used by the prophet is now taken to be a wooden tablet (s. Hyatt in 'Bibl. Arch.' VI 75–6).

[4] Hebr. גִּלָּיוֹן.

[5] Is. viii 1.

[6] Thus the LXX[B] translate it τόμον χάρτου καινοῦ. In the Mishnah the same Hebrew word means 'margin' as the blank and unwritten part of the page.

[7] Hebr. חֶרֶט (s. pp. 84–5).

[8] Galling *Bibl. Reallex.* 464.

[9] Hebr. דֶּלֶת 'door' and then 'column' (s. p. 84) goes back to some such usage (Galling ibid. 464; cp. Torczyner 'Lachish' I 80 on 4 3).

[10] S. p. 16.

[11] S. p. 78.

[12] Cp. Exod. xxxii 15.

[13] S. pp. 121–2.

[14] Hyatt ibid. VI 76.

of preserving and afterwards putting together inspired teachings would go far to account for the lack of order so often observable in the form in which they have been handed down to posterity.[1]

Neither leather nor papyrus are mentioned in connexion with writing in the Old Testament; they were, however, in common use in the countries bordering on Palestine[2] and were perhaps employed also there*.

The literary evidence for the use of leather is abundant, and it is enough here to recall that Ctesias[3] reported that the Persian royal records were kept on 'skins'[4] of sheep or goats and that the Avesta was said to have been written on skins of oxen;[5] and Herodotus[6] reports that those of sheep and goats were used by the Ionians, and that in his own time many barbarians wrote on skins. The first mention of documents on skin amongst the Egyptians goes back to the IVth dynasty (*c.* 2900–2650 B.C.), but the earliest extant of such documents from Egypt are a roll of leather of the XIIth dynasty (*c.* 2000–1788 B.C.), reported to be in Berlin,[7] a mathematical text of the seventeenth century B.C. now in the British Museum,[8] and a parchment dated *c.* 1288 B.C. and said to have come from Thebes.[9] There is also a scrap of leather with a few broken lines of Aramaic text of the fifth century B.C. from Elephantine,[10] followed by an important collection of fourteen Aramaic letters belonging to 411–408 B.C. or thereabouts.[11] A few Greek and Iranian documents on leather or parchment dated in the last two centuries B.C. have also been recovered from Dura-Europos[12] and the Avroman Dagh.[13] The method of preparing skins at this remote period is not known, but the evidence of extant Hebrew scrolls of fairly early date suggests that it included a general system of tanning the skin and of carefully treating, especially in the matter of

[1] The Accadian scribes ensured that their tablets were read in the correct order by giving the first line of the following tablet as a catch-line at the end of the preceding tablet, as the old printers used to add the first word of the following page at the bottom of the preceding page; they gave, too, the number of the tablet and often also added the number of lines on it at the end of each tablet (s. pp. 43–4).

[2] S. pp. 16–17 for a discussion of the question whether or to what extent leather and papyrus were employed for writing in Babylonia and Assyria.

[3] Diodorus Siculus *Bibl. Hist.* II xxxii 4.

[4] Gk. διφθέραι.

[5] Bailey 'Zoroastrian Problems' 151–7.

[6] In *Hist.* V 58.

[7] Minns in 'J.H.S.' xxxv 24.

[8] Lewis *ap.* Torczyner 'Lachish' I 192.

[9] Virey in *M.M.A.F.C.* I ii 481–510.

[10] Sachau *Aram. Pap. u. Ostr.* xxviii–xxix.

[11] S. pp. 122–3.

[12] Cumont in *Fouilles de Doura-Europos* 281–337.

[13] Minns ibid. 22–65 and Nyberg in *M.O.* XVII 182–230.

making smooth, the surface destined to receive the written words; normally only the smooth face of the roll was used to take the text,[1] but the address of letters might be written on the back.

Papyrus,[2] owing to its great cheapness in comparison with skins, was the commonest writing material for all ordinary purposes in Egypt (s. pl. 30), where it grew in profusion in ancient times and whence it was exported to Phoenicia as early as the eleventh century B.C.[3] It also grew in small quantities round Lake Ḥûlah in northern Palestine, though probably not in sufficient quantities for commercial use.* The earliest written papyri go back to the Vth dynasty (*c.* 2750–2625 B.C.) in Egypt, while the Judaeo-Aramaic papyri of the fifth century B.C. from Elephantine are amongst the most famous;[4] and its use lasted through Greek and Roman times right down to the Arab conquest of Egypt. The part of the plant used was the pith cut vertically into slices. In order to make a sheet of paper, these slices were laid crosswise, some vertically and others horizontally, pressed together and dried in the sun; uneven patches were then smoothed or pressed away and the sheets glued into a long strip[5] which was cut to the required length and then rolled up.[6]

Either leather or papyrus is implied in every reference of prophet and Psalmist[7] to 'a roll of a book'[8] and the like, since only these could be rolled up;[9] but papyrus would be more easily cut with a knife and burn more readily than leather.[10] After the canonical period legend[11] told of a splendid copy of the Law written in letters of gold on leather which was sent to king Ptolemy of Egypt in 285 B.C., and Jewish tradition without doubt reflected ancient custom in requiring all copies of the Law to be written on leather in the form of a roll or scroll,[12] although

[1] Thompson 'Introd. to Gk. and Lat. Palaeogr.' 28.

[2] Lat. *cyperus papyrus*. The Greek *πάπυρος* is an Egyptian loan-word (s. p. 16 n. 4) for which the correct word is *βύβλος*, whence *βιβλίον* 'book' and 'Bible' are derived (s. p. 91 n. 4).

[3] Erman in *Z.Ä.S.* XXXVIII 10–11.

[4] S. pp. 122–3.

[5] It is uncertain whether the juice or sap of the plant itself supplied the adhesive matter or whether an artificial gum or glue was employed.

[6] Cp. Plin. *Hist. Nat.* XIII xxiii 74–xxvi 83.

[7] Jer. xxxvi 2, 4, Ezek. ii 9, Ps. xl 7.

[8] Hebr. מְגִלַּת סֵפֶר, for which LXX$^{B}$ have *χαρτίον* (= papyrus) *βιβλίου* in Jer. xxxvi [xliii] 2, 4.

[9] Cp. Hos. xiii 12 (Hebr. צרר = Arab. *ṣarra* 'bound up, tied up.' N.Ė.B.)

[10] Jer. xxxvi 23–5, 32.

[11] Aristeas *Ep. Phil.* § 176; Josephus *Ant. Jud.* XII 89–90.

[12] In *Mass Sôp̱.* i 1–3; cp. Mishn. *M$^{e}$gill.* ii 2. An Egyptian tomb of the XVIIIth dynasty (*c.* 1580–1350 B.C.) states that laws were written on rolls of leather (Hyatt in 'Bibl. Arch.' VI 74–5).

the 'Five Rolls'[1] might be written on properly prepared parchment.[2]** At the same time papyrus was used for copies of or extracts from the Scriptures; for example, the so-called Nash Papyrus, which is dated between the first century B.C.[3] and the second century A.D.,[4]* contains a Hebrew text of the Decalogue and part of the *Š<sup></sup>ma'*,[5] and the Chester-Beatty Papyri contain the bulk of the Greek text of the Old Testament. The probability therefore is that the costly leather was reserved for important or official documents and the relatively cheap papyrus was used for matter intended for private use or of a merely ephemeral nature.[6] No leather or papyrus from Palestine itself, however, has survived, except in caves round the Dead Sea, owing to the dampness of the soil. Such documents as were thought worthy of preservation were kept in earthen jars, which were very fragile; and excavation has proved that clay-tablets were so stored not only in Babylonia[7] but also in Palestine,[8] while the Bible attests their use in the case of other materials, whether papyrus or leather.[9]

The word commonly translated now 'letter' and now 'book'[10] in the Old Testament has a variety of meanings. Thus it serves not only for 'letter' in the sense of epistle[11] but also for legal documents, such as Jeremiah's deed of purchase whereby he bought his cousin's field[12] or a wife's bill of divorce[13] or an indictment.[14] In the sense of a 'book' it describes collections of poems,[15] genealogical lists or registers[16] and chronicles,[17] and codes of law;[18] and once the plural 'books' connotes the Scriptures.[19]

[1] Namely Ruth, Song of Songs, Ecclesiastes, Lamentations, Esther.

[2] Mishn. *M<sup></sup>gill.* li 2.

[3] Albright in 'J.B.L.' LVI 145–76.

[4] Cook in 'P.S.B.A.' xxv 34–56.

[5] The Hebrew confession of faith (Deut. vi 4–5).

[6] St. Paul probably referred to copies of parts of the Old Testament when he asked for τὰ βιβλία, μάλιστα τὰς μεμβράνας (II Tim. iv 13).

[7] S. pp. 74–6.

[8] Sellin *Tell Ta'annek* 141–2 (*Abb.* 40) and Driver 'Judaean Scrolls' 7, 40, 49, 388, 391.

[9] Jer. xxxii 14; cp. 'Assumption of Moses' i 17.

[10] Hebr. סֵפֶר which could be rolled up (Is. xxxiv 4) like a scroll (Jer. xxxvi 2, 4). It might perhaps denote also an 'inscription' (Exod. xvii 14, E; Jb. xix 23) like the Phoen. and Aram. ספר (s. Lidzbarski *E.S.E.* III 223 b 14 and Euler in *Z.At.W.* LV 290–1)*.

[11] Cp. Esth. ix 25 w. 26, where סֵפֶר 'letter' and אִגֶּרֶת 'epistle' are used interchangeably.

[12] Jer. xxxii 10–14.

[13] Deut. xxiv 1, 3 (D).

[14] Jb. xxxi 35.

[15] Numb. xxi 14 (JE), Josh. x 13 (JE), II Sam. i 18.

[16] Gen. v 1 (P).

[17] I Ki. xiv 19+.

[18] Exod. xxiv 7 (E), Deut. xxviii 61 (D).

[19] Dan. ix 2.

The book took the form of a 'scroll',[1] whether leather or papyrus, that could be rolled up,[2] and the text was written not crosswise but lengthwise in 'columns',[3] to the number required.[4] The roll might be of any length, being cut to the length of the book,[5] and varied in depth from 5 to 15 in. with an average of about 10 in. for literary texts, while the column was from 2 to 3½ in. wide. The writer or reader began at the right and proceeded to the left end, winding up the scroll as he finished each column with his right hand and unwinding the other end with his left hand so as to uncover a fresh blank surface or the next column as the case might be; thus 'he spread out'[6] a document to read it. The text was usually written only on the inner side but might occasionally be continued on the outer side like Ezekiel's roll written 'within and without' with lamentations and mourning and woe.[7] A tag attached to and hanging down from one end of the roller round which the scroll was wound gave the title, at any rate in Graeco-Roman times, of the work which it contained.

The oldest instrument of writing was a crude 'stylus'[8] or 'pen'[9] whether 'with a point of a diamond' or rather 'emery'[10] or 'of iron', as Jeremiah says;[11] such would be an instrument with which any common man acquainted with the alphabet could scratch letters on the surface of a stone, a brick or a potsherd. It was therefore probably 'the pen of a man'[12] which

[1] Hebr. and Aram. מְגִלָּה (cp. Jer. xxxvi 2, 4 w. 6 and Ezr. vi 2).*

[2] Is. xxxiv 4; cp. Rev. vi 14.

[3] Hebr. דְּלָתוֹת (s. p. 80 n. 9). [4] Jer. xxxvi 23.

[5] The earlier rolls tended to be longer than the later, and one of 150 ft. containing the whole Iliad and Odyssey is known; but a roll of this length was very inconvenient to handle, whence Callimachus said *μέγα βιβλίον μέγα κακόν* in reference to the form and not to the matter of such works.

[6] Hebr. פרש (Is. xxxvii 14); cp. 1 Macc. iii 48.

[7] Ezek. ii 9–10. [8] Hebr. חֶרֶט. [9] Hebr. עֵט.*

[10] Thompson 'Dictionary of Assyrian Chemistry and Geology' 133.

[11] Jer. xvii 1; cp. Jb. xix 24, where the Massoretic text says 'with an iron pen and lead' (Hebr. בעט ברזל ועפרת). As a pen of lead would make no impression on a rock, Jewish tradition explained the phrase as meaning that the letters, after being incised with a pen of iron, were filled up with lead in the modern fashion; but no such custom has been found in antiquity. Another view is that the lead is parallel to the rock as the substance on which the pen works, like the *μολύβδινοι χάρται* of the Greeks, as the Vulgate's *plumbi lamina* suggest; this perhaps requires the alteration of 'and lead' into 'in lead' and of the following 'and' into 'or' (Driver & Gray 'Job' I 170–1, II 126), but it is supported by the discovery of Hittite texts engraved on lead (s. p. 15 n. 8)*.

[12] Hebr. חֶרֶט אֱנוֹשׁ.

was thus distinguished from that of the professional scribe,[1] and which Isaiah was bidden to take and use on a tablet at God's bidding.[2]

Nothing that has yet been recovered by excavation has been identified with certainty as a stylus, but mention may here be made of several curious objects which have been claimed as such, two from a Syrian grave of which the exact site is unknown but which may have been at Gebal, and one from a grave at Megiddo.[3] The first from Gebal is a rod of bronze encased in a glassy paste; the upper part of the handle has a band of gold with a granulated ring fixed above it and a small golden disk above it on the knob at the top, while its lower part is plated with gold-leaf, of which the top has a band of granulated work patterned in triangles; its original length seems to have been about 19–20 cm. The second must have been of similar work but has been recovered only in a very imperfect state of preservation (s. pl. 31 A). That from Megiddo, which is much impaired by weathering and the oxidization of the bronze, is of the same type but is not decorated with gold; its point is lost but may once have been furnished with a tip of some metal, probably also bronze (s. pl. 31 B). Both are dated *c.* 1800–1650 B.C., and the probability is that that found at Megiddo originates from the same source as the Syrian and that all three are Syrian work. There are also two similar instruments from Asshur, dated *c.* 1000 B.C.,[4] which are supposed to have been intended for the same purpose, whatever that may have been. This has been a subject of conjecture, but the general view seems to be that all five objects are some kind of writing implement or stylus. The suggestion has some degree of plausibility but is only a guess, like the identification of many objects of archaeological study.

The stylus must be distinguished from the 'pen',[5] called 'the pen of the scribes',[6] as the instrument of the professional writer. This was normally of reed[7] for use with ink on sherds or any

[1] S. pp. 78–9. So 'the cubit of a man' was an ordinary cubit as distinct from that which might be expected amongst giants (Deut. iii 11).

[2] Is. viii 1, where the M.T.'s חרט is translated *stilus* in the Vulgate.

[3] Watzinger *Tell el-Mutesellim* II 9–12.

[4] Galling *Bibl. Reallex.* 199–200.

[5] Hebr. עֵט, by which both 'stylus' and 'pen' may be loosely designated.

[6] Hebr. עֵט . . . סֹפְרִים (Jer. viii 8).

[7] S. pp. 30–1; cp. Ps. xlv 2, where עֵט is translated κάλαμος by the LXX, *stilus* (Jer. *iuxt. Hebr.*) and *calamus* (Jer. in *Ps. Rom.*)

other suitable surface;[1] for this purpose the point was prepared by splitting the ends of the fibre which were thus loosened and softened so as to resemble the hairs of a paint-brush. Only sculptures of Assyrian origin show how such a pen was held in writing;[2] in some of these it seems to be held in such a way that it rests with its top against the middle finger while the forefinger presses the writing end against the thumb (s. p. 22 fig. 4A); in others it is held lightly between the thumb and the forefinger (s. pls. 23, 2 and 24).

The 'ink'[3] employed in writing books and so on was apparently a composition of carbon, being soot mixed with a solution of gum or olive-oil on parchment, but a metallic composition when papyrus was used; both kinds are mentioned in the Talmud.[4] Analysis, too, of the ink of one of the letters from Lachish has suggested a mixture of iron in the form of oak-galls or copperas and carbon.[5] The expressed juice of the cuttle-fish was also employed, at any rate by the Romans.[6] Whichever Oriental scribes used, it did not sink deep below the surface and was easily washed off with a sponge or the like.[7] Alternatively the 'penknife'[8] might be used for erasure if the surface permitted it, but its chief purpose was that the leather or papyrus might be cut to the required shape as to depth and length, its ends and edges tidied and so on, and that the reed-pen might be trimmed; it might also serve for the destruction of a roll, as the story of Jehoiakim shows.[9] The 'inkhorn'[10] was not so much an ink-pot as a palette with a slot in which the pens were kept and hollowed places in which the ink was put, generally two for black and red ink; for the Hebrew word was an Egyptian loan-word and the palettes used by the Egyptian scribes were of this type (s. pl. 32).[11]

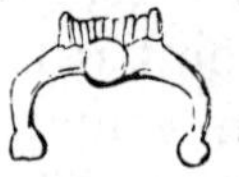

FIG. 33. Supposed ink-pot or pen-rack.

[1] Cp. διὰ χάρτου καὶ μέλανος (II Jn. 12) and διὰ μέλανος καὶ καλάμου (III Jn. 13).

[2] S. pp. 22–3.

[3] Hebr. דְּיוֹ (Jer. xxxvi 18).

[4] Bab. Talm. *Šabb.* 23a (carbon) *Šabb.* 104b, 133b *Giṭṭ.* 11a 19a (oak-galls)*.

[5] Lewis 'Lachish' I 188–95.

[6] Persius *Sat.* iii. 13.

[7] Numb. v 23 (P).

[8] Hebr. תַּעַר הַסֹּפְרִים.

[9] Jer. xxxvi 23.

[10] Hebr. קֶסֶת הַסֹּפְרִים (Ezek. ix 2, 3, 11). The Hebr. קֶסֶת like the Gk. κάστυ (Aq. and Theod. *ad locum*; cp. Hippolytus *Comm. in Dan.* IV lvii 248), which is a mere Hebraism, is a loan-word from the Eg. *gst(y)* 'writing outfit' (Müller in *O. Lz.* III 49–51).

[11] Glanville in 'J.E.A.' XVIII 53–61, where a number of such writing outfits made of various substances (wood, slate, limestone, alabaster, ivory) are described.

They were also well known to Syrian scribes, since three have been found on Aramaean inscriptions and one is depicted on an Aramaean monument[1] where the scribe carries it 'on his loins' or 'at his side' (s. pl. 33, 1), as described by the prophet,[2] just as the Accadian scribe carried his 'in the sash'[3] in accordance with a custom still observed in the East.[4] Whether the curious object depicted on several Aramaean monuments[5] (s. p. 86 fig. 33 and pl. 33, 2) is another kind of ink-pot, as sometimes supposed, or something in the nature of a stand or rack for pens, or indeed is anything connected with writing, is uncertain*

## 2. Diffusion of Writing

Writing, though not so old nor so widely diffused in the West as in the East, was well known there between *c.* 2000 and 1000 B.C., which is the period of the earliest attempts so far revealed by excavation.[6]

Apart from outcrops of cuneiform writing, there was no written literary composition in the ordinary sense till the middle of this period, when the earliest Phoenician inscriptions with a continuous text appear,[7] possibly 500 years before the Song of Deborah,[8] which is generally regarded as the earliest portion of the Old Testament. Approximately contemporary with these inscriptions was the Hebrew Calendar of Gezer, now dated about the tenth century B.C.;[9] and various fragments, mostly in verse, embedded in the Old Testament fall between these

[1] Sachau *Aram. Pap. u. Ostr.*, *Texte* 244 & *Tafeln* 68/3; Aimé-Giron in *B.I.F.A.O.* XXXIV 83–91 and XXXVIII 47–57.

[2] Ezek. ix 2, 3, 11.

[3] S. p. 31.

[4] Curiously enough, this writing outfit is omitted on Assyrian sculptures depicting scribes at work (Thureau-Dangin *Til-Barsib* 56).

[5] Clermont-Ganneau *Album d'Antiquités* xlvi (*Br-rkb*) and Von Luschan *Ausgrabungen in Zendschirli* IV 329–30/239 and 374–7/273).

[6] The assertion that the primary basis of Pentateuchal criticism was the assumption that writing was unknown to the Hebrews of the Mosaic age was long ago disproved (s. S. R. Driver 'I.L.O.T.'[9] 158), and this argument was surely never adduced by any responsible, certainly by any recent, scholar (s. Orr 'The Problem of the Old Testament' 374); one of the last scholars even to refer to it only asked tentatively whether writing was then feasible on a large enough scale for the recording of the Law and disclaimed the argument as in any sense decisive (Reuss *Die Geschichte der heiligen Schriften alten Testaments*[2] [1890] 96; cp. Naville 'The Text of the Old Testament' 45).*

[7] S. pp. 104–6.

[8] Jud. v 2–31.

[9] Cp. Albright in 'B.A.S.O.R.' LVIII 29 w. Aimé-Giron in *A.S.A.É.* XLII 331–8.

dates and the ninth and eighth centuries B.C.,[1] to which the Moabite Stone and some Aramaic royal inscriptions belong.

Books were already known before the establishment of the monarchy, when Samuel wrote 'the manner of the kingdom' in a book,[2] and royal records were kept thus in Solomon's time.[3] The compilers, too, of the earliest narratives of the Pentateuch in the tenth or ninth century B.C. were familiar with books, whether they contained collections of ancient poems[4] or the laws of Moses.[5] A knowledge of writing was assumed before the monarchical period in a leader like Moses,[6] in a number of ordinary Israelites[7] and even in a young citizen of Succoth.[8] Under the monarchy a number of prominent persons could write; such were the two kings David[9] and Jehu,[10] an unnamed king of Syria,[11] and even the queen-consort Jezebel,[12] while two of the prophets of the eighth century B.C., Hosea[13] and Isaiah,[14] could do so, if the text in each or any of these instances is to be taken in the literal sense.[15] Isaiah, too, could speak of the trees of a forest being so few that a child could write them;[16] every Israelite householder was bidden to write the words of the Law upon his doorposts and gates,[17] and writing was regularly used for legal purposes.[18] Yet writing and reading were not widely spread accomplishments. The court required a scribe,[19] although royal persons might read and write,[20] and 'one that knew writing'[21] was clearly an uncommon person;[22] hence the prophet Jeremiah employed Baruch as his scribe, and king Jehoiakim had what was written read to him by Jehudi.[23] In fact, a knowledge of writing was probably a rare accomplishment and quite unusual amongst common folk,[24]

[1] Such as parts of the Blessing of Moses (Gen. xlix 2–27) and fragmentary poems concerning the Israelite conquest of the Amorites and Moabites (Numb. xxi 21–xxiv 25).

[2] I Sam. x 25.

[3] I Ki. xi 41.

[4] Numb. xxi 14 (JE); cp. Josh. x 13 (J) and II Sam. i 18.

[5] Josh. i 8($R^D$) viii 31–2 ($R^D$) xxiii 6 ($R^D$); cp. xxiv 26(R).

[6] Exod. xvii 14 (JE); cp. xxxii 32–3 (JE), where Moses refers to God's book.

[7] Josh. xviii 2–9 ($R^D$).

[8] Jud. viii 14 (E), where the R.V.'s translation of כתב 'he wrote' by 'he described' is quite unjustified (as in Josh. xviii 4, 6, 8, 9 R)*.

[9] II Sam. xi 14.

[10] II Ki. x 1.

[11] II Ki. v 5 (where however שלח, not כתב, is used).

[12] I Ki. xxi 8.

[13] Hos. viii 12.

[14] Is. viii 1.

[15] Cp. II Chron. xxx 1 (Hezekiah) and xxxii 17 (Sennacherib) where the lateness of the source throws additional doubt on the tradition*.

[16] Is. x 19.

[17] Deut. vi 9 xi 20 (D).

[18] Deut. xxiv 1, 3 (D), Jer. xxxii 10, 12; cp. Jb. xiii 26 xxxi 35.

[19] Hebr. סֹפֵר (s. p. 16 n. 7).

[20] Cp. Deut. xvii 18–19, II Ki. xix. 14; s. pp. 72–3.

[21] Hebr. יוֹדֵעַ סֵפֶר.

[22] Is. xxix 11–12.

[23] Jer. xxxvi 4, 21.

[24] S. pp. 122–3.

who resorted to professional scribes[1] in the bazaar or market-place when they wanted anything written then as to-day in the East, being content, like unlettered Babylonians and Assyrians,[2] to leave a 'mark' in place of their signature.[3] There was therefore no specific word for reading, and a man said that another had 'recited' and that he had 'heard'[4] what was written to him; and these terms were applied not only to high officers of state but even to professional scribes*.[5]

In spite of an occasional reference to 'disciples'[6] in the Old Testament,[7] professional 'teachers'[8] are apparently not mentioned anywhere in it till a comparatively late date, perhaps even the Hellenistic epoch.[9] There were, however, 'families of scribes'[10] and perhaps also guilds or companies of scribes,[11] amongst whom the mysterious art would be handed down from father to son or other relation;[12] thus according to legend Ahiqar,[13] a 'wise and expert scribe' in the service of Esarhaddon, having no son, taught his wisdom to his sister's son.[14] Children destined to become scribes were presumably taught the alphabet, while still quite young,[15] by a master endlessly repeating the letters to them and listening to them reciting them after him. Thus the drunkards of Ephraim, mocking the prophet, liken him to a dull drone of a schoolmaster as they cry

> 'whom will he teach knowledge?
> whom will he make to understand the message?
> them that are weaned from the milk
> and drawn from the breasts?
> for it is *ṣ–ṣ, ṣ–ṣ,*
> *q–q, q–q*—
> (you) boy, there, (you) boy there!'

[1] Such persons were not above forgery (Josephus *Ant. Jud.* xvi x 319).

[2] S. pp. 62–3.

[3] Hebr. תָּו (Ezek. ix 4, 6; s. p. 211). This word is also the name of ת *t* (s. p. 162).

[4] Jer. xxxvi 11 (שׁמע; s. p. 70 n. 11) and li 61 (וראית וקראת), 63 (לקרא).

[5] The Jewish-Aramaic papyri from Egypt often contain a statement that such and such a scribe wrote the document 'according to' (Aram. בכפי) or 'at the mouth of' (Aram. על פם or כפם) such and such a person (Cowley 'Aram. Pap.' $2^{18}$ $3^{21}$ $5^{15}$ $6^{16-17}$ $8^{27-8}$ $9^{16}$ $10^{20-1}$ $11^{16}$ $13^{17}$ $14^{11-12}$ $18^{3-4}$ $20^{16}$ $25^{17}$ $28^{14-15}$; cp. $15^{37-8}$ $26^{23}$ $43^{11}$ $45^{9}$).

[6] Hebr. לִמֻּדִים.

[7] Is. viii 16.

[8] Hebr. מְלַמְּדִים.

[9] Ps. cxix 99, Prov. v 13.

[10] 1 Chron. ii 55.

[11] 1 Macc. vii 12.

[12] The Jewish-Aramaic papyri from Egypt give the names of several scribes who apparently were father and son (Cowley 'Aram. Pap.' $10^{21}$ $13^{17}$, father; $18^{3-4}$ $20^{16}$ $25^{17}$, son) or brothers (ibid. $5^{15}$ $11^{15}$ $8^{27-8}$ $28^{14-15}$).

[13] Aram. ספיר חכים ומהיר (cp. Ps. xlv 2, Ezr. vii 6).

[14] Cowley 'Aram. Pap.' '*Aḥ*. 1, 18.

[15] Cp. Is. x 19 xxviii 9.

In other words, the prophet is but a schoolmaster reciting *ṣ–q* to the answering *ṣ–q* of his pupils, first this lad and then that lad;[1] for *ṣ* and *q* are two successive letters of the Hebrew alphabet, as *p–q* are successive letters of the English alphabet*.[2] Thus the 'alphabet',[3] which was wont to be recited in a kind of sing-song, was called apparently by an onomatopoeic word describing continuous or repeated sound, rumbling, groaning, moaning, murmuring, musing, and meditation. After learning the alphabet the learner must have proceeded to reading and writing, but nothing is known of this stage in the Hebrew scholar's education; a potsherd however has been recovered by excavation at Samaria containing roughly scribbled and barely intelligible writing (s. pl. 55, 2) which may represent a child's early attempt to scribble a few letters of the alphabet.[4]*

## 3. Undeciphered Marks and Inscriptions

What are apparently the earliest attempts at writing in the West come from a place now called Teleilat-elGhassûl[5] in the centre of the plain of Moab, where excavations have yielded a large number of inscribed objects, including carved stones and pebbles, seals, bricks and potsherds (s. pl. 34, 1);[6] these have been found in all four layers, which are dated *c.* 2500–1800 B.C. Some 150 of the 300 potsherds found here have only

[1] Is. xxviii 9–10. The traditional translation of צַו לָצָו and קַו לָקָו is 'precept upon precept' and 'saw upon saw' (A.V., R.V.); but קַו (*qaw*) 'line' means a 'cord' or 'measuring line', not a 'line of writing', and צו (*ṣaw*) 'saw' in the sense of 'maxim, proverb' does not otherwise occur but is invented for the purpose of explaining the present passage, as though derived from צִוָּה (*ṣiwwāh*) 'commanded' (s. pp. 167–8). Further, the neuter 'a little' hardly makes sense in such a context, while the masculine 'a lad' echoes the last clause of the preceding verse (s. Procksch *Jesaia* 354–5). Ought then שׁ(י)ם זְעֵיר 'attend, child' to be read?*

[2] Kennett 'Hebrew Social Life and Custom' 12; cp. the English 'p's and q's' for the choice of letters late in the alphabet.

[3] Hebr. הִגָּיוֹן (*higgāyôn*) 'alphabetic poem' (Ps. ix 17; s. Wutz *Psalmen* 17) = Syr. *hegyānâ* 'rudiments of letters' and Arab. *hijâ* 'alphabet'; elsewhere 'thrumming' a harp (Ps. xcii 4) whose strings were repeatedly struck as the single note was not resonant enough to maintain accompaniment to a singer's voice (s. Galpin 'Music of the Sumerians' 44) and continued 'muttering, musing' (Ps. xix 15). The verbs are the Bibl. Hebr. הָגָה (*hāgāh*) 'growled, groaned, moaned, muttered, mused' and Mishn. Hebr. הָגָה (*hāgāh*) 'spelled' and the Arab. *hajâ* 'spelled; satirized, scolded' (s. Driver in 'J.T.S.' XLIII 151).

[4] Sukenik in 'Q.S.' LXV (1933) 155. Nothing is known of libraries; for that ascribed to Nehemiah is undoubtedly fictitious (II Macc. ii 13).

[5] Arab. تليلة الغسّول 'the hillock of wild mallow'.

[6] Duncan in 'Q.S.' LXIV (1932) 71–7.

one sign, others have from two to six signs each; and approximately 170 stones are similarly inscribed. The marks, all incised or scratched on the objects with a pointed flint or some kind of graving tool, are of a very crude type; the same signs, too, are often repeated and all are much alike, thus constituting a well-characterized group in which straight lines predominate, while curves are very rare. These marks cannot for the most part be compared with the more or less contemporary marks found on pottery from various sites in Egypt,[1] but some of them recall if they do not resemble Canaanite or Phoenician alphabetic signs. The number and variety of the objects so marked indicate constant use amongst the inhabitants of the locality; the signs therefore were probably intended as makers' or owners' marks. If this were so, it would suggest that the origin of writing in this part of the world was to be sought not in economic needs but in the necessity for the identification of property.

Such inscribed stones, if rightly regarded as having been intended to indicate ownership by means of distinguishable symbols, must probably be distinguished from the scored pebbles found in a field near Sidon (s. pl. 34, 2).[2] These are beach-pebbles of rather hard finely grained limestone, roughly elliptical or nearly circular in shape, having a diameter on an average of approximately 2 in. and being about ½ in. thick. They are scored on both sides with shallow grooves made with a wheel and cut in straight lines in every variety of number and arrangement, no two patterns being exactly alike; but the pattern on the one face is more or less exactly reproduced on the other face of the same pebble. The scoring therefore is not accidental but intentional, being made with a view to rendering each pebble clearly recognizable and distinct from all the others; but the differences are not so marked as those which distinguish the letters of an alphabet from one another. The most plausible conclusion then is that these pebbles were not intended as marks of ownership, whether alphabetic or otherwise, but for use in some kind of game; but no conjecture can be made as to the nature of this game. Their date is equally uncertain, for nothing likely to throw any light on it has been found in their immediate neighbourhood.

The ancient Gebal,[3] whose Greek name was Byblos,[4] a

[1] S. pp. 102–3. [2] Torrey in 'A.A.S.O.R.' II–III 119–25.

[3] Arab. جَبْلَة ' hill' or جُبَيْل 'hillock'.

[4] Apparently Gebal was so called because *βύβλος* 'papyrus' (s. p. 82

Phoenician town on the coast not far to the north of Beirut, was the scene of persistent attempts to develop an alphabetic script.[1] These were a result of the commercial activity of the rulers and merchants of Gebal, whose position on the shores of the Mediterranean Sea made it an important link on the trade-routes between the East and the West.

This place has yielded an important group of inscriptions on stone and metal contemporary with the Egyptian Middle Kingdom (*c.* 2100–1700 B.C.) written in a pseudo-hieroglyphic script which conceals a language or languages still defying interpretation.[2] They are briefly described in the following list:

(i) a large slab of stone with ten lines of text, of which half the left side and perhaps also the bottom are lost, containing 38 distinct signs (s. pl. 36, 1);

(ii) a small slab of stone with five lines of text, of which top and bottom and both sides are lost, running vertically down and not horizontally across the five columns and containing 17 distinct signs (s. pl. 37, 3);

(iii) one fragment of stone with remnants of four lines and one other fragment with traces of three lines of text, in which scarcely a single sign is fully legible, both probably portions of the same monument;

(iv) a piece of stone with four signs running down, not across, it (s. pl. 37, 1);

(v) a large tablet of bronze with 13 lines of text on the obverse and two on the reverse side, containing 53 distinct signs (s. pl. 38);

(vi) a small tablet of bronze with 22 lines of text on one side and 19 lines on the other, containing 64 distinct signs (s. pl. 39);

(vii) a small spatula of bronze inscribed on only one side with three lines of text containing eleven distinct signs (s. pl. 37, 2);

(viii) a small spatula of bronze inscribed on one side with four and on the other with three lines of text, in which the words are apparently separated by vertical strokes;

(ix) a large spatula of bronze inscribed on one side with five and on the other with four lines of text, in which the signs can only be made out with difficulty owing to the oxydization of the metal but in which the words can be seen to be divided by vertical strokes;

n. 2) was originally imported from Egypt through Gebal into Greece; but the change of name was helped by the assonance*.

[1] S. pp. 104–6.

[2] Dunand *Bybl. Gr.* 71–86. The recently announced decipherment of these inscriptions is said to show that they are written in a form of the Phoenician language (Dhorme in *C.R.A.I.B.-L.* 1946, 360–5 and 472–9)*.

(x) a spatula of bronze inscribed on one side with four and on the other with three lines of text containing fifteen distinct signs of which some on the side with four lines are facing in the opposite direction to that otherwise observed in these texts (s. fig. 34).

There are also from the same place a spatula of bronze with traces of pseudo-hieroglyphic signs on one side and a Phoenician inscription on the other side and a block of stone with an inscription, of which unfortunately only the beginning of the three lines of the text are preserved, set in a rectangular frame (s. pl. 36, 2);[1] in this the signs have some affinity with those of the pseudo-hieroglyphic script from the same place but in other respects so closely resemble the earliest forms of the Phoenician letters, that Grimme may be reasonably followed in reading בגבל *b-gbl* 'in Gebal' and רב *rb* 'master' in the second line.[2]

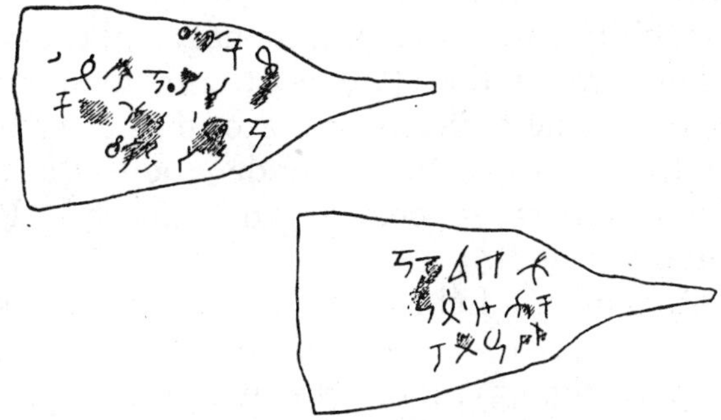

FIG. 34. Spatula from Gebal.

The signs in the inscriptions on all the objects just described are clearly not numerous enough for a pictographic or even for a syllabic script, but they are equally clearly too numerous for an alphabet; in appearance most of them are pseudo-hieroglyphic but some of them strongly recall various forms of the Phoenician letters. In other words, these inscriptions present a system of writing lying midway between the Egyptian hieroglyphic script and the Phoenician alphabet, possibly an elaborated alphabet combined with a certain number of signs having determinative values. At the same time, their script on the one hand shows no affinity to that of the Sinaitic inscriptions, and the two systems must probably be regarded as parallel developments; on the other hand many of the signs resemble those of the epigraphs

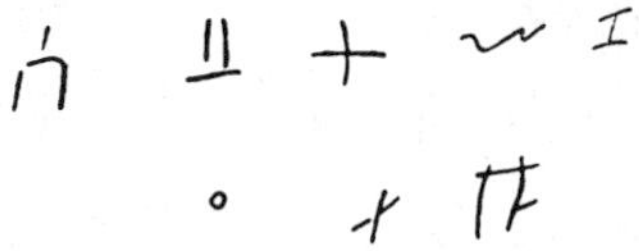

FIG. 35. Potter's marks from Lebe'ah.

[1] Dunand *Bybl. Gr.* 85–6 and 135–8; s. Albright in 'B.A.S.O.R.' LXIII 10–11, Grimme in *Muséon* XLIX 85–98, Gaster in 'P.Q.S.' LXIX [1937] 56, Böhl in *Z.D.P.-V.* LXI 17*.

[2] In *Altsin. Forsch.* 117–8.

found at Lachish,[1] which may be due to borrowing on the one side or the other or perhaps rather to common influences. These inscriptions therefore are of the greatest importance for the history of the development of the alphabet, and the absence either of texts of sufficient length or of a single bilingual text to facilitate their decipherment is a matter of the greatest regret. They remain, therefore, for the moment as tantalizing evidence of the earliest Phoenician gropings after an alphabet, parallel to the attempts being made about the same time by other Semites both in central and southern Palestine and in the Sinaitic mines.

A tomb at Lebeʿah beside the road from Sidon to Jezzîn, dated *c.* 1840–1790 B.C., has yielded some potters' marks (s. p. 93 fig. 35); these closely resemble early forms of letters of the Phoenician alphabet, but their identity cannot be proved as they are not likely to have been intended to be and obviously cannot be read as a coherent sentence. Unfortunately, too, there is as yet no connecting link between these markings and the earliest intelligible Phoenician inscriptions, which greatly increases the difficulty of interpreting them.*

## 4. Sinaitic Inscriptions

Leibovitch[2] has recently republished two fragmentary texts from the district of Sinai which have been long known but have not yet been deciphered (s. fig. 36). Several of the signs on these inscriptions resemble others on the inscriptions from Gebal just discussed or on the Sinaitic inscriptions and on the potsherd from

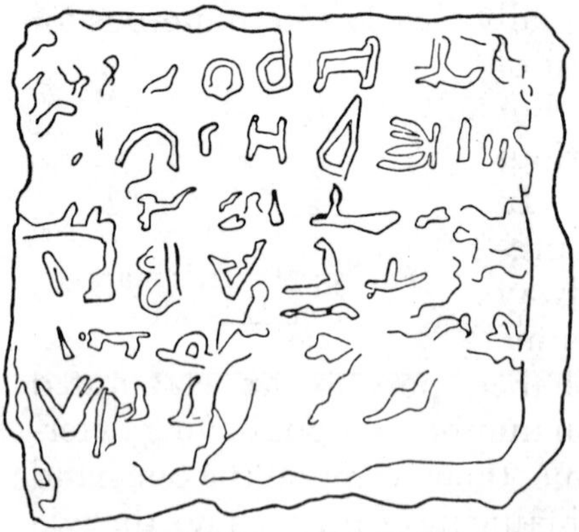

A. Inscription from Wâdī Mukattab.[3]

B. Inscription from Wâdī Qan'ah.[4]

Fig. 36. Inscriptions from Sinai.

[1] Guiges in *B.M.B.* I 42–4.

[2] In *B.I.É.* XVI 177–81. [3] Arab. وادى آلمكتّب 'the inscribed ravine'.

[4] Arab. وادى القناة 'the ravine of the subterranean stream'.

Beth-Shemesh which follow. Even with this help there seems to be no chance of discovering their sense, but they are useful as evidence of an early script.

FIG. 37. Inscriptions from mines of Sinai.

The next group of inscriptions, also from Sinai, is the most important of this early period. They are those of which Flinders Petrie[1] announced the discovery in the winter of 1904–5 in the temple of Sarâbîṭ-alḪâdim in the Sinaitic peninsula and of

[1] In 'Researches in Sinai' 129–31.

which Gardiner and Peet[1] published copies in 1916.[2] These ill-written texts are apparently the work of Semitic labourers employed by the Egyptians in the Sinaitic mines, and they have been variously dated *c.* 1850 B.C. (Sethe) or *c.* 1600 B.C. (Gardiner) or *c.* 1500 B.C. (Petrie).[3] The script displays a multiplicity of forms, for which the reason is disputed; the most plausible is either that the signs were originally written in a somewhat cursive form with pen and ink on potsherds[4] or that they were tentative copies of Egyptian hieroglyphs.[5] However this may be, these inscriptions contain between 20 and 30 different signs; but the exact number is uncertain as it is still doubtful whether some of them are distinct signs or variant forms of the same sign. This low number shows that they represent not a syllabary, which may require an immense number of signs, but an alphabet, for which any number between 20 and 35 will suffice.[6] Many if not most of these signs more or less closely resemble various forms of Egyptian hieroglyphs and/or proto-Semitic letters (s. p. 95 fig. 37); the language, however, is certainly not Egyptian but in all probability a Semitic, and most likely a North-Semitic, dialect*.

Several attempts, as ambitious as they are unsatisfactory, have been made to solve the riddle of these, unfortunately all

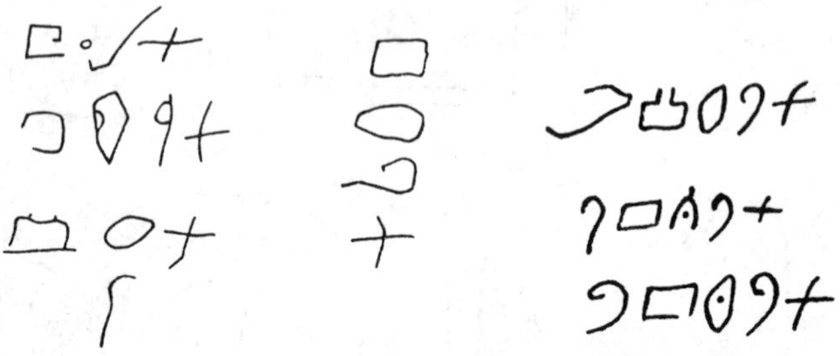

A. B.

FIG. 38. A divine name alone (A) and with a preposition (B).

damaged or fragmentary, texts but only three or four words have up till now been plausibly explained on them (s. pl. 40). First, Petrie,[7] recognizing a group of four or five signs which recurred

[1] In 'Inscriptions of Sinai' I lxxxii–lxxxiii (hand-drawn copies).

[2] Other fragments have been found recently by American expeditions (Lake & Blake in 'H.T.R.' XXI 1–8 and Lake & Barrois ibid. XXV 95–121; Starr & Butin in 'S.D.' VI 31–42), so that some thirty are now known; cp. Barrois in *R.B.* XXXIX 595 (s. xxvi/4), who speaks also of a bilingual text.

[3] Cp. Leibovitch in *B.I.É.* XVI 24.

[4] Sprengling in 'Alphabet' 3, 50.

[5] Février in *J. As.* CCXX 376–7.

[6] S. pp. 140–4.

[7] In 'Researches in Sinai' 129.

several times, suggested that they concealed a religious phrase, and Gardiner[1] proposed (ל)בעלת (*l*)*b*ʿ*lt* '(for) Baalat' (s. p. 96 fig. 38). This reading was inferred from two facts: that these signs resembled the figures from which four Phoenician letters were thought to have been derived and that the inscriptions had been found in a temple of Ḥatḥor, an Egyptian goddess

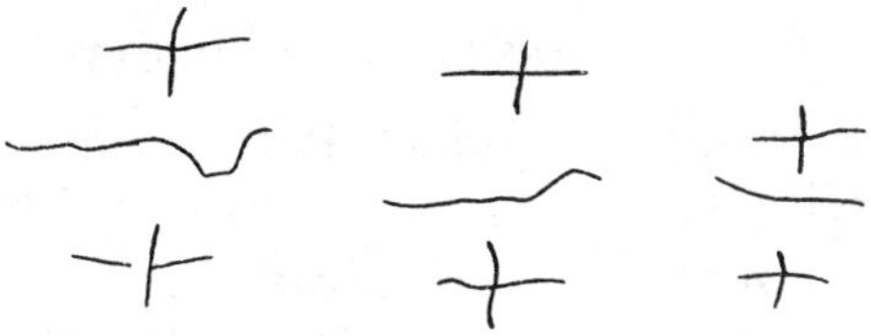

FIG. 39. A verbal noun.

equated with the Semitic Baalat, the female counterpart of the Biblical Baal, by ancient theologians. Second, Lidzbarski[2] and Sethe,[3] apparently independently of each other, read another group of signs as תנת *tnt* with almost equal probability (s. fig. 39).[4] The former took this to denote the Punic goddess Tanit, almost certainly wrongly since her cult was late, being Tunisian or North-African; Sethe's view, therefore, that the word was an abstract noun, comparable to the Hebr. תֵּת *tēt̲* 'giving', used in the concrete sense of 'gift', has won the day. Third, Eisler[5] and Grimme[6] both detected a proper name in מאהבעלת *m'h*(*b*)-*b*ʿ*lt* 'Beloved of Baalat', which occurs twice in these texts (s. fig. 40); this is equivalent to *mryy-ḥtḥr* 'Beloved of Ḥatḥor', an Egyptian name which actually occurs in one of the inscriptions found in this temple[7] and so lends colour to the proposed reading of this group of signs.[8]*

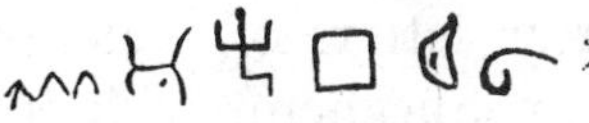

FIG. 40. A personal name.

These identifications then may be accepted as reasonably sure and, if right, prove the language of these non-Egyptian Sinaitic inscriptions to be a Semitic speech. Leibovitch,[9] however, has suggested Midianite or the language of the Maziu,

[1] In 'J.E.A.' III 15; cp. 'P.Q.S.' LXI (1929) 49–50*.

[2] In *T. Lz.* XLVI 50–1.

[3] In *Z.D.M.G.* LXXX 48–9.

[4] Cp. Cowley in 'J.E.A.' III 18, 21, XV 206, and Grimme *Lös. d. Sinaischrift-probl.* 65.

[5] In *Ken. Weihinschr.* 31–5.

[6] In *Althebr. Inscr.* 43 (cp. 67–8).

[7] Ibid. 9, 42.

[8] Cp. Butin *ap.* Starr & Butin in 'S.D.' VI 37–8 for another instance of this name.

[9] In *B.I.É.* XVI 27–30 and *M.I.É.* XXIV 9–26, 108.

since the territory of this people reached well into Sinai, and Sprengling[1] calls it 'Seʿirite'[2] for approximately the same reasons; but these guesses can be neither proved nor disproved, as scarcely a word of either language is known. The fact, however, that *'hb* 'loved' occurs in Hebrew and Ugaritic alone of the Semitic languages suggests a Canaanite dialect.

## 5. Early Inscribed Objects*

Several inscribed objects found in Palestine are approximately contemporary with the Sinaitic inscriptions, but the signs on them are not so markedly pictographic.[3] A potsherd from Gezer[4] in southern Palestine dated *c.* 1800–1650 B.C. carries

Fig. 41. Potsherd from Gezer.

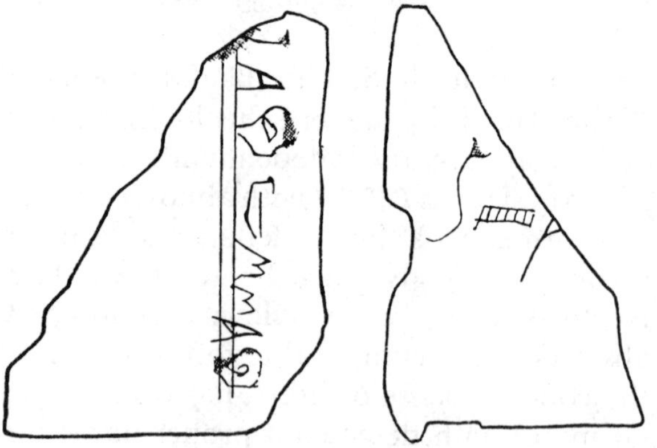

Fig. 42. Plaque from Shechem.

three letters of a clearly Sinaitic type[5] (s. fig. 41); a plaque from Shechem[6] with (obv.) eight and (rev.) three signs (s. fig. 42) and one from Tell-eṣṢârem[7] with eight signs scratched on it (s. fig. 44) belong to approximately the same period. Unfortunately the texts of all four fragments defy interpretation. There is also a dagger of bronze from Lachish,[8] dated *c.* 1700–

[1] In 'Alphabet' 50–7. [2] From *Śēʿîr*, a poetical name for Edom.

[3] S. pp. 198–9 for the proposed interpretations of the objects described in this section.

[4] Taylor in 'J.P.O.S.' x 17, s. Böhl in *Z.D.P.-V.* LXI 19–20, Gaster in 'P.Q.S.' LXVII (1935) 133, Sprengling 'Alphabet' 45 and Diringer *Iscrizioni* 296–7.

[5] Butin in 'H.T.R.' XXV 200–1; cp. Albright in 'B.A.S.O.R.' LVIII 28–9 (s. pp. 141–2).

[6] Böhl ibid. 21–5; cp. Kahane in 'B.J.P.E.S.' XII 30–9.

[7] Böhl ibid. 24–5 and Sukenik in *Kedem* II 15.

[8] Starkey in 'P.Q.S.' LXIX (1937) 239–40/viii 1, Gardiner in 'Times' 16 July 1937 (12–iv), Böhl ibid. 20–1, Obermann in 'P.A.O.S.' IX 25–33.

1550 B.C., bearing four clearly incised signs running down one side of the blade (s. p. 99 fig. 43 and pl. 41); these probably convey the owner's name, but what that is remains a mystery. Mention must also be made of a number of marks on so-called 'Amorite' pottery[1] found at Tell-elḤesy[2] in a layer dated archaeologically

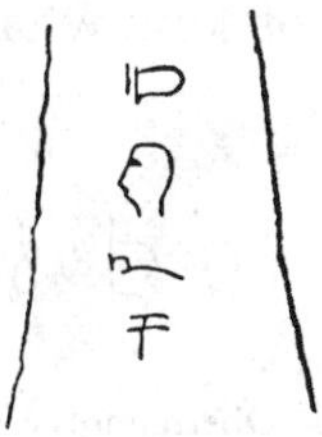

FIG. 43. Dagger from Lachish.

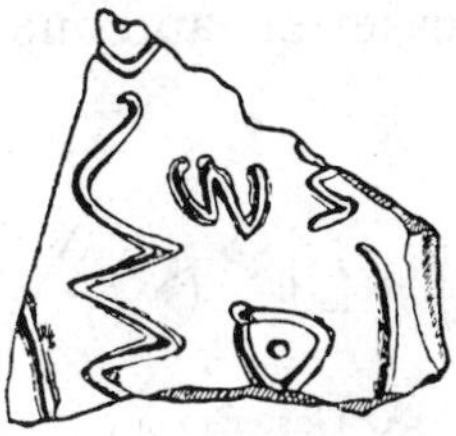

FIG. 44. Plaque from Tell-eṣṢârem.

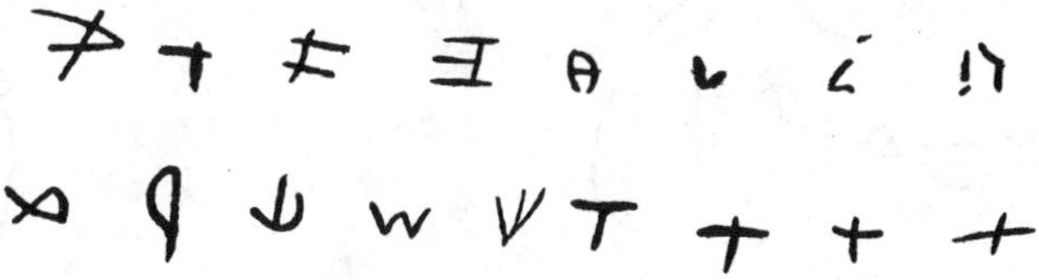

FIG. 45. Potters' marks from Tell-elḤesy.

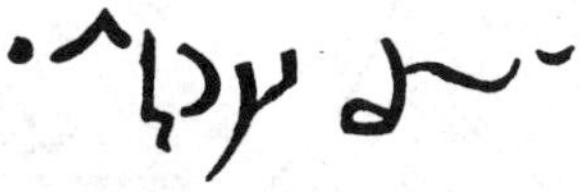

FIG. 46. Potsherd from Tell-etTaʿajjul.

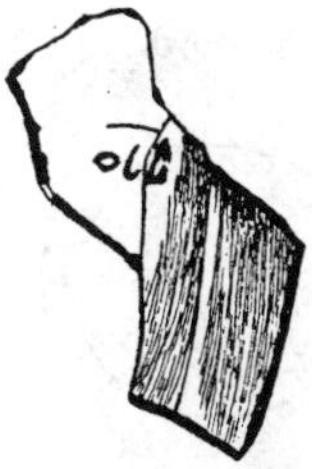

FIG. 47. Potsherd from Tell-elḤesy.

before 1600 B.C. (s. fig. 45); several of the marks closely resemble letters on inscribed objects of the subsequent periods[3] rather than signs of the preceding centuries.

The next period in Palestine runs approximately from 1400 B.C. to 1100 B.C. Even now the writing on such fragments as have been found is barely intelligible, but the period overlaps

[1] Diringer *Iscrizioni* 303.
[2] Arab. تل الحسى 'the mound of sandy soil'.
[3] S. pp. 115–17.

that in which several completely intelligible Phoenician inscriptions appear.

Two fragments are assigned to the first part of this period, namely, *c.* 1400–1300 B.C. The one is a potsherd from Tell-etTaʿajjul[1] with unintelligible signs cut or scratched on it (s. p. 99 fig. 46). The other is a potsherd from Tell-elḤesy[2] with two perfect letters and one damaged letter of somewhat Sinaitic

A. Gaster's copy.

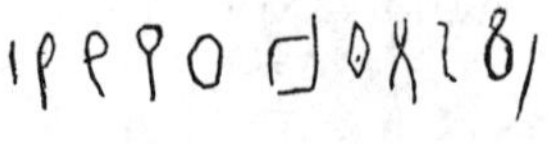

B. Obermann's copy.

FIG. 48. Potsherd from Lachish.

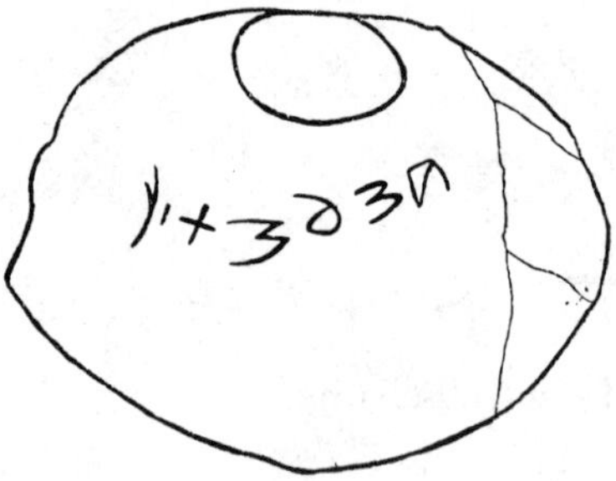

A. Bowl.

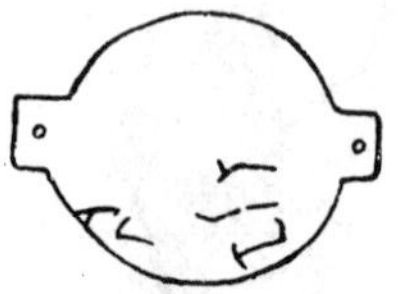

B. Lid of censer.

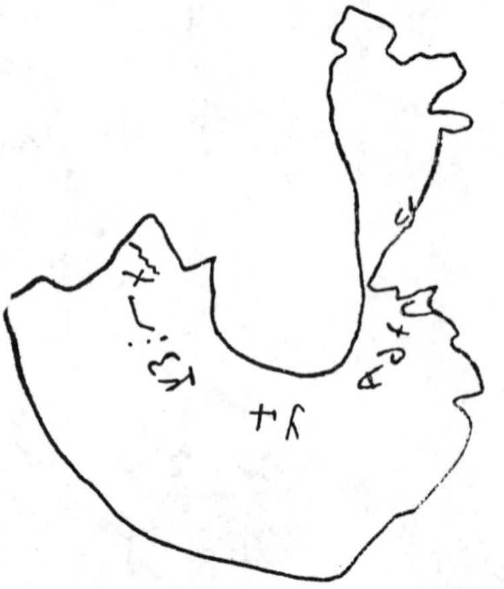

C. Ewer.

FIG. 49. Inscribed pottery from Lachish. (s. pl. 43)

appearance[3] (s. p. 99 fig. 47); these may be read בלע *blʿ* as the name of the owner of the object of which it is a fragment.[4] A large potsherd from Beth-Shemesh, now ʿAin Shems,[5] inscribed

[1] Petrie 'Gaza' II pl. XXX no. 1109.

[2] Bliss 'A Mound of many Cities' 88–9.

[3] Cp. Butin in 'H.T.R.' XXV 201–2, who thinks ב Sinaitic, ל Phoenician, and ע intermediate in type.

[4] Cp. Hebr. בֶּלַע *Belaʿ*, a Hebrew and Edomite name found in the Old Testament.

[5] Arab. عين شمس 'the spring of the sun'.

on both sides, is dated *c.* 1400–1200 B.C. (s. pl. 42);[1] the text consists of a number of symbols which resemble early known forms of Phoenician letters, but the surface has unfortunately been so badly damaged that it must be regarded as unlikely ever to be deciphered. Interpreters who have attempted to read it agree over scarcely a single letter.

Four pieces of pottery from Lachish[2] belong to the second part of this period, all dated *c.* 1250 B.C. by the archaeologists who have published them; all carry symbols which are unmistakably the letters of an alphabet. The first is a potsherd[3] in bad condition carrying what looks like a text of ten or eleven symbols scrawled on it in black ink or paint; these have been read both ways up, as Egyptian signs and as Hebrew letters (s. p. 100 fig. 48), but no sense has been made of them; several of the letters resemble masons' marks found on stones at Jerusalem.[4] The second is a piece of a censer[5] showing traces of several letters in red ochre which have not been satisfactorily explained (s. p. 100 fig. 49 B). The third is a bowl[6] which has been almost completely restored from broken fragments found close together and has a text of some half a dozen signs (s. p. 100 fig. 49 A and pl. 43, 1); the four middle letters seem to be שלשת *šlšt* 'three', which may be part of a note indicating its capacity. The fourth[7] is a fragment of a ewer, originally about 2 ft. high, with an inscription of which a dozen letters survive (s. p. 100 fig. 49 C and pl. 43, 2), running from left to right against the usual direction of Semitic writing; the first word is thought with some probability to be מתן *mtn* 'gift', even though this reading of it has been disputed, and the last is generally agreed to be אלת *'lt* 'goddess'. The interpretation of the two remaining words is disputed, but enough has been made out to suggest that the text is a dedicatory inscription.

[1] Grant 'Ain Shems' I pl. x; s. Diringer *Iscrizioni* 312, Vincent in *R.B.* XLI 281–4 and Gaster in 'P.Q.S.' LXVII (1935) 133–5.

[2] Arab. تل الدوير 'the mound of the little convent'.

[3] Starkey in 'P.Q.S.' LXVI (1934) 172–3/viii 3, Gaster ibid. LXIX (1937) 54–5, Obermann in 'P.A.O.S.' IX 33–8, and Gaster *ap.* Tufnell, Inge & Harding 'Lachish' II 55–7/xxix 12.

[4] S. p. 115.

[5] Starkey in 'P.Q.S.' LXVIII (1936) 180, Obermann in 'P.A.O.S.' IX 28–41.

[6] Stawell ibid. LXVIII (1936) 97–101, Gaster ibid. LXIX (1937) 55–6, Obermann in 'P.A.O.S.' IX 17–25.

[7] Starkey in 'P.Q.S.' LXVI (1934) 172–3, Burrows ibid. LXVII (1935) 87–9, Obermann in 'P.A.O.S.' IX 8–17, Yeivin in 'J.P.O.S. XV 98–100, and Gaster *ap.* Tufnell Inge & Harding 'Lachish' II 49–54/lx 3.

There belong also to this period two other objects bearing unintelligible legends. The first is a ring of gold from a tomb at Megiddo, dated *c.* 1350–1250 B.C. (s. fig. 50);[1] the script shows affinities on the one hand with that of the Old-Byblian texts,[2] of the potsherd from Beth-Shemesh[3] and of the bowls from Tell-edDuweir,[4] and on the other hand with that of Aḥiram's

FIG. 50. Ring from Megiddo.

FIG. 51. Scaraboid seal.

inscription;[5] but the suggested interpretations of the text on these lines make no sense. The second is a scaraboid seal which probably, if not certainly, belongs here (s. fig. 51);[6] its exact provenience is unknown but is vaguely said to be Asia Minor, and the legend on it, though written apparently in a form of the North-Semitic alphabet, defies interpretation*.

Attention may here be drawn to a large number of marks on various objects found in Egypt in the course of various excavations. The objects so marked are of stone and wood, pottery and papyrus, and the marks are now incised and now daubed with paint or ink (s. pl. 35); they are found not only on prehistoric pottery but also on objects of the XIIth to the XIXth dynasties (*c.* 2000–1205 B.C.).[7] On the one hand the earlier marks found on objects assigned to the prehistoric period cannot be letters of the future alphabet; on the other hand, it becomes difficult not to see more or less crude attempts at reproducing North-Semitic letters in many of the later marks, which are obviously of a type posterior to those found in Moab and of non-Egyptian origin, especially as there were almost always considerable groups of

[1] Guy 'Megiddo Tombs' 173–6.
[2] S. pp. 91–3.
[3] S. pp. 100–1.
[4] S. p. 101.
[5] S. p. 105.
[6] Zakharov in *A.O.* VII 36 (pl. vi no. 7) and Gaster in 'P.Q.S.' LXIX (1937) 57–8.
[7] Edwards in *Actes du 8me Congrès International des Orientalistes* II iv/3, 209–18; Petrie 'Kahun, Gurob, and Hawara' xxvii–xxviii and 'The Formation of the Alphabet' i, vii.

Semitic workers scattered about the country. Indeed, one such group of signs or letters inscribed round a wooden rod (s. fig. 52) has been plausibly read as אחטוב *'ḥṭwb* 'Aḥiṭûb' or the like,[1] which is a known Semitic personal name.[2] Clearly all such markings, whether symbols or letters, are marks of ownership, but when mere symbols become letters cannot be said in the present state of knowledge.

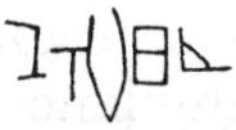

FIG. 52. Semitic name on a wooden rod from Egypt.

## 6. Cuneiform Tablets

Meanwhile, during the period *c.*1425–1350 B.C., clay-tablets were extensively used for correspondence between the local princes of Syria and Palestine on the one side and between them and their Egyptian overlords on the other side. The vast majority of the texts of this period were found at Tell-el-Amarna, a mound lying about 300 km. to the south of Cairo on the eastern bank of the Nile; they were written in the Babylonian language influenced, if not corrupted, to a considerable extent by the Semitic idiom of southern Syria and Palestine, the speech of the Canaanite populace (s. pl. 44, 1). A few tablets of very different periods have also been found by excavation at several sites in Palestine (s. pl. 44, 2). Another small but very important collection of clay-tablets comes from the ancient Ugarit, which is mentioned half a dozen times in the correspondence from Tell-elAmarna and is situated by the modern Râs-ashShamrah, lying about 12 km. to the north of Latakia on the Syrian coast.[3] These tablets are dated *c.* 1425–1350 B.C.; they deal almost exclusively with mythological or religious subjects, written in a new Semitic dialect and a simplified cuneiform script (s. pl. 45). Its decipherment by Virolleaud and Dhorme working with Bauer, who joined them in Paris, revealed a Canaanite dialect showing a remarkably close affinity to the Hebrew and Phoenician languages but also not a few peculiarities of Aramaic and Arabic origin.[4] The script contained 29 or 30 signs representing the letters of a full Semitic alphabet and was therefore not a syllabary but an alphabet; the

[1] Eisler *Ken. Weihinschr.* 123–7.

[2] Cp. I Sam. xxii 12, II Sam. viii 17 = I Chron. xviii 16.

[3] S. pp. 78–9.

[4] This decipherment was based on the inscriptions of two axe-heads, reading respectively *ḥrṣn rb khnm* 'the axe of the chief of the priests' and *rb khnm* 'the chief of the priests' (s. pl. 44) *.

only relic of the syllabic stage of development was the use of three distinct signs for *'ālep* according to the vowel (*ả*, *ẻ*/*ỉ*, *ủ*) which accompanied it. The resemblance, too, or apparent resemblance of the signs to those of the Accadian cuneiform syllabary on the one side and to the earliest forms of the Phoenician letters on the other side aroused lively controversy: was the Ugaritic alphabet the parent of the Semitic alphabet, or was it derived either from the Accadian syllabary or from the Phoenician alphabet, or was it a connecting link between these and/or other early alphabets? The discovery, however, of texts from Sinai and Gebal in which words in an early form of the Phoenician alphabet can be certainly read deprives the Ugaritic cuneiform alphabet of its brief pride of place and shows it to have been but an experimental attempt to adapt the cuneiform to the alphabetic system in the light of the Phoenician alphabet.[1]

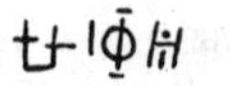

FIG. 53. Non-Semitic script from Ugarit.

Further, a bowl of silver, of the period of the destruction of Ugarit, found in a chamber near the library, bears five letters (s. fig. 53) which resemble signs in the Cypriot syllabary but cannot be interpreted.[2]

## 7. PHOENICIAN INSCRIPTIONS*

The story now returns to Gebal, where the earliest inscriptions in a North- or West-Semitic language that can be fully understood have been found. These inscriptions are those of several kings of Gebal[3] who reigned between the 17th and 9th centuries B.C. The first is that of Shaphaṭbaal (שפטבעל)[4] which is engraved on a stone from the wall of a spring or well (s. pl. 50, 2) and is assigned by the finder to the 15th if not the 17th century B.C.; for he says that archaeologically it belongs to the time of the XIIth (*c.* 2000–1788 B.C.) or XIIIth (*c.* 1788–? B.C.) dynasty of Egypt, while palaeographically he holds Shaphaṭbaal to be as far from Aḥiram as Aḥiram is from Mesha' king of Moab (*c.* 850 B.C.).[5] A date before 1500 B.C., however, is hardly possible, although the forms of *b* and *q*, as well as of other

[1] S. pp. 148–52. The Ugaritic like the Babylonian cuneiform script runs from left to right; but one or two tablets have a script running from right to left in the Phoenician fashion (De Langhe *Ugarit* I 234–5).

[2] Schaeffer in *Syria* XIII 22–3. [3] S. pp. 91–2.

[4] Dunand *Bybl. Gr.* 146–51.

[5] S. pp. 108–9. Maisler however makes Shaphaṭbaal son of Elibaal and grandson of Yeḥimilk (s. Albright in 'B.A.S.O.R.' CIII 14–15).

letters, are indisputably anterior to any hitherto found. The next are two inscriptions from the tomb of Aḥiram (אחרם), the one a notice by the entrance to the sepulchral chamber (*s.* fig. 54)[1] and the other the memorial text on the actual coffin (s. pls. 51, 2 and 52).[2] The various dates proposed for this king include the 13th century[3] or the 11th or 10th century[4] or *c.* 975 B.C.;[5] but

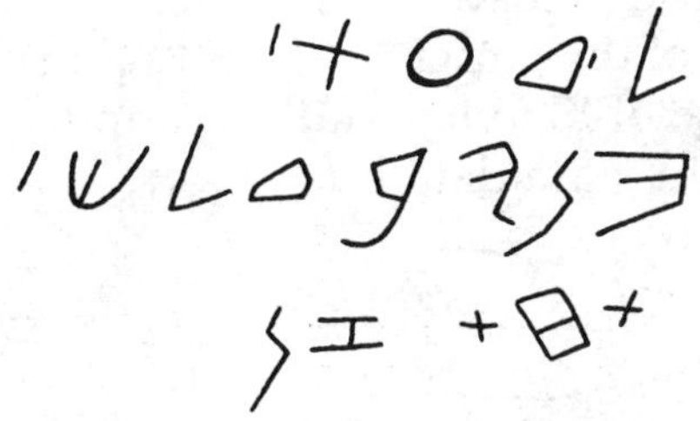

FIG. 54. Notice over a tomb at Gebal.*

the later date is now generally preferred, although on the earlier the absence of any development in the script between Aḥiram on the one side and Abibaal and Elibaal on the other side would be easily explained by the unsettled state of the country in the following two and a half centuries, which would have made progress in the arts of peace more or less impossible. The next inscriptions are that on a building erected by Yeḥimilk (יחמלך),[6] which cannot be certainly dated but perhaps belongs to a period approaching the preceding rather than the following inscriptions (s. pl. 53, 1),[7] those of Abibaal[8] (אבבעל) and of Elibaal[9] (אלבעל). These give the only tolerably

[1] Dussaud in *Syria* V 142–4, Bauer in *O. Lz.* XXVIII 135–7, Vincent in *R.B.* XXXIV 183–93/viii B, Gaster in 'P.Q.S.' LXIX (1937) 57 (Byblos I A).

[2] Dussaud in *Syria* V 135–41, Bauer in *O. Lz.* XXVIII 129–35, Lidzbarski ibid. XXX 456–7, Vincent in *R.B.* XXXIV 183–9/viii B, Torrey in 'J.A.O.S.' XLV 269–79 and 'J.P.O.S.' VII 122–7, Ronzevalle in *M.U.B.* XII 3–40, Bruston in *R.H.P.R.* VI 157–63 (Byblos I B).

[3] Diringer in 'Antiquity' XVII 86; cp. De Langhe *Ugarit* I 254.

[4] Cowley *ap.* Aimé-Giron in *A.S.A.É.* XLII 321.

[5] Aimé-Giron ibid. XLII 331–8, Albright in 'B.A.S.O.R.' XCII 19–21 and CIII 14–15*.

[6] Dunand in *R.B.* XXXIX 321–31/xv (Byblos II).

[7] Cp. Diringer in 'Antiquity' XVII 86, who assigns Yeḥimilk to the 12th century B.C.

[8] Montet in *R.B.* XXXV 322, 463/vi 1 = vii 3 (Byblos III A); Clermont-Ganneau in *R.A.O.* VI 74–8/ii, Lidzbarski *E.S.E.* II 167–9, Dussaud in *Syria* V 145–7 and VIII 81, Bauer in *O. Lz.* XXVIII 137–8, Torrey in 'J.A.O.S.' XLV 278–9 (Byblos III B).

[9] Dussaud in *Syria* VI 101–17, Montet in *R.B.* XXXV 323, 463/vi 2, Torrey in 'J.A.O.S.' XLVI 237–40, Aimé-Giron in *A.S.A.É.* XLII 328–31 (Byblos IV).

certain dates for this group of Phoenician inscriptions; for that of Abibaal is engraved on a statue of the Egyptian king Shishak I (*c.* 945–924 B.C.) and that of Elibaal on one of Osorkon I (*c.* 924–895 B.C.). They cannot be before, although they may be after, these dates.

There are two other small inscriptions from Gebal of this period which call for mention. The first is a piece of pottery bearing the name of the potter *ʿAbdâ* (עבדא) in characters which are as old as those of Shaphaṭbaal's inscription and may even, as the editor thinks, ante-date it (*s.* pl. 51, 1).[1] The *b* certainly

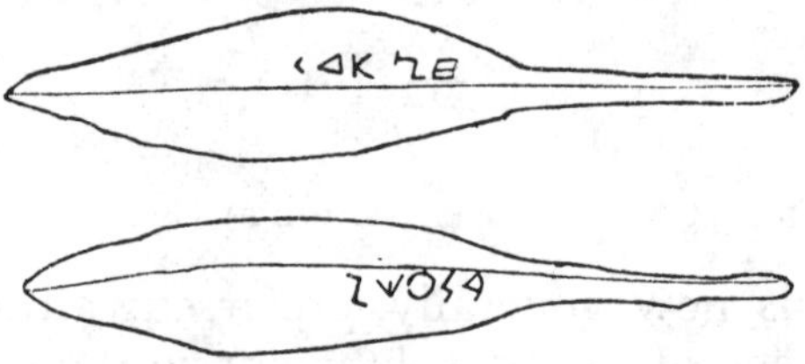

FIG. 55. Arrow-head from Ruwaisah (Nabâṭîyah).

has the same tail turned back rightwards as Shaphaṭbaal's, but the six different letters which the text contains are insufficient evidence to allow the date to be more than approximately fixed. There is also an inscribed spatula of bronze from the temple of Baalat bearing a text of which the sense is not entirely clear, although almost every character is legible, and known as the spatula of ʿAzarbaal (עזרבעל) from the owner's name (s. pl. 53, 2);[2] the editor is now inclined to put this before Aḥiram, although the script hardly seems to bear out so early a date and only suggests one somewhere between him on the one hand and Abibaal and Elibaal on the other hand.[3] Finally, there is an inscribed arrow-head from Ruwaisah in the Lebanon with the owner's name (אדי בן עכי or אדא) engraved on it (s. fig. 55);[4] it may be dated between Yeḥimilk and Abibaal*.

[1] Dunand *Bybl. Gr.* 152–3; s. 197–200.

[2] Dunand *Bybl.* I 28 and in *B.M.B.* II 99–107, Obermann in 'J.B.L.' LVIII 229–42.

[3] Dunand *Bybl. Gr.* 155–7. The editor's arguments that the spatula is of the same shape as those bearing pseudo-hieroglyphic texts (s. pp. 92–3) and indeed that it has traces of such signs on one side have no real value; every spatula must be of roughly the same shape and the hieroglyphic and Phoenician texts may have no connection with one another, since the spatula may be an old one re-used.

[4] Dussaud in *Syria* VIII 185–6, Savignac in *R.B., N.S.* XXVII 257, Ronzevalle & Guignes in *M.U.B.* XI 325–58.

The next and only other monument of importance is the inscription of Kilamuwa from Zinjîrlû, dated *c.* 900–800 B.C.;[1] this is of some interest as the script is Phoenician and the language Phoenician showing traces of Aramaic influence, while the king is ruler of an Aramaean state. After this almost perfect text of sixteen lines there are Honeyman's Cypriot inscription[2] and the Cypriot bowl, dated possibly *c.* 700 B.C.;[3] only part of its inscription which runs round the top of the outer edge has been recovered, but enough remains to show that the characters are as developed as they are beautifully shaped. In this respect they

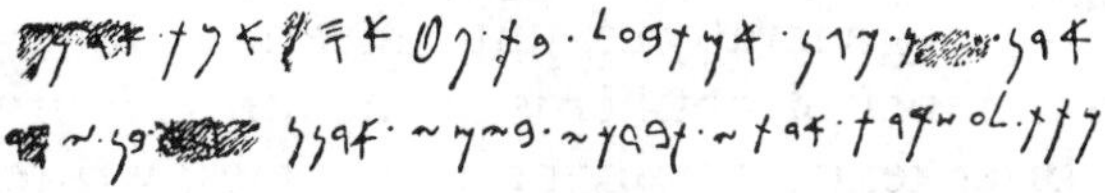

FIG. 56. Phoenician inscription on ivory from Ur.

resemble those of Kilamuwa's inscription and are totally unlike the crude, almost coarse, lettering of Aḥiram's inscription; but, unlike the former and like the latter, they show curious variations of size. The brief and badly worn inscriptions from Nora and Bosa,[4] recording the dedication of a pillar, may also belong to the last half of the 8th century B.C., but their date is disputed.[5] After a considerable interval of time there comes a brief inscription of two lines[6] found buried beneath a pavement of Nebuchadrezzar (604–562 B.C.) at Ur[7] (s. fig. 56). This text is engraved on the lid of a box of ivory in neat characters showing traces of Aramaic influence such as may be expected

[1] Lidzbarski in *E.S.E.* III 218–38*. [2] In *Iraq* VI 106–8.

[3] In *C.I.S.* I i 22–6 5. The bowl has also been dated *c.* 900–850 B.C. (Albright in 'B.A.S.O.R.' LXXXIII 16–17) or *c.* 750–700 B.C. (Bauer in *O.Lz.* XXVIII 138), but the objects found with it perhaps suggest a date even in the 7th cent. B.C. It is usually called Cypriot from its discovery on a hill near Limasol, but the inscription shows it to have been an offering made by the servant of one Ḥiram, king of Sidon, to the Baal of the Lebanon.

[4] In *C.I.S.* i 190–3 144 and 145, 211 162.

[5] Dates early in the 9th century B.C. (Albright in 'B.A.O.S.R.' LXXXIII 16–21) or at the end of it (Bauer in *O. Lz.* XXVIII 138) or *c.* 900–800 B.C. (Diringer *Alfabeto* 408–9) seem too early, as the *k* is of a form not otherwise found before the Cypriot bowl, and allowance must be made for the possibility that archaic forms of the letters may linger in remote and outlying districts for some time after becoming obsolete on the mainland; but the Punic element in the language is hardly marked enough to justify a date so late as the 6th century B.C. or thereabouts (Harris 'Gramm. Phoen. Lang.' 157).

[6] Burrows in 'J.R.A.S.' 1927, 791–4/viii.

[7] S. p. 124.

at a time when summaries in that language were being added to native Babylonian documents.[1] Others of this period from the Phoenician homeland are that of Yeḥawmilk king of Gebal,[2] recording his gifts to the Baalat of Gebal, and that of king *'ztwd* from Karatepe, found in 1946*.

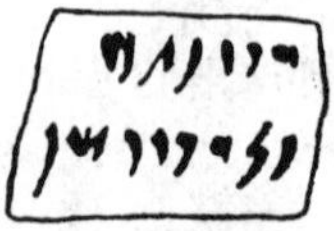

FIG. 57. Phoenician potsherd.

Mention may further be made of a few small objects with Phoenician inscriptions from several countries. Such are Phoenician seals, mostly of native origin though often exhibiting foreign, whether Aramaean or Assyrian or Egyptian, influence;[3] they are generally of quite uncertain date. There are also a small number of potsherds of the 5th century B.C. from Egypt with brief texts, usually proper names, written on them with ink in an Aramaizing script (s. fig. 57).[4] Curiously enough there is only a solitary Phoenician papyrus, which is tentatively assigned to the 4th century B.C., from Egypt;[5] it contains 13 lines of text on the obverse and 5 on the reverse side, all so badly damaged that consecutive sense can hardly be made of it. Finally there are two monuments of calcareous stone, of unknown date, from Larnaka, which is thought to be the ancient Citium;[6] these are peculiar in having the text, which relates to work on a temple of Astarte, painted on them in black and red colouring matter, in a script betraying Aramaic influence.[7]

## 8. Moab and Palestine

The earliest completely intelligible inscription recovered from the soil of Palestine is without doubt the Calendar of Gezer[8] with a summary list of farming operations arranged by months carved on kaolin (s. pl. 54, 1). This on linguistic and possibly also on palaeographical grounds is dated *c.* 1100–900 B.C.; for the script is archaic rather than the work of an unpractised hand.

After a gap of some considerable length the Moabite Stone[9]

[1] S. p. 122.

[2] In *C.I.S.* I 1–8 1; cp. Cooke 'N.-Sem. Inscr.' 18–25 3 (Byblos V).

[3] Levy *Sieg. u. Gemm.* 22–32, 53–4.

[4] Clermont-Ganneau in *R.A.O.* III 70–4 and Lidzbarski *Phön. u. Aram. Krugaufschr.* 4–19.

[5] Aimé-Giron in *B.I.F.A.O.* XXXVIII 1–18.

[6] In *C.I.S.* I i 92–100 86–7.

[7] Cp. Harris 'Gramm. Phoen. Lang.' 158–60, where a list of Phoenician inscriptions with the relevant literature is given.

[8] S. R. Driver 'Samuel'[2] vii–viii (with photograph) and Diringer *Iscrizioni* 1–20.

[9] S. R. Driver op. cit. lxxxiv–xciv and Cooke 'N.-Sem. Inscr.' 1–4.

is the next written monument, dated *c.* 850 B.C. This stele of Mesha' king of Moab[1] is of great importance as the sole historical monument of the Moabite kingdom and a record of historical relations between Moab and Israel which are glossed over or omitted from the Old Testament. It further reveals Moabite as a Semitic dialect almost identical with Hebrew and proves the advanced stage of writing in a petty kingdom lying off the main historical routes in the 9th century B.C. The text in its present condition contains 34 lines of which 27 are perfectly preserved; the following 7 lines are in an increasingly bad condition and the end has been lost. It is beautifully carved in a remarkably advanced form of script. This already shows a tendency to become cursive in the lengthening of the tails of

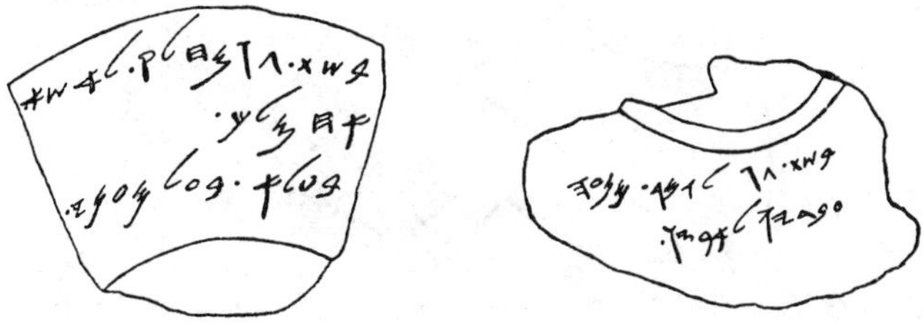

A. B.

FIG. 58. Inscribed ostraca from Ahab's palace.

several letters (*k*, *m*, *n*, *p*) towards the left as though to be connected with the following letters and in the simplification of some forms such as that of *ḥ* whose cross-strokes are reduced from three to two or one; and it is distinguished from that of all other early North-Semitic inscriptions by dividing both words and clauses, the former by points and the latter by strokes.[1]

Samaria has been prolific in inscribed potsherds*. The most important of these is a collection of seventy-five uncovered by excavation on the floor of Ahab's palace and originally dated *c.* 875–825 B.C.;[2] but they perhaps belong rather to the time of Jeroboam II, *c.* 774–766 B.C. (s. fig. 58).[3] The text, which is put on the surface with a reed in some ink-like substance and consists of one to eight lines, in most cases complete or nearly so, deals with supplies of oil and wine, to which the names of the persons concerned and the number of the year, presumably the regnal year of the king, are appended. These

[1] Cp. II Kings iii 4–27. [2] Cp. Lidzbarski *N.-Sem. Epigr.* 175.

[3] Reisner 'Samaria' I 227–46 and Diringer *Iscrizioni* 21–68; cp. Albright 'Arch. and Rel. of Isr.' 214, where these ostraca are now assigned to the reign of this king.

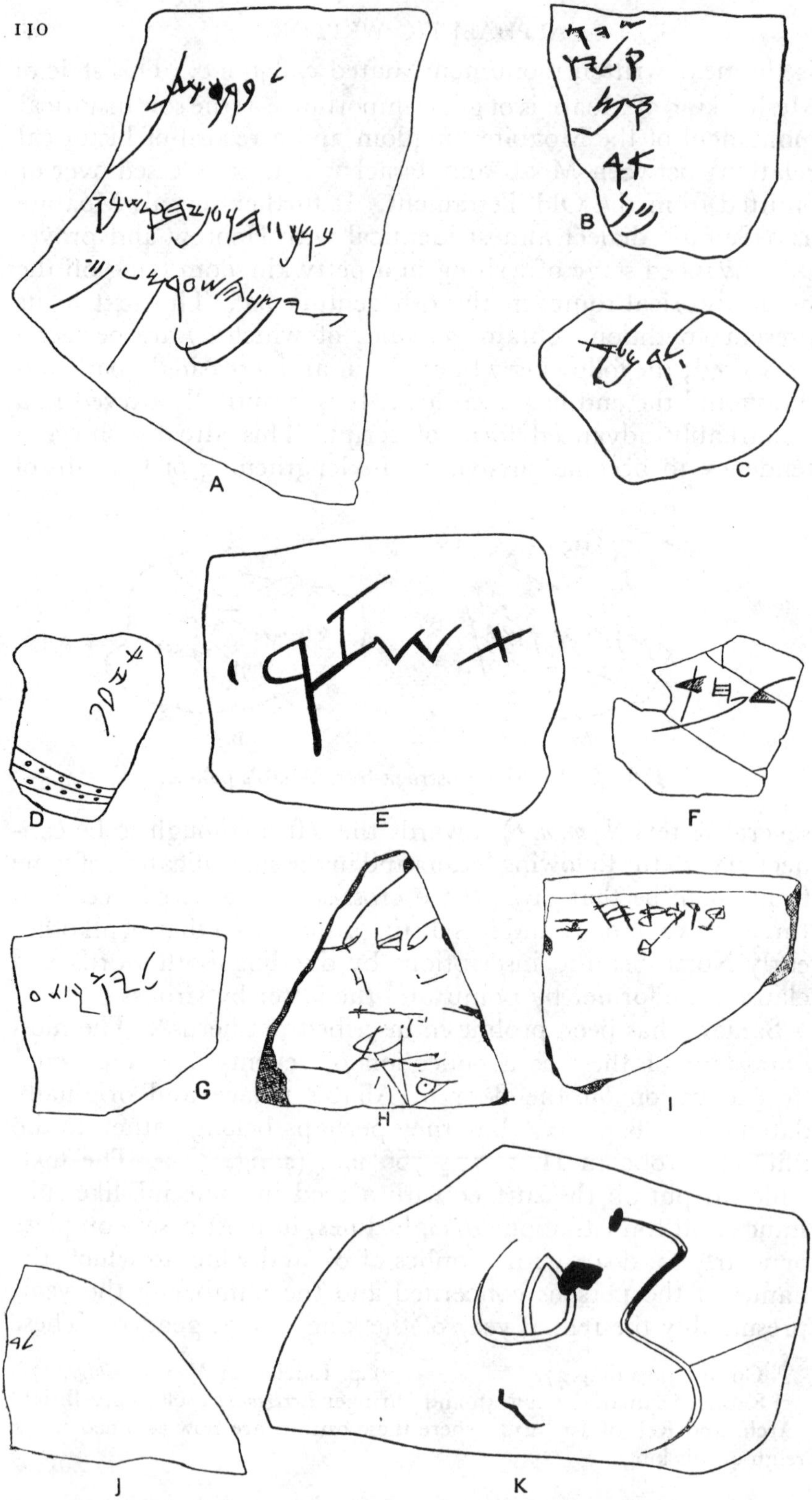


Fig. 59. Inscribed Samaritan potsherds.

documents are of great importance for the study both of the alphabet and of the language. The script is a cursive type, showing great regularity of form and an easy familiarity on the part of the scribe, and the language is Biblical Hebrew with some archaic and dialectal forms. There are also a dozen or so miscellaneous ostraca having brief texts incised or scratched on their surface; these belong to the same or the immediately following period (s. p. 110 fig. 59). They are, however, of slight

A. Jerusalem.

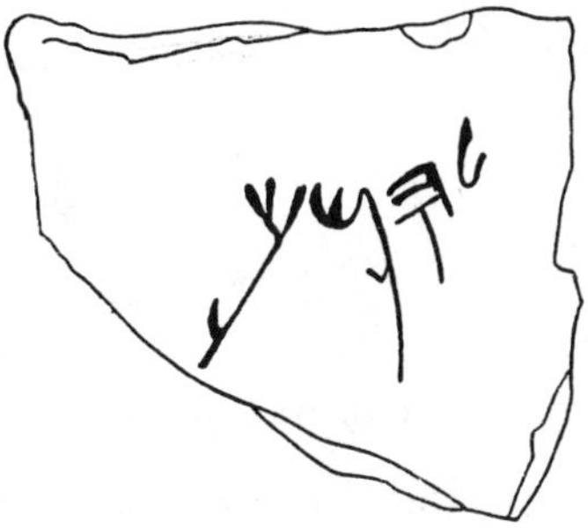

B. Tell-elḤesy.

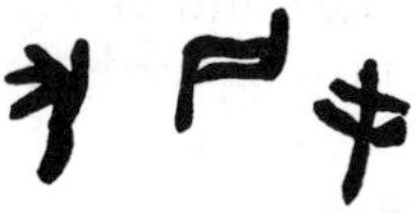

C. Beth-Shemesh.

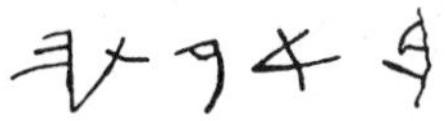

D. Megiddo.

FIG. 60. Inscribed potsherds from Palestine.

importance as they are often fragmentary and not always easily interpreted, and their dates are not so surely determined.

There are also a few potsherds from other places which can hardly be exactly dated but belong approximately to the same or the following century as the Samaritan sherds. Amongst these are an almost illegible potsherd from Mount Ophel,[1] one from Jerusalem[2] (s. fig. 60 A) and another from Beth-Shemesh[3] (s. fig. 60 C), neither precisely dated, one from Tell-elḤesy[4] (s. fig. 60 B) and another from Megiddo[5] (s. fig. 60 D) which are dated *c.* 750 B.C. on archaeological grounds. In addition there is a fragment from Ezion-geber at the head of the Gulf of ʿAqabah bearing an inscription of six letters (s. fig. 61) which

[1] Diringer *Iscrizioni* 74–9. [2] Ibid. 314–15.

[3] Mackenzie 'Excavations at Ain Shems' 87/10.

[4] Petrie 'Tel-el-Hesy' 50 and Hooke in 'P.Q.S.' LXVIII (1936) 38; cp. Vincent *Canaan* 180.

[5] Schumacher 'Tell-el-Mutesellim' I 109 and Diringer *Iscrizioni* 301.

is dated *c.* 700–600 B.C.;[1] it is worth mention if only because it comes from a district which has not yielded much inscribed matter beyond a few seals. The interpretation of all these fragments is uncertain.*

Another fact attesting the diffusion of writing in the pre-

A. Albright's copy.

B. Harding's copy.

FIG. 61. Inscribed potsherd from Ezion-geber.

Exilic period, from *c.* 1000 B.C. to *c.* 600 B.C., in Palestine is the popularity of seals, of which a large number have been recovered, belonging both to royal officers and to private persons (s. fig. 62); a few, too, have come from the surrounding countries (s. p. 113 fig. 63).[2] These seals, of which the number now exceeds one hundred

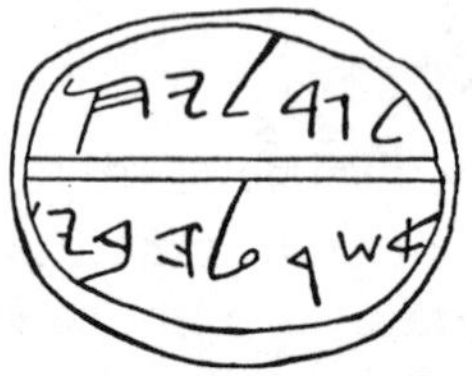

FIG. 62. Israelite seal from Palestine.

and is steadily rising, are of some ten main types; they carry from one to four lines of legend according to the amount of information given to identify the owner and the space available, which varies with the size of the seal, and much of this on large seals is

[1] Albright in 'B.A.S.O.R.' LXXI 17–18, and Harding ibid. LXXII 9.

[2] Cp. Lidzbarski *E.S.E.* III 279 (Ammon). Some two-thirds of extant North-Semitic seals emanate from countries neighbouring on Palestine, whether by excavation or purchase, and it is not easy to decide from what country they originate, owing to the close resemblance between the Ammonite, Edomite, Moabite, and kindred dialects with the Hebrew, Aramaic, and Phoenician languages; certainty is possible only when the place of excavation is definitely known or the owner's name reveals something characteristic, such as the name of the god of his country of origin (s. Reifenberg in 'P.Q.S.' LXXI [1939] 195).

occupied by ornamental designs. The seal is usually carved out of some semi-precious stone of considerable hardness; the script on the earliest specimens, so far as they can be arranged in any order of development, is coarse, but that on some of the latest is exceedingly fine.[1] Many types are known not from the original seal, which has not survived, but through their impressions on clay

A. Seal from Ammon. B. Seal from Edom. C. Seal from Moab.

FIG. 63. Semitic seals from countries adjacent to Palestine.

which have been recovered with the objects to which they are attached (s. pls. 57 and 58, 1).[2] Stamps impressed on fragments of jars, chiefly jar-handles, and similar objects belong to the same class as seals,[3] since they generally indicate ownership. These mostly bear a person's name with some other specification, such as his father's name (s. pl. 56, 2), often accompanied by a simple pattern of geometrical or heraldic design (s. fig. 64). Especial mention may be made of two peculiar classes of stamps found

A. B.

FIG. 64. Decorated stamps on jars found in Palestine.

on jars. The first class bear letters generally read as the divine name, mostly in an abbreviated form, namely, *Y* or *YH* or *YHW* for 'Yahweh' (s. p. 114 fig. 65). The purpose of these stamps is much disputed, but it has been plausibly conjectured that the jars to which they were affixed belonged to the temple and were used for collecting offerings or tribute in kind. It must, however, be admitted that it is not universally agreed that these letters stand in this connexion for 'Yahweh', which indeed is

[1] Diringer *Iscrizioni* 159–261.

[2] The papyrus on which Gedaliah's seal (s. pl. 58, 2) was impressed has left its mark, still visible, on the clay-sealing (Hooke in 'P.Q.S.' LXVII [1935] 195–6).

[3] Diringer *Iscrizioni* 110–57.

*a priori* not likely to have been used on profane objects in daily use, and it is possible that their true meaning has not yet been found.* Such stamps have so far come exclusively from the two towns of Jericho and Jerusalem. The second class are royal stamps from jars inscribed למלך *l-mlk* 'for the king', usually followed by the name of one of four places; these are Hebron, Socoh, Ziph, and an otherwise unknown place called ממשת *Mmšt* (?), possibly Mampsis to the east of Beersheba[1] (s. pl. 56, 1)*. The purpose of these stamps is equally uncertain; suggested

A. B. C.

FIG. 65. Stamps bearing the *tetragrammaton* on jars found in Palestine.

explanations, for example, are that the jars were manufactured in royal potteries or were destined for the collection of royal dues in kind at these places. Most of these stamps belong apparently to the last two centuries before the Exile, although a few may be earlier and some later than these centuries. Palaeographically they are interesting as showing a less formal and so a more

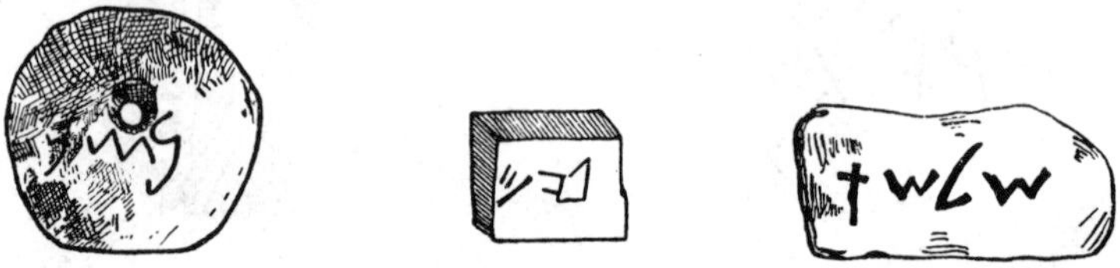

A. B. C.

FIG. 66. Hebrew weights.

cursive type of script than the seals, on which the letters, as often on stone, tend to be angular and indeed at times almost stylized.

Another interesting type of inscribed object belonging to this period are weights.[2] These are pieces of round, oblong or oval or square, stone, which are cut to the size of the required weight and occasionally also pierced so as to be carried on a cord (s. fig. 66). The unit, usually a fraction of a shekel, is engraved on

[1] Hommel *Ethnol. u. Geogr. d. Alt. Or.* 615³.

[2] Diringer *Iscrizioni* 263–90; cp. 'P.Q.S.' LXXIV (1942) 82–103 for a number of similar inscribed weights from Lachish.

the stone in rather rough lettering; occasionally numbers take the place of words in stating the unit. In this connexion it may be convenient to draw attention to a few fragments of jars which bear a legend stating their cubic capacity, which may be fixed according to the royal standard (s. pl. 55, 1). None of these objects is of much interest from a palaeographical point of view, especially as it is not as a rule easy precisely to determine their

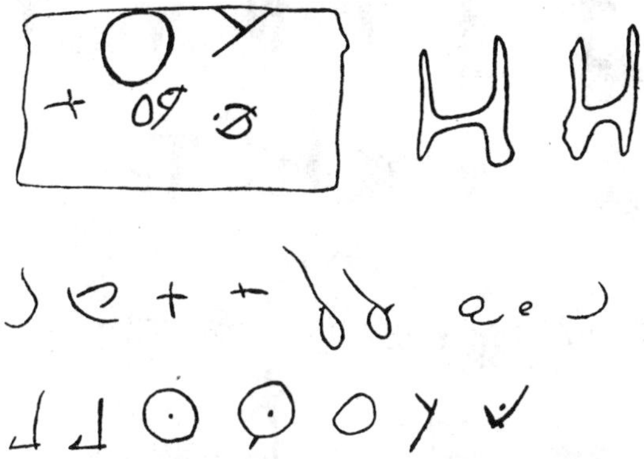

FIG. 67. Masons' marks on stones, Jerusalem.

date, but they are of great value in converting ancient Hebrew weights and measures into modern terms*.

Notice must also be taken of a number of masons' marks which have been found at a few important centres such as Megiddo, Samaria and Jerusalem, incised or scratched on dressed stones. The earliest of such signs, which come from Jerusalem[1] and are of quite uncertain date, can hardly be recognized as letters and perhaps are not such (s. fig. 67); yet one or two of the signs closely resemble letters on potsherds from Lachish.[2] If they are not letters, the workmen must have used them as pictorial mnemonic devices. The marks on the stones from Ahab's palace and other buildings at Samaria[3] belong to the early Israelite period (s. p. 116 fig. 68 A); some are evidently mere signs but others are certainly letters, while the marks on the backs of the ivories from the palace[4] are without doubt letters of the alphabet (s. p. 116 fig. 68 B), like those at Arslan Tash.[5] The very similar marks on stones at Megiddo,[6] dated *c.* 800–750

[1] Warren & Conder 'S.-West. Pal., Jerusalem' 151–2, who suggest quarry-marks; s. Diringer *Iscrizioni* 292–3. [2] S. pp. 100–1.

[3] Reisner 'Samaria' I 119–20; s. Diringer *Iscrizioni* 294–5.

[4] Crowfoot 'Early Ivories' 6–8/xx, xxv. [5] S. pp. 119–20.

[6] Schumacher *Tell-el-Mutesellim* I xxx e–f; s. Diringer *Iscrizioni* 293–4.

B.C., in several cases closely resemble those at Samaria and are also in all probability mostly letters of the alphabet (s. fig. 69). Their purpose was to show the workers the order in which the pieces were to be laid in the building. Last and perhaps most important of all these marks is the series of five letters carved on the vertical face of one of the steps of the palace at Lachish,[1]

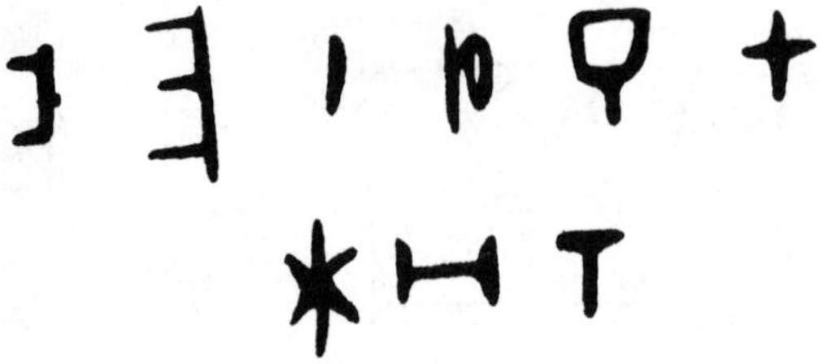

A. On stones.

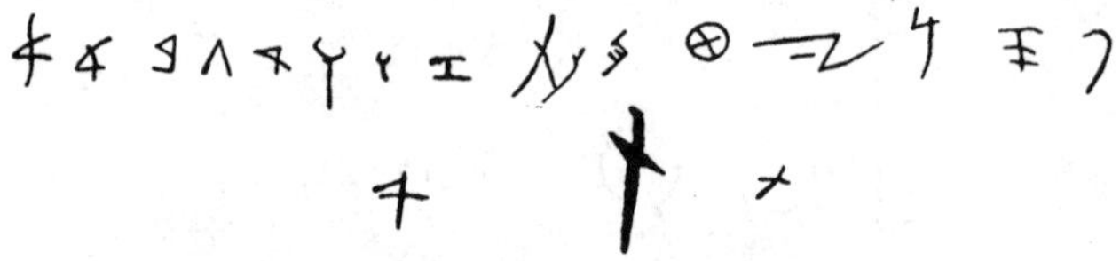

B. On ivories.

FIG. 68. Masons' marks, Samaria.

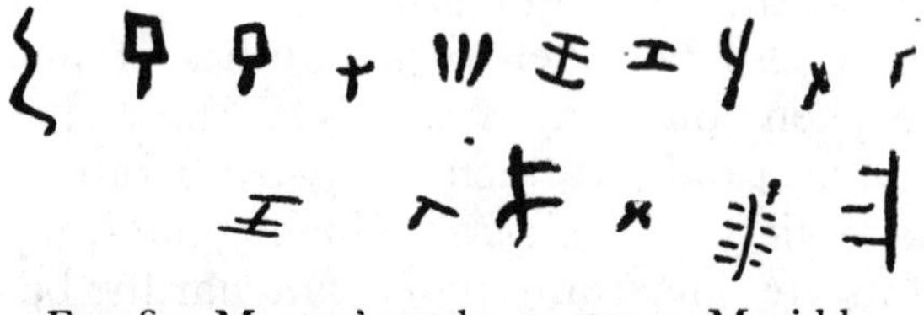

FIG. 69. Masons' marks on stones, Megiddo.

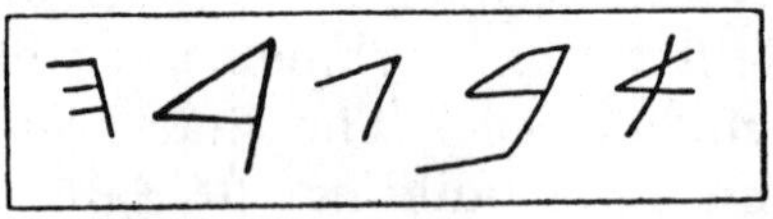

FIG. 70. Masons' alphabet, Lachish.

dated *c.* 600 B.C. (s. fig. 70); these are the first five letters of the alphabet in their traditional order, for which this is the earliest evidence.[2] Whether they were thus engraved in their proper order as a *memoria technica*, to which the masons could look to remind themselves of it as they laid the stones, or were the work of someone who was learning or teaching the alphabet,

[1] Published by an anonymous writer in the 'Times' of 26 May 1938 (7-v).

[2] S. p. 181.

cannot now be said; in either case their author could not have guessed the interest which they would rouse many centuries afterwards.

These marks on pottery and masonry, flints, bone and ivory, have not received the attention that they deserve in the history of the alphabet; for it is difficult to believe that these signs, whose variety is almost exactly equal in number to the letters of the alphabet and which can all with little imagination be identified with the letters of the alphabet, are not in fact letters. The following analysis shows their distribution:

Tell-elḤesy (א, ב, ג, ד or ר, ח, ל, ר or ד, ש, ת)
Gezer (א, ד or ר, ו, ז, ח, נ, ס, ק, ר or ד, ש, ת)
Tell-elJemmah (ח, ל, מ, נ, צ, ש, ת)
'Ain Shems (א, ת)
Tell Bêt Mirsim (כ)
Ta'annak (א, ת)
Megiddo (א, ג, ד or ר, ו, ז, ח, כ, ל, מ, נ, ס, ק, ש, ת)
Samaria (א, ד or ר, ו, ח, צ, ק, ת)
Jerusalem (א, ב, ו, ח, ט, ל, ע, פ, ק, ר or ד, ת)
Ḫirbat-aṭṬubêqah (א, ו, ק)

with others from Central Palestine but of unspecified place and date (א, ד or ר, ו, י, ר or ד, ש, ת). The coincidence indeed of number and resemblance is too striking to be overlooked; and in any case masons' marks would have been useless unless they fitted into a sequence of order or number. Further, these marks range over a whole millennium, from *c.* 1600 B.C., when those from Tell-elḤesy are dated, past those at Samaria in the 9th and at Megiddo in the 8th centuries B.C., down to those at Ḫirbat-aṭṬubêqah which belong *c.* 500 B.C. to the beginning of the Hellenistic age.[1] If then these marks are rightly identified as alphabetic signs or letters, the origin and order of the alphabet may go back as far as *c.* 1600 B.C.,[2] a time not so long after the coming of the Phoenicians to their historic home.[3]

Caution, however, must be exercised against a too ready assumption that masons' and potters' marks are necessarily letters of the alphabet; for there is naturally always a chance

[1] Cf. Petrie 'Tell-el-Hesy' 53 for similar marks on pottery from Ḫirbat 'Amûdah of uncertain date. [2] S. pp. 127, 196–7.

[3] The first reference in literature to the Phoenicians is the mention of the *Fnḫw* by Ahmose I king of Egypt (*c.* 1580–1557 B.C.), who reached their country in the course of his northern conquests and speaks of them as working in his quarries (Breasted 'Ancient Records of Egypt' II 12–13 § 27).

that they are meaningless figures.[1]* Such figures, often strangely like letters of the alphabet, appear on seals not only of the Israelite period (s. fig. 71 A) but also of the Neo-Babylonian period in Palestine (s. fig. 71 B) as elsewhere; similar figures,

A. Ta'annak. B. Nêrab.

FIG. 71. Seals with grotesque animal figures.

too, of the Hellenistic period, carved on tablets of stone, have been found in Palestine (s. fig. 72).

During all this period of little things, there is no inscription of any length or intrinsic importance between the Calendar of

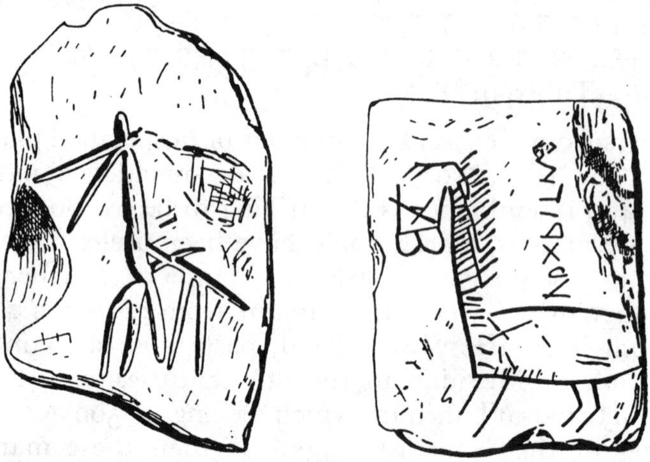

FIG. 72. Tablets of stone with grotesque animal figures from Gezer.

Gezer and the Moabite Stone and that carved in the tunnel connecting the Virgin's Spring with the Pool of Siloam at Jerusalem,[2] assigned on historical grounds to the reign of Hezekiah, king of Judah, *c.* 700 B.C. (s. pl. 54, 2).[3] The text is not quite

[1] Modern Arab marks of ownership on cattle often closely resemble ancient letters which, however, they cannot be (s. Banks 'Bismya' 41); the fact is that the number of possible combinations of points, curves, and strokes, is not unlimited.

[2] Cp. II Kings xx 20.

[3] Cooke 'N.-Sem. Inscr.' 15–17; Driver 'Samuel'[2] viii–x (with photograph).

complete, as something is missing at the beginning, and it consists now of six lines in a slightly archaic form of Hebrew telling how the gangs of workmen excavating the tunnel from opposite ends successfully effected a junction, so that the waters flowed from the Spring to the Pool. The writing may fairly be assigned to the same general stage of development as that represented by the Moabite Stone but is lighter and more flowing, while some of the letters have considerably altered their shape.

Then there is a gap of a century between the inscription over the Pool and the final monument of the southern kingdom. This is the now famous collection of letters from Lachish (s. pl. 58, 3),[1] in which the art of writing on potsherds reaches its peak. These letters, twenty in number, represent all that is left of the correspondence between the commander of a small advanced post of Hebrew soldiers in the field and the military governor of Lachish as the Babylonian army closed in on the doomed city *c.* 586 B.C. They are written in ink in a bold cursive script, in perfect Biblical Hebrew, easy to read and understand except where the text has been damaged or destroyed from its long sojourn in the soil. They are thus documents of almost equal value from the palaeographical as from the historical point of view.

## 9. Aramaean Documents

Syria yields no texts in the Aramaic language before the 9th century B.C.; for she had no great commercial centres looking east and west, as Phoenicia had, and was broken up into a number of petty warring states.

The earliest Aramaic inscriptions[2] come from Tell Ḥalaf[3] and Arslan Tash[4] and Buraij,[5] all three places near Aleppo; these texts are assigned to a period *c.* 850 B.C., the first perhaps a little before, the second and third a little after that date*. The texts from Tell Ḥalaf[6] include five clay-seals with Aramaic legends, all badly preserved, and a similarly inscribed piece of stone, now broken into three pieces (s. p. 120 fig. 73), which evidently

[1] Torczyner 'Lachish' I 19–183 and תעודות לכיש 1–220.

[2] Aramaic inscriptions can be recognized by the open tops of some letters (*b*, *d*, ', *r*) and the straight tails of other (*k*, *m*, *n*) letters.

[3] Friedrich *Tell Halaf* 71–8; s. Bowman in 'A.J.S.L.' LVIII 360–1 and Dussaud in *Syria* XXIII 106–8.

[4] Thureau-Dangin *Arslan-Tash*, *Atlas* xxvi/20, xlvii/112.

[5] Dunand in *B.M.B.* III 65–76; Albright in 'B.A.S.O.R.' LXXXVII 25–6.

[6] Anciently Ass. *Guzāna* = Hebr. גּוֹזָן on the river Ḫābûr (II Kings xvii 6 xviii 11 xix 12, Is. xxxvii 12, I Chr. v 26).

comes from an altar, and in its present condition not much sense can be extracted from it. The only inscription from Arslan Tash is on a piece of stone, again unfortunately broken into three

FIG. 73. Fragmentary inscription from Tell Ḥalaf.

pieces (s. fig. 74), but these fragments when put together suffice to give some indication of the sense. There come also from the same place a few letters incised on the backs of ivories intended

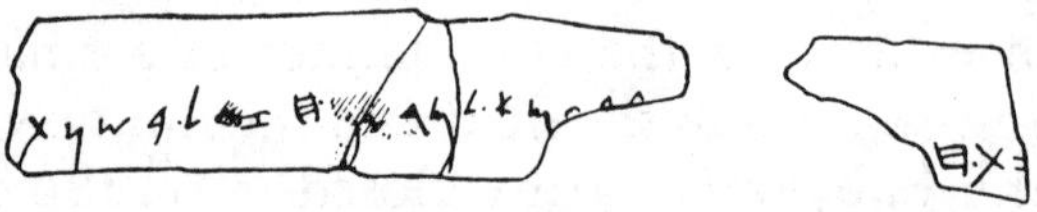

FIG. 74. Inscription from Arslan Tash.

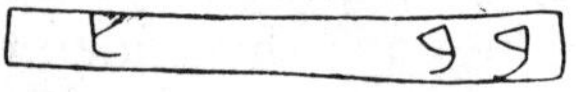

FIG. 75. Craftsmen's marks at Arslan Tash.

for use on the inner walls of the palace (s. fig. 75) of exactly the same type and workmanship as those found in Ahab's palace at Samaria.[1] The third inscription of this period is that from

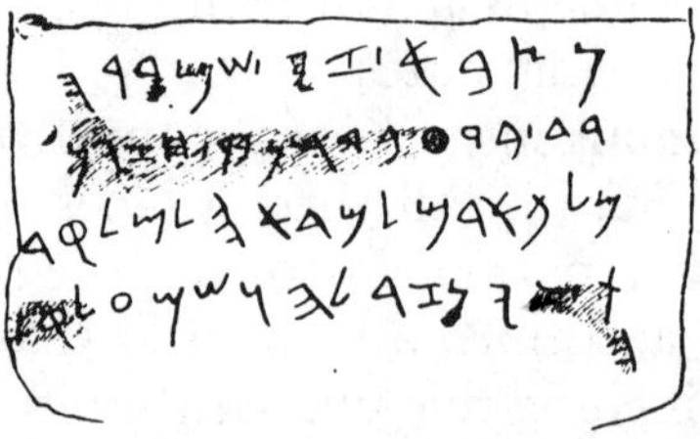

FIG. 76. Inscription from Buraij.

Buraij (s. fig. 76), which is fortunately in an almost perfect state of preservation except for a little weathering of the stone and can be easily read; it is a dedication of the monument, of which it is a part, to the god Melqart, and is written in a classical form of the Aramaic language.

The next century produces a number of long and important historical inscriptions, of which several have been known now

[1] S. pp. 109–11.

for many years. These are those of Panammû I from Zinjîrlû[1] (incomplete at end; 34 lines), of Zakir king of Hamath (incomplete; 46 lines),[2] and of Mati'el from Sûjîn (incomplete; 90 lines),[3] all three dated *c.* 800–750 B.C., and those of Panammû II also from Zinjîrlû (complete; 23 lines)[4] and Bar-Rākib his son (complete; 20 lines), dated *c.* 750–700 B.C.*.[5] These texts already show signs of a cursive form of script, for instance, in the development of ⌶ into Z (*z*) and of φ into φ or ϙ (*q*), and so on.[6]

In the seventh century Syria produces only a curious magical text in a mixed Phoenico-Aramaean jargon from Arslan Tash;[7] but the end of this or the beginning of the next century produces two finely executed funeral inscriptions from Nêrab, a small village lying to the south-east of Aleppo, in an Aramaic dialect showing, like the sculptures, Assyrian influence (s. pl. 59).[8] In the late 6th or early 5th century B.C. there are two inscriptions from Têmâ in Arabia, recording the introduction of a new cult to that place; some of the forms are archaic but most are fully characteristic of the middle period of the Aramaic script.[9]

The 7th and 6th centuries B.C. witnessed also an extension in the use of the Aramaic language in Babylonia and Assyria; and in fact this simple and flexible instrument of communication was destined after a few centuries utterly to displace the cumbersome cuneiform system of writing and the very languages which it enshrined.

Aramaic potsherds are rarely found in Babylonia (s. pl. 60, 2) or Assyria, but one fine ostracon with a political letter written on it in ink comes from Asshur (s. pl. 62, 2);[10] it belongs probably to the age of Ashurbanipal (668–626 B.C.). There is evidence, too, of an attempt to use clay-tablets for Aramaic documents, since several clay-tablets from Asshur have been

[1] Cooke 'N.-Sem. Inscr.' 159–71.

[2] Pognon *Inscr. Sémit.* 156–78 and Lidzbarski *E.S.E.* III 1–11.

[3] Ronzevalle in *M.U.B.* XV 237–60 and Bauer in *A. Of.* VIII 1–16.

[4] Cooke 'N.-Sem. Inscr.' 171–80.

[5] Ibid. 180–4.*

[6] Cp. Lidzbarski *N.-Sem. Epigr.* 187.

[7] Mesnil du Buisson in *M.S.* I 422–5; s. Albright in 'B.A.S.O.R.' LXXVI 5–11*.

[8] Cooke 'N.-Sem. Inscr.' 186–91. These two monuments of priests of the moon-god can be dated between 605 B.C., when the Medes destroyed Ḥarrān the centre of the worship of that deity, and 552 B.C., when Nabonidus restored it (Clermont-Ganneau cited by Cooke).

[9] Ibid. 195–9 (s. Smith 'Isaiah: chapters xl–lv' 143[103]).

[10] Lidzbarski *Altaramäische Urkunden* 5–15; s. Bowman *ap.* Waterman 'Royal Correspondence' IV 275–82.

preserved containing purely Aramaic texts;[1] these are all brief receipts and belong approximately to the same period (s. pl. 60, 2). There is also a small number of Mesopotamian cylinder-seals with Aramaic legends (s. pl. 61, 1); these differ from the West-Semitic seals not only in their form, being usually cylindrical instead of scaraboid or conical, but also in the stylized and occasionally somewhat bizarre script often found on them, under the influence of Assyro-Babylonian art.

Otherwise the use of Aramaic in these countries was as yet incidental rather than essential; it conveyed not the main text but a translation or summary of it. Thus Assyrian weights which might be expected to have an international currency had the statement of their weight inscribed on them in both languages during the Neo-Assyrian period, *c.* 727–681 B.C. A certain number, too, of Assyrian private commercial documents are provided with Aramaic endorsements or summaries of their contents; these come from Asshur itself during this period[2] and after the fall of the Assyrian empire from Nêrab, *c.* 603–486 B.C.;[3] similar endorsements were added to cuneiform texts of the same class from Babylon during the 6th century B.C. (s. pl. 17, 1).[4] These endorsements contain a high percentage of Jewish names, and Aramaic summaries may have been necessary to facilitate the work of merchants and clerks not very well acquainted with the cuneiform script; for it is noteworthy that these do not begin on Assyrian texts till after Sargon's deportation of the Hebrews of the Northern kingdom (*c.* 721 B.C.), and those on Babylonian tablets only follow Nebuchadrezzar's carrying of the Jews of the Southern kingdom into captivity (597–586 B.C.). However this might be, Aramaic had by the end of this period become so widely known and used that even royal bricks bore inscriptions in both languages (s. pl. 17, 2).[5]

This wide diffusion of the Aramaic language is equally attested by two considerable and important collections of documents, one written by Persian officers and the other by Jewish colonists in Egypt. The first consists of some fourteen documents or fragments of documents of an official nature, the second of nearly a hundred official and private documents, dated from 495 to 400 B.C.; the material of the first is leather (s. pl. 62, 1)[6] and of the second papyrus (s. pl. 61, 2).[7] There

[1] Lidzbarski ibid. 15–20. [2] Delaporte *Épigr. Aram.* 23–49.
[3] Dhorme in *R.A.* xxv 53–82. [4] Delaporte ibid. 51–86. [5] S. p. 30.
[6] Borchardt *Kleinigkeiten* 47–9, *Bl.* 16; s. G. R. Driver *Aramaic Documents of the 5th Century B.C.* [1954]. [7] Cowley 'Aram. Pap.' 1–203.

was also found with this last collection the story of Aḥîqar, which lies behind the apocryphal book of Tobit, and fragments of an Aramaic version of the famous trilingual inscription of Darius I at Bisutûn.[1] All are written in ink in a bold flowing hand, in classical Aramaic. These collections then show that writing by the time of the Exile was not an affair of the court and the priesthood but had established itself amongst various classes of the people; it does not, however, follow that any common man could read and write, and the practice of it probably remained in the hands of a professional class to which those who wished to have something written for them would resort.[2]

### 10. Earliest South-Semitic Inscriptions

Four or five inscriptions in a script akin to the South-Semitic scripts must be noticed. The first,[3] which comes from Baluʿah

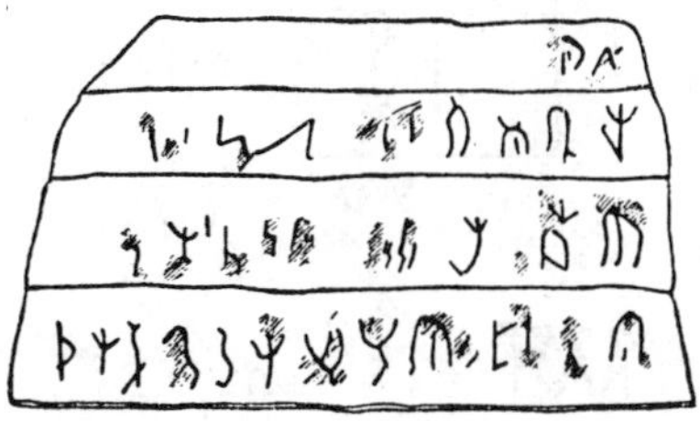

Fig. 77. South-Semitic inscription from Baluʿah in Moab.

in Moab and is dated *c.* 1200–1100 B.C. by the archaeologists, is of interest from the fact that its letters show affinity on the one side to the Sinaitic and on the other to the South-Semitic (s. fig. 77); its resemblances, however, are to letters now of one and now another of these alphabets, suggesting either a date before the differentiation of the various forms of these scripts or an eclectic script based on arbitrary choice between or indistinct recollection of them. Unfortunately the monument, on which a worshipper confronting two deities is depicted, is so badly worn and damaged that the forms of many of the letters are blurred or uncertain, and the text cannot be interpreted.[4]

[1] Cowley 'Aram.-Pap.' 204–71. [2] S. pp. 88–9.

[3] Horsfield & Vincent in *R.B.* XLI 417–44; cp. Drioton ibid. XLII 353–65, Crowfoot in 'P.Q.S.' LXVI (1934) 76/i, Gaster ibid. LXIX (1937) 49–52, and Albright in 'J.A.O.S.' LVI 129 (who suggests the 3rd millennium B.C. for the inscription as distinct from the relief; s. 'Arch. and Rel. of Isr.' 189[53]).

[4] A potsherd from Beth-shean has some markings which perhaps recall the letters on the inscription from Baluʿah (Fitzgerald 'Beth-shan' II/ii 21; xlii/5).

There is also a fragmentary bowl from Ezion-geber[1] in southern Palestine on which some signs, part of a South-Arabian inscription, are still legible. The other three[2] inscriptions were all found in a temple at Ur, just beneath a pavement of Nebuchadrezzar, and therefore very probably belong to the 7th century B.C.[3] (s. fig. 78). Of these the first (A) and second (B), being incised on bricks, are tolerably well preserved and fairly intelligible as most of their letters can be readily identified by comparison with those of the South-Semitic alphabets; but the third (C) is a mere *graffito* and cannot be deciphered, although conjectural

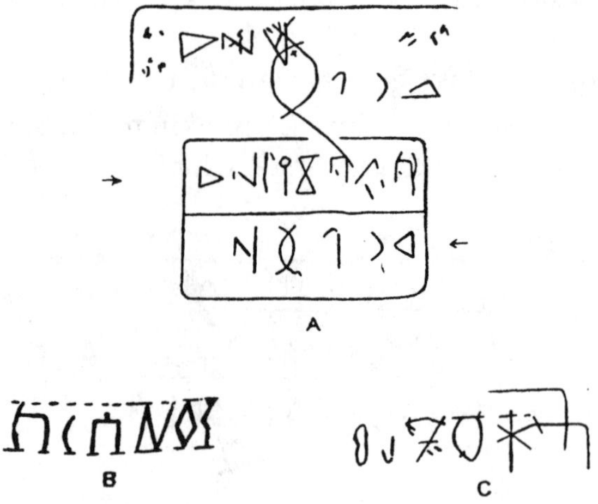


FIG. 78. South-Semitic inscriptions from Ur.*

identification of some of the letters is possible by the same method of comparison. It may be added that the text of the first (A) is written 'as the ox ploughs',[4] namely from left to right in the first and from right to left in the second line; this method of writing, though otherwise most unusual in Semitic texts, is not infrequently found on Sabaean inscriptions and is quite normal in early Greek inscriptions.[5]*

## 11. Problems of Interpretation

Attempts to discover the meanings or values of the symbols found in texts of the early period *c.* 2000–1500 B.C. have so far met with little success;[6] but the detection of two or three

[1] Glueck in 'B.A.S.O.R.' LXXI 15.

[2] Burrows in 'J.R.A.S.' 1927, 795–802.

[3] S. pp. 107–8.

[4] Gk. βουστροφηδόν.

[5] Writing βουστροφηδόν was common in Greek inscriptions down to the 7th century B.C.; it lingered on stone into the 6th century and on vases into the 5th century B.C., when however it was something abnormal.

[6] S. pp. 198–9.

recognizable Semitic names or words in an obviously early form of the Phoenician alphabet in the Sinaitic and Gebalite or Old-Byblian inscriptions may be held to have proved the existence of the alphabet long before the date to which its invention has usually been assigned.[1] The same comparisons or identifications of signs are not always proposed with others occurring within or without this group of documents and, even when these are such as to command general assent from the point of view of the form, a satisfactory interpretation of word or sentence is rarely achieved. The causes of this failure are obvious. First, there is the paucity of the documents hitherto available for study; for, apart from the cuneiform texts, which are in a category by themselves, there are less than 50 documents for a period of more than 500 years. The gaps therefore are immense; they are measured almost in centuries rather than decades. Secondly, nearly every document is imperfect, either damaged or hardly legible, and none exceeds ten lines in length, while several seem to contain or to have contained only a single word, probably nothing but a proper name. Thirdly, signs resembling each other in form might have different values in the various centres where they were used. Fourthly, it is probable, if not certain, that these texts are not all in the same language; for the appearance of certain inscriptions from Gebal suggests a non-Semitic language. Even if all are written in a Semitic language, it does not follow that they are all in the same dialect, and differences of this kind may offer no small obstacles to interpretation. Consequently there is or may be no continuity either of script or of language, and the wide gaps requiring to be bridged make interpretation a matter almost entirely of guess-work, and scholars have given free rein to their imagination, uncontrolled by philology or grammar, by probability or common sense. Thus one decipherer,[2] having read certain signs in the Sinaitic texts as 'Manasseh', concluded that he had found 'Moses' under another name and supported his view by recalling that there is one passage of the Old Testament in which מנשה[3] $M^{n}\check{s}h$ 'Manasseh' has been substituted for מ[ו]שה *M*[*w*]*šh* 'Moses' out of deference to the memory of the great lawgiver.[4]

[1] S. pp. 91–3.

[2] Grimme *Althebr. Inschr.* 92–6.

[3] The *nûn* was written 'suspended' because it was a Rabbinical insertion not in the original text.

[4] Jud. xviii 30, where the reason for the alteration of the text was that the Levite in the story had acted not as a descendant of Moses should have acted or might have been expected to act but after the fashion of the

Another interpreter[1] of these same texts does not hesitate to mix the dialects from which he draws his forms, postulating now a Phoenico-Hebrew and now an Aramaic plural ending, here a Byblo-Phoenician and a Hebrew and there an Accadian and Phoenician (and occasionally Aramaic and Hebrew) relative particle. Yet another,[2] in an attempt to interpret the text of three words on the bowl[3] from Lachish, produced a sentence containing words from two different Semitic languages, of which one figured in Aramaic spelling with a Hebrew pronominal suffix, while there was no antecedent for the first pronoun; consequently, the sense which he wrested from it was in the highest degree uncertain if not improbable! Such vagaries of interpretation do not inspire confidence, and the wisest course is perhaps to hold one's hand until enough matter becomes available to enable the development of script and language to be traced with some degree of probability and a sure foundation to be laid for profitable study.

Fortunately, Phoenician and Hebrew inscriptions from the 15th to the 10th centuries B.C. and Aramaic inscriptions of the 9th century B.C. can be and have been read with reasonable certainty. The true course therefore is to wait for future excavation to bring fresh texts to light and to hope thus to be able to work backwards from the Phoenician to the earlier rather than forwards from the Egyptian to the later texts.

impious king Manasseh (Cooke 'Book of Judges' 170–1). Is משה ever written מושה in the Massoretic text? If not, the ground is cut away from under the theory.*

[1] Butin in 'H.T.R.' XXI 38 (plural *-m*) and 45–6, 50 (plural *-n*), 38–9, 63 (relative *z*) and 59 (relative *'š*).

[2] Langdon in the 'Times' 5 Oct. 1935 (8–iii); s. G. R. Driver ibid. 10 Oct. 1935 (10–iv). Langdon has also claimed to have discovered the origin of the Hebrew vowel-signs in this text, although they are known to have been introduced in approximately the 8th century A.D. (Kahle 'Geniza' 84–6, 108–10)!*

[3] S. pp. 100–1.

# CHRONOLOGICAL TABLE OF INSCRIPTIONS[1]



## CUNEIFORM

| B.C. | |
|---|---|
| 1425–1350 | Tell-elAmarna |
| 1425–1350 | Râs-eshShamrah |

## PROTO-SINAITIC[2]

| B.C. | |
|---|---|
| 2500–1800 | Tell-elGhassûl |
| 2100–1700 | Gebal A and B |
| 1850–1600 | Sinai |
| 1840–1790 | Lebeʿah |
| 1800–1650 | Gezer and Shechem |
| 1700–1550 | Lachish |
| 1600 | Tell-elḤesy |
| 1500 | Gebal Ċ |
| 1400–1300 | Tell-etTaʿajjul, Tell-elḤesy |
| 1400–1200 | ʿAin Shems |
| 1250 | Lachish |
| 1200 | Dêr ʿAllā. |

## NORTH-SEMITIC[2]

### Phoenician

| | |
|---|---|
| c. 1500 | Byblos, *Špṭbʿl* |
| 1000 | Byblos I and II |
| | Ruwaisah (Nabâṭîyah), arrow |
| | Byblos, spatula |
| 1000–900 | Byblos III |
| 900 | Byblos IV |
| 900–800 | Zinjîrlû, *Klmw* |
| c. 800 | Karatepe, *'ztwd* |
| 725–700 | Sidon, Cypriot bowl |
| | Nora and Bosa, pillars |
| 700–600 | Arslan Tash, incantation |
| 575 | Ur, ivory |
| 550–350 | Seals, potsherds, papyrus |
| 500–400 | Byblos V |

### Aramaic

| | |
|---|---|
| 850 | Tell Ḥalaf, Buraij, Arslan Tash |
| 800–700 | Zinjîrlû, *Pnmw* I and II and *Br-rkb* |
| | Sûjîn, *Mtʿ 'l* |
| | Hamath, *Ẓkr* |
| c. 725–680 | Assyrian weights |
| 720–450 | Endorsements on cuneiform tablets |
| 700–600 | Nêrab, funerary monument |
| 675–625 | Asshur, potsherds and tablets |
| 675–330 | Seals |
| 500–400 | Têmâ |
| 495–400 | Documents from Egypt |
| 411–407 | Documents from Susa and Babylon |

## WEST-SEMITIC

### Hebrew

| | |
|---|---|
| 1000 | Gezer, calendar |
| 1000–600 | Seals and stamps, weights |
| 900–600 | Jerusalem, Samaria, Lachish, Megiddo, masons' marks |
| 775 | Samaria, potsherds and ivories |
| 750 | Jerusalem, Megiddo, ʿAin Shems, Tell-elḤesy, potsherds |
| 700 | Siloam |
| 700–600 | Ezion-geber |
| 590–585 | Lachish, letters on potsherds |

### Moabite

| | |
|---|---|
| 850 | *Mšʿ* |

## SOUTH-SEMITIC

| | |
|---|---|
| 1200–1100 | Baluʿah |
| 700 | Minaean inscriptions |
| 575 | Ur, bricks |
| 500 | Sabaean inscriptions |

[1] The dates are in round figures, since early documents can rarely be assigned to a definite year; only the Assyrian and Babylonian contracts with Aramaic endorsements and the Aramaic papyri from Egypt, or rather some of them, bear exact dates which can be correlated with those of the Gregorian Calendar.

[2] Cp. Flight *ap.* De Langhe *Ugarit* I 251[2] for a comparable table of dates (1938).

# III

# THE ORIGIN OF THE ALPHABET

*ΚΑΔΜΗΙΑ ΓΡΑΜΜΑΤΑ*
'Oriental letters'
(Herodotus 'Histories' v 59.)

## 1. Theories regarding the Origin of the Alphabet

Ancient writers held various opinions regarding the origin of writing and the alphabet*. Herodotus,[1] the 'father of history', expressing no view on its origin, remarked simply that the Phoenicians, who came to Greece with one Cadmus, introduced it there, amongst other arts, and that letters were therefore called καδμήια or φοινικήια γράμματα after the country whence they had been brought. Diodorus Siculus[2] held that the Syrians were the inventors of the alphabet, and that the Phoenicians, having had it from them, modified the forms of some of the letters and Cadmus brought them to Greece; and by Syrians he perhaps meant Assyrians[3] in accordance with the statement of the elder Pliny[4] that *litteras semper arbitror Assyrias fuisse*, though adding *sed alii apud Aegyptios a Mercurio ut Gallius, alii apud Syros repertas volunt*. Yet neither Diodorus nor Pliny felt any certainty in the matter; for the former noted the claim of the Egyptians παρ' αὐτοῖς τὴν τῶν γραμμάτων εὕρεσιν γενέσθαι, and the latter went on to say that *Anticlides in Aegypto invenisse quendam nomine Menon tradit . . . idque monumentis adprobare conatur*, with the comment that the Babylonians were known to have used letters for astronomical calculations from a very remote age, *quo apparet aeternus litterarum usus*. Other writers were divided into two schools of thought, the one favouring the Egyptian and the other the Phoenician claim. Thus Plato[5] named an Egyptian called *Θευθ* as the inventor of letters, and the Syrian Philo Byblius[6] in the 1st century A.D. only repeated this legend when he declared that a certain *Τάαυτος* invented it; for these

[1] In *Hist.* v 58–9.

[2] In *Bibl. Hist.* I lxix 5 (Egyptians), v lviii 3 and lxxiv 1 (Syrians).

[3] Cp. Nöldeke in *Hermes* v 443–68. Clearly the כתב אשורי(ת) 'Assyrian script' into which Ezra was said to have transposed the Hebrew scriptures was the Syrian (Aramaean) form of the alphabet (s. Lidzbarski *N.-Sem. Epigr.* 189–90)*.

[4] In *Nat. Hist.* VII lvi 192–3.

[5] In *Phileb.* 18 b–c and *Phaedr.* 274 c–275 a.

[6] Eusebius *Evang. Praep.* [31 d–32 a] i 9.

two names clearly reproduce that of the Egyptian god Thoth[1] and represent a tradition that the invention was of Egyptian origin*. Tacitus,[2] too, was of this opinion, saying expressly that *primi per figuras animalium Aegyptii sensus mentis effingebant*, and that the Phoenicians transmitted them to Greece. Such was the older and better opinion, which reflected tradition if not knowledge; later opinion was little more than speculation coloured by tradition or pious fancy. Thus Critias[3] in the 1st century B.C. declared that *Φοίνικες εὗρον γράμματα ἀλεξίλογα*, Lucan[4] wrote that *Phoenices primi, famae si creditur, ausi | mansuram rudibus vocem signare figuris*, and Pliny[5] affirmed that *ipsa gens Phoenicum in magna gloria litterarum inventionis*, thus disregarding other views which he had expressed elsewhere in the same work. Suidas,[6] a Greek lexicographer of uncertain date, repeated the Phoenician legend, which Photius,[7] another Greek lexicographer of the 9th century A.D., embellished with the name of an inventor; this, according to him, was one Agenor the son of Phoenix. Similarly, the Jewish historian Eupolemus,[8] in the second century A.D., claimed Moses as the inventor of the alphabet, seeking to glorify his race. There is no need to take these self-evident speculations too seriously; they show that ancient writers can have had no sure tradition, even though as by chance they enshrine or reflect a measure of the truth, namely that the Egyptians invented the alphabet, as in a sense they did, and that the Phoenicians carried it into Europe. There is, however, no reason to suppose that Cadmus was an historical person; his name merely typified the person or people who introduced letters to the Greeks as being of Eastern origin.[9]

Modern views regarding the origin of the alphabet are almost as numerous as those just described. Thus it has been

[1] Eg. *Ḏḥwt(y)* and Copt. ⲑⲟⲟⲩⲧ god of writing (s. Sethe in *Göttingen* 1916, 101³); cp. Cicero *D. Nat. Deor.* III xxii 56, where *Thoth* is the form given in Orelli's text.

[2] In *Ann.* xi 14.

[3] Kaibel *Athen. Deipnosoph.* 164 50 28 c.

[4] In *Pharsal.* iii 220–1.

[5] In *Nat. Hist.* v xiii 67.

[6] Adler *Suid. Lex.* I 538.

[7] Porson *Φωτ. Λέξ. Συναγ.* II 652, where the author adds that letters were called *φοινικήια γράμματα* according to the Cretans *ὡς εὑρέθη ἀπὸ τοῦ γράφειν ἐν φοινίκων πετάλοις*.

[8] Müller *Hist. Fragm. Graec.* III 220.

[9] The Gk. *Κάδμος* is a proper name based on the Hebr. קֶדֶם and Aram. קַדְמָא 'East' (cp. I Ki. Gk. iv 30 = Hebr. v 10 where the wisdom of 'all the sons of *Qeḏem*' is equated with that of the Egyptians). To what alphabet Philo's *ἀπόκρυφα Ἀμμουνέων γράμματα συγκείμενα* and his *πάγχαια γράμματα* (Eusebius *Evang. Praep.* [32 b] i 9, [60 b] ii 2) refer is unknown (s. Eissfeldt *Ras Schamra u. Sanchunjaton* 9–12 and Humbert in *A. Of.* XIII 161).

sought in the Egyptian systems whether hieroglyphic or hieratic or demotic, in the cuneiform systems whether Sumerian or Accadian, in the Hittite hieroglyphs, and the Cretan and Cypriot linear scripts.[1] Recent discoveries of inscriptions in Palestine and Sinai, however, seem to exclude the Cypriot script on chronological grounds, while to use the still undeciphered Cretan or Hittite systems, if indeed chronology does not exclude them, for the purpose is simply to attempt to explain *obscurum per obscurius*. The present examination of the problem therefore is restricted to a discussion of the claims of the Egyptian and Accadian, including the Ugaritic, systems of writing to be the source, mediate or immediate, of the so-called Phoenician and thus also of the Greek alphabet *.

## 2. The Cuneiform Scripts and the Phoenician Alphabet

Lidzbarski[2] has adduced various cogent arguments against the theory of the Accadian origin of the Phoenician alphabet, and these may be briefly summarized here, although detailed disproof is hardly required. The Accadian (Assyro-Babylonian) signs had lost all resemblance to the original Sumerian pictographs by *c.* 3000 B.C., some thousand years before the earliest conceivable date for the invention of the Phoenician letters; the Phoenician characters, therefore, since they cannot possibly be dated before *c.* 2000 B.C., can by no means be derived from the cuneiform pictographs. Resemblances between odd signs of the two systems can indeed be detected but prove nothing; either they are due to the accidents of transmission, whereby for example the Sumerian 𒄞 or 𒄞 *GUD* = Accadian 𒄞 *alpu*(*m*) 'ox' has retained enough of its primitive form to have a passable likeness to the Phoenician 𐤀 = Hebrew א (*'ālep̄*),[3] or the values are totally different and prove that the likenesses are purely a matter of chance and have no evidential value, as shown by a comparison of the Accadian 𒈠 *ma* or 𒀾 *áš* with respectively the Phoenician 𐤄 *h* or 𐤎 *s*. Moreover, such comparisons are few and often specious; they rest only too often on an arbitrary choice of comparable forms from widely different periods, and this fact seriously impairs their value.

[1] Cp. Bauer & Leander *Hist. Gr. d. Hebr. Spr.* I 61, Contenau *Man. Arch. Or.* I 258–9, Gardiner in 'J.E.A.' III 1–5, 11–12, and Diringer in 'Antiquity' XVII 77–82, where the various views are listed under the names of their authors.

[2] In *E.S.E.* I 128–32, 268–9.

[3] So called from the Sem. **'alp* 'ox' (s. p. 163).

They are thus apt to be either fortuitous or external, and attempts have therefore been made to enhance their appeal on other grounds. Thus it has been argued that, for example, there is an inner connexion between the Sumero-Accadian sign for an ox and the Phoenician sign for *'ālep̠* because both stand *pars pro toto*; both take the head alone to represent the whole beast. The Egyptian  and the Cretan , however, are equally *pars pro toto*, and this principle underlies so many hieroglyphs that it has no value for the present argument. It has also been urged that, as the Phoenicians, like the Accadians, had separate signs for various forms of the same object, such as those for the hand with the arm (Acc. ; Phoen. z) and the hand alone (Acc. ; Phoen. ), their two systems were necessarily connected, since the same idea is not likely to have occurred independently to the Accadians and the Phoenicians; but this argument is easily countered by showing that the Egyptians, too, had distinct signs for the hand with the arm (, ) and the hand alone (, , , , ), varying according to their positions. This line of argument therefore does not prove that the Phoenicians must have derived their system of writing from the Accadians. Yet other reasons have been brought forward to support this theory; but the best refutation of all such arguments will be found in the evidence cited hereafter in favour of the Egyptian origin of the Semitic alphabets.[1]

The proto-Elamites in the East and the Hittites and the Mitanni in the north devised their own systems of pictographic and cuneiform writing; but none of these peoples introduced any improvements on the Sumero-Babylonian system or took any steps towards the invention of an alphabet. The Chaldians of the district between Mount Ararat and Lake Van (*c.* 859–585) used the Assyrian syllabary for historical texts in their own language, retaining confusion of kindred sounds but refraining from using more than one sign for any given syllable, and employing less than fifty ideograms;[2] they thus effected some improvement on the cumbersome Assyrian system. The Neo-Elamites of the late Persian period, indeed, devised a simplified cuneiform syllabary of 113 signs, with which they combined a limited number of ideograms,[3] and the Achaemenid Persians devised a syllabary containing only fifty-one cuneiform signs[4]

[1] S. pp. 136–9.

[2] Lehmann-Haupt *C.I.C.* I 14–15.

[3] Weissbach *Keilinschriften der Achämeniden* xxxix–il, lxxvii–lxxxii.

[4] Weissbach ibid. l–lxix, lxxxiii–lxxxiv.

based on the principle of, but almost entirely different from, the old Sumero-Accadian syllabary;[1] but, while they isolated three of the vowels, they did not succeed in designing an alphabet by isolating the consonants and representing them by distinct signs without inherent vowels (s. fig. 79). Thus they only devised yet another syllabary, not an alphabet, and cannot therefore be

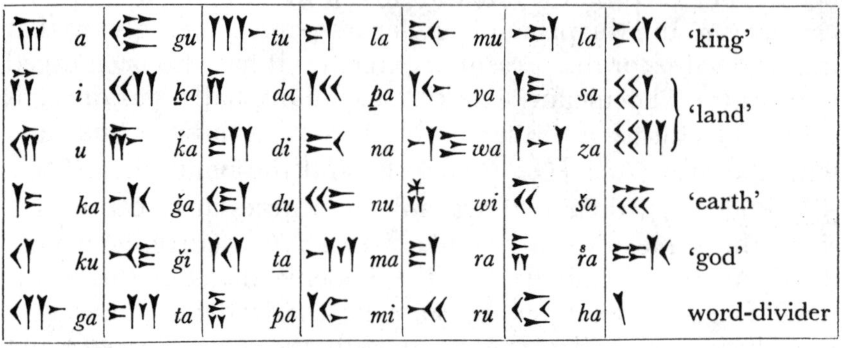


FIG. 79. Old-Persian syllabary.

included in the search for the inventors of the alphabet; they merely simplified and improved the Accadian system.

## 3. THE EGYPTIAN PSEUDO-ALPHABET

The fourth millennium B.C. was apparently the period in which the Egyptian, like the Sumerian, system of writing arose, and the probability is that the idea and the method of writing were borrowed by the Egyptians from the Sumerians; for, while other traces of Sumerian influence have been detected in Egypt, there is no evidence of any influence working in the opposite direction. Clay, however, was not used, except at a comparatively late date in the correspondence found at Tell el'Amarna as well as at Ugarit (*c.* 1400–1350 B.C.). The materials used by the Egyptians were principally stone for hieroglyphic and papyrus for hieratic and demotic texts; but alabaster and ivory, wood and metal, as well as leather, were also employed. The script was pictographic in origin; while, however, the cuneiform signs in the earliest known texts were already degenerating into unrecognizable symbols in consequence of the clumsy method of writing on clay which the Sumerians had adopted,

[1] Very few Persian signs are identical in form with, even though different in value from, Accadian signs (for example, Acc. *ma* = Pers. *ra*, Acc. *iz/s/ṣ* = Pers. *ba*).

the artistic taste and suitable material of the Egyptians preserved the hieroglyphs as true pictures almost in their original freshness for many centuries. When, however, wood and papyrus came to be commonly used, the script became increasingly cursive as it passed through the hieratic and demotic stages, until the original forms became as unrecognizable as those of the cuneiform signs.

Like the Sumerian, the Egyptian system is by no means primitive; it is only partly pictographic but is also at the same time to a considerable extent ideographic. In the first place, a sign depicting a common object was stretched to represent also a cognate idea: for example, the picture of the sun stands not only for the sun itself but also for the word denoting a day, the figure of a man in an attitude of prayer expresses the conception of worship, and so on. Beside primary symbols there are also combinations of pictorial signs serving for concepts too complicated for representation by simple pictures. For the most part, however, the hieroglyphs are not merely ideographic or expressive of words or concepts; they are phonetic, expressing sounds, whether words or syllables. For the Egyptian pictographic system revealed the same defects as the Sumerian system. The signs, therefore, which in origin pictorially represented concrete objects, were unsuited to express abstract conceptions but had to be adapted to this purpose; for this a sign depicting one object might be used also to represent or indicate a homonymous word denoting something totally different; so 𓆼 *ḫꜣ* 'lotus' came to stand also for *ḫꜣ* 'thousand' and 𓆣 *ḫpr* 'beetle' came to stand also for *ḫpr* 'became'.[1] In consequence of the ambiguity resulting from this practice, the Egyptians like the Sumerians used a number of so-called determinative signs to indicate the class to which the intended object belonged, and so give the reader a hint of the intended meaning;[2] these require no illustration. Like Sumerian, again, the Egyptian syllabary as originally devised was incapable of indicating grammatical inflexions or writing phonetic complements, which came to be widely used to assist the reader in identifying the hieroglyph before him, since no ordinary man could carry many hundreds of hieroglyphs with their manifold meanings in his head or read them fluently; and it was quite useless for representing

[1] As though the picture of a 'bee' might be used also for 'be' as a verb and ultimately even for '-be-' as a mere syllable within another word in writing the English language!

[2] S. pp. 61–2.

foreign words, especially proper names, for which no native symbols were available and which had therefore to be somehow or other spelled out.

Consequently, the Egyptian scribes began to use signs with simple values to represent not the original words but the mere sounds, in themselves meaningless, of those words as syllables or letters, whether a combination of consonants or a single consonant. Thus *mn* 'to remain' might and indeed was used not only for the homonymous *m(a)n* 'so and so' but also for *m-n* as a syllable forming an element in any word in which this combination of consonants occurs, without regard to the division of syllables: for example, in *m(e)nf(ʿ)r* 'Memphis', *m(o)nm(ʿ)n* 'to move', *m(ū)n(ʿ)q* 'to finish', *sm(ī)n(ʿ)t* 'to fix', and so on.[1] Further, since the Egyptian language at a very early state of its development already contained a high percentage of roots consisting of only one strong consonant and one or even two weak consonants which showed an increasing tendency to fall away, it was an easy step to disregard or drop these and use the surviving strong consonant as a mere letter. Thus the sign for *rꜣ* or *rỉ* 'mouth' came readily to be used for *r(a)*, *r(e)*, *r(i)*, *r(u)*, and finally for *r* alone, and that for *ỉd* 'hand'* came equally easily to be used for *d*; similarly but less easily the sign for *qꜣꜣ* 'hill' came to serve for *q* and even more easily that for *s* 'bolt' served for the consonant *s*. It was usually the initial consonant but occasionally also the final consonant that, if strong, survived as the letter which came thus to be represented by the hieroglyph, and words of two rather than three consonants were generally preferred; also only words representing common and well-known objects were chosen for this purpose. By this means a pseudo-alphabet of twenty-four consonants was devised, but it was not much used except for spelling out foreign words and phonetic complements (s. p. 135 fig. 80).[2]

The principal function of these consonantal or alphabetic signs was to spell out the phonetic complement indicating the pronunciation of the hieroglyph which it accompanied, though more or less imperfectly. For thus only the first or last or a

[1] Sethe in *Göttingen* 1916, 117[3]; cp. *V. Bilde z. Buchstaben* 36. The old Egyptian system is purely consonantal and the vowels are generally supplied from the late Coptic forms.

[2] Sethe *Göttingen* 1916, 151–8. The Cypriot syllabary was used in a somewhat similar fashion to indicate consonants alone, as in Cypr. *ka-se* = *kas* for Gk. καὶ 'and' and Cypr. *ta-mi-ti-ri* for Gk. Δάματρι (Δήμητρι) 'for Demeter'.

couple of the consonants, even though at times all the consonants, of a word might be written beside the hieroglyph itself as

| | Word furnishing sign with pronunciation and meaning[1] | | Sign with object depicted and consonantal value | | |
|---|---|---|---|---|---|
| I. Words containing (i) one consonant | 𓄿𓏤 | *ꜣ* 'vulture' | 𓄿 | 'vulture' | *ꜣ* (א) |
| | 𓇋𓇇𓏥 | *i* 'reed' | 𓇋 | 'reed' | *i* (י/א) |
| | 𓂝 | *ꜥ* 'hand, arm' | 𓂝 | 'forearm' | *ꜥ* (ע) |
| | 𓆑𓏏[2] | *f.t*[3] 'horned viper' | 𓆑 | 'horned viper'[4] | *f* |
| | 𓈖𓏏𓈗 | *n.t*[3] 'water' | 𓈖 | 'water' | *n* |
| | 𓉔𓏤 | *h* 'courtyard' | 𓉔 | 'courtyard' | *h* |
| | 𓊃𓏤 | *s* 'bolt' | 𓊃 | 'bolt' | *z* |
| | 𓏏 | *t* 'loaf' | 𓏏 | 'loaf' | *t* |
| (ii) one strong and one weak consonant | 𓊪𓏤 | *pi* 'plinth, seat' | 𓊪 | 'stool' | *p* |
| | 𓂋 | *rꜣ* or *ri* 'mouth' | 𓂋 | 'mouth' | *r* |
| | 𓐍𓏤 | *ḫi* 'placenta' (?) | 𓐍 | 'placenta' (?) | *ḫ* (خ) |
| | 𓄡𓏏 | *ẖꜣ.t* 'interior of trunk' | 𓄡 | 'animal's belly with teats' | *ẖ* (*ch*) |
| (iii) one weak and one strong consonant | 𓂧[2] | *ἰd** 'hand' | 𓂧 | 'hand' | *d* |
| (iv) one strong and two weak consonants | 𓈙𓏤 | *šꜣi* (?) 'pool' | 𓈙 | 'pool' | *š* |
| | 𓈎𓄿𓄿𓈎 | *qꜣꜣ* 'hill' | 𓈎 | 'hill-slope' | *q* |
| (v) two weak and one strong consonant | 𓆓𓏏 | *wꜣḏ.t*[3] 'cobra' | 𓆓 | 'cobra' | *ḏ* (*dj*) |
| II. Words not known | | | 𓅱 | 'quail-chick' | *w* |
| | | | 𓃀 | 'foot' | *b* |
| | | | 𓅓 | 'owl' | *m* |
| | | | 𓎛 | 'twisted hank' | *ḥ* (ح) |
| | | | 𓋴 | 'folded cloth' | *s* |
| | | | 𓎡 | 'basket' | *k* |
| | | | 𓎼 | 'jar-stand' | *g* |
| | | | 𓍿 | 'tethering rope' | *ṯ* (*tj*) |

[1] Taken from the most primitive known writing.
[2] Form not actually found but inferred.
[3] Final *t* indicating feminine gender (s. p. 158 n. 1).
[4] Or perhaps rather 𓅱𓆑𓇋𓆙 *wfi* 'horned viper'.

FIG. 80. Egyptian pseudo-alphabet.

in the following examples, in which the phonetic complement distinguished two uses of the same sign, as in

𓂻 *šm* 'went' and *ἰw* 'came'

distinguished in writing as

[1] $^{š}šm$ 'went' and $iw^{w}$ 'came'

or merely indicated the pronunciation, as in

ʿnḫ written also $ʿnḫ^{n}_{ḫ}$ 'lived'

qmꜣ written also $^{q}qmꜣ^{ꜣ}$ 'throw-stick'

inr written also $^{i.n}inr$ or $^{in}_{r}inr$ 'stone',

where several or all of the letters of the word represented by the ideogram are repeated. By this means the reader was helped in finding the correct pronunciation of the hieroglyph, especially when it was polyphonous.[2] Such an alphabetic use of the hieroglyphs was also the sole method by which grammatical inflexions and foreign words, and especially proper names, could be represented. Indeed, the Egyptians practically restricted the use of this pseudo-alphabet to these purposes and employed it in consecutive writing only once by way of experiment in the Saʿite period (*c.* 600 B.C.), largely through the foreign example of alphabetic scripts. Consequently, they too fell short of devising a true alphabet; for, although they succeeded in writing consonants without vowels, they failed to represent vowels without consonants.

Sethe[3] has adduced a number of arguments which may here be summarized, as they are evidently conclusive, to show that the Phoenician alphabet was derived ultimately if not immediately not from the Sumero-Accadian cuneiform syllabary but from the Egyptian hieroglyphic system of writing.

The Phoenician alphabet in its earliest known form is found engraved on stone or metal or painted on potsherds, like Egyptian hieroglyphic and hieratic writing. Further, papyrus is attested as an Egyptian import into Phoenicia *c.* 1100 B.C. and may even have been manufactured in northern Palestine;[4] this was a common writing material also in Egypt, but no Phoenician papyri have survived. Clay, however, was used only for two brief periods in Syria and Palestine, where a suitable kind was not easily obtained,[5] and attempts to use it for Aramaic (Phoenician) writing were shortlived, obviously because it was ill-suited to a linear script;[6] it was, however, well suited to the cuneiform script, which indeed was devised for it. Thus the writing materials suggest Egyptian rather than Sumero-Accadian affinities. Again, the Phoenician script is clearly pictographic,

[1] The two signs are here combined into a single sign.

[2] S. pp. 59–60.

[3] In *V. Bilde z. Buchstaben* 48–55.

[4] S. pp. 82–3.

[5] S. pp. 8–9, 78–9.

[6] S. pp. 28–9.

as the Egyptian still visibly is, whereas the pictorial origin of the cuneiform signs is almost entirely obscured even in the earliest known texts. Even when the pictorial origin of a sign has ceased to be evident in a North-Semitic letter, it can often still be recognized in its South-Semitic counterpart. In form, too, then, the Phoenician alphabet approximates rather to the Egyptian hieroglyphic than to the Sumero-Accadian script; its letters admit curves and show no sign of being based on wedges. Further, the Phoenician like the Egyptian script ran from right to left, since the scribe naturally began at the point nearest to the tip of the pen; if it had been derived from or even been influenced by the Sumero-Accadian writing, it would certainly have followed that in running from left to right. If it had been so derived or influenced, the retrogressive step of changing the direction in favour of writing from right to left, with the risk of defacing what had already been written, would be incomprehensible; it would have been to revert to a stage of development beyond which the Egyptians never advanced and to adopt a method which the Greeks tried, only to reject it. The advantages of writing from left to right are as great with ink as on clay; the direction is immaterial only on stone.

Again, Egyptian and Phoenician are the sole kinds of writing that represent only the consonants and leave, at any rate in the first instance, the vowels unrepresented. The nature of the Semitic languages is such as to make this omission tolerable, as the vowels are not essential to the root but serve only to indicate modifications of its meaning; the practice continues to the present day in Arabic and Hebrew writing without causing much difficulty in simple texts, but serious misunderstanding may and indeed does occasionally arise.[1] All the Semitic languages therefore were driven in course of time to devise various means of obviating this difficulty, such as the use of half-consonants (', *h*, *w*, *y*,) to indicate long vowels and ultimately also points above or below the line to indicate short vowels; similarly, late Egyptian texts employ weak or half-consonants as vowel-signs in spelling foreign names, and the Greeks from the beginning adapted the signs for certain Semitic consonants not required by their own language for use as vowel-letters.[2] If then the Phoenician script were based on the cuneiform syllabary which had distinct signs for the four main vowels (*a*, *e*, *i*, *u*),[3]

[1] For example, the Arab. قتل (*qtl*) can be read *qatal*(*a*) 'he killed' or *qutil*(*a*) 'he was killed', and the context alone decides the sense.

[2] S. pp. 178–9.

[3] S. pp. 58–9.

it would have been a retrogressive step to have picked out only signs for consonants and to have discarded those for vowels at the cost of having subsequently to invent new signs for the vowels. The omission of the vowels then is explicable only on the assumption that those who were inventing and working out the Phoenician alphabet had none before them in the model on which their system was being based; that must have been the Egyptian system, in which the omission of the vowels was inherent in a method derived from pictography and which did not till a relatively late date advance beyond that stage.

Finally, while a syllabic script can be evolved from a purely consonantal alphabet, as the Ethiopic syllabary[1] shows, syllabic writing is a blind alley from which there is no escape. Neither a purely consonantal alphabet nor one of consonants and vowels was ever evolved from the Sumero-Accadian syllabary; the best that was achieved was the simplified Old-Persian syllabary which reduced the number of signs by eliminating polyphones and dispensing with those that represented vowel + consonant and consonant + vowel + consonant.[2] The Ugaritic alphabet was no exception, because it was certainly influenced by an early Canaanite alphabetic script.[3] It is indeed remarkable that the Accadians with all their devotion to philological and literary studies never thought of an alphabet to take the place of their elaborate and clumsy syllabary of 285 signs (exclusive of ideograms); but the reason lay probably in the fact that they were using a syllabary designed for a totally different non-Semitic language and so never succeeded in freeing themselves from its complications and implications. On the one hand, too, there was the convenience of using ideograms as a kind of shorthand. On the other hand, a syllable in which consonant and vowel are welded into a firm and indissoluble phonetic unity is a barrier to the separation of the distinct sounds such as an alphabet presupposes. The Egyptians were not so wedded to the syllabic system as the Accadians, and only languages which exhibited a functional distinction between consonants as expressing the notion or conception of the root and vowels as marking the form of the root and so indicating modifications of its meaning could succeed in splitting up words and syllables into their individual component elements; for the consonants,

[1] The earliest Ethiopic inscriptions were written in a purely consonantal script based on the South-Semitic scripts; but already by the 5th century A.D. the consonants were so modified that each was given seven forms varying slightly according to the vowel (*a*, *ū*, *ī*, *ā*, *ē*, *e*, *ō*) which followed it.

[2] S. pp. 131–2.

[3] S. pp. 148–52.

which could not by themselves alone and without vowels be pronounced, could only so be treated as independent sounds. It was not Sumerian but Egyptian that could and did so treat the consonants, and it was not the former but the latter that Phoenician followed in similarly distinguishing consonants from vowels.

Thus every factor in writing—papyrus and potsherd, reed-pen and ink, still recognizably pictorial signs, direction of writing, absence of vowel-signs—points indisputably to a close connexion between the Egyptian and Phoenician scripts; and no single factor clearly or indisputably suggests any connexion between the Sumero-Accadian and Phoenician scripts.

Yet the borrowing of the Phoenician alphabet can hardly have been immediate. On the one side, the Egyptian signs or letters, alike in their hieroglyphic or pictographic and their hieratic or cursive forms, show few, if any, close resemblances to the Phoenician letters even at their earliest appearance; and, when the picture underlying any two signs or letters is clearly the same, the value of the signs does not generally agree. For example, the zigzag line depicting water is the sign for the Egyptian *n* but the Phoenician *m*, that representing the mouth is the Egyptian *r* but the Phoenician *p*, and so on. These differences are naturally due to differences of language; for the Egyptian *r*(ꜣ) but the Semitic **puw* mean 'mouth'.[1] On the other side, the pictures to which the Phoenician letters go back unmistakably agree with the names which they bear, and these are genuine Semitic or Canaanite words and in most cases approximately fit the object depicted and so speak for the Canaanite origin of the alphabet. Moreover, that these names are intelligible Canaanite words, whereas the names of the Greek letters have no meaning in the Greek language, is indisputable evidence that it was the Greeks who borrowed the alphabet from the Phoenicians, not the Phoenicians who borrowed it from the Greeks. Further, if the Phoenicians had derived it from the Greeks, they would hardly have discarded the use of special signs for the vowels; the Greeks, however, diverted certain signs, for which their language had no use, to serve as vowel-signs, since the vowels were an indispensable and essential element which could not be disregarded in their language.[2] The forms and values and names of the letters are thus indissolubly bound up with one another, and they can only have come from a Semitic and not an Egyptian source. Even

[1] S. p. 161 n. 2. [2] S. pp. 154–5, 178–9.

the direction in which the pictures look is different in Egyptian and Phoenician writing; the Egyptian signs usually look rightwards,[1] the Phoenician always leftwards. In this respect, too, the two systems are obviously independent of each other. All this argues a considerable lapse of time between the Egyptian syllabary and the Phoenician alphabet.

## 4. The Sinaitic Script

Seeing then that there was some connexion between the Egyptian hieroglyphic and the Phoenician alphabetic systems of writing, and that a period of several centuries would be required to allow adequate time for the invention, development and perfection, of the alphabet, Gardiner[2] suggested that the Sinaitic inscriptions might furnish the missing link between the two systems. These recently discovered inscriptions were written in an unknown script; this at first sight appeared to consist of roughly engraved Egyptian hieroglyphs but on close inspection revealed signs belonging to no known Egyptian style of writing.[3] All the monuments found in the same locality showed strong signs of Egyptian influence but might well be of non-Egyptian workmanship. Further, the writing, however crude, could not have been the work of indigenous Semitic nomads eking out a bare existence in the Sinaitic Peninsula from time immemorial; and neither miners nor their foremen are likely inventors of an alphabet.[4] These monuments were rather the work of strangers from other parts who accompanied the Egyptians on their expeditions and to whom Amenemḥe III (*c.* 1849–1801 B.C.) referred in one of his inscriptions, even though they came no farther than from Palestine or the Lebanon.

The script is not the Egyptian hieroglyphic script, but many of the signs are evidently borrowed from or based on it (s. pp. 142–3 fig. 81). Such are those depicting an ox's head, the human head and eye, and water; and there are others probably depicting a man's hand, a snake, and a fish. All these symbols occur indubitably in both the Egyptian and the Phoenician scripts. Then there are signs which are not so clear, such as those depicting a house or courtyard, plant or an open hand, mountains or teeth, a mark or a cross, but which may possibly be identified with signs in one or other or in both of these scripts.

[1] In the fount here used the Egyptian hieroglyphs look, as only rarely in actual texts, leftwards instead of rightwards.

[2] In 'J.E.A.' III 12–16.

[3] S. pp. 94–8.

[4] Cp. Bea in *St. T.* [126] VI 23–4.

Yet in these as in other cases the resemblances are often neither compelling nor convincing.[1] The number of types is apparently thirty-two; this is too few for a pictographic or syllabic script[2] but is approximately that required for an alphabet,[3] as everyone has recognized. A majority of these signs have self-evident affinity with Byblo-Phoenician signs; and the identification of three or four words proves the language of these inscriptions to have been Semitic.[4]

These Sinaitic texts, then, may represent the missing link between the Egyptian hieroglyphs and the Phoenician alphabet; but not only is the interpretation of them largely a matter of speculation but also the connecting link between them and the earliest decipherable Byblo-Phoenician inscriptions is a very tenuous chain of fragmentary inscriptions. In view of this fact, it is only possible to draw up tables of the signs found in each of them without attempting translation and to compare them on the one side with the Egyptian and on the other side with the Phoenician signs which they most closely resemble (s. pp. 142–3 fig. 81);[5] but the student must not forget that similarity of form does not necessarily import identity of value, as the comparison of several Egyptian hieroglyphs with the corresponding Phoenician letters shows.[6] At the same time such tables, however imperfect, already contain enough forms to suggest if not to prove that all the Phoenician characters are not derived either through normal development or by attrition from Sinaitic signs;[7] but they can hardly yet be used for purposes of interpretation, which must await the discovery of continuous texts which alone can raise translation above the level of mere conjecture, however plausible or probable.

[1] Cp. Bea *St. T.* [126] vi 24–7.

[2] The Sumero-Accadian system contains over 550 signs, of which 285 may be used as syllable-signs or letter-signs. The Egyptian hieroglyphs are over 700 in number, of which some 70 to 100 may be used syllabically and 24 may be used alphabetically with letter-values.

[3] The Ugaritic and South-Semitic alphabets have 26–29 and the Arabic alphabet has 28 letters against the 22 letters of the Phoenico-Aramaeo-Hebrew alphabet.

[4] S. pp. 96–7.

[5] Sethe in *Göttingen* 1917, 442–3 (cp. *Z.D.M.G.* lxxx 36–7) and *V. Bilde z. Buchstaben* 58, Bauer *Urspr. d. Alph.*, *Taf.* iii–v, Grimme *Althebr. Inschr.* 101–2, Obermann in 'P.A.O.S.' ix iii, Sprengling 'Alphabet' 55, Dunand *Bybl. Gr.* 122–31, Butin in 'H.T.R.' xxv 139, Gaster in 'P.Q.S.' lxvii (1935) 135 i–ii and lxix (1937) 44, 46, Diringer in 'Antiquity' xvii 78–80; cp. Butin *ap.* Starr & Butin in 'S.D.' vi 36–8.

[6] S. p. 163.

[7] Cp. Sethe in *Göttingen* 1917, 463.

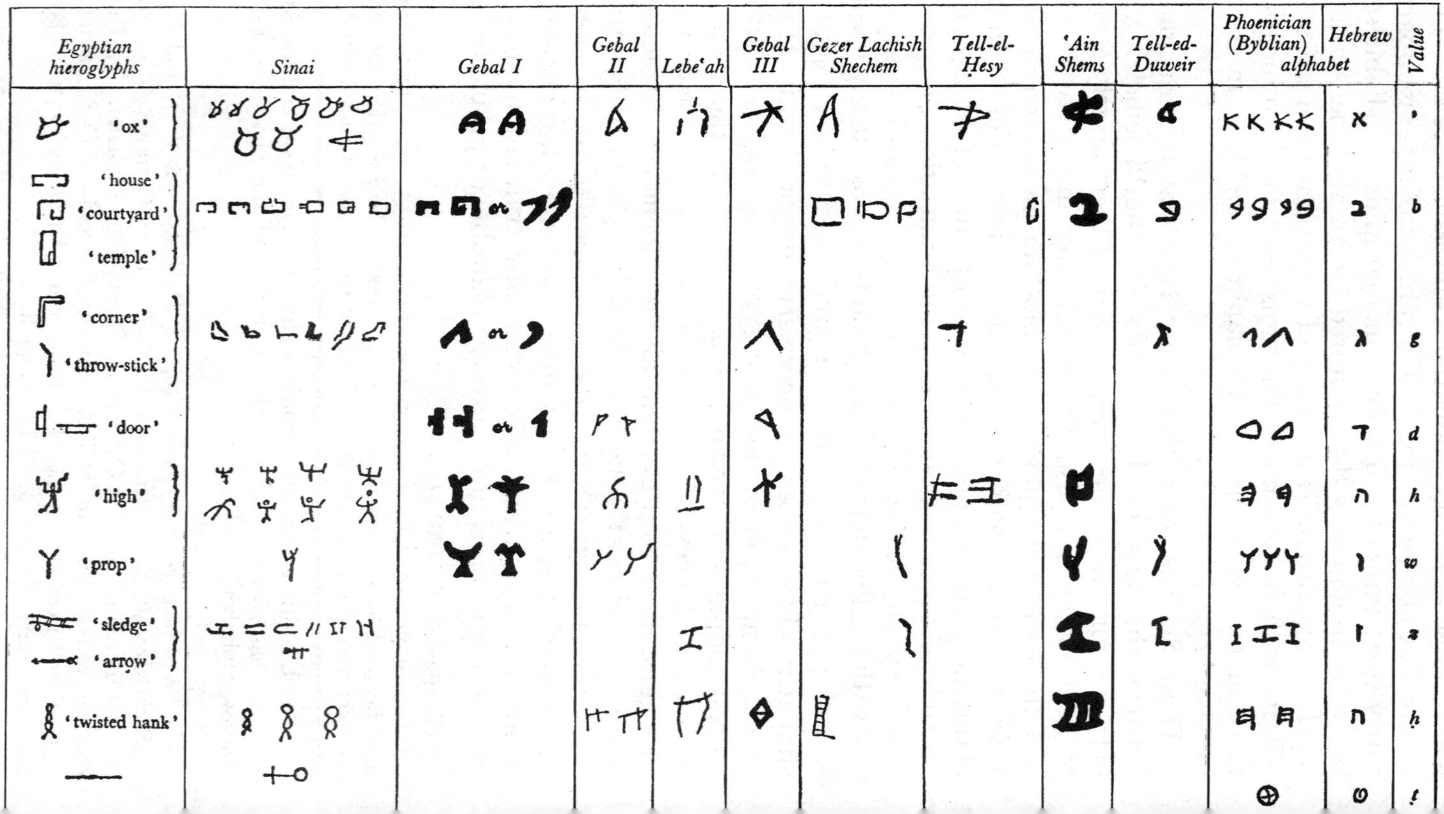
Egyptian hieroglyphs
Sinai
Gebal I
Gebal II
Lebeʿah
Gebal III
Gezer Lachish Shechem
Tell-el-Ḥesy
ʿAin Shems
Tell-ed-Duweir
Phoenician (Byblian) alphabet
Hebrew alphabet
Value
'ox'
'house'
'courtyard'
'temple'
'corner'
'throw-stick'
'door'
'high'
'prop'
'sledge'
'arrow'
'twisted hank'
א ʾ
ב b
ג g
ד d
ה h
ו w
ז z
ח ḥ
ט ṭ

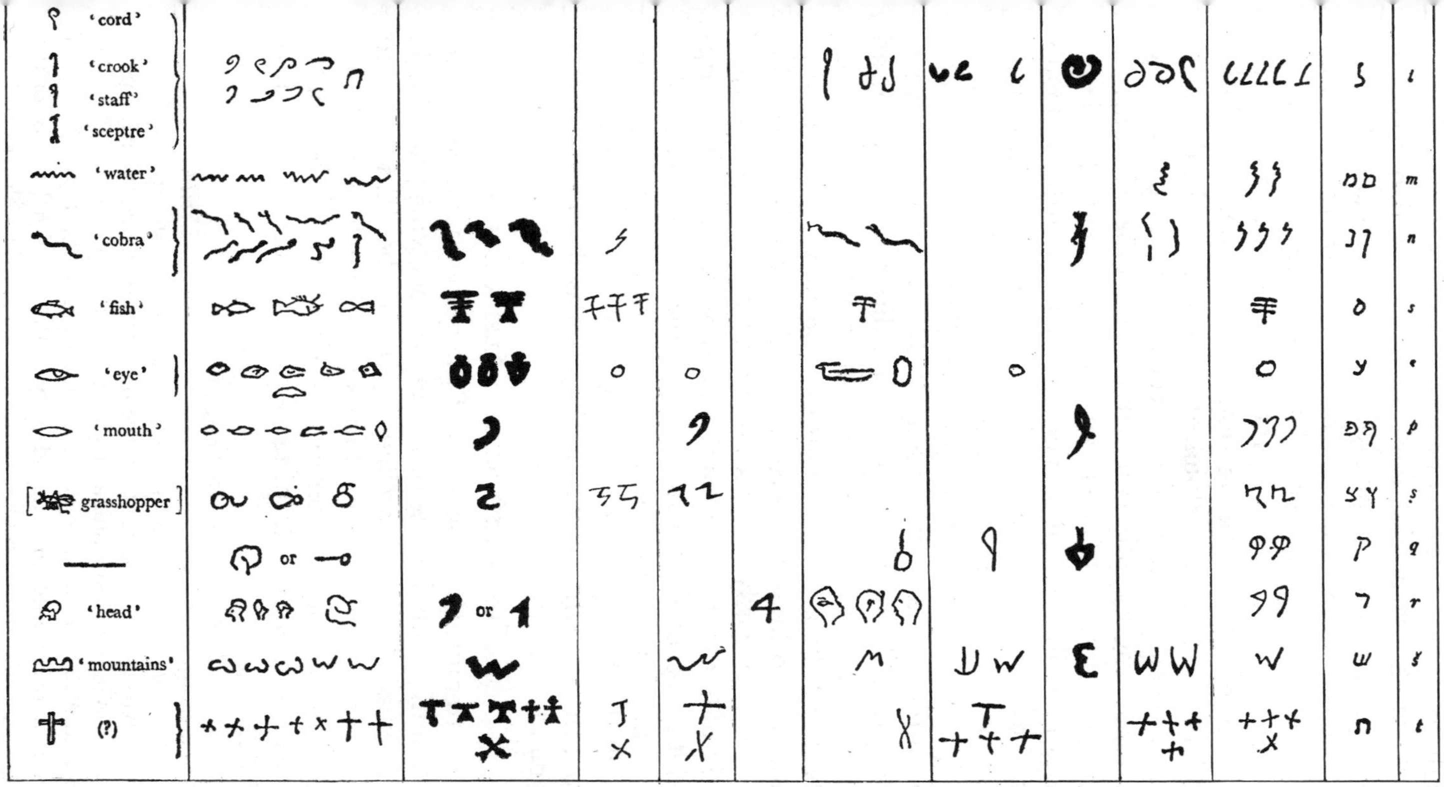


FIG. 81. Egyptian hieroglyphs and Sinaitic and kindred signs compared with Phoenician letters.

The discovery of these Sinaitic inscriptions has revolutionized the study of the early alphabet. Before this Lidzbarski[1] had indeed expressed the opinion that the Phoenician alphabet was in all probability loosely connected with the Egyptian script.[2] Afterwards, however, Sethe[3] felt able to express the opinion that the Egyptian script was in respect to external form the archetype of[4] but in respect to its inner formulation the model[5] of the Semitic alphabet; in other words, the forms of the Phoenician letters were directly derived from those of the corresponding Egyptian hieroglyphs, but otherwise only the general idea of the alphabet, and not the particular details of it, was modelled on the Egyptian system. Gardiner[6] finally carried the argument a stage further by reference to the Sinaitic inscriptions, of which he says that 'if the new Sinaitic script is not the particular script from which the Phoenician and South-Semitic alphabets are descended, I can see no alternative to regarding it as a tentative essay in that direction, which at all events constitutes a good analogy upon which the Egyptian hypothesis can be argued'. This opinion may be accepted at any rate as a working hypothesis, even though it is liable to be, and indeed may easily be, upset by future discoveries. Already the early date to which Dunand assigns Shaphaṭbaal's inscription,[7] if it is accepted, threatens to rob the Sinaitic script of its priority; and, if the Phoenician inscriptions are pushed much further back, the alphabet in which they are written will regain its primacy while the Sinaitic script will recede into the background.

### 5. The South-Semitic Alphabets.

Before attempting a discussion of the individual letters of the North-Semitic alphabets with a view to following each back, so far as possible, to its archetype, it will be convenient to consider the South-Semitic alphabet, of which some letters present forms obviously closer to the archetype than those of the North-Semitic alphabets (s. p. 145 fig. 82).[8] Further, that these

[1] In *E.S.E.* I 134–5.
[2] Germ. *nur eine freie Anlehnung an die ägyptische Schrift.*
[3] In *Göttingen* 1917, 455–6. [4] Germ. *Urbild.*
[5] Germ. *Vorbild.* [6] In 'J.E.A.' III 16. [7] S. pp. 104–5.
[8] Cp. Lidzbarski *E.S.E.* II 361 (whence the accompanying table has been adapted) and Winnett 'Lihyanite and Thamudic Inscriptions' x. The signs from Sinai and Baluʿah as here given are intended to illustrate identity of forms without necessarily implying identity of values. Further, six of the letters (*ṯ, ḏ, ḫ, ḍ, ẓ, ġ*) are peculiar to the South-Semitic dialects and have no corresponding forms in the North-Semitic alphabets.

two alphabets are independent inventions is improbable; for it is difficult to believe that two branches of the same race can

| Sinai[1] | Byblos[2] | Balu'ah[3] | Ur[4] | Minaean / Sabaean | Lihyânian | Thamûdean | Ṣafâitic | Value |
|---|---|---|---|---|---|---|---|---|
| | | | | | South Semitic—Arabian | | | |
| | | | | | | | | ' |
| | | | | | | | | b |
| | | | | | | | | g |
| | | | | | | | | d |
| | | | | | | | | ḏ |
| | | | | | | | | h |
| | | | | | | | | w |
| | | | | | | | | z |
| | | | | | | | | ḥ |
| | | | | | | | | ḫ |
| | | | | | | | | ṭ |
| | | | | | | | | ḏ |
| | | | | | | | | y |
| | | | | | | | | k |
| | | | | | | | | l |
| | | | | | | | | m |
| | | | | | | | | n |
| | | | | | | | | s[5] |
| | | | | | | | | ʿ |
| | | | | | | | | ġ |
| | | | | | | | | p, f |
| | | | | | | | | ṣ |
| | | | | | | | | ḍ |
| | | | | | | | | q |
| | | | | | | | | r |
| | | | | | | | | š |
| | | | | | | | | t |
| | | | | | | | | ṯ |

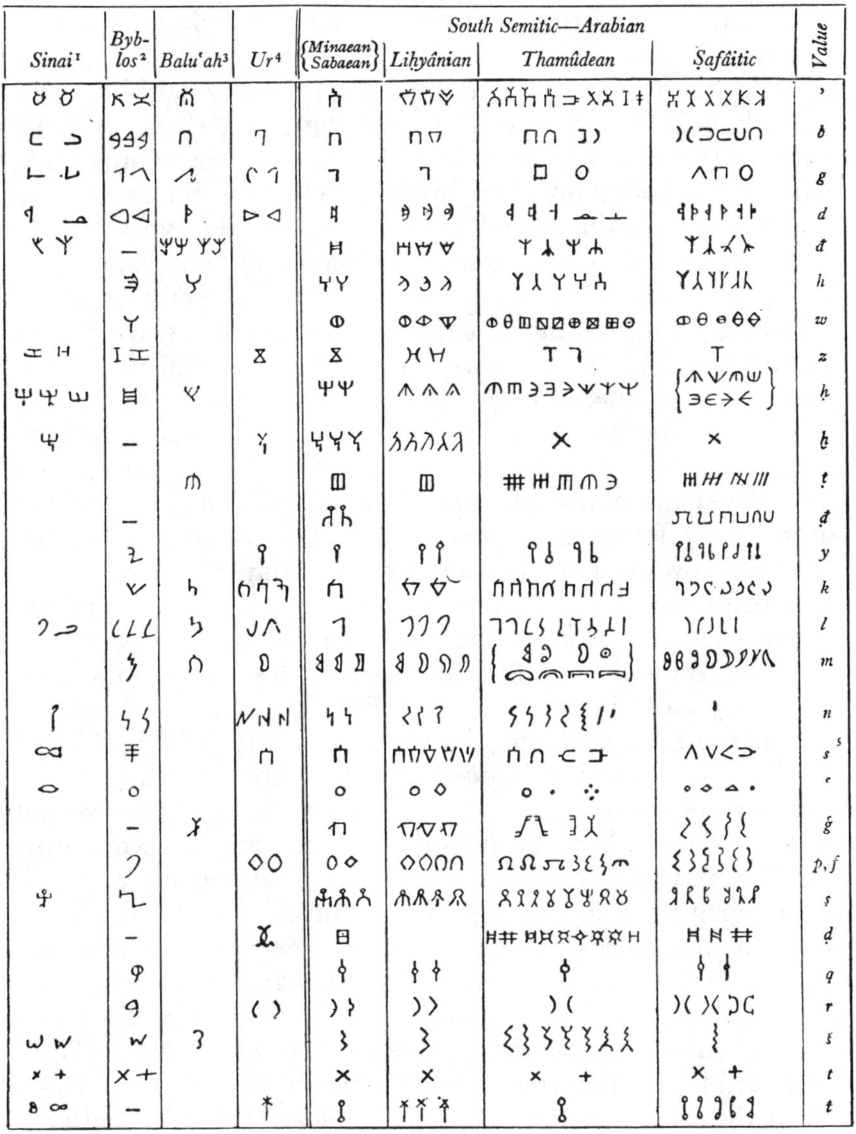

[1] S. pp. 94-8.    [2] S. pp. 104-7.    [3] S. p. 123.
[4] S. p. 124.    [5] Or ∩ = š (ﬡ) and X = s (ﬢ).

FIG. 82. Comparative table of Sinaitic and South-Semitic signs.

have almost simultaneously invented alphabets and devised closely similar symbols without some degree of contact with or influence on one another.

Lidzbarski[1] has subjected these South-Semitic scripts to close examination with a view to determining their age in relation to that of the North-Semitic scripts. Unlike the latter, which almost from the beginning reveal a tendency towards simplification and the development of cursive forms, due without doubt to the practice of scratching the letters or daubing them with ink on potsherds beside that of engraving them with the chisel on stone, the former show hardly a trace of any such tendencies throughout their history. Thus the South-Semitic alphabets are distinguished by the elegant and symmetrical, if somewhat stiff and formal, appearance of their letters; in this respect they recall the artistic designs of South-Arabian architecture and sculpture, carving and engraving, which are similarly marked by a stylized symmetry of form. Even the direction of writing *βουστροφηδόν*, which early South-Semitic and Greek inscriptions alike exhibit,[2] may be due partly to a desire for a balanced arrangement of the lines. This architectural *motif* is seen in the upright stance of a majority of the letters whose forms are based on a scheme resembling pillars erect in a row (ΠΠΠ); and others reflect a simple form of monogram or armorial bearing. This *motif* reveals itself also in the separation of the rows of the text by lines which serve as an elaborate frame to set off the actual text; this is most noticeable when letters and lines are cut in relief and stand out from the stone like the features, especially the ornament, of a building.[3] The building effect is enhanced when the letters standing on the lower line reach the upper line. The same *motif* had a strong influence on the shape of the letters, which might be modified in such a way as to conform to it; thus what became 𐤄 and 𐤎 in the north became 𐩠 and 𐩯 in the south. So artificial a script argues a long period of development behind it[4] but does not necessarily demand a date posterior to that of the Phoenician alphabet. The internal evidence of the South-Semitic script perhaps throws some light on the problem of its date. Thus, for example, on the one hand the South-Semitic X *t*, which clearly diverges from the Egyptian ⊹, is identical rather with the earlier X than the later † or × of the North-Semitic alpha-

[1] In *E.S.E.* I 113–28.

[2] S. p. 124.

[3] Such a phenomenon appears but rarely in early Aramaic inscriptions, in which it is probably due to Hittite influence.

[4] Cp. Montgomery 'Arabia and the Bible' 134–5, who says that 'the script is evidently of a secondary "Gothic" character and must have had a long preceding history'.

bets; this suggests a connexion with the earlier, not the later, forms of these alphabets. Again, the resemblance of the South-Semitic 𐩬 *n* is not to the Egyptian ⌐ but to the Phoenician 𐤍, by which it has clearly been influenced. On the other hand, the South-Semitic ⊓ *b* and ◊ *p* correspond respectively not to the Phoenician 𐤁 and 𐤐 but to the Egyptian ⊓ and ⬭, which they clearly recall,[1] while the South-Semitic ▯ or ⊳| *d* clearly stands midway between the Egyptian ▯ or ⊂⊃ and the Phoenician ◁ or 𐤃, and so on. The conclusion therefore is irresistible: the South-Semitic alphabet is derived directly neither from the Egyptian hieroglyphs, even though some signs seem rather to reflect them, nor from the Byblo-Phoenician alphabet, although this has left marked traces of its influence on some of the letters.

It may then be suggested that the South-Semitic and North-Semitic alphabets were influenced by the Egyptian hieroglyphs, possibly through a common ancestor or ancestors, and were evolved in their earliest stages in close contact with one another. The intermediate link may have been the Sinaitic and probably also some early Canaanite form of the North-Semitic alphabet that preceded its branching off into the specific Phoenician and Aramaic, Hebrew and Moabite alphabets. Further, the pot-sherds and other fragments found at Shechem and Beersheba, Gezer and Lachish,[2] suggest that the scene of this evolution of the Canaanite script was central or southern Palestine. It is, therefore, interesting to find that the only North-Semitic place mentioned in South-Semitic inscriptions is Gaza in that very district;[3] and this town has been an Arab stronghold from very early times till the present day. Such a conclusion, too, does not clash with the evidence of the inscription from Balu'ah which proves the existence of a form of the South-Semitic script in Moab about the twelfth century B.C.

At the same time, the South-Semitic alphabet is probably posterior to the Canaanite alphabet, if the Arabic names of the letters may be called in evidence; for several of them are demonstrably not South-Semitic but North-Semitic words. Thus *'alif* and *qâf* are merely Arabizing forms of *'ālep̱* 'ox' and *qôp̱* 'monkey (?)' which occur only in the North-Semitic and not in the South-Semitic dialects; and *ṣâd* is a meaningless abbreviation of *ṣādê* 'grasshopper', which is an Aramaic but not an Arabic word.[4] Too much stress, however, ought not to be laid on this argument until the date of these South-Semitic forms of the

[1] Cp. Sethe in *Göttingen* 1917, 457–8.
[2] S. pp. 98–103.
[3] Cp. Lidzbarski *E.S.E.* I 128¹.
[4] S. pp. 167–8.

names has been determined; for they are hitherto attested only in post-Islamic Arabic literature.

Unfortunately, the date of the earliest South-Semitic, the Minaean and Sabaean, kingdoms is very variously estimated; thus the Minaean, centred at Ma'în in Edom, has been put *c.* 1300–700 B.C.,[1] but the date generally accepted for this and the Sabaean which apparently displaced or succeeded it is *c.* 700–500 B.C.[2] This agrees with that of the earliest known inscriptions certainly written in a form of the South-Arabian script, namely those found beneath a pavement of Nebuchadrezzar (*c.* 604–562 B.C.) at Ur.[3] If then a round 500 or 750 years may be allowed for the evolution of the artificial script just described as found even on the oldest monuments, the invention of this alphabet will have taken place *c.* 1500–1250 B.C., the period to whose end the inscription from Balu'ah belongs; and the script of this shows so little elaboration that it may confidently be regarded as reflecting the earliest period of its development. This line of argument, too, then indicates a period between the Egypto-Sinaitic and the Byblo-Phoenician inscriptions soon after the emergence of the proto-Canaanite script.

## 6. The Ugaritic Alphabet

How the Ugaritic alphabet is related on the one side to the Accadian syllabary and on the other side to the North-Semitic and South-Semitic alphabets is disputed*.

On the one hand Ebeling[4] has attempted to derive every Ugaritic sign from an Accadian sign, and indeed there are striking resemblances (s. p. 149 fig. 83). Some forms are identical (*g*, *s*), others very similar, as though they were derived from the corresponding symbols by turning them round 90° (*b*, *d*) or by dropping superfluous strokes, for example by halving their number (*z*/*ṣ*, *m*) and so on. The basis of these comparisons, however, is in many cases suspect or unsound, as the Accadian forms are chosen from widely different periods, whether Old-Babylonian (*ti*, *ka*) or Neo-Babylonian (*ḫe*) or Neo-Assyrian (*da*, *ḫa*); the first of these periods is long anterior, the second and third almost as far posterior to the date of the

[1] Hommel *ap.* Nielsen *Altarab. Altertumsk.* I 67.

[2] Montgomery 'Arabia and the Bible' 136–7; cp. Hommel *Ethn. u. Geogr. d. Alt. Or.* 142, where the Sabaean kingdom is dated *c.* 700–500 B.C., and Albright in 'Arch. and Rel. of Isr.' 56–7, where the earliest South-Arabian inscriptions are assigned to the 8th or 7th century B.C. and the latest to the 6th or 7th century A.D.*

[3] S. p. 124. [4] In *Berlin* 1934, 10–15; s. *Forsch. u. Fortschr.* x 193–5.

Ugaritic texts. Several, too, of these Accadian signs do not apparently occur in the exact form postulated for the purpose of this comparison (*e, lu, ma, se, ṣu, qa, ša, šu*). Moreover, one of the values required (*gi*) seems to be found only in Sumerian texts. Further, such Ugaritic signs as closely resemble or are

| Accadian | | Ugaritic | | Phoenician | | Accadian | | Ugaritic | | Phoenician | |
|---|---|---|---|---|---|---|---|---|---|---|---|
| 𒀀 | a | | à | K 𐤀 | ' | | ma | | m | | m |
| | e | | ĕ, ī | | . | | na | | n | | n |
| | u | | ù | | | | ša | | s | | |
| | bi | | b | 𐤁 | b | | se | | ṣ | | s |
| | gi | | g | | g | | ḫa | | ʿ | O | ʿ |
| | da | | d | | d | | pa | | p | | p |
| | ḫe | | h | | h | | ṣa | | ṣ | | ṣ |
| | wa | | w | Y Y | w | | ṣu | | ẓ | | |
| | za | | z | I I | z | | qa | | q | | q |
| | ḫa | | ḥ } ḫ | | ḥ, ḫ | | ra | | r | | r |
| | ṭi | | ṭ | | ṭ | | ša | | š | W | š |
| | ya | | y | | y | | šu | | ṣ́ | | |
| | ka | | k | V | k | | ti | | t | + | t |
| | lu | | l | | l | | qa | | ġ | | |

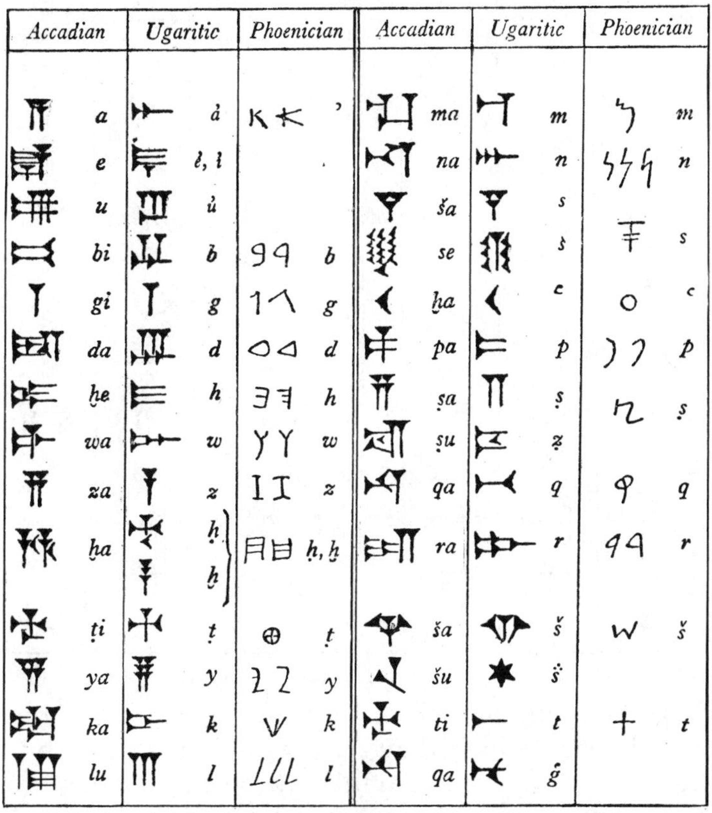

FIG. 83. Ugaritic compared with Accadian and Phoenician signs.

identical in form with Sumerian or Accadian signs usually have different values.[1] On the other hand, not a few Ugaritic signs are tolerably like the corresponding Phoenician signs, especially when allowance is made for the fact that the former are impressed in clay while the latter are incised in stone (*g, h, w, z, k, m*); and these resemblances exceed those between the Old-Persian and the Babylonian cuneiform signs.[2]

On the other hand Sprengling and Olmstead [3] have made comparisons of the Ugaritic signs with the Sinaitic signs on the

[1] For example Sum. *gi* = Ugar. *g* and Acc. *u* = Ugar. ', but Acc. *be* = Ugar. *q*, Acc. *aš* = Ugar. *t*, and Acc. *nu* = Ugar. *ġ*.

[2] S. pp. 131-2.    [3] In 'Alphabet' 54-67.

one side and with the South-Arabian letters on the other side (s. fig. 84). Resemblances can indeed be traced between the Sinaitic and Ugaritic signs, but rather in their general appearance, notably in the direction in which they look, than in any particular details. Yet the comparison is vitiated by doubts

| Sinaitic | Ugaritic | South-Semitic | | Sinaitic | Ugaritic | South-Semitic | |
|---|---|---|---|---|---|---|---|
| | | | ' | | | | k |
| | | | | | | | l |
| | | | | | | | m |
| | | | b | | | | n |
| | | | g | | | | s |
| | | | d | | | | ʿ |
| | | | ḥ | | | | p |
| | | | w | | | | ṣ |
| | | | z | | | | q |
| | | | (ḥ)ḫ | | | | r |
| | | | ṭ | | | | š |
| | | | y | | | | t |

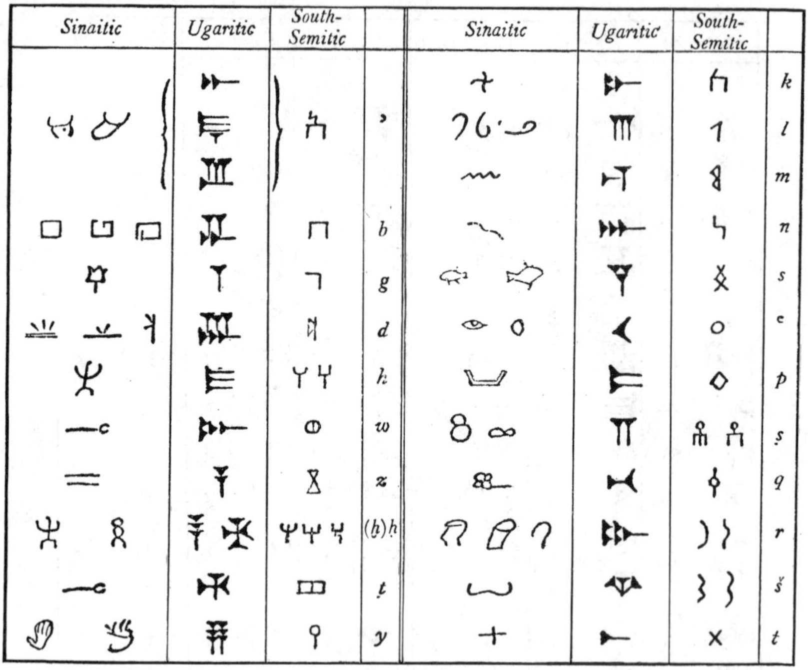

FIG. 84. Ugaritic compared with Sinaitic and South-Semitic signs.

regarding the identification of most of the Sinaitic signs; for example, the sign which they read as *w* is read as *ṭ* by most other scholars. The same thing may be not unfairly said of their South-Semitic comparisons, of which none would be likely to have occurred to them if they had not previously known the value of all the signs in both alphabets.

In this connexion it is important to remember that the number of possible combinations of lines and strokes is limited, and especially so in the case of a cuneiform script which does not tolerate curves,[1] and experiments with children have shown what remarkable coincidences can result from their efforts to create artificial alphabets.[2] Fortuitous resemblances, therefore, cannot be ruled out also in real scripts. For example, the primitive Sum. ≈ or ⑊ (Acc. ⑊⑊) *A* 'water' and the Eg. ⌇ *n.t* 'water' have a certain likeness to one another in consequence of their representing the same thing; but the likeness of the

[1] S. pp. 28–9, 36–7.      [2] Cp. Bauer *Urspr. d. Alph.* 35–6.

primitive Sum. ∃ (Acc. 𒂊) *e* to the Phoen. 𐤄 (Hebr. ה) *h* which became the Gk. *E* is purely accidental, as their history shows that they have no connexion with one another. It is, therefore, dangerous to build too much on the resemblance between the various forms of the letters unless every stage in their development can be traced, and doubly so when the values of all but half a dozen are conjectural or disputable.[1]

Whatever may be thought, then, of such resemblances, Bauer[2] has rightly remarked that the inventor has introduced novelties found in no other Semitic alphabet, such as three signs for *'ālep̄* according to the vowel accompanying it and several signs for various sibilant sounds which have not yet been satisfactorily explained. He has sought to explain these divergences from the Semitic norm by supposing the Ugaritic alphabet to have been originally invented for a non-Semitic (presumably Hurrian or Horite) language and only subsequently adapted to a Semitic speech; but they are hardly enough to sustain such a theory.[3]

The inventor of this alphabet was in any case no mere copyist but rather an experimenter who was not afraid of novelties which might not and in fact did not survive his system. He was acquainted with the use of writing clay and the cuneiform script and chose it perhaps because it was more suitable for long records than stone and less perishable than papyrus; but, being aware of the difficulties inherent in a syllabary, he preferred to devise an alphabet on the Egyptian or Phoenician model, of which he must have been aware, since recent excavation has shown that the Phoenician alphabet antedates the Ugaritic texts and Egyptian influence has been traced at Ugarit*. Excavation, too, has shown that the period *c.* 1750–1000 B.C. was one in which experiments in writing were being made, and the obvious conclusion is that the Ugaritic method was one of

[1] Cp. Burrows in 'J.R.A.S.' 1936, 271–7, arguing for a mixed origin, post-Sinaitic but pre-Phoenician, of the Ugaritic script and a date *c.* 1500 B.C.*

[2] In *Urspr. d. Alph.* 38–41.

[3] Bauer argues that the absence of these additional letters from the Phoenician alphabet proves it to have been dependent on the Ugaritic alphabet; it has discarded what is foreign or superfluous to a Semitic dialect. The argument, however, is hardly valid. The additional sibilants may represent sounds which the North-Semitic group of languages has not generally felt the need of representing by specific signs, just as the South-Semitic group still represents such and similar additional sounds; and the three forms of *'alif* may have resulted from an attempt to indicate the vowels, made too late to affect the Phoenician alphabet. This then may be prior to the Ugaritic alphabet, as also other considerations suggest.

these experiments. The inventor would be likely to borrow what seemed to him suitable or advantageous in the experiments being made by neighbouring workers and add or adapt it to his own system; for almost every invention is based on previous discoveries. His system, however, was invented too late to oust the Phoenician method which already held the field; and indeed it scarcely lasted a generation, since clay was not so convenient and handy a medium of writing as papyrus, which therefore won the day. Date, medium and method, combined to ensure its defeat*.[1]

## 7. The Evidential Value of the Names of the Letters

Gardiner[2] has examined the names of the Semitic letters with a view to determining their antiquity and origin. These, if they are ancient, may throw light on the transmission of the signs from the pictographic to the alphabetic stage, whereas if of relatively recent creation they have no evidential value; for the meaning of the name ought to give a hint of the picture from which any given sign has been derived when it has become obscured in the course of centuries.

The Septuagint[3] and Eusebius[4] are the earliest authorities for the Hebrew forms of these names (though in Greek garb),[5] which therefore go back at any rate to the second or third century B.C., but their true Greek forms are attested so far back as the fourth and fifth centuries B.C. It is, however, the general view that this nomenclature is prior to the fifth century B.C. and in fact that it goes back to the very invention of the alphabet.

Anthropological analogy indeed suggests that the Semitic script will have been pictographic in origin, and the signs are therefore likely to have borne names denoting the objects which they must originally have represented. The probability of this suggestion is heightened by the fact that the primitive forms of several Phoenician letters seem roughly to correspond to the shapes of the objects denoted by their names. On the one hand, of course, this correspondence may be fortuitous, especially when it rests on the testimony of a minority of the witnesses. For example, neither the Phoenician 9 nor the Greek 8 but only the (South-Semitic) Sabaean ∏ *b* in any sense looks like a 'house'

[1] Cp. De Langhe *Ugarit* I 261–3. A solitary Ugaritic tablet has been found at Beth-Shemesh in Palestine (Barton in 'B.A.S.O.R.' LII 5–6 and Albright ibid. LIII 18–19; s. Virolleaud in *Syria* XVI 186–7)*.

[2] In 'J.E.A.' III 5–10.

[3] In Ps. [cxviii] cxix.

[4] In *Evang. Praep.* [474 b–d] x 5.

[5] Cp. Nöldeke *Beitr. z. Sem. Sprachw.* 126–9.

(Sem. **bayt*); only the Phoenician 𐤊 or 𐤊 but neither the Sabaean 𐩫 nor the Greek ꓘ *k* resembles a 'hand' or 'frond' (Sem. **kapp*).[1] On the other hand, when the principal witnesses all agree on this point, such resemblances cannot be accidental. For example, the Phoenician o and the Sabaean o and the Greek o all obviously depict an 'eye' (Sem. *'*ayn*),[2] and Phoen. + or × and Sabaean X and Greek T alike depict a cross or 'mark' (Hebr. *tāw*). In many cases the resemblance does not immediately strike the eye: for example, neither the Phoenician K or 𐤀 nor the Greek A nor the Sabaean 𐩱 at first sight calls up the image of an 'ox' (Sem. *'*alp*); but the Egyptian 𓃾 'ox' shows roughly what the Phoenician sign must have been intended to resemble and the Sumerian 𒄞 or 𒄞 (𒄞) 'ox' compared with the (South-Semitic) Liḥyânian 𐩱 or 𐩱 (but not the Sabaean 𐩱) shows how the Sabaean sign has been treated.[3]

So soon as the similarity of certain of the letters to the objects denoted by their names has been admitted to be due to design, an important criterion has been found for establishing which forms are early and which are late; and here it must be kept in mind that the later scripts may have preserved earlier forms through isolation or little use, while the earlier scripts may present only later forms through degeneration due to much use resulting in a cursive style or the influence of neighbouring styles. Thus the Sabaean ◊ rather than the Phoenician 𐤐 preserves the original form of the human 'mouth' (Sem. **puw*).

The names of the letters may then assuredly be regarded as primary; for they agree fairly with the objects which the forms of fourteen out of the twenty-two letters of the Phoenician alphabet seem intended to suggest, and it is conceivable that this number may be increased on examination. If, too, the names are primary, it is easy to see why some of the forms of the letters in these Semitic alphabets resemble the objects denoted by their names more than others; it is because time and use have dealt unequally with them, preserving some in a rough likeness to their original forms and simplifying others out of all recognition. If, however, the names are secondary and are held to have been given by the Phoenicians to the letters *c.* 700 B.C., they are in the majority of cases inexplicable, since by that date many of the letters bear no conceivable likeness to their prototypes. Some, however, of the names may be conceded as secondary;

[1] S. p. 163.

[2] Namely, an eye without the pupil, which is shown only in the Egyptian and Sinaitic forms of the sign (Sethe in *Gött. Gel. Anz.* 1917, 456).

[3] S. p. 54.

and this must be the case when a letter has two names, since it is very improbable that it will have received both at the same time*. Thus the sign for *n* is called *nûn* ' fish ' by the Hebrews[1] but *nahās* 'serpent' by the Ethiopians.[2] The reason for the change may be that at some point of its development the sign was thought to resemble less the object which it originally depicted than some other object, and its name was accordingly changed; but it is important to remember that the later language may occasionally have by some chance preserved the older name.[3]

Other arguments supporting the view that the names of the letters are ancient may be drawn from a philological examination of their forms.

The peculiar defect of the Phoenician alphabet from the point of view of a person wishing to adapt it to an Indo-European language lay in the absence of any special signs for the vowels; it was a purely consonantal alphabet.* The Greeks obviated this difficulty by using the signs for those Semitic sounds which did not occur in their language to represent the vowels. It was natural that *yôḏ* (*y* or *i*) and *wāw* (*w* or *u*) should be taken for ι (*i*) and υ (*u*), since they are phonetically related to these vowels*; indeed, the Hebrews somewhat similarly used them to indicate *î* (*ê*) and *û* (*ô*) when long. The use of *'ālep̄* (') for α, even though the Hebrews similarly used this letter to indicate long *â*, and of *hē'* (*h*) for ϵ and *ḥêṯ* (*ḥ*) for η was not so obvious a step; but Praetorius[4] has plausibly suggested that the *a*-sound attributed to the Phoenician ' (proto-Sem. *'*alp*; Hebr. *'ālep̄*) was probably due to the vocalization of its name with *a*; and similarly the *e*-sound in *hē'*[5] and the *ê*-sound in *ḥêṯ* accounted for the use of *h* for ϵ and of *ḥ* for η*. As the Greeks had no use for *'ālep̄* and *hē'* and little for *ḥêṯ*, on the acrophonic principle

[1] S. p. 165.

[2] The change of name would not be so difficult if the fish were an eel.

[3] Ethiopic names such as *'alf* and *gaml* and also *dant* for (*dalt*) reflect the primitive monosyllabic character of a common type of Semitic nouns, therein agreeing with the Greek against the Hebrew and Aramaic names. This suggests that they are of Phoenician origin, since Phoenician nouns of the same class retain the proto-Semitic vocalization (Nöldeke *Beitr. z. Sem. Sprachw.* 131–4). Ethiopic tradition may then be trustworthy in the case also of other letters.

[4] In *Über den Ursprung des kanaanäischen Alphabets* 10.

[5] Bauer (*Urspr. d. Alph.* 40–1) remarks that Ugaritic texts use *h* where the Hebrew and Aramaic languages have *ai* > *ê* (as in proto-Sem. **bayt* = Ugar. *bht* ' house ') ; but this phenomenon may be due to Aramaic influence (cp. Hebr. *bôš* w. Aram. *bᵉhēṯ*).

(ʾ)*alp* became α (ἄλφα) while (*h*)*ē*ʾ became ε (εἶ or ἒ ψιλόν) and (*ḥ*)*ê*ṯ became η (ἦτα). The reason for using ʿ*ayin* (ʿ) for ο is not so clear; but Bauer[1] has pointed out that in Ugaritic texts long *ô* is written once with ‹ (ע) and once with ⓒ‹ (ʿ*ayin* enclosed in a circle as though to indicate a peculiar usage), and it is also noticeable that *a* and *i* tend to become *u* (*o*) in the neighbourhood of emphatic and guttural sounds.[2] At the same time, it was the last letter still available for the purpose. Gardiner[3] therefore claims that the letter-values assigned by the Greeks to ʾ*ālep̱* (א), *hē*ʾ (ה) and *ḥêṯ* (ח), as well as ʿ*ayin* (ע), prove that the names of the letters were already in use when the Greek values of these letters were determined; and this conclusion seems irresistible*.

The pronunciation of the names of the letters as handed down by tradition is not uniform. Some appear to be Phoenician (*bêṯ*, *mēm*),[4] others are genuinely Hebrew (*wāw*, *tāw*, *kap̱*, *qôp̱*, *zayin*, ʿ*ayin*), and others are equally clearly Aramaic (*rêš*, *ṣāḏê*, ʾ*ālep̱*, *dāleṯ*, *lāmeḏ*, *sāmeḵ*). In several cases the Septuagint have preserved proto-Semitic or Phoenician forms (αλφ, σαμχ)[5] which are philologically older than those in current use, in others relatively late Hebrew (δελτ)[6] forms*. Some seem to have been artificially differentiated (unless they are derived from a hitherto unknown dialect) from the expected form of the noun with which they are ostensibly connected (*yôḏ* for *yāḏ* 'hand', *pē*ʾ for *peh* 'mouth', *šîn* for *šēn* 'tooth'), and one is peculiar, since its Hebrew vocalization is questionable in any Semitic language and its true form can only be recovered from its Ethiopic name (*gīmel* or *gimmel* for *gaml* 'throw-stick'). The Septuagint's ζαι[7] for *zayin* is probably not so much an alternative name for this letter as an attempt to represent its bare pronunciation with the addition of the necessary vowel; for probably most if not all of the letters could at one time be thus named monosyllabically like the Gk. μῦ and νῦ, ῥῶ and so on, with the vowel suited roughly to the nature of the consonant. Other examples may be

[1] In *Ursp. d. Alph.* 40–1.

[2] Cp. Hebr. עֲמֹרָה (ʿ*ămōrāh*) = Gk. Γομόρρα (Gomorrah); s. Brockelmann *Vergl. Gr. d. Sem. Spr.* I 125.

[3] In 'J.E.A.' III 10–11.

[4] Cp. Phoen. σαμημ and *samem* w. Hebr. *šāmayim* 'heaven' (Schröder *Phön. Spr.* 175); apparently always sing. מם (Gr. μημ) but plur. מימין in Hebrew sources (Nöldeke *Beitr. z. Sem. Sprachw.* 126[7]).

[5] Cp. Phoen. αλφ (as transliterated in Greek letters) w. Hebr. ʾ*elep̱* 'ox' (Schröder op. cit. 90, 168).

[6] Acc. *daltu* but Massoretic Hebr. *deleṯ* 'door'. [7] In Ps. [cxviii] cxix 49.

seen in *ṣaw* (*ṣau* or *ṣô*) for *ṣ* and *qaw* (*qau* or *qô*) for *q*.[1] Twelve of the Arabic letters are thus pronounced with a helping *â* (*b*, *t*, *ṯ*, *ḥ*, *ḫ*, *r*, *z*, *ṭ*, *ḍ*, *ḏ*, *f*, *h*, *y*), and the Eth. *zay*/*zāy* for *z* and *may*/*māy* for *m* are instances of the same formation; further, the Eth. *ḥaut* for *ḥ* as also *śaut* for *ś* and *sāt* for *s* are formed in the same way with the addition of the deictic *t* attached also to two of the Hebrew names.[2]

The fact then that the forms of the names can be referred some to the Phoenician, others to the Hebrew, and yet others to the Aramaic, language suggests that they go back to an early date before the complete differentiation of the various Semitic dialects into distinct languages; and the preservation by the Septuagint of primitive beside late forms,[3] as well as the survival of other demonstrably primitive forms in the Ethiopic alphabet,[4] are additional arguments for the high antiquity of these names and increase the confidence with which they can be used in investigating the origin of the alphabet.

## 8. The Relation of the Form of the Letter to its Name

If then the names of the letters, or at any rate those of them that are primary, go back to the very beginning of the alphabet, the question whether the form of the letter preceded and so dictated its name or the name preceded and so dictated the form of the letter must be asked.

Lidzbarski[5] has remarked that certain of the names fall into three or four well-defined groups. First, there are the names consisting of one strong and one weak consonant (*hē'*, *pē'*); second, there are those beginning and ending with the same consonant, namely the letter which they represent (*wāw*, *mēm*, *nûn*); third, there are those which begin with the letter which they represent and terminate in one of two formative elements common to all the Semitic languages namely *n* (*zayin*, *'ayin*, *šîn*) or *t* (*bêṯ*, *ḥêṯ*, *ṭêṯ*). This fact has so far received little considera-

[1] S. p. 89–90, 167–8.

[2] The Gk. ζῆτα, which is formed not from the Hebr. *zayin* but from the pseudo-Gk. ζαι (LXX at Ps. cxviii [cxix] 49), on the analogy of ἦτα, is another instance of this type of formation (s. p. 159). The final α which is added to most of the Greek letters seems to have been intended to give them a Graecized appearance; thus the Sem. **gaml* (s. pp. 163–4) becomes the Gk. γάμμα on the analogy of γράμμα 'letter'*.

[3] A caution, however, must be uttered in regard to paying too much attention to the forms in the LXX, since it is not known when these may have been inserted in the text (Ps. cxviii = cxix).

[4] S. pp. 163–4, 165 n 5.

[5] In *E.S.E.* II 132–4.

tion and no satisfactory explanation, and indeed the problem can be solved only in the light of its origins; and for the present purpose the provisional assumption may be made that the Phoenician letters are somehow or other derived from or influenced by (whether immediately or mediately is for the moment no matter) the Egyptian hieroglyphs.[1]

The Semitic inventors of the alphabet chose a number of familiar objects, whether parts of the body or beasts or weapons or other things in common use, whose names began with the letter which they were intended to represent; but obviously they might, as indeed they did, have a very considerable number of words from which they could make their choice. For example, why was the picture of a cross chosen as the symbol or sign for *t*, for which the Egyptians used the picture of a loaf, rather than that of any other concrete object for which the Semitic word began with that letter—for example *tayiš* 'goat' or *tāmār* 'palm-tree'?[2] Any of these words would have served their purpose equally well; they denoted familiar objects more or less easily depicted and began with the required letter. The answer is perhaps not far to seek. The principle on which the inventors worked was evidently acrophonic,[3] but they operated it in a somewhat different fashion from the Egyptians. The Semites began by looking for a word reproducing the consonantal sound with, so far as possible, nothing else but the vowel required to render possible its pronunciation; for example, they found only one monosyllabic word beginning with *p* which could be used for that sound, namely *peh* (*pē'*)[4] 'mouth' and they therefore adopted this as the name of the *p*-sound and consequently took the picture of a mouth as its symbol or sign. The Semitic languages, however, had very few such words representing concrete objects.[5] The inventors, therefore, so soon as they had exhausted the only words available for their purpose, next chose words beginning and ending with the same consonant as echoing *tout simple* the required sound; in this way they chose *mayim* (*mēm*) 'water(s)' as reproducing the *m*-sound and

[1] S. pp. 161–71.

[2] The words chosen as examples are selected from the Hebrew vocabulary as likely to be the best known of the Semitic languages to most readers.

[3] Based on the principle of acrophony, namely the use of an originally pictographic symbol of an object to represent the initial sound or letter of the name of that object.

[4] For the purpose of the argument the final *h* or ' can be discounted as a weak letter.

[5] Obviously an abstract term like *pōh* 'here' could not be depicted.

therefore suited to be the name of that phoneme and therewith, of course, the picture of water to be its symbol. In this case indeed the choice was especially easy; for the Acc. *mû* 'water' shows that this word, too, was originally a monosyllable, whose primitive form was afterwards preserved in the Gk. μῦ, while the final *-m* was merely the North-Semitic plural ending. In the case of *wāw* and *nûn* there was no such transitional form but the principle underlying the choice of the name was the same. Again, there were few such words available and the stock was soon exhausted. The inventors then proceeded to the third method. They took the consonant and added the necessary vowel to enable it to be pronounced and so produced forms resulting in such names as *ši-* for *š* and *be-* for *b*, which however were meaningless sounds as they stood, as there were no such monosyllabic words in the Semitic languages; they thereupon added one or other of the formative elements common to all the Semitic languages, namely *n* or *t*,[1] to these bases in order to convert them into seeming if not actual Semitic words. Such were *šîn* and *bêṯ*, the names respectively of *š* and *b*; the former still meant nothing while the latter was a real word. However, *šin* could easily be identified with the proto-Semitic **šinn* (Hebr. *šēn*) 'tooth; peak' while *bêṯ* was naturally identified with the Sem. **bayt* (Hebr. *bayiṯ*) 'house',[2] and so *š* and *b* came readily to be represented by symbols modelled on the hieroglyphs respectively for a chain of mountains and a house.

Two arguments seem to strengthen the probability of the method of invention here suggested. First, the names of *ḥ* and *ṭ*, which are secondary letters, namely *ḥêṯ* and *ṭêṯ*, were obviously formed by the addition of a formative *t* to the monosyllabic base (*ḥê-* and *ṭê-*);[3] they remained, however, onomatopoeic but meaningless names since no words with which they could be identified (as *bêṯ* for *b* was identified with the Sem. **bayt* 'house') existed. There are traces, too, of this type of formation in the names of several other Phoenician and Ethiopic letters.[4]

[1] Of these two letters *n* is a common affix in the formation of Semitic nouns and is also the Aramaic and Arabic plural ending (corresponding to the Phoenician and Hebrew *m*), and *t* is the universal Semitic feminine ending. In origin the first is merely a nasal prolongation and the second a deictic element and therefore the plural or feminine significance, which is a relatively late development, does not here come into play; cp. Phoen. *z* and *zn* or *zt* 'this', all of the masculine gender, Phoen. *z'* and *z't* and Hebr. *zōh* or *zô* and *zō't* 'this', all of the feminine gender, which show that the *t* is not a mark of gender but merely a formative element added to the primitive *z* (s. p. 162). [2] S. p. 163. [3] S. p. 167. [4] S. p. 167 n. 1.

Thus, secondly, the similarly onomatopoeic but meaningless *zây* or *zay* (*zê*) for *z*[1] was subjected to both procedures, becoming *zayin* in the Semitic and ζῆτα in the Greek alphabet; but in this case, while *zayin* 'weapon(s)' is the accepted Semitic name of the letter, it is improbable that *zay* (*zê*) was furnished with a formative *t* and assimilated to the Sem. **zayt* (Hebr. *zayiṯ*) 'olive' within the Semitic alphabet, since no second name for it is attested in these languages and its sign does not suggest such a meaning; further, no other instance of a letter having alternative names is known in the primitive period. It is preferable to suppose that this name was transformed into ζῆτα on the analogy of ἦτα[2] and θῆτα after its incorporation into the Greek alphabet.[3]

The procedure thus sketched out will account for about half the letters of the alphabet, and it is at first sight not clear why it stops at this point; for, as Lidzbarski[4] remarks, there are eminently suitable names for *g* and *d* in the Hebr. *gāḡ* 'roof' and *daḏ* 'breast', if not for others. Why then are they not used? This question cannot be answered except tentatively: the required words may not have been current in the dialect spoken by the inventors of the alphabet, or the pictures representing them may not have been easily reducible to mere symbols or suitable for conversion into linear forms.

However this may be, it remains a fact that the names of none of the remaining primary letters fall into any of the above-mentioned three or four groups and they must therefore be otherwise explained. In their cases the inventors of the alphabet normally had no simple monosyllabic word which naturally suggested itself to them on phonetic grounds as the name of any given phoneme. They therefore changed the procedure; they chose any well-known word beginning with the required consonant and representing an object easily drawn in linear script and took the thing represented by that word as the symbol of the letter with which it began, and they used this word to serve also as the name of the phoneme. For example, when they wanted a sign for the *r*-sound, they sought a suitable word beginning with *r* and, having chosen that for the human head, for

1 Cp. Arab. *zā'* or *zây* for *z* and so on.

2 Cp. also Gk. ἦτα = Copt. ϩⲏⲧⲁ (W. Schulze *Kl. Schr.* p. 717).

3 S. p. 164. Apparently its Phoenician and Hebrew name was the onomatopoeic *zay* till after its incorporation in the Greek alphabet; this is very probable, as *zayin* is not a Hebrew but an Egyptian and Aramaic word (Eg. *zin* 'arrow' = Aram. *zainâ* 'weapons')*. If so, the original Egyptian name was reflected in the Aramaic name, which was taken into the Hebrew language only at a relatively late date.

4 In *E.S.E.* I 133–4.

which the common Semitic term began with that letter, called the sign for *r* by the name of *rêš* 'head' and represented it by a picture of a head. Similarly, they took the well-known Sem. **yad* as the name for *y* and represented it by the picture of a hand.

On this theory of the origin of the names of the letters there is no entirely uniform principle underlying the formation of the whole alphabet. Indeed, it is useless to look for any single principle underlying almost any human invention; there is always the interplay of diverse motives, forces and influences. The inventors of the alphabet were not exempt from this law of nature and adopted various, often overlapping, methods for diverse reasons in carrying out their project. In the case of the primary letters they adopted the two methods outlined above, which may now be briefly summarized: first, they took the bare consonant with the necessary vowel, without which it could not be pronounced,[1] and after some slight modification, where required, identified it with or assimilated it to a Semitic word denoting some familiar object and, using this word as the name of the letter, adapted a picture illustrating that object to represent the letter in linear form; second, advancing on their previous procedure, they arbitrarily chose a word representing any well-known and easily depicted object as the name of the sound with which it began, i.e. of its initial letter, and took the object represented as the symbol of that letter. The case of the secondary letters, for which analogous methods were employed, does not call for consideration at this point, as the signs representing them are not primitive, and it will be discussed below.[2] For the present argument the important point in the two methods just summarized is that in the first the name arose naturally out of the sound which it represented while in the second it was arbitrarily chosen. Logically, therefore, the name preceded the sign, which was based on it, but that does not mean that it was not contemporary with it in point of time. The inventors of the alphabet, since of necessity they already had names for the letters of the first group, would be likely to have recognized the advantage of naming the letters and therefore to have adopted the words describing the signs *ab initio* as their names. In both

[1] The survival of one such name for a letter in its original meaningless form in the Hebrew alphabet of the Septuagint (ζαι) and of several in the Greek alphabet (μῦ, νῦ, πῖ, ῥῶ, ταῦ) gives a hint that all the letters of the alphabet must originally have been called by onomatopoeic monosyllables (s. pp. 167–8); their conversion into intelligible words will have been due to the introduction of signs depicting tangible objects to represent them.

[2] S. pp. 166–8, 170–1.

cases name and sign are so closely interwoven into a common pattern that the name is as meaningless without the sign as the sign is unintelligible without the name. The names must therefore be regarded as going back to the very beginnings of the alphabet*.

### 9. The Forms and Names of the Individual Letters

The acceptance of the historic names of the letters at their face-value allows their meanings to be used as pointers towards the objects which the letters may originally have depicted. It must, however, not be overlooked that tradition may err and that this or that name may lead the inquirer astray in his search for the origin of the letter which is called by it.

The Egyptians and the Semites owed the invention of their alphabets to the similar but distinct application of analogous principles. The Egyptians derived their alphabet from the peculiar structure of their language, whereby the letters or rather the consonants, as it were, fell into their hands, and only two dozen hieroglyphs depicting common objects whose names had undergone similar phonetic deterioration were required to make a workable consonantal alphabet.[1] The Phoenician alphabet then will have come into existence in a somewhat similar way, except that, whereas the Egyptian alphabet was discovered almost by accident, the Phoenician was due to a deliberate invention based on the Egyptian analogy; for the Semitic languages never reached the advanced stage of phonetic decay which the Egyptian had already reached before the invention of the Semitic alphabet, leaving it with a number of words consisting of only one strong consonant. Allowance must also be made for differences of language, so that corresponding Egyptian and Phoenician signs represented different letters in the two alphabets, because the names denoting the objects depicted by these signs were totally different words and did not necessarily begin with the same letter.

It is in some such way as this that the Semitic alphabet must have come into being, and traces of the process can be detected in the case of several letters;[2] for the inventors were obviously working on the analogy of the Egyptian system with which they

[1] S. pp. 133–6.

[2] In consequence of the meagreness of the known Phoenician vocabulary as recovered up to date the place of Phoenician must be taken by assumed Semitic roots, here marked by an asterisk, derived from a comparison of the forms of words found in the cognate languages, or by their actual forms as found in one or other of these languages.

were *ex hypothesi* acquainted. Thus they represented *y* after the first letter of the Sem. **yad* 'hand' (not *d*, as the Egyptians did, after the last letter of the Eg. *ỉd* 'hand') by the picture of a hand (inasmuch as they preferred to use the initial letters of the root, since these, even if weak, did not normally fall away in the Semitic languages); and similarly they represented *p* after the Sem. **puw* 'mouth' (not *r*, as the Egyptians did after the Eg. *rꜣ* or *rỉ* 'mouth') by the picture of a mouth. In the same way the sign of a nail or peg was used for *w* after the Hebr. *wāw* 'peg'* and that for a cross or mark after the Hebr. *tāw* 'mark'.[1] Terminations were, of course, disregarded; thus the sign for the Eg. *n.t* 'water', in which the final *t* marked the feminine gender,[2] became the Eg. *n* but served as the prototype of that for the Phoen. *m*, whose name was derived from the Sem. **muw* and took the form of the Hebr. *mēm* 'water' or 'waters', in which the final *m* was the mark of the plural number.

Possibly *h* may be put in this class; for it may be suggested that the sign for being high, which represented a man with his hands raised high above him and was used with determinative value before *ḥʿỉ* 'rejoiced' and *ḥꜣ* 'mourned', was the prototype of *h*, of which the name was identical with the Hebr. *hē*' 'lo!'.[3] This was an exclamation akin to the Eg. *h* and *ỉ*, the Aram. *hā*', the S.-Arab. (Ṣaf.) *h*, and the classical Arab. *hâ* 'ah!',[4] which supports the suggestion that *hē*', too, might have been an onomatopoeic monosyllable representing a shout of joy or grief.[5]

Words, however, consisting solely of one strong and one weak consonant were extremely rare in the Semitic languages, and no others probably were available to continue the process. The inventors of the alphabet were therefore driven to use words of three consonants, which were the norm in these languages, to go on with their alphabet. They continued even so to restrict themselves to the first letters of the words which they chose for their purpose.

In these cases the scheme of the Egyptian pictographs was followed in choosing common objects as symbols for the Phoenician letters, again without regard to their word-values or letter-values, when they had any, in the language whence they were taken (s. p. 169 fig. 92). The selection was quite arbitrary,

[1] Cp. Ezek. ix 4, 6 (s. pp. 88–9). The derived verb is הִתְוָה 'set a mark' (Ezek. ix 4).
[2] S. p. 158 n. 1.
[3] Cp. Dussaud *Arabes en Syrie* 95.
[4] Cp. Sethe *Göttingen* 1917, 444–5.
[5] The Eth. *hōy* as the name for *h* is similarly akin to the Hebr. *hôy* 'ah!' (Eisler *Ken. Weihinschr.* 112[2]).

since only a dozen or so signs were wanted out of many hundreds, and the only guiding principle was the need to choose simply drawn and easily recognized forms; as such head and eye, ox and serpent, house and door, and perhaps also certain well-known weapons, were chosen. In this way the picture of the human head became, from the Hebr. *rō'š* 'head', the sign for *r* and that of a door, from the Hebr. *delet̠* 'door', the sign for *d*. In the same way the pictures of an ox and an eye, from the Sem. **'alp* 'ox' and the Sem. **'ayn* 'eye', became the signs respectively for ' (*'ālep̠*) and ' (*'ayin*), two sounds which alone have symbols in and of which one is peculiar to the Semitic languages.

Fig. 85. Warrior carrying throw-stick or boomerang.

Pictograph and sign did not always correspond. Thus it was not the pictograph for a 'house' (⊏⊐) but rather that for a 'courtyard' (⌈⊔) that lay behind the sign for *b*, named *bêt̠* after the Sem. **bayt* 'house'.

Occasionally the Semitic name for the letter was equivocal and only a rare or obsolete meaning recalled the Egyptian hieroglyph on which it was modelled. Thus the Egyptian hieroglyph for 'rushes' is evidently the prototype of the Semitic sign for *k*, called **kapp*; this is rightly explained by the Hebr. *kap̠* 'palm of the hand' and also 'branch, frond (of palms)',[1] but the intended sense is not 'hand' (as usually supposed) but evidently 'frond'*.[2] Similarly, the pictograph for mountainous country was the model for *š*, called *šîn* after the Hebr. *šēn* 'tooth; point, peak (of rock)'.[3]

Complete or even approximate agreement between form and name in both languages was rare. The Eg. *qmꜣ* 'threw' and probably also 'throw-stick' (⟩) became the sign for *g* (1,ↄ), which was called *gīmel* or *gimmel* (s. fig. 85).[4] The form of the word

[1] Lev. xxiii 40 and cp. Is. lv 12. The Acc. *kapp*(*u*) 'hand; bough' shows both meanings to be early (s. p. 184). [2] Cp. Sethe in *Göttingen* 1917, 445.

[3] 1 Sam. xiv 4–5, Jb. xxxix 28; cp. post-Bibl. Hebr. *šᵉnānîm* 'rocks' and the Syr. *šnānt̠â* 'rocky height, mountain' from the same root. The hieroglyphic 𓈐 *šꜣ* 'pool with lotus-plants' and also *š* hardly comes into the question, as it seems to have acquired its consonantal value only at a very late date. Further, the Egyptian lotus is very rare in Palestine; the white lotus does not occur and the blue is found only at Râs-ul'ain and Ḥădêrāh. The distinction of שׁ and שׂ by a diacritical point is not original (s. Nestle in *Actes du IXme Congrès des Orientalistes* II, 62–3).

[4] Cp. Hommel *ap.* Lidzbarski *E.S.E.* I 269 and Eisler *Ken. Weihinschr.* 19; s. Butin *ap.* Butin & Starr in 'S.D.' 38*. The Eg. *q* might correspond

with such vowels, however, though confirmed by the Septuagint's γιμαλ, is a solecism, as such a vocalization of a Hebrew word is impossible and is due to the fact that its meaning had already been forgotten by the time of the Greek translation of the Hebrew Bible; the original form survived, however, in the Eth. *gaml* and was also reflected in the Gk. γάμμα, although these are but meaningless names in the languages preserving them, while only the Acc. *gamlu* 'throw-stick'[1] preserves its

A. Hand grasping arrows. B. Warriors carrying lances.

FIG. 86. Multiple weapons.

proper meaning*. Another possible instance of such agreement may occur in *z*, whose Semitic name is **zayn*, if the form of this letter is derived from the Egyptian hieroglyph for an 'arrow' (—•) used as a determinative sign for an arrow; for the Eg. *zin* or *zwn* 'arrow', which seems to have been the original reading of this hieroglyph, corresponds exactly to the Syr. (Aram.) *zain*(*â*) 'arms, weapons', which gives its name to the letter.[2] At the same time, its form seems to fluctuate between that of a single arrow in a vertical position and several held in a horizontal position (s. fig. 86); it may also originally have been influenced by the hieroglyphs for a 'bolt' (—), which was used for *z*, and by that for a 'folded cloth' (𓋴), which was used for *s*, in the same way that the sign for *l* may owe its form to a conflation or confusion of similar hieroglyphs.

The sign for *l* may be derived from the Egyptian hieroglyph used as a determinative sign for a 'coil of rope' (𓍢), as certain Sinaitic signs suggest (if indeed they correspond with either the Egyptian hieroglyph or the Byblo-Phoenician symbol); but its Phoenician forms strongly recall the hieroglyphs for a shepherd's 'crook' or a 'sceptre' (𓌂, 𓋾, 𓌀), which may have influenced the choice of a name for it (s. p. 165 fig. 87 and fig. 88). This is *lāmed*[3]

to the Sem. *g*/*j* and Eg. *ꜣ* might replace Sem. *l* as in Eg. *bꜣq* 'was bright, clear' = Hebr. *bālag* 'smiled' and Arab. *balaja* 'shone' and *balija* 'was gay' (Calice *Grundl. d. äg.-sem. Wortvergl.* 29).

[1] So-called as apt to recoil on the thrower (cp. Hebr. גָּמַל 'requited') like גָּמָל 'camel' as μνησίκακος (Bochart & Rosenmüller *Hierozoicon* I 5–6).

[2] S. p. 159 n. 2; cp. O.-Pers. (Avest.) zaēna, M.-Pers. zēn and N.-Pers. *zīn* 'weapon'.

[3] There is no objection to postulating two forms, one without and one with prefixed *m* (indicating the implement) from the same root, as *rekeb* 'chariotry' and then also 'chariot' and *merkāb* 'chariot' show.

'goading', an abstract noun otherwise unattested, used in the sense of the concrete Biblical *malmēḏ* 'goad'.[1]

The explanation of the names of two other letters has been found difficult. The Aramaic and Arabic name for *n* is *nûn* 'fish', which is confirmed by the Septuagint's νουν[2] and probably reflected in the Gk. νῦ; but it is objected to this identification that the sign at no stage of its development resembles a fish. If then a fish is meant, it must have been an eel, which is found in Palestine.[3] Its Ethiopic name, however, is *nahās* (*naḥās*) 'serpent' which exactly describes the Egyptian hieroglyph from which the Byblo-Phoenician sign seems to have been derived, and this must have been an early,[4] and may well have been the original, name of the letter;[5] for the Hebr. *nāḥāš* 'serpent' is a word attested in early literature, and it may have been replaced by the Aram. *nûn* 'fish', as this has the additional advantage of echoing the sound of the letter. The Aramaic name for *s* is *sāmeḵ* 'support',[6] but the sign hardly recalls any such object, even in the form of the Egyptian hieroglyph for a 'head-rest' (⌶). It may then perhaps rather be regarded as derived through the Sinaitic forms (again if these correspond on either side) from the Egyptian hieroglyph for the *bulti*-fish, and this suggestion receives some support from the fact that the name can then be easily explained in the light of the Arab.

Phoen. 𐤋 𐤋
(Hebr. ל)

FIG. 87. Egyptian nobleman holding a staff.

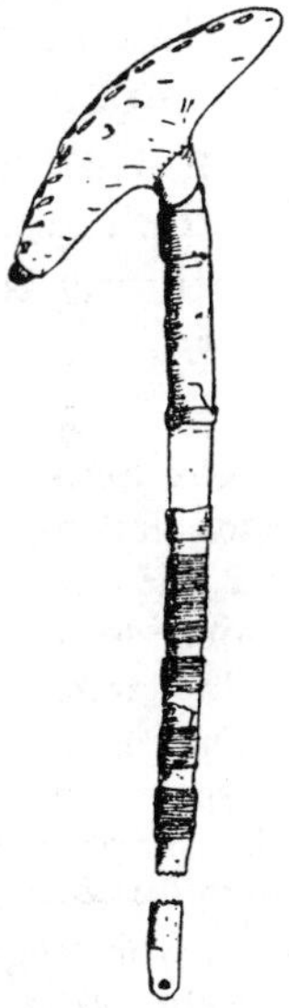

FIG. 88. Egyptian peasant's camel-stick.

[1] The alternative λαβδ or λαβεδ, which occurs occasionally as the name for *l* (LXX at Ps. cxviii [cxix] 89 and Eusebius *Evang. Praep.* [474 c] x 5; s. Nöldeke *Beitr. z. Sem. Sprachw.* 126–8), is only a phonetic variation of *lāmeḏ* (s. p. 168 n. 1); but the Arab. *labad*$^{u(n)}$ 'tangled, matted wool; felt' has been invoked somewhat improbably to explain it (Sethe *Göttingen* 1917, 445).

[2] Ps. cxviii [cxix] 105.

[3] Cp. Eisler *Ken. Weihinschr.* 111 (s. p. 154).

[4] There is no such word as *nahās* or *naḥās* 'serpent' in the Ethiopic language, nor is there any corresponding Arabic word, so that the Ethiopians must have taken over this name from a previous stage of the alphabet (cp. Lidzbarski *E.S.E.* I $132^2$).

[5] So the Eth. *gaml*, of which the Gk. γιμ(ε)λ (Eusebius *Evang. Praep.* [474 b, 475 a] x 5) is a weakened form, preserves the true form of the name for *g* (s. pp. 163–4).

[6] Syr. *sāmḵâ* 'prop, support' (s. p. 184 n. 2).

*samak* 'fish'.[1] Alternatively, Levy[2] may be right in regarding the sign for *s* (𐤎) as an augmented form of that for *z* (I, ⌶), when it will have received its name from the fancied resemblance of its shape to a fish with fins. It is hardly possible to decide which of these two forms of this explanation ought to be preferred; but, if he is right, this letter will belong rather to the following group of letters.

Thus far, explanations of eighteen letters have been offered, and four others remain for discussion.

Levy[2] and, apparently independently, Halévy[3] have both made the suggestion that the Phoenician sign for *ḥ* (𐤇, 𐤇) was developed as an intensive form of that for *h* (𐤄, 𐤄), from which it was distinguished by an additional stroke; but this does not exclude the possibility that its form was influenced by the Egyptian hieroglyph for a 'twisted hank' which was also used for *ḥ* (𓎛). They implausibly claim the sign for *ṣ* (𐤑, 𐤑, 𐤑) as developed from that for *z* (I, ⌶), since *ṣ* was intensive *z* in sound.[4] Again, Bauer and Leander[5] convincingly explain the sign for emphatic *ṭ* (⊕) as compounded of that for the simple *t* (+) enclosed in that for the guttural ʿ(O); and this explanation suggests that the sign for the emphatic *q* (𐤒) may have been analogously formed by combining that for the guttural ʿ(O) with that for the simple *k* (𐤊).[6]

[1] Cp. Sethe *Göttingen* 1917, 446. Hommel (s. Eisler *Ken. Weihinsch.* 23[4]) seems first to have suggested the Arab. *samak* 'fish', and the objection that this word does not appear to occur before the classical language is not serious; for the history of many words now known only in the post-Islamic Arabic language can be traced back to the pre-Christian Semitic vocabulary (s. Driver in 'J.B.L.' LV 101–20). So Lake Ḥûlah was called by the Greeks ἡ Σεμεχωνῖτις λίμνη 'the lake of fishes' apparently because it contained fishes διάφορα πρὸς τοὺς ἀλλαχοῦ γεῦσίν τε καὶ ἰδέαν, like the sea of Galilee (Josephus *Bell. Jud.* III x 7 §509) and ימא דסמכו in the Talmud. If so, there was a word cognate with the Arab. *samak* 'fish' in presumably an Aramaic or Hebrew dialect and there might well have been another in the Phoenician language and even in the earliest forms of West-Semitic speech, if the Ugar. *šmk* is rightly identified with this word (Virolleaud *ap.* Gaster in 'Iraq' IV 127[28]); if so, it was probably in origin a local appellative term describing fish, in districts where it was plentiful, as the main 'support' of life, just as bread was called the 'staff' of life (Is. iii 1) *.

[2] In *Phön. Stud.* I 52.

[3] In *Mél. d'Épigr. et d'Arch. Sém.* (1874) 179.

[4] Cp. Sab. 𐩠 *h* and 𐩢 *ḥ* and 𐩭 *ḫ* (s. Müller *Epigr. Denkm. a. Arab.* 16–19 for other South-Semitic examples of such formations).

[5] In *Hist. Gr. d. Hebr. Spr.* I 64–5; cp. Grimme in *Z.A.* XX 50–1.

[6] As though respectively *t*ʿ and *k*ʿ in origin. So the Sab. 𐩮 *ṣ* is probably

The names, however, of these last four signs have hitherto received no satisfactory interpretation. The name of *ḥ* is *ḥêṯ* which is modelled on *hē*', of which the origin has been shown to be exclamatory, with *ḥ* in place of *h* and a deictic or feminine *t* added to heighten the effect or bring out the distinction; in

Phoen. 𐤑, 𐤑, 𐤑 (Hebr. צ, ץ).

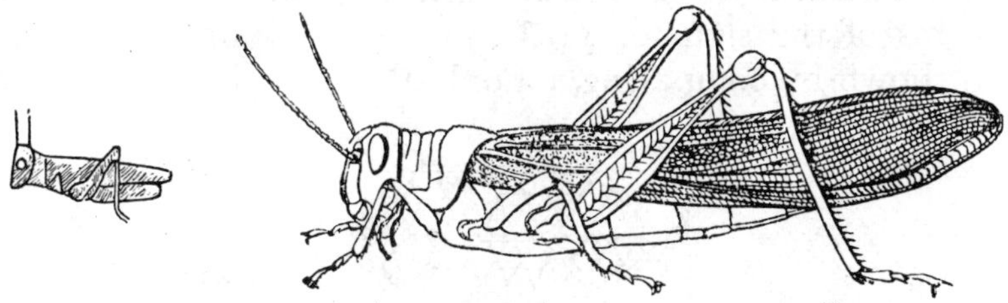

A. Engraved locust. B. Natural locust.

FIG. 89. Locusts.

the same way the name for *ṭ* is *ṭêṯ*, which can be explained as a modification of *tāw* with a similar *t* added to it to emphasize the distinction.[1] Neither name has any meaning, being merely

Phoen. 𐤒, 𐤒, 𐤒. Aram. 𐡒, 𐡒, 𐡒 (Hebr. ק).

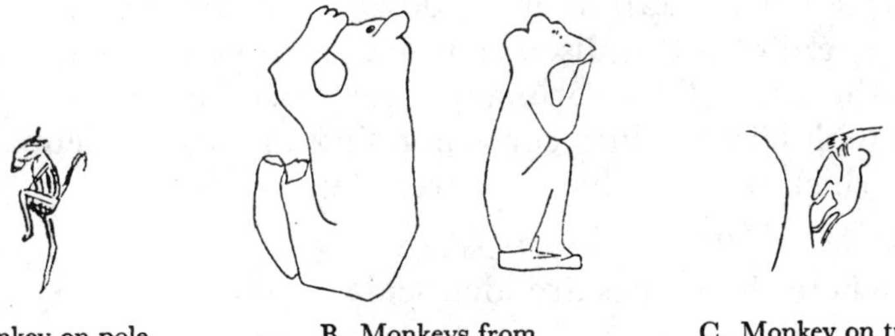

A. Monkey on pole on a Syrian seal. B. Monkeys from Gebal. C. Monkey on tree from Egypt.

FIG. 90. Monkeys in art.

onomatopoeic in origin. Like *ṭ*, both *ṣ* and *q* are uncommon in early texts, and this suggests that they too may have been late developments; and it agrees with this suggestion that there is no sign for *ṣ*, nor indeed for *ṭ*, in the Egyptian pseudo-alphabet. Further, like *zay* or *zai* beside *zayin* for *z*, both *ṣ* and *q* had respectively *ṣaw* or *ṣau* and *qaw* or *qau* as onomatopoeic names

a combination of ሰ *s* and o ʿ as the Eth. ጸ *ṣ* is a combination of ሰ *s* and ዐ ʿ (Grimme in *Z.A.* xx 55–7; cp. Hommel *Süd-arab. Chrestom.* 5)*.

[1] S. p. 158 n. 1. There is thus no need to identify the Hebr. *ḥêṯ* with the Arab. *ḫaiṭ* 'cord' (Eisler *Ken. Weihinschr.* 43). The Eth. *ṗait* for *ṗ* is similarly formed on the analogy of *ṭaiṭ*, in which *ṭ* for *t* is due to assimilation to the initial *ṭ*, (Dillmann & Crichton 'Eth. Gramm.' 18).

expressing simply the consonants themselves with the vowel or diphthong necessary to enable the sound to be enounced,[1] if the jingling *ṣaw lāṣāw* and *qaw lāqāw* really mean 'ṣ by ṣ' and 'q by q' as taught by master to pupil;[2] but their proper names were *ṣāḏê* and *qôp̄*. The first, which has hitherto remained without explanation, may be the absolute (uninflected) form of the Aram. *ṣād'yâ* 'cricket, grasshopper',[3] which the earliest forms of the sign for ṣ ( , , ) resemble tolerably well, as shown by comparing not only the Egyptian hieroglyph for a

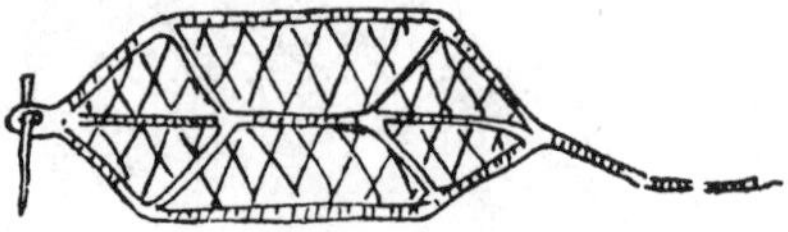

FIG. 91. Egyptian bird-trap.

'grasshopper' ( ) but also modern pictures of the locust (s. p. 167 fig. 89).[4] The second has been thought to be the Acc. *quppu* 'bird-trap'[5] (s. fig. 91) but is generally supposed to be the Hebr. *qôp̄* 'monkey' which will then have given its name to the sign for q from its fancied resemblance to a monkey on a pole or a tree with its tail hanging down (s. p. 167 fig. 90).[6]

The results of this discussion may now be summarized.

In the case of the primary signs, first, there are Egyptian signs with letter-values corresponding to various Semitic symbols, which however have different letter-values:

*d* (Eg. *id* 'hand') for *y* (*yôḏ*),

where the names are identical;

*r* (Eg. *rꜣ* 'mouth') for *p* (*pē'* 'mouth')

[1] Cp. Eth. *law* for *l*, of which the proper name had become unintelligible (s. p. 165 n. 1).

[2] Is. xxviii 10 (s. pp. 89–90).

[3] Literally perhaps 'clapper' from the noise which it makes; cp. Arab. *ṣadâ* (صدا) *manibus complosit*, whence *ṣadâ* (صَدا, صَدى) *insecti genus maius locusta, saltans ac noctu stridens* (Freytag), Aram. and Syr. *ṣdâ* (ܨܕܐ) *derisit* (Brockelmann).

[4] Locusts are fairly often represented in ancient Oriental art, especially on seals (s. Staples *ap.* Guy 'Armageddon' 49–50, 64–7).

[5] Sayce in 'P.S.B.A.' XXXII 220. This word, however, is not known in the Phoenician or Hebrew languages, while the cognate Syr. *qoppeṯâ* and Arab. *quffatun* 'basket' hardly give the required sense.

[6] The monkey on a pole is a known figure on seals (Frankfort 'Cylinder-Seals' xxvi e, xl o, xli e). Monkeys appear also frequently in Egyptian (Klebs *Rel. u. Mal. A.R.* 32–4, *Rel. u. Mal. M.R.* 48–9, 89, *Rel. u. Mal. N.R.* 37), and Phoenician (Dunand *Bybl.* I 137/59) art.

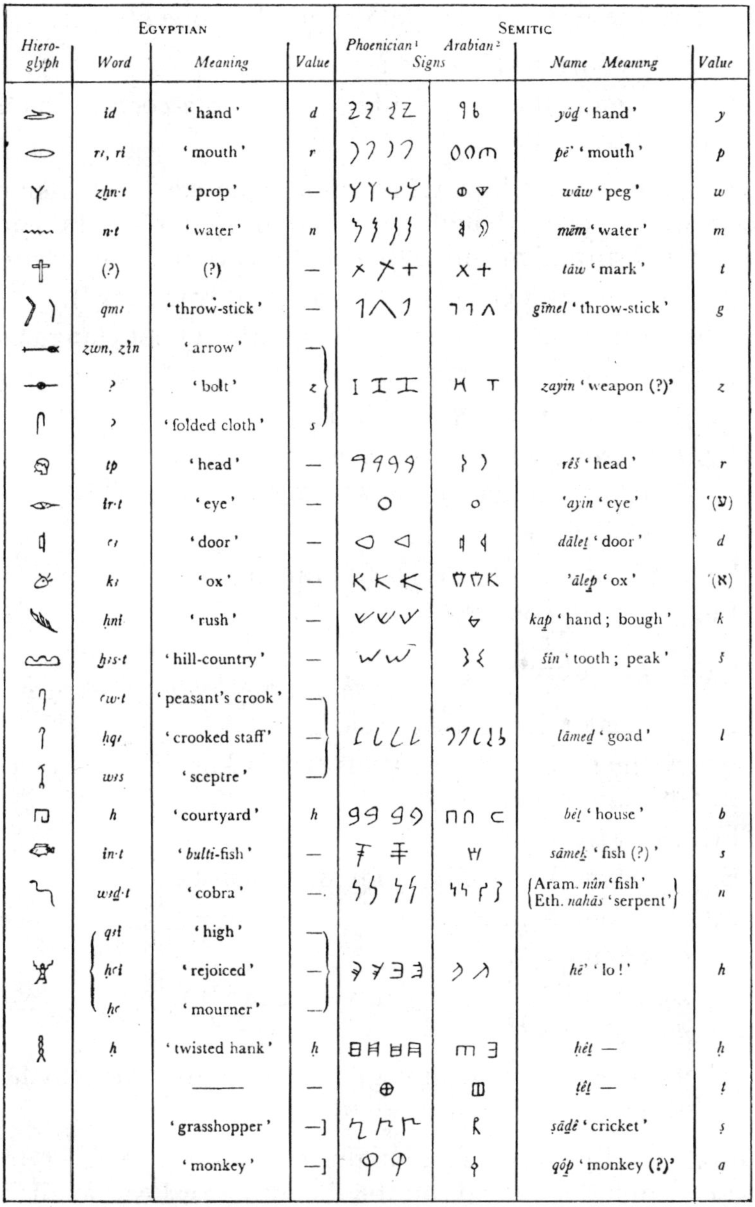

| Egyptian: Hieroglyph | Egyptian: Word | Egyptian: Meaning | Egyptian: Value | Semitic: Phoenician[1] Signs | Semitic: Arabian[2] Signs | Semitic: Name Meaning | Semitic: Value |
|---|---|---|---|---|---|---|---|
| | *id* | 'hand' | *d* | | | *yôḏ* 'hand' | *y* |
| | *rꜣ, ri* | 'mouth' | *r* | | | *pē'* 'mouth' | *p* |
| | *zẖn·t* | 'prop' | — | | | *wāw* 'peg' | *w* |
| | *n·t* | 'water' | *n* | | | *mēm* 'water' | *m* |
| | (?) | (?) | — | | | *tāw* 'mark' | *t* |
| | *qmꜣ* | 'throw-stick' | — | | | *gīmel* 'throw-stick' | *g* |
| | *zwn, zꜣn* | 'arrow' | — } | | | | |
| | ? | 'bolt' | *z* } | | | *zayin* 'weapon (?)' | *z* |
| | ꜣ | 'folded cloth' | *s* } | | | | |
| | *tp* | 'head' | — | | | *rēš* 'head' | *r* |
| | *ir·t* | 'eye' | — | | | *'ayin* 'eye' | '(ע) |
| | *ꜥꜣ* | 'door' | — | | | *dālet̲* 'door' | *d* |
| | *kꜣ* | 'ox' | — | | | *'ālep̲* 'ox' | '(א) |
| | *ḥni* | 'rush' | — | | | *kap̲* 'hand; bough' | *k* |
| | *ḫꜣs·t* | 'hill-country' | — | | | *šin* 'tooth; peak' | *š* |
| | *ꜥw·t* | 'peasant's crook' | — } | | | | |
| | *ḥqꜣ* | 'crooked staff' | — } | | | *lāmed̲* 'goad' | *l* |
| | *wꜣs* | 'sceptre' | — } | | | | |
| | *h* | 'courtyard' | *h* | | | *bêt̲* 'house' | *b* |
| | *in·t* | '*bulti*-fish' | — | | | *sāmek̲* 'fish (?)' | *s* |
| | *wꜣḏ·t* | 'cobra' | — | | | {Aram. *nûn* 'fish' / Eth. *nahās* 'serpent'} | *n* |
| | { *qꜣi* | 'high' | — } | | | | |
| | { *ḥꜥi* | 'rejoiced' | — } | | | *hē'* 'lo!' | *h* |
| | { *ḥꜥ* | 'mourner' | — } | | | | |
| | *ḥ* | 'twisted hank' | *ḥ* | | | *ḥēt̲* — | *ḥ* |
| | | ——— | — | | | *ṭêt̲* — | *ṭ* |
| | | 'grasshopper' | —] | | | *ṣādê* 'cricket' | *ṣ* |
| | | 'monkey' | —] | | | *qôp̲* 'monkey (?)' | *q* |

[1] Taken only from inscriptions dated *c.* 1300–900 B.C.
[2] Chosen from the South-Arabian alphabets without regard to dialect with a view to comparison with the corresponding Phoenician letters.

FIG. 92. Comparison of Egyptian and Semitic letters.

*n* (Eg. *n·t* 'water') for *m* (*mēm* 'water'),
where the names differ but denote the same objects;

*h* (Eg. *h* 'courtyard') for *b* (*bêt* 'house'),
where again the names differ but denote cognate though not identical objects.

Second, there were Egyptian signs for common or well-known objects which, even though they had no letter-values, corresponded in form and meaning to those for various Semitic letters:

(Eg. *qmꜣ* 'throw-stick') for *g* (*gīmel* 'throw-stick'),
where the name of the objects is the same in both languages;

(Eg. *zẖn·t* 'prop') for (*wāw* 'peg') *w*

(Eg. *tp* 'head') for (*rêš* 'head') *r*

(Eg. *ỉr·t* 'eye') for (*'ayin* 'eye') *ꜥ*

(Eg. *ꜥꜣ* 'door') for (*dāleṯ* 'door') *d*

(Eg. *kꜣ* 'ox') for (*'ālep* 'ox') *'*

(Eg. *ḥnỉ* 'rushes') for (*kap̱* 'branch, frond') *k*

(Eg. *ḫꜣs·t* 'hill-country') for (*šîn* 'peak') *š*

(Eg. *wꜣḏ·t* 'cobra') for { (*nûn* 'fish' / *nahās* (i.e. = *nāḥāš*) 'serpent')[1] } *n*

(Eg. ? ? ) for + (*tāw* 'mark') *t*,[2]
where the names of the objects (when known) are different in both languages;

(Eg. *zỉn* 'arrow') —
(Eg. ? 'bolt') *z*
(Eg. ? 'folded cloth') *s*
} for (*zayin* 'weapon') *z*

(Eg. *ꜥw·t* 'crook'
(Eg. *ḥqꜣ·t* 'staff'
(Eg. *wꜣs* 'sceptre'
} for (*lāmeḏ* 'goad') *l*,
where several similar or cognate Egyptian signs may have influenced the Phoenician letter.

Third, an Egyptian sign might exist corresponding to a Semitic symbol but, as no suitable Semitic word was available, the name of the letter was based on a pseudo-onomatopoeic principle, as in:

(Eg. *ḥꜥỉ* 'rejoiced') for (*hē'* 'lo!') *h*.

The secondary signs were formed either by augmenting the sign for a kindred phoneme, sometimes but not always influenced

[1] S. p. 165 n. 4. [2] Cp. Ezek. ix 4, 6 and Jb. xxxi 35.

by Egyptian models, or by combining the two signs for the phonemes of which the new phonemes were composed and giving them names after the objects which they were supposed to represent or on onomatopoeic principles:

ǂ (*sāmeḵ* ' fish ') enlarged from ⌶ *z*
 but influenced by 𓆛 (Eg. *blty* ' fish ')

ᗷ (*ḥêṯ*, meaningless) enlarged from ⱻ *h*
 but influenced by 𓎛 (Eg. *ḥ* ' hank ') *ḥ*,
 where the name is onomatopoeic and meaningless but given a pseudo-Semitic form;

ꜧ, ꜧ *ṣ* (*ṣādê* 'grass-hopper') possibly not the original name, but one subsequently given to it by Aramaean scribes;

ψ, ✗ *k* (*kap̱*) + o ' ('*ayin*) = φ (*qôp̱* ' monkey ') *q*

+ *t* (*tāw*) + o ' ('*ayin*) = ⊕ (*ṭêṯ*, meaningless) *ṭ*,
 where the principle is that of combination. These letters are purely Semitic in origin, and their names are onomatopoeic or explanations of their forms.

The signs for and the names of the letters as thus explained are of two classes, according as they are primary or secondary. The former are those signs which correspond to Egyptian hieroglyphs and of which the letter-values are reproduced by the initial letters of their Semitic names; the latter are the signs which are formed by modifying other signs and which are then called by the names of objects which they are thought to resemble or by an onomatopoeic name when no suitable word suggests itself.

The idea of an alphabet, then, was Egyptian but the form which it took was Semitic, though often influenced by Egyptian models.*

## 10. The Greek Alphabet

The Greek alphabet is admitted to be of Phoenician origin in the sense that the Greeks must have obtained it from or through Phoenician, Aramaean or Syrian, trading centres, whatever its ultimate origin may have been*. This is the burden of ancient legend;[1] and the forms and names of the letters and even their order in the alphabet combine to confirm this derivation. The time of its acquisition and adoption by the Greeks, however, is a much vexed question, and various dates have been proposed: for example, the eleventh (Larfeld), the tenth (Kenyon, Szántó),

[1] S. pp. 128–9.

the tenth or ninth (Beloch), centuries, and many intervening epochs. The latest writers on the subject advocate extreme dates, Ullmann[1] the twelfth or eleventh century and Carpenter[2] *c.* 700 B.C.

Some light will perhaps be thrown on the problem if the earliest Greek alphabets are compared letter by letter to see which of the Semitic alphabets they resemble (s. p. 174 fig. 93)[3]:

*A*: Attic and Theran *A* resemble א at Gezer with the cross-stroke traversing the two V-strokes (not merely touching the point where they meet, as in the Byblian inscriptions);

*B*: Theran *B* with a looped bottom (or rather top) resembles the early Byblian *B* with the bottom curved (not straight as in subsequent forms);

*Γ*: Greek *Γ* has nothing noteworthy;

*Δ*: Greek *Δ* resembles the ד of Elibaal and the Moabite Stone in having its right leg of the same length as its left leg (not prolonged, as usually elsewhere) and its sides like Elibaal's and the Cypriot ג (not rounded, as those of Aḥiram and Yeḥimilk and often thereafter);

*E*: Theran and Melian *E* resemble Aḥiram's ה with the vertical stroke reaching only to the horizontal upper and lower horizontal strokes (not running beyond them above or most often below as in subsequent forms);

*F*: Greek *digamma* is peculiar in having the head facing sideways to a marked degree, perhaps to differentiate it from *Y*, since both are derived from the same Phoenician prototype;

*Z*: Attic and Cretan *Z* come most close to Aḥiram's ז with both cross-strokes extremely short (not so long as to exceed the length of the upright strokes, as often in subsequent scripts);

*H*: Attic, Theran and Cretan, *H* resembles the ח of Aḥiram, of the Lebanese arrow-head, and of Gezer, with the upright strokes reaching only to the upper and lower cross-strokes (not extended beyond them as in many Byblian forms and usually thereafter);

*Θ*: Greek *Θ* is, like the ט of Aḥiram and at Nora, round (not oblong, as on the Cypriot bowl);

[1] In 'A.J.A.' XXXVIII 359–81. [2] Ibid. XXXVII 8–29 and XLII 58–69.

[3] S. p. 175. Only Phoenician and Hebrew engraved inscriptions are taken for the purpose of the present comparison; the Aramaic alphabet tends to develop its own peculiarities (s. p. 119 n. 2), while the brush soon gives a cursive form to the letters, whichever the language may be.

*I*: Theran *I* like Abibaal's י has its top flat (not rounded, like most other forms), while the Greek form generally is peculiar in having no cross-bar;

*K*: Greek *K* generally corresponds with the כ, ך from Gezer onwards in having the right stroke prolonged like a tail (not equal to the left stroke as in all Byblian and Lebanese forms);

*Λ*: Greek *Λ* resembles the ל of the late Byblian and Lebanese inscriptions and of that from Gezer in being pointed (not rounded, as from Zinjîrlû generally onwards);

*M*: Early Greek *M* resembles the מ, ם from Zinjîrlû onwards in having the upper strokes at a sharp angle to the lower stroke (not running in a continuous line with it as in all preceding forms);

*N*: Greek *N* is like the Byblian and Lebanese נ, ן in having the outer strokes more or less equal (not unequal, with one prolonged into a tail as from Zinjîrlû onwards);

*Ξ*: Theran and Melian and also Corinthian *Ξ* are identical with the Phoenician ס down to that on the Cypriot bowl, having the upright stroke running through the transverse strokes (not stopping short of them as at Arslan Tash and Ur);

*O*: Greek *O* as compared with the Phoenician ע shows no peculiarities;

*Π*: Theran and Cretan and occasionally Attic *Π* follow the פ, ף of Yeḥimilk, found also at Gezer and Zinjîrlû, in having the top rounded (not pointed as in the Lebanon);

Ϻ: Theran and Cretan *san* is most like the Byblian and Moabite צ, ץ with the outer strokes of equal length (not with one elongated into a tail as from Zinjîrlû onwards);

Ϙ: Attic, Theran and Cretan, Ϙ is that of Gezer and Zinjîrlû, with its head rounded (not curved inwards at the top like that of Yeḥimilk nor crossed like that on the Cypriot bowl);[1]

*P*: Greek *P* has nothing significant for the purpose of comparison;

*Σ*: Greek *Σ* generally resembles the Byblian and Lebanese ש and that of Gezer in having the two angles wide (not narrow as at Zinjîrlû and to a certain extent on the Cypriot bowl);

*T*: Greek *T* like Aḥiram's ת is upright (not standing crosswise like that of Yeḥimilk nor slantwise as at Zinjîrlû and

[1] The form with an open head at Arslan Tash is Aramaic (s. pp. 119–20).

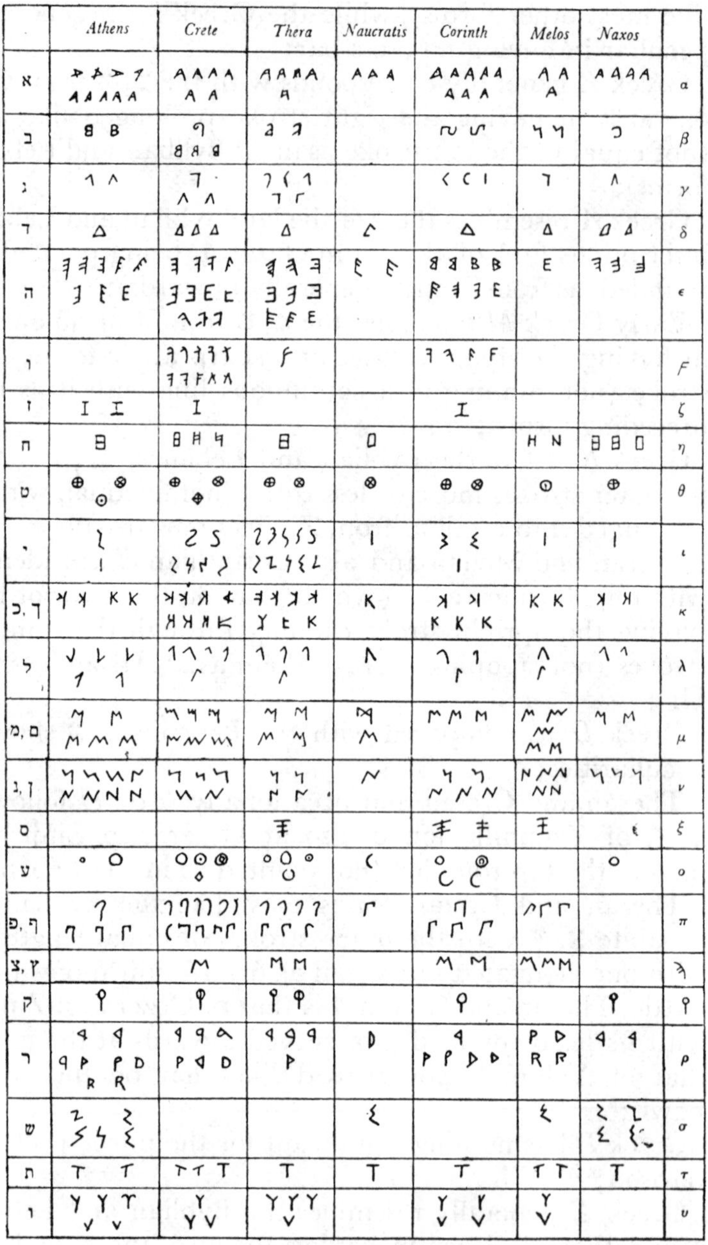
Athens
Crete
Thera
Naucratis
Corinth
Melos
Naxos

FIG. 93. Early Greek alphabets.

Gezer), but it never has the upright bar pass through the cross-bar as in all Phoenician forms.

*Υ*: Greek *Υ* resembles most closely the ו at Zinjîrlû in having the head pointed or *v*-shaped (not rounded or *u*-shaped like the Byblian and Lebanese forms).

The resemblances between the Phoenician or Aramaeo-Hebrew and the Greek alphabets revealed by this examination may be set out in the following table:

| | *c.* 1500–1000 (?) | | *c.* 1000 (?) | | *c.* 900 | | *c.* 850 | | *c.* 725–700 B.C. | |
|---|---|---|---|---|---|---|---|---|---|---|
| | Aḥi-râm | Yeḥî-milk | Nabâṭ-îyah | Gezer | Abi-baal | Eli-baal | Zinjîr-lû | Moab | Cyprus | |
| א | ... | ... | ... | × | ... | ... | ... | ... | ... | Α |
| ב | × | × | × | ... | ... | ... | ... | ... | ... | Β |
| ג | × | ... | ... | ... | ... | ... | ... | × | ... | Γ |
| ד | ... | ... | ... | ... | ... | × | ... | ... | ... | Δ |
| ה | × | ... | ... | ... | ... | ... | ... | ... | ... | Ε |
| ו | ... | ... | ... | ... | ... | ... | ... | ... | ... | Υ |
| ז | × | ... | ... | ... | ... | ... | ... | ... | ... | Ζ |
| ח | × | ... | ... | × | ... | ... | ... | ... | ... | Η |
| ט | × | ... | ... | ... | ... | ... | ... | ... | ... | Θ |
| י | ... | ... | ... | ... | ... | ... | ... | ... | ... | Ι |
| ך, כ | ... | ... | ... | × | ... | ... | × | ... | ... | Κ |
| ל | ... | ... | ... | × | × | × | ... | ... | ... | Λ |
| ם, מ | ... | ... | ... | ... | ... | ... | × | × | ... | Μ |
| ן, נ | ... | ... | ... | ... | × | × | ... | ... | ... | Ν |
| ס | × | ... | ... | × | × | ... | × | × | × | Ξ |
| ע | × | × | × | × | × | × | × | × | × | Ο |
| ף, פ | ... | × | ... | × | ... | ... | × | ... | ... | Π |
| ץ, צ | ... | ... | ... | ... | × | × | ... | × | ... | ϡ |
| ק | ... | × | ... | × | ... | ... | × | ... | ... | Ϙ |
| ר | × | × | ... | × | × | × | × | × | × | Ρ |
| ש | × | × | × | × | × | × | ... | × | ... | Σ |
| ת | × | ... | ... | ... | ... | ... | ... | ... | × | Τ |
| ו | ... | ... | ... | × | ... | ... | × | ... | ... | F |

Such comparisons, however, must be taken with considerable caution in matters of detail in view of the extreme paucity of texts hitherto available on both sides. In fact, only six Phoenician inscriptions are as yet known for a period of three hundred years, an average of two to every century; the number of Greek inscriptions available for comparison is considerably greater but they are spread over an immeasurably larger field in which local peculiarities play a considerable part. Further, the whole alphabet is often not represented in any given inscription, and indeed several letters in both alphabets are of quite rare occurrence.

Yet, with this caution in mind, some attempt at defining the period at which the Phoenician alphabet may be held to have made its way by the islands into Greece must and can be made.

The most numerous contacts of the Greek alphabet are with that of Aḥirâm, while there are many with the inscriptions from Gezer to Zinjîrlû and even with the Moabite stone, after which the two scripts begin clearly to diverge. The extreme dates therefore are *c.* 1200–1000 B.C. (according to the date assigned to Aḥirâm)[1] and 850 B.C. Certain letters, whose forms are crucial for this inquiry, however, certainly allow these limits to be considerably reduced. On the one hand, the Phoenician ד has no tail before the inscription from Zinjîrlû (*c.* 850 B.C.) on which one makes its first appearance; consequently the Greek *Δ*, which never has a tail, is likely to have been borrowed before that date.[2] On the other hand, the Phoenician כ, ך first acquires a tail on the same inscription; it never has one before and always has one after it, so that the Greek *K* will probably have been borrowed after that date. In other words, both *Δ* and *K* must have been borrowed very close to 850 B.C., the former hardly after and the latter hardly before that date. So, too, the gradual curving of the tail of *B* and the gradual straightening of that of *M* tell the same tale*. Neither *terminus a quo* nor *terminus ad quem*, however, is absolute. Old forms may not become obsolete everywhere at the same time or may have remained in use long after the latest known instance of their occurrence; or again, new forms may have come into use long before the earliest example so far discovered. The evidence therefore hardly goes beyond suggesting that the Greek alphabet must have been based on forms of the Phoenician letters current about the middle of the eighth century B.C. (s. pp. 192–3 figs. 96–7)*.

Such a date agrees reasonably well with the archaeological and historical evidence. The second millennium B.C. shows little if any trace of Phoenician penetration into Aegean lands, and indeed there seems to have been little Phoenician colonization in them before the eighth century B.C.; scarcely any distinctively Phoenician objects have been found on any Aegean site before that date.[3]

[1] S. p. 105.

[2] Similarly, this sign has no tail on the Hebrew calendar from Gezer (*c.* 1000 B.C.) but one on the inscription in the Pool of Siloam (*c.* 700 B.C.). The tail disappears momentarily from the Phoenician ד on the Cypriot bowl (*c.* 725–700 B.C.), but this is too late to affect the discussion (s. p. 107).

[3] Although the presence of Phoenicians in the West cannot be proved

The earliest period to which written documents in Greece can be assigned is the eighth century B.C. Homer's poems will probably have been orally transmitted in the form of lays for some time before being written down, and the works of Hesiod, who is assigned, though somewhat tentatively, to the same century, may be the first literary compositions to have been immediately committed to writing. This, however, is conjecture of which there is no confirmation, and it does not prove the Greeks to have been generally acquainted with writing in this century. That Lycurgus of Sparta *c.* 800 B.C. was traditionally reported not to have written down his laws has little evidential value either way, as law was often handed down by word of mouth for many generations; Rome had only unwritten laws for several centuries after the introduction of writing, as proved by inscriptions, and before the promulgation of the Twelve Tables. On the other hand, both Zaleucus at Locri *c.* 675 B.C. and Draco at Athens *c.* 625 B.C. had their laws written down, thus attesting the use of writing for official purposes in the seventh century B.C.

These facts tally with the evidence of the earliest inscriptions, which may be approximately dated thus:

| | B.C. |
|---|---|
| Athens (Hymettus, Dipylon) | 750–600 |
| Argolis | 700–600 |
| Corinth | 675–600 |
| Rhodes, Colophon, Teos | *c.* 650 |
| Crete | 650–600 |
| Thera | 625–600 |
| Miletus | 600–550 |
| Samos, Siphnos, Melos, Ceos, Sparta | 600–500 |
| Naucratis (Abû Simbel) | *c.* 590 |
| Argos | 575–550 |
| Naxos | 525–475 |

The earliest possible date for inscriptions therefore appears to be the middle of the eighth century B.C. Other facts are approximately in harmony with this conclusion. The Olympic lists begin with 776 B.C., but their accuracy before the sixth century is disputed, and it is not known when oral tradition may have given place to written record, possibly not till a century after their commencement; and the lists of Athenian

before the 8th–7th centuries B.C., this is only a negative conclusion; their influence may well have reached some of the Mediterranean islands before this, possibly so far back as the 11th century B.C. (Albright in 'B.A.S.O.R.' LXXXIII 20–1).

archons begin with 683 B.C. These points suggest that, although odd words or brief texts were put privately on vases and so on in the eighth century, writing was not developed enough for public inscriptions much before the seventh century B.C.

In conclusion, then, if the Greeks borrowed the alphabet not long before or in the middle of the ninth century B.C., the following two centuries would be a period of adaptation and experiment; during this time the changes necessary to convert it from use with the Phoenician to use with the Greek language would occur and enough enterprising persons, merchants and artists, and the like, would familiarize themselves with the new invention to carry it across the islands to the mainland of Greece; and by the middle of the seventh century it would be sufficiently well known to be suitable for public purposes*. An artist may sign a work of art or a merchant may keep his accounts by methods known only to himself, but public notices which no one but the draughtsman can understand are inconceivable; private invention and experiment normally precede the public adoption of a novelty, and time must be allowed for both these factors as well as for the slow *tempo* of ancient life and travel in the development of the alphabet.

The Greeks, when they took over the Semitic alphabet, at the same time adapted it to the needs of an Indo-European language and so made it to all intents and purposes universal.

In the Semitic languages the fundamental element in the root of a word is the consonants, while the vowels are accidental; they are, of course, essential to its pronunciation but they serve merely to modify its basic sense: for instance, while the idea of killing was inherent in *q-t-l* as the root, the distinction between *qatal*(*a*) 'he killed' and *qutil*(*a*) 'he was killed' was shown only by the changed vocalization. Every consonant was thus followed by a vowel and this might in certain circumstances even fall away. Consequently, the Semites could write only the consonants and leave the reader to supply the vowels as the context and his own sense suggested. In the Greek language the vowels were of equal value with the consonants and had therefore to be represented in the written word; words consisting entirely or almost entirely of vowels could not in fact have been written in any Semitic script.

The Greeks, however, found certain symbols in the Phoenician alphabet representing sounds which they did not possess. These were the glottal *'ālep̄* (א) and *hē'* (ה), the pharyngeal *ḥēṯ* (ח) and *'ayin* (ע), and the so-called half-vowels *wāw* (ו) and *yôḏ* (י). They therefore took the symbols for *'ālep̄* and *hē'* for the vowels which seemed to their ears to begin these words, namely *A* and *E*, disregarding the initial sounds (' and *h*). They similarly took *ḥēṯ* for *H*, since that sound immediately followed the discarded initial sound (*ḥ*). They then took the half-vowels or half-consonants *wāw* (*w* or *u̯*) and *yôḏ* (*y* or *i̯*) for respectively *Y* and *I*, to whose sounds as half-vowels they were most closely akin. Finally, they took the pharyngeal *'ayin* as the last unwanted consonant for *O*, partly because *O* was the only vowel still unrepresented and partly because the Semitic ' showed a preference for the *o*-sound.[1] The augmentation of the sign for *O* or ο (short *ŏ*) to produce *Ω* or ω (long *ō*) was an inner-Greek development which had no connexion became obsolete at a very early date. Second, the Phoenician

Two of these Phoenician letters served also other purposes. First, the Phoenician *wāw*, besides supplying the symbol for *Y*, supplied also that for Ϝ (*digamma*), which represented its original and proper sound; but this letter, like Μ (*san*) and Ϙ (*koppa*),[2] became obsolete at a very early date*. Second, the Phoenician *ḥēṯ*, which represented a hard *ḥ* (pronounced like the Scotch *ch*), was broken up into ⊢ or L (ʽ) to serve as the rough breathing indicating the presence of an *h*-sound and ⊣ or ⅃ (') to serve as the smooth breathing indicating the absence of any *h*-sound.

Thus the Greeks created the first true alphabet in which both vowels and consonants were represented by distinct signs; they added, indeed, three other double consonants (*Φ*, *X*, *Ψ*), but these like the long vowels (*H*, *Ω*) were ultimately found superfluous and disappeared from the derived alphabets*. Other peoples have subsequently revived certain of the old letters or have introduced new letters, but the alphabet of the civilized world is still substantially the Greek alphabet as adapted from its Semitic prototype.

## 11. The Order of the Letters of the Alphabet*

The order of the letters of the Phoenician alphabet, which is substantially the same as that of the Greek alphabet, is a problem that requires some discussion; for, while it is in itself firmly established on trustworthy evidence, the reasons for it are by no means clear and have been keenly disputed.

The Babylonian and Assyrian scribes seem to have established a conventional order for the arrangement of their signs. Thus

[1] Bauer *Urspr. d. Alph.* 41.

[2] These three signs survived only with numerical values (Ϝ = 6, Μ = 900, Ϙ = 90); but the identity of Μ with ϡ is not certain.

Thureau-Dangin[1] has shown that the order of the vowels was *u-a-i-e*; this order is beyond doubt phonetic. Peiser,[2] too, has examined lists containing some 400 signs and by considering overlapping passages has succeeded in reconstituting the order of 200 of them as regularly followed by the scribes; but he admits that the grounds on which this is based have eluded him and is content to suggest that it may have rested on graphic and phonetic principles, in other words now on the forms of the signs and now on the sounds represented by them. Finally, Zimmern,[3] subjecting this list of 200 signs to examination, has remarked on the curious fact that eight or nine of the Sumerian signs, when translated into Accadian words, are not only identical with the names of letters of the Phoenician alphabet but also stand in an order relatively identical with, though distributed into two groups in inverse order to, that of the Phoenician letters. These words may be set out in the following list, in which the Accadian terms are given in the left column and their Hebrew names are set against them in the right column, each accompanied by the number signifying its place in the list or alphabet as the case may be and its meaning:

| | | | |
|---|---|---|---|
| (1) | *mû* 'water' | (1) | *'ālep* 'ox' |
| (17) | *nûnu* 'fish' | (2) | *bêṯ* 'house' |
| (42) | *ênu* 'eye' | (4) | *dāleṯ* 'door' |
| (51) | *pû* 'mouth' | (10) | *yôḏ* 'hand' |
| (52) | *rêšu* 'head' | (11) | *kap* 'palm of hand; bough' |
| (105) | *alpu* 'ox' | | |
| (139) | *idu* 'hand'[4] / *kappu* 'palm of hand; bough'[4] | (13) | *mēm* 'water' |
| | | (14) | *nûn* 'fish' |
| | | (16) | *'ayin* 'eye' |
| (147) | *bîtu* 'house' | (17) | *pē'* 'mouth' |
| (153) | *daltu* 'door' | (20) | *rêš* 'head' |

The author of this scheme then claims that it is only necessary to put *mû–rêšu* after *alpu–daltu* in the Accadian list in order to obtain correspondence with the Phoenician list. This inversion of the two parts of the Accadian list, however, constitutes a great difficulty in the way of accepting the scheme; and the fact that *idu* or *kappu* (whichever reading is chosen) has to be omitted to obtain such correspondence as it has finally destroys its value. What coincidence of order there is can only be fortuitous.[5] The only possible conclusion is that the Accadian

[1] S. pp. 58–9. [2] In *Z.A.* I 95–125. [3] In *Z.D.M.G.* L 667–70.

[4] Sum. *Á* or *ID* = Acc. *idu* and *kappu* (Howardy *C. C.* 600–1 311 13, 17).

[5] There are also words omitted, such as *gamlu* 'throw-stick' and *zânu* 'ornament, equipment', possibly because they are represented by com-

list has no connexion with the Phoenician alphabet, strange as the coincidence may appear; but truth may be stranger than fiction.[1] In fact, it would be more surprising if there was any connexion between the two lists, since the inventors of the Phoenician alphabet were otherwise quite unaffected by the Sumero-Accadian syllabary.

The order of the Phoenician alphabet is attested by the evidence of the Hebrew scriptures and confirmed by external authority. The earliest evidence here is fragmentary; it is the series *ṣ*(צ)–*q*(ק) in the schoolmaster's repetition, if that is rightly so interpreted,[2]* and the series '(א)–*b*(ב)–*g*(ג)–*d*(ד)–*h*(ה) on the step at Lachish.[3] The order of the whole alphabet is assured primarily by various acrostic passages in the Old Testament, although some of these in their present form are corrupt or incomplete[4] and several of them agree in putting *p*(פ) before '(ע),[5] even though this controverts the Greek evidence. The Greek alphabet, too, which provides secondary evidence, shows substantially the same order as the Hebrew. Finally, it agrees with the late numerical values of the letters. The Arabic order partly agrees and partly disagrees with the Hebrew, while the Ethiopic is entirely different*.

The most fantastic reasons for the order of the letters have been suggested based, for example, on astral or lunar theories, even to the extent of using South-Semitic meanings of cognate words to explain the North-Semitic names.[6] Another method has been to seek for mnemonic words which the successive letters when combined into words may spell out; thus '(א)–*b*(ב)–*g*(ג)–*d*(ד) can be made to spell '(*a*)*b*(אב)–*g*(*a*)*d*(גד) 'father–grandfather', and a similar series of common and easily remembered words, now lost, is supposed to have underlain the order of the remaining letters.[7] The idea, however, is open to

pound ideograms, while the list in question contains only simple ones, and *šinnu* ' tooth ', obviously because it is represented by the same ideogram as *pû* ' mouth ', in the Sumerian vocabulary.

[1] S. p. 208. [2] S. pp. 89–90. [3] S. pp. 116–17.

[4] Nah. i 2–14, Pss. ix–x (s. pp. 200–6), xxv, xxxiv, xxxvii, cxi, cxii, cxix, cxlv, Lam. i–iv, Prov. xxxi 10–31, J. b. Sir. li 13–29.

[5] Ps. x 7–8, Lam. ii 16–17, iii 46–51, iv 16–17; cp. Prov. xxxi 25–6 (LXX), J. b. Sir. li 23–5.

[6] The attempt to explain the order of the North-Semitic alphabet by astronomy is particularly absurd, since both Hebrews and Phoenicians seem to have had singularly little interest in it as compared with the Babylonians, who laid its foundations as an exact science*.

[7] Such attempts go back to early Christian writers (Eusebius *Evang. Praep.* [474 b–d] x 5).

several objections.[1] First, the theory, if pursued to its logical end, is liable to produce a succession of consonants that imply words of a form impossible in any Semitic language or, if possible, of unknown meaning; and in fact no such attempt has yet been carried beyond the first half-dozen letters of any Semitic alphabet. Second, even the mnemonic device for the first four letters just mentioned does some violence to the language; for, while *'*ab* 'father' is a North- as well as a South-Semitic word, as attested in extant literature **gad* 'grandfather' is an exclusively South-Semitic word; as such it would be unlikely to have figured in a North-Semitic mnemonic tag, whose purpose would have been defeated by an unfamiliar or unknown word. Third, the theory implies that the nomenclature of the letters preceded their arrangement in order, and this was very possibly what happened; but the mnemonic sentences, on which that order is supposed to be based, are so absurd that there is great difficulty in supposing that anyone could have invented them and then have proceeded to take them as determining the order of the letters.

*Peiser's tentative explanation of the order of the signs in the Accadian syllabaries may or may not be right as applied to them, but it suggests principles which may be applied to the Phoenician alphabet.[2] On such a scheme the alphabet falls into three groups. The first consists of four plosive, the first unvoiced and the other three voiced, (', *b*, *g*, *d*), followed by four fricative (*h*, *w*, *z*, *ḥ*) sounds, and in this last group *h* and *w* are further connected by kinship of usage;[3] and these two sub-groups

[1] The final *reductio ad absurdum* of the theory appears in its application to the Ethiopic alphabet. Its opening letters are *h-l-ḥ-m-ś-r* which have been combined and read as *h(a)-l(e)ḥ(e)m ś(ᵉ'ē)r* 'the bread (is) flesh' (Bauer in *Z.D.M.G.* LXVII 501–2) or 'the fish (is) an omen' (Bartels *ibid.* LXIX 52–8), which is supposed to have been the mnemonic sentence responsible for their order. These, however, are all Hebrew or Arabic words, including the definite article, which finds no place in the Ethiopic language, while *śr* is a solecism for *ś'r*; and no reasons are offered to explain why the Ethiopians made *'alf* the thirteenth letter instead of the sixth letter in their alphabet, when it could have taken its proper place in *ś'r*, nor indeed why they used a foreign language to establish the order of their own alphabet!*

[2] Cp. Taylor 'Alphabet' I 192–5.

[3] For example, the pronominal suffix of the singular third person is written *-ōh* (ה) in pre-classical but *-ô* (ו) in classical texts; the usage of these two letters must have fluctuated in the archaic period (Bauer & Leander *Hist. Gr. d. Hebr. Spr.* I 65). Further, Aramaic often has *h* where Hebrew has *w*, as in Aram. *bᵉhēṯ* (בהת) = Hebr. *bôš* (בוש) 'he was ashamed' (Brockelmann *G.V.G.S.S.* I 52–3). It is further worthy of notice that the Moab. *w* (Y) seems to have given its form to the S.-Sem. *h* (Ψ), which again suggests an affinity between these letters (Lidzbarski *E.S.E.* III 39).

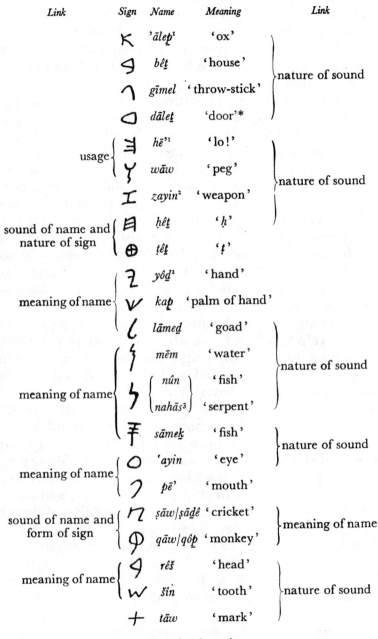

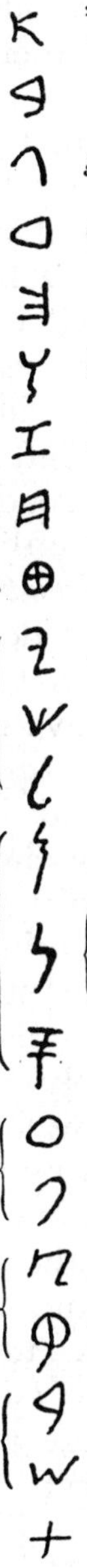

| *Link* | *Sign* | *Name* | *Meaning* | *Link* |
| --- | --- | --- | --- | --- |
| | | *'ālep̱*[1] | 'ox' | nature of sound |
| | | *bêṯ* | 'house' | |
| | | *gīmel* | 'throw-stick' | |
| | | *dāleṯ* | 'door'* | |
| usage | | *hē'*[1] | 'lo!' | nature of sound |
| | | *wāw* | 'peg' | |
| | | *zayin*[2] | 'weapon' | |
| sound of name and nature of sign | | *ḥêṯ* | '*ḥ*' | |
| | | *ṭêṯ* | '*ṭ*' | |
| meaning of name | | *yôḏ*[2] | 'hand' | |
| | | *kap̱* | 'palm of hand' | |
| | | *lāmeḏ* | 'goad' | nature of sound |
| meaning of name | | *mēm* | 'water' | |
| | | *nûn* / *nahās*[3] | 'fish' / 'serpent' | |
| | | *sāmeḵ* | 'fish' | nature of sound |
| meaning of name | | *ʿayin* | 'eye' | |
| | | *pē'* | 'mouth' | |
| sound of name and form of sign | | *ṣāw/ṣāḏê* | 'cricket' | meaning of name |
| | | *qāw/qôp̱* | 'monkey' | |
| meaning of name | | *rêš* | 'head' | nature of sound |
| | | *šîn* | 'tooth' | |
| | | *tāw* | 'mark' | |

[1] Connected as glottal sounds.

[2] Connected as fricative sounds.

[3] S. p. 165, n. 4.

FIG. 94. Factors determining the order of the letters of the alphabet.

are linked by beginning with phonetically similar sounds, since ʼ and *h* are both glottal sounds, although the manner of articulation is different. Then *ḥ* (*ḥêṯ*) is followed by *ṭ* (*ṭêṯ*), inserted here because of the assonance of their names; further, their juxtaposition is re-inforced by the fact that both are secondary or compound signs. As then the first group terminates (apart from the inserted *ṭ*) with fricative sounds, so the fricative *y* begins the second group. This is arranged in four overlapping sub-groups. In the first the fricative *y*, which is at the same time a liquid sound, is naturally connected with the liquid *l*-*m*-*n*, but the sequence is interrupted by *k*, inserted here because the names of *y* (*yôḏ*) and *k* (*kap̄*) are similar in meaning, since the former denotes 'hand' and the latter denotes or may denote 'palm of hand',[1] which *l* (*lāmeḏ*) 'goad' follows as denoting an instrument held in the hand; in the third *l*-*m*-*n* are all sonants; in the fourth *m* (*mēm*)–*n* (*nûn*)–*s* (*sāmeḵ*) are brought together on the score of meaning, the first denoting 'water' and the second two 'fish'[2] which live in that element. Again, as the last sub-group ends with the fricative *s*, so the fricative ʻ opens the next group. This begins with ʻ (*ʻayin*) and *p* (*pēʼ*), meaning respectively 'eye' and 'mouth' and therefore put together as describing organs of the body; but these letters also represent respectively a fricative and a plosive sound and are naturally followed by two other letters representing respectively a fricative and a plosive sound, namely *ṣ* (*ṣāw*) and *q* (*qāw*), which seem originally to have had assonant names and subsequently to have acquired other names possibly with kindred meanings,[3] and further are both compound signs for which there is no other obvious place. These are followed by the only alveolar sounds in the old alphabet, namely *r* (*rêš*) and *š* (*šîn*), and their juxtaposition may have been aided by the meaning of their names, since the first denotes 'head' and the other may for this purpose have been explained as 'tooth', whatever it may originally have denoted.[4] Finally *t* is added at the end as having some affinity with *š*, whose place it takes in certain circumstances in the Aramaic dialects. Possibly, too, the forms

[1] See p. 163.

[2] Incidentally, if *sāmeḵ* means 'support' (s. pp. 165–6), its position at the end of the middle group is not easily explained.

[3] S. pp. 166–7. The alternative order of פ–ע–צ–ק (s. p. 179) may have been due to doubt regarding the order of the fricative-plosive-fricative-plosive or plosive-fricative-fricative-plosive sounds. So שׂ originally preceded שׁ (Nestle *Actes du XI^me^ Congrès des Orientalistes* IV 113–16)*.

[4] S. p. 163.

of the letters have contributed something to their order:[1] for example, the signs for *y* and *k*, those for *m* and *n* and for ʿ and *p*, respectively have certain resemblances which may have suggested or confirmed their juxtaposition (s. p. 183 fig. 94)*.

It is then submitted that this explanation of the arrangement of the alphabet, even if it is fanciful in parts, is not so wholly fantastic as those based on celestial theories; at the same time it is in harmony with Semitic modes of thought, since similar principles can be shown to be at work in other parts of the Semitic world. Thus, as Lidzbarski[2] has shown, three distinct mnemonic principles have played a part in the ordering of the signs in the native Accadian syllabary commonly called *Syllabar A*: signs of similar shape ([cuneiform], [cuneiform]; [cuneiform], [cuneiform]; [cuneiform], [cuneiform]; [cuneiform], [cuneiform]) or with similar syllable-values (*li*, *la; zu*, *za; nu*, *na; ma*, *mu*) or with similar word-values (*ênu* 'eye', *pû* 'mouth', *rêšu* 'head', *libbu* 'heart'; *abu* 'father', *ummu* 'mother') are grouped together. In the Arabic alphabet the shape of the signs is a dominant factor, as in ب ت ث (*b–t–ṯ*), ج ح خ (*j–ḥ–ḫ*) and د ذ ر ز (*d–ḏ–r–z*); sometimes shape and/or phonetic value both operate, as in س ش ص ض ط ظ (*s–š–ṣ–ḍ–ṭ–ṭ/ḏ̣*) and ف ق ك (*f–q–k*);[3] and similarity of use also plays its part, as in ه و ي (*h–w–y*).[4] In the Ethiopic alphabet shape accounts for the order of ሀ ለ ሐ መ ሠ (*h–l–ḥ–m–š*) and ኀ ነ አ ከ (*ḫ–n–ʾ–k*) and ወ ዐ (*w–ʿ*) and phonetic value accounts for that of ፈ ፐ (*f–p*), while a combination of phonetic value and assonance of name determines the order of ጠ ጰ ጸ ፀ (*ṭ–p̣–ṣ–ḍ*), since the first two and the last are plosive and the first and the last two are alveolar sounds.[5] It may be added that the reason why the meanings of the names are not factors is that they have been corrupted or lost in the Arabic alphabet and that few traces of them remain in the Ethiopic alphabet*. The value of these comparisons, however, lies in utilizing them not as proof of a theory but as showing that that theory is within the bounds of human possibility.

## 12. The Time and Place of the Invention of the Alphabet

An attempt must now be made to find answers to the two questions of the time and place of the invention of the alphabet.

[1] Cp. Kautzsch & Cowley 'Hebr. Gr.' 29–30.
[2] In *E.S.E.* I 135–6.
[3] Cp. Petrie 'The Formation of the Alphabet' 20.
[4] Cp. Schwarz in *Z.D.M.G.* LXIX 59–62; s. Jensen *Gesch. d. Schr.* 131.
[5] Cp. Nöldeke *Beitr. z. Sem. Sprachw.* 131[5]. The form is a late factor in determining the order of the letters.

In this connexion Sethe[1] has drawn attention to the following points and reaches certain tentative conclusions. He argues that the earliest Byblian inscriptions show a fully developed system of writing requiring very little improvement to meet future needs, and that it has undergone no essential modification in subsequent centuries, at any rate as applied to a Semitic speech. These inscriptions are so written that the signs follow one another in logical order and in regular lines, and the words are separated by a dividing mark[2] such as Accadian scribes very rarely[3] and Egyptian scribes never employed. So advanced a stage of writing demands a long period of evolution and development; the script cannot have sprung from its inventor's head so perfect an instrument of expression as it is found to be already in the fifteenth century B.C. or thereabouts. Its inventor or inventors, moreover, had no particular or practical acquaintance with the Babylonian system, although that was known in Syria and Palestine from *c.* 2750 B.C. till 550 B.C. and was in full use, though probably only in strictly limited circles, in these countries in the fifteenth and fourteenth centuries B.C. These facts put back its invention before *c.* 1500 B.C. Albright,[4] indeed, argues that the Phoenician alphabet must have been posterior to the reduction of the North-Semitic sounds to twenty-two, since the additional sounds are still distinguished in the Egyptian phonetic transliterations of foreign words in texts of the XVIIIth dynasty (*c.* 1500–1400 B.C.);[5] but the argument is without force, since the Phoenicians, unlike the Arabs,

[1] In *Göttingen* 1916, 55–60 and 1917, 467–8.

[2] S. p. 42. Phoenician inscriptions from Gebal, except that of Abibaal, have the words divided by a stroke, while that from Zinjîrlû uses points for this purpose The Hebrew Calendar of Gezer has some strokes in the first two lines but then drops them; the Samaritan *ostraca* and the inscription from Siloam regularly use points, while the *ostraca* from Lachish fluctuate in their use of them. The early Aramaic inscription from Arslan Tash and those from Zinjîrlû have points, that from Buraij has occasional points and that from Hamath has strokes, while that from Sûjîn does not indicate the division of the words. The Moabite Stone is unique in separating both words and clauses, the former with points and the latter with strokes. Inscriptions and *papyri* of the Persian period introduce the custom of leaving a space between the words*.

[3] S. pp. 42–43.

[4] In 'J.P.O.S.' VI 81–4.

[5] The South-Semitic alphabets distinguish ح (*ḥ*) and خ (*ḫ*), ع (ʿ) and غ (*ġ*), ت (*t*) and ث (*ṯ*), د (*d*) and ذ (*ḏ*), ط (*ṭ*) and ظ (*ṭ/ḏ*), ص (*ṣ*) and ض (*ḍ*). The LXX recognizes some of these distinctions in the Greek transliteration of Hebrew words, thus showing that the Hebrews still made them in speech although they did not feel the need of indicating them in the script*.

may have thought the distinctions not clear or important enough to require recognition in the written language.[1] The date therefore of the invention of the alphabet must have been well before 1500 B.C., but that it antedates the Sinaitic inscriptions (*c.* 1850–1500 B.C.) cannot be proved but is possible. The same fact, that the inventors show no knowledge of the Sumero-Babylonian system, suggests that the locality of their invention must be sought outside Canaan, in some place where Babylonian influence cannot have been felt; for the lands in which Canaanite dialects were spoken were from *c.* 2500 to 1250 B.C. strongly influenced by Babylonian culture. At the same time the Phoenician alphabet shows marked traces of Egyptian influence; it cannot, however, have been invented on Egyptian soil, where it would have been stifled at birth or if born have made no progress against the dead-weight of Egyptian tradition, already of hoary antiquity and in the hands of a powerful priesthood. The place therefore where the Byblo-Phoenician alphabet was invented was in all probability somewhere not only outside Canaan and beyond the wide range of Babylonian influence but also outside Egypt and out of danger from Egyptian vested interests; the obvious place would be a district in the immediate neighbourhood of Egypt occupied by a Semitic people preferably of Canaanite stock. In the same way the period would be one when there was a culturally advanced Semitic race or tribe in such a district and when the rulers of Egypt were well-disposed towards Semitic settlers on their borders, even if they were not actually of Semitic stock.

Some of Sethe's arguments, indeed, have weight, but others are disputable; and the weakest link in the chain is the disregard of the distinction between the pictographic and linear forms of the North-West Semitic scripts. Consequently Obermann[2] is clearly on the right track when he argues that, just as there are four or, if the Ethiopic script is included, five types of South-Semitic script preceding the final Arabic script, so there may well have been several North-Semitic types preceding the historic Phoenician type; accordingly he derives the Phoenician form of the North-Semitic group from a proto-Semitic complex set in a wider rather than a narrower context. He sees this pre-Phoenician script as the parent of four distinct types of scripts, that of Shechem and Lachish, the Ugaritic and Phoenician, and the Graeco-Italic scripts. In theory, in so far as it concerns

[1] Several pairs of sounds (*t-ṭ*, *d-ḍ*, *ṭ-ṭ*, *ʿ-ġ*) are not distinguished in the Ethiopic alphabet or apparently language. [2] In 'P.A.O.S.' IX 2–3, 43–4.

the first three types, this may be accepted as a reasonable hypothesis; but the inclusion of the third and fourth types is open to the objection that there is considerable evidence of a direct connexion between the Phoenician and the Greek alphabets at a very different epoch, namely the ninth century B.C.[1]

Bea,[2] approaching the problem from the same point of view, tries to press the argument farther home. He argues that, while the proto-Sinaitic script was certainly earlier than those of Shechem and Lachish, all three are interconnected; for what was the source of these two later scripts, if they were independent of the Sinaitic script? But they evidently owed their linear form to the Byblian inscriptions, since there was nowhere else whence it could be derived. Two distinct types of script, the pictographic Sinaitic and a non-Sinaitic linear script, therefore, must already have existed side by side. The South-Semitic scripts, however, although they show clearly Sinaitic traits, exhibit also non-Sinaitic peculiarities; obviously therefore these and the North-Semitic scripts, which, though demonstrably pictographic in origin, are clearly linear in their earliest known form, have a common element which did not lie in the Sinaitic system. Again, the North-Semitic system was clearly known to the inventor of the Ugaritic script. On the one hand, his use of clay and wedge-shaped signs, often strongly recalling those of the Sumero-Accadian syllabary, as well as three separate signs for *'ālep̱* according to the accompanying vowel (*a*, *e* or *i*, *u*) proves his acquaintance with the East-Semitic system;[3] on the other hand, his simplification of it by otherwise employing only signs representing consonants without inherent vowels and his development of a number of signs closely resembling those of the West-Semitic alphabet equally proves his acquaintance with that system. This argument, too, then postulates the existence of a proto-Semitic script, though one from which both the Byblo-Phoenician and the Ugaritic alphabets may be derived.

Now Scharff[4] has shown that the Egyptian hieroglyphs for hand, ear and eye, originally bore Semitic names, although these afterwards gave way to Egyptian names with the eventual development of the native language;[5] and he thinks that the hieroglyphic script came into being shortly before 3000 B.C.

[1] S. p. 176. [2] In *St. T.* [126] VI 28–33. [3] S. pp. 58–9.

[4] In *Bayern* 1942 III 68–71.

[5] Namely *ỉd** [afterwards called *ğr.t*] 'hand' (cp. Hebr. *yāḏ* 'hand'), *ʿyn* ['beautiful' and afterwards *ỉr.t*] 'eye' (cp. Hebr. *ʿayin* 'eye'), *ỉdn* (*w*) ['vicegerent' and afterwards *msğr*] 'ear' (cp. Arab. *'uḏn* 'ear').

Thus it was considerably later than the Sumerian cuneiform script, whose beginning went back to a period before 3500 B.C.[1] There was, of course, no external connexion between cuneiform and hieroglyphic systems, but their inner forms had so much that was common to each that Falkenstein[2] was able to claim that the Egyptian was closely related in type to the Babylonian system.

Bea[3] then argues that a knowledge of the Sumerian pictographic script would seem to have reached the Egyptians at some point where they had dealings or lived in contact with Semites and that these had then evolved a form of script essentially resembling the pictographic system of the Sumerians; such a district might well be the eastern Delta. This argument would presuppose that there was already in use *c.* 3000 B.C. in a non-Babylonian territory a pictographic script which, like the Babylonian cuneiform script, was derived from the Sumerian pictographs but had preserved the pictographic forms more truly than the Sumerians and Babylonians, because its West-Semitic inventors were using a different medium of writing than their Mesopotamian kinsmen, for example, stone rather than clay. Such a common origin of Babylonian cuneiform and a western-proto-Semitic pictographic script would account for the resemblances between a number of signs in both systems (e.g. the Sum. ⇨ and the Phoen. ≮ 'ox') and would also explain why not a few Ugaritic signs can be derived with equal plausibility from the Babylonian cuneiform and the Phoenician linear scripts. This western proto-Semitic script naturally became much simplified during the third millennium B.C. and underwent development in the direction of a linear script but with a different rhythm in the various centres or districts where it was employed, though most speedily in the Phoenician coastal towns. Possibly the half-pictographic Byblian inscriptions and that from Baluʿah were two representatives of this development, which, however, failed to come to full fruition and was ultimately checked by the growing use of the Phoenician variety. Once the idea of an alphabet had been evolved, on the Phoenician coast the forms of the letters became attached to these linear scripts while in other parts of the West-Semitic world they clung to the prevailing, more or less pictographic, scripts. Such a twofold development would explain how the scripts from Sinai, Lachish and Shechem, exhibited a predominantly pictographic type, whereas the Byblo-Phoenician type was linear in form as early as *c.* 2000–1780 B.C.; for the fact that Montet has published a jar from a Byblian

[1] S. pp. 6–7. [2] In *Uruk* 65. [3] In *St. T.* [126] VI 33–4.

tomb of this period on which a linear Sem. *ʿ*ayn* and **kapp* are inscribed[1] (s. fig. 95 A) proves that the origin of the linear script can be pushed back to, if not before, such a date. Thus, while the fragments from Shechem and Lachish furnish evidence of a non-Phoenico-linear alphabet, the Byblian jar just mentioned is proof, if the signs inscribed on it are rightly read as letters, of a proto-Phoenician linear script; and the Phoenicians, of whose presence on the Syrian coast there is no evidence before the

A. Supposed alphabetic. signs.

B. Early dynastic trade-marks.

FIG. 95. Marks on early Byblian vases.

sixteenth century B.C.[2] forfeit their claim to have been the inventors of the alphabet, although the credit of this achievement still belongs to the Semites.

Bea's arguments are not altogether sound. Thus there is no shred of evidence to prove the existence of any West-Semitic alphabet in the first half of the third millennium B.C., and nothing is known of any direct contact between the earliest Babylonians and the western Semites whom he supposes to have occupied the eastern Delta in the third millennium B.C. The resemblances, too, between individual cuneiform signs and the earliest possible forms of Phoenician letters, when they are in any degree plausible, are restricted to the representation of common objects, e.g. an ox, which must in their very nature be more or less similarly reproduced all the world over. Finally, the signs on the Byblian vase, to which he appeals, may indeed not be letters but rather the marks of the workman or the workshop, as their finder prefers to regard them (s. fig. 95 B). Yet, if Grimme's recognition of several well-known Semitic words in the three lines of text carved on a Byblian block of stone which is dated *c.* 2100–1700 B.C. (s. pl. 36, 2) is correct,[3] the Semitic alphabet must by then have been fully developed, albeit in an early form, and must already have had a considerable history behind it. Bea, then, in spite of objections to his presentation of the case, is clearly right in postulating the existence of a proto-Phoenician linear alphabet before the appearance of the Sinaitic

[1] In *Byblos et l'Égypte*, *Texte* 159–61; cp. Dussaud in *Syria* XVII 393, who suggests *c.* 1800 B.C.

[2] S. p. 117 n. 2.

[3] S. pp. 92–3.

script. He is also right in detecting some sort of connexion between the various Phoenician and Palestinian scripts and the Sinaitic scripts of the second millennium B.C. and in seeing something common to the North-Semitic and South-Semitic alphabets that must be referred to some other source than the Sinaitic script. The very existence, too, of these diverse scripts argues a long period of experiment before the eventual development of them in their earliest known form,[1] and this must in all probability put back the invention of the alphabet well into the second half of the third millennium B.C.

If then no exact date can be fixed for the invention of the alphabet, the difficulty of identifying its inventor or inventors is greatly increased; the question, indeed, can hardly be answered in the present state of knowledge.

The *Ḫabirū* obviously come into the picture so far as chronology is concerned. They appear in documents *c.* 2750–1350 B.C. as people of various occupations, labourers or even slaves, mercenaries, soldiers of fortune, adventurers or bandits, and they seem to have constituted an element in the 'Hyksos' as also in the early Hebrews. Yet it may also be doubted if the *Ḫabirū* can have reached the West early enough or been culturally advanced enough to have invented or perfected the alphabet; but they must have known of the cuneiform system, even though they may not have made use of it. In any case Moses hardly comes into the question; for, even if dated *c.* 1200 B.C., he has perhaps only been introduced in this connexion after the common practice of attaching great inventions to famous names, just as Ezra the scribe has been credited with the invention of the square Hebrew script.[2] What is the work possibly of many persons spread over several generations is crystallized in a single person by a kind of simplified history.

One of the most advanced, both politically and culturally, of the Semitic peoples at this period were the *Amurrû* of the cuneiform inscriptions. They appeared for the first time in the West

[1] For example, if the proposed decipherment of the proto-Byblian inscriptions (s. pp. 90–1) is proved correct, allowance will have to be made for a stage when some signs still had syllabic values while others had already acquired consonantal values as also for the transition from the time when a complicated syllabary was a priestly mystery till that when a simple alphabet was every man's possession (Dhorme in *C.R.A.I.B.-L.* 1946, 473–5).

[2] Cp. Lidzbarski *N.-Sem. Epigr.* 188–99, where the ancient authorities are fully set out and evaluated.

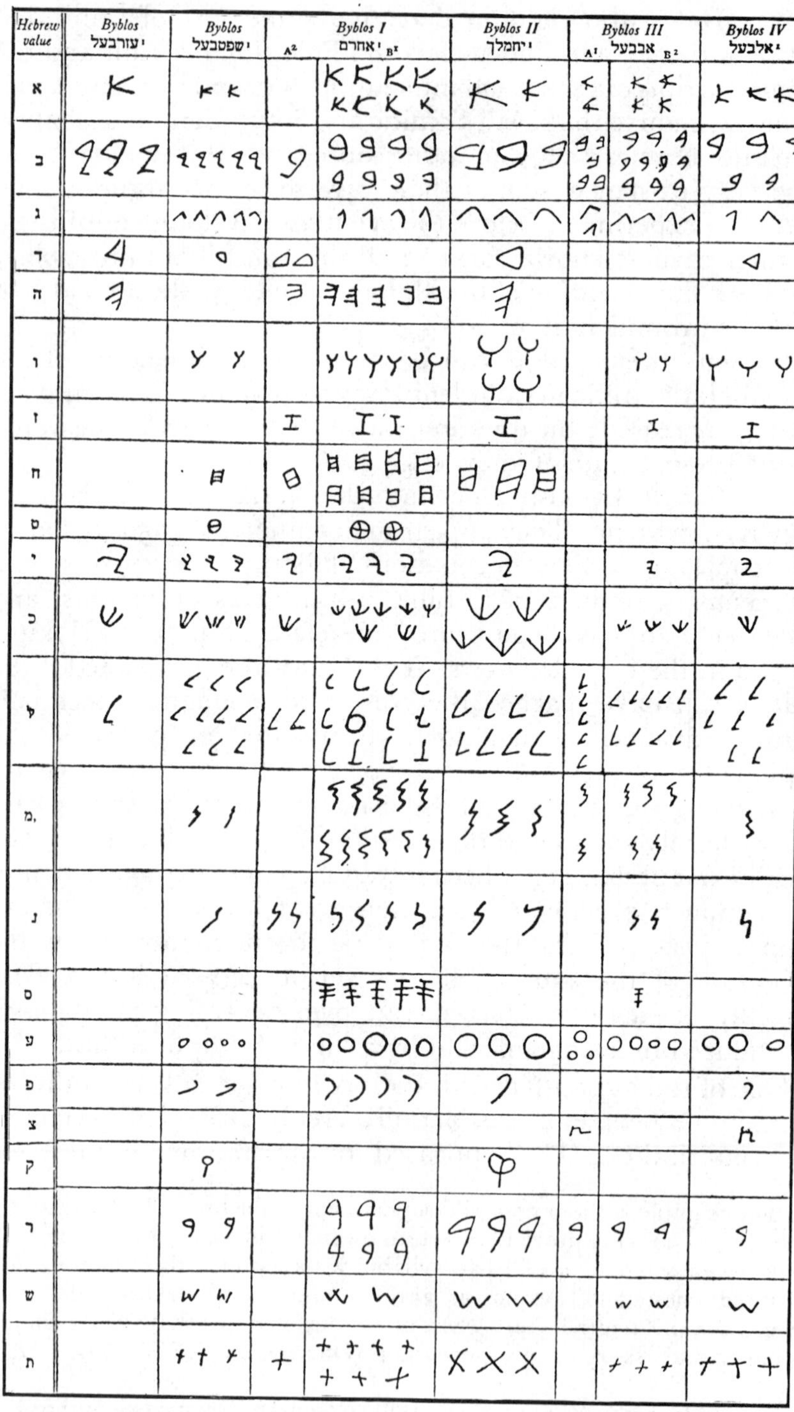
Hebrew value
Byblos עזרבעל¹
Byblos שפטבעל¹
Byblos I A² אחרם¹ B¹
Byblos II יחמלך¹
Byblos III A¹ אבבעל B²
Byblos IV אלבעל¹
א
ב
ג
ד
ה
ו
ז
ח
ט
י
כ
ל
מ
נ
ס
ע
פ
צ
ק
ר
ש
ת

¹ Taken from photographic reproductions. ² Taken from hand-drawn copies.

FIG. 96. Byblo-Phoenician alphabet*.

| Spatula of עורבעל [1] | אדי | Zinjirlu כלמו [2] | Sidon Cypriote bowl [1] | Nora [1] I II | Arslan Tash [1] | Ur [2] | Hebrew value |
|---|---|---|---|---|---|---|---|
| | | | | | | | א |
| | | | | | | | ב |
| | | | | | | | ג |
| | | | | | | | ד |
| | | | | | | | ה |
| | | | | | | | ו |
| | | | | | | | ז |
| | | | | | | | ח |
| | | | | | | | ט |
| | | | | | | | י |
| | | | | | | | כ |
| | | | | | | | ל |
| | | | | | | | מ |
| | | | | | | | נ |
| | | | | | | | ס |
| | | | | | | | ע |
| | | | | | | | פ |
| | | | | | | | צ |
| | | | | | | | ק |
| | | | | | | | ר |
| | | | | | | | ש |
| | | | | | | | ת |

[1] Taken from photographic reproductions.    [2] Taken from hand-drawn copies.

FIG. 97. Phoenician alphabet*.

in the reign of Sargon of Agade (*c.* 2751–2696 B.C.) and in the East they gave Babylon its brilliant first dynasty (*c.* 2169–1870 B.C.);[1] thereafter they played a considerable part in Semitic history for many centuries, while in the fifteenth and fourteenth centuries B.C. they established a state in the Phoenician *hinterland* of which the capital city was possibly Kadesh on the Orontes, penetrating also into Palestine proper, where they survived after the twelfth century B.C. as a legendary people under the name of 'Amorites' in the pages of the Old Testament.[2] They were perhaps not so much an ethnic as a political unit, as perhaps the Hebrews were after them, and as such might be the most likely group from which the genius who invented the alphabet might have sprung. Their kinsmen, the Moabites, who were also a Semitic people, might also be thought worthy of consideration in this connexion; for the earliest inscribed objects so far discovered in territory occupied by Western Semites are those from Teleilat-elGhassûl in Moab, dated *c.* 2500–2100 B.C.,[3] and the earliest form of the South-Semitic alphabet is that found on the fragmentary inscription dated *c.* 1250 from Balu'ah in the same country,[4] while the Moabite Stone of the ninth century B.C. shows the most advanced form of the North-Semitic script known at that period.[5] Clearly the Moabites had evolved a civilization as highly developed as that of any neighbouring Semitic people at a very early date and might well have been capable of inventing an alphabet. Of these three peoples, then, the *Ḫabirū* seem unlikely on several grounds, while either the Amorites or the Moabites may on the same grounds have invented or have played some part in inventing and developing the alphabet; but proof is lacking to clinch the argument. Too little is as yet known of their respective histories to know to which, if to either, of them the honour belongs. Time alone may settle the question.

The authors of the Sinaitic inscriptions, which may be dated at some time between 1850 and 1500 B.C.,[6] may have come out of Egypt, as the bilingual (Egyptian and Sinaitic) sphinx suggests, although this is not conclusive evidence. Already by the middle of the XIIIth dynasty (*c.* 1788–? B.C.) the valley of the Nile had been subject to an ever increasing stream of Semitic immigrants who served as soldiers of fortune and workers of various kinds; and in course of time some of these

[1] Or preferably 1894–1595 B.C. on the new chronology (Smith 'Alalakh' 27–31).
[2] Forrer in *Rl.A.* I 99–100.
[3] S. pp. 90–1.
[4] S. p. 123.
[5] S. pp. 108–9.
[6] S. pp. 94–8.

attained high positions, as the stories of the Beni Hasan, Abraham and Joseph, show. These people were the precursors of the 'Hyksos', a Semitic shepherd-people of Canaanite origin, who overran Egypt from the East towards the end of this dynasty and established there a dynasty which lasted till their defeat, *c.* 1600–1550 B.C., when they fell back on Palestine*. If then the inventors of the Sinaitic script came from Egypt, they might be someone like the *ʿꜣm·w* of the *Rṯn·w*[1] mentioned on the monuments of Ammenemet III (*c.* 1849–1801 B.C.). They are unlikely to have been the Hyksos themselves who, although they acquired a certain amount of Egyptian culture during their sojourn in Egypt, were at heart a nomad and pastoral people and have left no written records of their brief glory.[2] During this period the Sinaitic peninsula had come to be permanently occupied by an Egyptian garrison owing to the importance of the turquoise extracted from its mines, and the nomad Semitic tribes of the neighbourhood, called the *Mnṯy·w*, were kept in subjection by force of arms; what little, however, is known of these tribes does not suggest that they could have been the inventors of any alphabet, since they were pure Bedouin without even the barest elements of a civilization. In any case, whoever invented the Sinaitic script, it was probably not so much 'the missing link'[3] between Egyptian hieroglyphs and Phoenician alphabet as one link in a complex chain of development which has not yet been fully unwound.[4]

The Phoenicians, according to ancient tradition, came from the shores of the Indian Ocean, including the Persian Gulf.[5] From their name, if the Greek *φοῖνιξ* 'palm-tree' is its source, they came from a land of palm-trees such as Arabia is and Phoenicia is not; and one of their gods, called *Μωτ* in Greek sources, has left his name not only in the Arabian 'Ḥaḍramaut' which may mean 'the settlement of *Môt*', but in a number of early place-names in Palestine and elsewhere;[6] and the texts from Ugarit give a hint of Phoenicians in this same district. Possibly then they were a Semitic tribe which reached the Mediterranean coast as part of the same great movement which brought the

[1] Cp. Butin in 'H.T.R.' XXV 155 and Eisler in 'J.R.A.S.' 1923 179.

[2] Cp. Bea in *St. T.* [126] VI 22–3.

[3] S. pp. 141–4.

[4] Cp. Diringer in 'J.A.O.S.' LXIII 24–30.

[5] Herodotus *Hist.* i 1, vii 89.

[6] Hebr. חצרמות and Arab. حضرموت; this is the same name as the Mysian *Adramyttium* and the Tunisian *Hadrumete*. Other place-names containing the name of this god are עַזְמָוֶת (LXX, *Αζμωθ*) and יַרְמוּת (LXX, *Ιεριμουθ*) in Palestine (s. p. 199 n. 4). Cp. *Ιερμωθ* (Eusebius *ap.* Lagarde *Onom. Sacr.* 169. 63).

Aramaeans and Hebrews to their historic homes in the West; and it is significant that the first mention of them occurs in Egyptian inscriptions *c.* 1575 B.C.[1] It might therefore be conjectured that the Phoenicians or a branch of them played a part, if not in the invention, at any rate in the transmission of the alphabet from the south to the north, whence the knowledge of it was spread far and wide by their commercial activity, as Greek and Latin historians averred. They were certainly quick-witted and practical enough to see the advantages of the new invention and to turn it to their own use but probably not culturally gifted enough to have made so remarkable a discovery, even if that were chronologically possible; they were 'adapters rather than inventors'.[2] Yet here again, as so often in life, the genius who makes the discovery is forgotten while his successor, who turns it to practical use, gives his name to it.

The conclusion of the matter then is this. The Sumerians invented writing on clay by means of pictographic signs and devised a method of using these to render syllables; they also accidentally isolated four of the five vowels. The Babylonians developed the use of these signs for syllables and employed this syllabic script in continuous texts of every kind, interspersed with ideographs; the Persians invented the simplest form of syllabic script based on the cuneiform system. The Egyptians had early devised their own system of hieroglyphs which they carried forward through the hieratic and demotic stages of cursive writing; they also adapted their signs for occasional use as syllables and even as consonants but never used them so in continuous texts except for a brief experimental period. It was the merit of the western Semites that they saw the importance of this discovery and, discarding the whole cumbrous machinery of ideographic and syllabic scripts and providing that each sound was represented by only one sign, made a simple alphabet the vehicle of written thought. Who first took this step is and may always remain unknown; all that can be said is that he or they were sprung in all probability from one or other of the Semitic peoples who came into contact with the Egyptians *c.* 2500–1500 B.C. and that it was taken in or near Egypt, and that the invention was developed in Palestine and perfected on the Phoenician coast.[3] At this early

[1] S. p. 117 n. 2. [2] Rawlinson 'Phoenicia' 59–61.

[3] The theory of Conder and Naville, that the Pentateuch can have been written only in the Babylonian language and in the cuneiform script on tablets of clay (s. Cowley 'Aram. Pap.' xxv–xxvi) is not supported by the history of the alphabet (s. p. 79 n. 9).

stage three types of alphabetic script were evolved, a mixed pictographic-linear, a cuneiform, and a true linear script; the two former soon died out while the latter survived to be carried by the Phoenicians overseas to Greece, where separate signs were devised and whence the completed alphabet passed to all the nations of the western hemisphere—one, and only one, of the gifts of the Semites to mankind.

# APPENDIX

## I

THE following samples of the proposed interpretations of the principal pre-Hebraic inscriptions found in Palestine will show how diverse and therefore uncertain they are.

P. 98 fig. 41: *ḥ-w-m* (Taylor in 'J.P.O.S.' x 17) or *b-l-y* (Taylor ibid. 79–81), *b-n y-* . . . = 'son of Y. . . .' or *b-n-y* = . . . 'sons of . . .' (Butin *ap.* Taylor ibid. 80; s. 'H.T.R.' xxv 155, 200–1), *'-y-b* = 'Job' (Grimme in *A.Of.* x 268) or *ṭ-y-b* = 'incense' (Grimme *Altsin. Forsch.* 114; s. *Muséon* LV 57–8), [*l*-]*k-l-b* (Ginsberg *ap.* Yeivin in 'P.Q.S.' LXIX [1937] 186–7)*.

Ibid. fig. 42: *r-'-š š-'-r-'* = 'the top of the gate (Böhl in *Z.D.P.-V.* LXI 21–4), *b-z r-g-m-m-z-r* = 'in this (place lies) Regem-mazzir' (Grimme *Muséon* LV 51–4), [. . .]*d r-ḥ m-m '-r* = '. . . of wind, water, light' (Obermann in 'J.B.L.' LVII 248–51), (?)*-d-r-y/k-š-š-*$\frac{(?)}{b}$*-r* with *b* corrected by another letter written over it (Kahane in 'B.J.P.E.S.' XII 30–5), *r-ḥ-m-m y-r-ḥ* 'have mercy indeed, O Yerach'[1] (Maisler in 'J.P.O.S.' XVIII 283–6).

Ibid. fig. 43: *d/ṣ-r-n-t* (Gardiner in 'Times' 16 Jul. 1937, p. 12 col. iv), *d-r-n-s* (Gaster ibid. 30 Jul. 1937, p. 10 col. ii), *d-r n-s* = 'the house of the banner' or *d-r m-s* = 'house of tribute' or 'the house of the banner' or 'the house of Ra'mose (Obermann in 'P.A.O.S.' IX 31–3), *b-r n-s* = 'the son of the fugitive' (Böhl in *Z.D.P.-V.* LXI 20–1), *b-r-l-m* (Yeivin in 'B.J.P.E.S.' V 8–9), *s-r-y z* = 'this (is) Seraiah'[2] (Grimme in *Muséon* LV 56–7).

P. 99 fig. 44 A: *y*-symbol of death-*m* (Grimme *ap.* Bea in *St.T.* VI 8), (?)*-ḥ-*(?) (Böhl in *Z.D.P.-V.* LXI 25).

Ibid. fig. 44 B: *m-š-'-l* | *l-'-m* (Sukenik in *Kedem* II 15).

Ibid. fig. 46: *l y-r-g*(?) (Gaster in 'P.Q.S.' LXIX [1937] 57), *l y-r-d* (Böhl in *Z.D.P.-V.* LXI 17).

Ibid. fig. 47: *b-l-'* = 'swallow'[3] (Sayce *ap.* Albright in *A.Of.* V 151; s. 'P.Q.S.' XXV [1893] 31) or 'Bela'[4] (Albright in *A.Of.* V 150–2)*.

P. 100 fig. 48: *'-n*(?)*-t-'-b-'-l-l-l* = 'Anata'-Ba'llil'[5] (Langdon in 'Times' 17 Oct. 1936 p. 8 col. iii); [. . .]*l-z-q w-b-'-h n-s-k* = '[vessel] for straining and testing the libation' (Grimme *Altsin. Forsch.* 165–7); [*'-n-p w-*]*g-p-r y-'-d w-ḥ-l-ṣ* = '[he was angry but] he forgave, he threatened but he rescued'[6] (Obermann in 'P.A.O.S.' IX 37–8).

[1] A name of the moon-god.

[2] Cp. Hebr. שְׂרָיָה(וּ).

[3] Verb, not noun.

[4] Cp. Hebr. בֶּלַע.

[5] A supposed syncretistic deity composed of ענת and *Ba'al-lil* 'the lord of the night' or 'of the wind' after the model of the Jud.-Aram. ענתביתאל = 'Anath (consort) of Bēth-'ēl and ענתיהו = 'Anath (consort) of Yāhû in Egypt.

[6] Cp. Hos. vi 1.

Ibid. fig. 49 A: *z-d-q-w q-t-.-y w-(?)-y-(?)-h* = 'his righteousness (is) my hand and . . .' (Langdon in 'Times' 5 Oct. 1935 p. 8 col. iii; s. Driver ibid. 10 Oct. p. 10 col. iv), [*z-w k-p*]*-k t-š-l-š d-* . . . = 'this (is) thy bowl for a threefold [libation]' (Stawell in 'P.Q.S.' LXVIII [1936] 97–9), *b-š-l-š-t* [. . .] = 'because of three . . .' (Albright in 'B.A.S.O.R.' LXIII 9), *b-š-l-š-t y-m y-*[*r*]*-ḥ* = 'on the third day of the month' (Dussaud in *Syria* XVI 419), *b-š-l-š-t y-*[*m-g-r ṣ-ḥ*] = 'for a third time may he overthrow . . .' (Yeivin in 'P.Q.S.' LXIX [1937] 180–4), *b-š-l-š-t h-n y-s-k* or *y-n h-s-k* (Torczyner *ap.* Leibovitch in *A.S.A.É.* XL 117–18), *d-š-l-š-t* = 'of (a person named) *Šlšt*' (Obermann in 'P.A.O.S.' IX 21–3); *p š-l-š-t y-ʿ-y ʾ-ḥ* = 'here (are) three shovels of the brazier' (Grimme *Altsin. Forsch.* 119–20).

Ibid. fig. 49 B: *z g-w* = 'this is (the) back' (Gaster in 'P.Q.S.' LXIX [1937] 142–3), *q-n z b-ʿ-*[*l* . . .] 'vessel which Baal . . .' (Obermann in 'P.A.O.S.' IX 40), *l-g q-n-h* 'a log[1] of aromatic reeds' (Grimme *ap.* Obermann ibid. 41[59]). *z-g y-n-h* = 'the jar of her[2] wine' (Grimme *Altsin. Forsch.* 167–8; s. *Muséon* LV 58–9).

Ibid. fig. 49 C: *m-t-n š-g-*[. . .]*-t g-d-l-t* = 'gift of a large . . .' (Gaster in 'P.Q.S.' LXVI [1934] 176–8), *m-t-n ś-g-ʾ* [*l*]*-g-ʾ-l-t* = 'a great gift for redemption' (Eisler *ap.* Grimme in *A.Of.* X 276–7), *m-t-n š-w-*[*r m*]*-t w-ʾ-l-t* = 'gift to Shor[3] Mot[4] and Elat' (Burrows in 'P.Q.S.' LXVI [1934] 179–80 and LXVII [1935] 87–9), *m-t-n š w-*[. . .] *t-w-ʾ-l-t* [*l-* . . .] = 'a gift of a sheep and . . . (as) a favour [to . . .] (Albright in 'B.A.S.O.R.' LXIII 9), *m-t-n š-b .* [*m*]*-ḥ-b ʾ-l-t* = 'gift of *Šb*[5] beloved of the goddess' (Obermann in 'P.A.O.S.' IX 14–15), *m-t-r š-p l-*[*r-*]*ṣ-p ʾ-l-t* = 'reserve' or 'residue: bowl for the glowing stones[6] of the goddess' (Grimme *Altsin. Forsch.* 118–19; s. *A.Of.* X 277–9); *ś-g-*[*ʾ m*]*-t-g ʾ-l t-*[*r-p*] = 'be exalted, have dominion, O God, preserver' (Stawell in 'P.Q.S.' LXVIII [1936] 100–1)*.

P. 102 fig. 50: *g-l-n š-t-r-b-ʾ* (Bea in *St.T.* VI 11).

Ibid. fig. 51: *n-k-g/p-š-t*(?) (Gaster in 'P.Q.S.' LXIX [1937) 58).

Obviously reading and translation in all these cases are mere guess-work. The extreme paucity of the texts and their almost invariably damaged and incomplete state make interpretation extremely hazardous, while their brevity and lack of context render control impossible; consequently imagination is apt to run riot. The transcriptions are often more or less arbitrary and incapable of translation, the translations (when attempted) are equally often based on dubious philology and yield an uncertain, if not improbable, sense. No confidence can be felt in them and no theory of the alphabet can be built on them.[7]

[1] A Hebrew liquid measure (Lev. xiv 10, 12, 15, 21, 24).
[2] Namely, of the goddess.
[3] Cp. Ugar. *Šr* the bull-god.
[4] Cp. Ugar. *Mt* god of death (s. p. 195 n. 6).
[5] Cp. Hebr. שְׁבִי/שְׁבָי and שׁוֹבָב.
[6] Cp. 1 Ki. xix 6 (R.V., marg.).
[7] Cp. Cross in 'B.A.S.O.R.' CXXXIV (1954) 15–24.

## II*

The text of Psalms ix–x [1] is of considerable interest in connexion with the subject of these lectures; for, although it is in some disorder, most if not all of its errors can be remedied by ingenious or skilful emendation, when the acrostic arrangement of the verses is seen to agree with the traditional order of the letters in the Hebrew alphabet.[2]

| | | |
|---|---|---|
| א | אודה יהוה בכל־לבי | אספרה כל־נפלאותיך: |
| | אשמחה ואעלצה בך | אזמרה שמך עליון: |
| ב | בשוב אויבי אחור | יכשלו ויאבדו מפניך: |
| | כי־עשית משפטי ודיני | ישבת לכסא שופט־צדק: |
| ג | גערת גוים אבדת רשע | שמם מחית לעולם ועד: |
| | . . . . . . . . | . . . . . . . . |
| ד | דַּמּוּ הָאוֹיֵב אָבַד זִכְרָם | חֲרָבוֹת וְעָרִים נָתַשְׁתָּ לָנֶצַח |
| | . . . . . . . . | . . . . . . . . |
| ה | הָמָה יְהוָֹה לעולם יָשַׁב | כונן למשפט כסאו: |
| | והוא ישפט תבל כצדק | ידין לאמים במישרים: |
| ו | וַיְהִי יהוה משגב לדך | משגב לעתות בצרה |
| | וַיִּבְטְחוּ בך יודעי שמך | כי־לא עזבת דרשיך יהוה: |
| ז | זמרו ליהוה יושב ציון | הגידו בעמים עלילותיו |
| | כי־דרש דָמָם אֲוָתָם זכר | לא־שכח צעקת עניים: |
| ח | חננני יהוה ראה עניי | מְנַשְּׂאִי וּמְרוֹמְמִי משערי מות |
| | למען אספרה כל־תְּהִלֹּתֶיךָ | בשערי בת־ציון אגילה בישועתך: |
| ט | טבעו גוים בשחת עשו | ברשת זו־טמנו נלכדה רגלם: |
| | נודע יהוה משפט עשה | בפעל־כפיו נוקש רשע: |

הגיון סלה

| | | |
|---|---|---|
| י | ישובו רשעים לשאולה | כל־גוים שכחי אלהים |
| | שיתה יהוה מורה להם | ידעו גוים אנוש הֵמָּה: |

[1] Properly one Psalm, as in the Septuagint and the Vulgate version.
[2] S. p. 181.

IX 2 I will confess, Jehovah, with all my heart,
I will recount all Thy wondrous deeds.
3 I will be glad and exalt in Thee,
I will sing a psalm to Thy name, O (Thou) Most High;
4 because[1] mine enemies are turned back,
(because) they stumble and perish at Thy presence.
5 For Thou hast executed my judgement and my cause,
Thou hast sat on the throne (as) a righteous judge.
6a Thou hast rebuked the heathen, Thou hast destroyed the wicked man,
Thou hast blotted out their name for ever more.
6b . . . . . . . .
. . . . . . . .
7a The enemy are stilled, their memory is perished;
Thou hast utterly uprooted (their) palaces and cities.
7b . . . . . . . .
. . . . . . . .
8 Jehovah long since has thundered and taken his seat,
He has set up his court to do justice.*
9 So now he will judge the world in righteousness,[2]
He will give doom to the nations with equity;
10 So Jehovah became a high retreat to the crushed,
a high retreat against times of need*,
11 and they that knew Thy name did trust in Thee;
for Thou didst not forsake them that sought Thee, O Jehovah.
12 Sing a psalm to Jehovah that sitteth on Zion,
declare His deeds among the peoples,
13 that He that requires their blood has remembered their desire,[3]
(and) has not forgotten the cry of the afflicted.
14 Jehovah, be gracious unto me, behold my affliction,
(Thou) that liftest me up and raisest me from the gates of death,
15 that I may recount all Thy praises
(and) rejoice in Thy salvation in the gates of the daughter of Zion.
16 The heathen are sunk in the pit (that) they have made,
their foot is caught in the net that they have hidden.
17 Jehovah has made Himself known, He has executed judgement,
and the wicked man is ensnared in the work of his own hands.
18 The wicked rush headlong* to Sheol,[4]
(even) all the heathen forgetful of God.
21 Teach them, O Jehovah, a lesson[5]
(that) the heathen may know (that) they are mere men,

[1] Cp. Cheyne 'Book of Psalms' [1888] 22.
[2] Literally 'according to righteousness'.
[3] Or 'lament' in view of the parallel term (s. p. 206, n. on x 17).
[4] Cp. Ps. xc 3.
[5] Literally 'set them . . . a lesson' (s. p. 204, n. on ix 21).

כ כי־לא לנצח ישכח אביון    תקות־ענוים תאבד לעד
קומה יהוה אל־יעז אנוש    ישפטו גוים על־פניך
סלה

ל למה יהוה תעמד ברחוק    תעלים לעתות בצרה
בְּגֵאוּת רשע ידלק עני    יִתְפְּשׂוּ במזמות זו־חָשָׁב :
מ מְהֻלָּל רשע על־תאות־נפשו    ובצע ברך רָשַׁע:
. . . . . . . . .    . . . . . . . . .
נ נאץ יהוה כגבה־אפו    אין אלהים כל־מזמותיו
אָמַר בְּלִבּוֹ בל־ידרש    בל אמוט לדור ודור :
ס סָרִים משפטיך מנגדו    כל־צורריו יפיח בהם
יחילו דְרָכָיו בכל־עת    אַשְּׁרוֹ לא־ברע אלה
* ע עיניו לחלכה יִצְפֹּנוּ    יארב במסתר כאריה בְסֻכָּה
יארב לחטף עני    יחטף עני במשכו ברשתו :
* פ פיהו מָלְאוּ מִרְמוֹת ותך    תחת־לשונו עמל ואון
ישב במארב רַצָּחִים    במסתרים יהרג נקי :
צ ⟨צַדִּיק⟩ יִדְכֶּה ישח    וְנָפְלוּ בעצומיו חלכאים
אמר בלבו שׂכח אל    הסתיר פניו בל־ראה לנצח :
ק קומה יהוה אַל־יִנָּשֵׂא    אל־תשכח אֵל עניים
על־מה נאץ רשע אלהים    אמר בלבו לא־תדרש :
ר רָאִתָה כי־אַתָּה עמל וכעס    תביט לָתֵתוֹ בידך
עליך יעזב חלכה וְיָתֹם    אתה היית עוֹזְרוֹ :
ש שבר זרוע רָשָׁע וָרָע    תדרש רשעו כָּלוֹ תמצא

19 When the poor shall not be utterly forgotten
nor the hope of the humble perish for ever.
20 Arise, O Jehovah, let not mere man prevail;
let the heathen be judged in Thy presence.
1 Why standest Thou afar off, O Jehovah,
(and) hidest (Thine eyes) in times of need*?
2 In swelling pride the wicked man hotly pursues the afflicted
(that) he may take him in the schemes that he has devised.
3 Frantic is the wicked man for his soul's desire
and, reaping unjust gain, he blesses wicked courses.*

. . . . . . . .

. . . . . . . .

4a + c He has contemned Jehovah in his haughtiness
(and) all his schemes are Godless;
6a + 4b he has said in his heart 'He will not require (it);
I shall not be moved to endless generations'.
5b + c Thy judgements pass out of his sight,
he puffeth at all his foes;
5a his ways are stable at all time(s),
6b—7a (if) his feet flag, (it is) not in wrong-doing.*
Deceitful thoughts and oppression fill his mouth,
on his tongue are mischief and naughtiness;
8 he lingers where murderers lurk
(that) he may slay the innocent in secret places.
His eyes spy out the wretched
9 (as) he lurks in secrecy like a lion in its lair;
he lurks to carry off the afflicted,
(that) he may carry off the afflicted by drawing him into his net.
10 The righteous man is crushed (and) bowed down
and the hapless fall by his prowess.
11 He has said in his heart 'God has forgotten,
He has veiled His face; He has not seen (it) at all'.
12 Arise, O Jehovah, let not the down-trodden be forgotten;
O God, forget not the afflicted.
13 Wherefore has the wicked man contemned God?
He has said in his heart 'Thou wilt not require (it)'.[1]
14 Thou hast seen that mischief and spite are with him,
Thou lookest to deliver him into Thy hand.
15 The hapless and the orphan leaves (his plaint) with Thee;
for Thou hast been his helper.
16 Break the arm of the wicked and evil man;
do Thou require his wickedness (of him), finding it all,

[1] Literally 'according to his wickedness' (s. p. 205, n. on x. 3).
[2] Namely, the reason is that he does not expect his wickedness to be required of him.

בל־יוסיף עוד לשפט יתום ודך    לערץ אנוש מן־הארץ

ת תאות־ענוים שמעת יהוה    תָּכֵן־לבם תקשיב אזנך

יהוה ימלך עולם ועד    אבדו גוים מארצו

---

IX 1 אודה] אודך (Houbigant w. SVS$^{H}$), needlessly in view of the changes of person throughout the Psalm[1] or if יהוה is taken in the voc. case and אודה taken with כל־נפלאותיך (cp. Ps. lxxxix 6).

7 האויב תמו] דַּמּוּ הָאֹיֵב (Abbott in *Z.At.W.* xvi 292) or דָּמוּ (Buhl); the substitution of ת for ד is an error of ear (cp. Prov. i 11).

חרבות לנצח transferred after נתשת unchanged (Gunkel) or as altered to לְחָרְבוֹת נֶצַח (Buhl; cp. Ps. lxxiv 3).

וערים] וְעָרֵימוֹ ≐ וְעָרֵיהֶם (Schlögl w. VT).

Alternatively חֳרָבוֹת וערים נתשת לנצח, on the assumption of a Hebr. *חֲרְבָּה = S.-Arab. *mḥrb(n)* 'castle, fortified place' and Arab. *miḥrâb* 'pavilion' (Daiches in 'J.Q.R.' xx 637–9), whence LXX's *οἰκόπεδα* and Vulg.'s *habitationes* in Ps. cix 10 and LXX's *τόποι* in II Chron. xxxiv 6; cp. Is. xliv 26 Ezek. xxxvi 4, 10, 33 (‖ עיר), Is. xliv 26 (w. קומם), Is. lviii 12 Ezek. xxxvi 10, 33 Mal. i 4 Jb. iii 14 (w. בנה) and also Ezek. xxxviii 12 (w. ישב).

לנצח 'to a pre-eminent degree, utterly' transposed after נתשת (Gunkel).

אבד זכרם transposed after †דמו האויב† to preserve the alphabetic order (Gunkel).

7–8 המה : ויהוה] הֵמָּה אָבְדוּ וַיהוָֹה (Ley *Leitf. d. Metr.* 35–6)*.

8 ישב] יָשַׁב (Gunkel) in view of the ‖ כונן; לְעוֹלָם 'from long ago'.*

10 ויהי] וַיְהִי w. SVS$^{H}$ (Merx in *Festschrift . . . Chwolson* 204); otherwise 'that He may be(come) . . .' (s. S. R. Driver 'Tenses'[3] § 62).

11 ויבטחו] וַיִּבְטְחוּ (Gunkel).

13 דרש דמים] דָּמָם (Gunkel w. PVEth.) דָּרַשׁ (Gunkel).

אותם] אַוָּתָם (Gunkel).

14 חנני] חֲנָנֵנִי (Merx ibid. 204 w. 'AJ$^{H}$) } which hardly improve the sense.
ראה] רָאָה (Merx ibid. w. S$^{A}$'AJ$^{H}$) }

משנאי] מְנַשְּׂאַי (Merrick w. H. Mss.).

מרוממי] וּמְרוֹמְמִי (Gunkel w. H. Mss.).

15 תהלתיך] תְּהִלָּתֶךָ (Baethgen w. SΣΘPVJ$^{H}$T.)

17 נוקש] נוֹקַשׁ (Ewald w. SVJ$^{H}$T).

21 שיתה . . . המה transposed after v. 18 (Duhm).

מורה Namely *mawrāh* from √*wrh* = מוֹרָה 'lesson' as *maṣwāh* from √*ṣwh* = מִצְוָה 'command'; cp. Symm.'s *νόμον*, Pesh.'s ܢܡܘܣܐ and Arab.$^{L}$'s سُنَّة النَّامُوس.

X 1 תעלים] תֵּעָלֵם (Houbigant w. T), unless עיניך omitted by ellipse (cp. Is. lvii 11 where Michaelis rightly changes מעולם into מעלים w. SVS$^{H}$).

[1] There is generally no need to emend fluctuations of person in Hebrew poetry, since the same practice, called الْتِفَات by Arab grammarians, is found in Arabic and Persian poetry (Sperber in *Z.A.* xxxii 23–33).

18 (that) he judge not again the orphan and the crushed
(nor) drive mere man by tyranny from the land.
17 Thou hast heard the lament of the meek, O Jehovah;
Thine ear inclines to hear the purpose of his heart.
19 Jehovah shall reign for evermore,
(and) the heathen are perished out of His land.

---

2 בגאות] בְּגֵאוּת (Nowack) or בְּגַאֲוָתוֹ (Olshausen) unless archaic בְּגַאֲוָת = בְּגַאֲוָה.

יתפשו] יִתְפְּשׂוּ (Halévy in *Rech. Bibl.* III 33).

חשבו] חָשֵׁב (Graetz).

3 כי־הלל] מְהַלֵּל (Abbott in *Z.At.W.* XVI 292) or rather מְהֹלָל (Driver *ap.* Leveen in 'J.T.S.' XLV 17). Early Hebrew *k* and *m* are very alike (s. p. 195).

ובצע ברך] ובצע ברך רָשָׁע *i.e.* 'and he flatters himself on successful crime', obtained by transferring רָשָׁע, which is not wanted in first clause, as רָשָׁע to end of second clause*.

בל־ידרש transferred after אמר בלבו in following verse (Leveen ibid. 16).

אין אלהים 'godless' (Driver ibid. 17–18).

מרום] סָרוּ (Abbott ibid. 292 w. S) or סוּרִים (Leveen ibid. 18).

6 אמר בלבו transposed before בל־ידרש in v. 4.

בל אמוט לדר ודר transposed after בל־ידרש in v. 4.

אשר] אֲשֻׁרָיו (Graetz).

6–7 אשר לא־ברע : אלה] אֲשֻׁרוֹ לא־ברע אלה : transposed to follow יחילו דרכו בכל־עת, which lacks a parallel clause*.

7 מלא ומרמות] מְלָאוּ מִרְמוֹת (Delitzsch).

8 חצרים] רֹצְחִים (Graetz) or רַצָּחִים (Driver *ap.* Leveen ibid. 18).

יצפנו] יִצְפֹּנוּן (Hare w. SPV Jer[H]; cp. Ps. xxxvii 32); does a similar error lurk in Prov. i 11 (if נצפנה is an error for נִצְפֶּה־נָּא or some other energic form; cp. Jud. v 26, Is. xxvii 11, xxviii 3, Ob.[13], Prov. i 20, Jb. xvii 16, and Hab. ii 17) and i 18 (where יצפנו may be an error for יִצְפֹּנֻן), as Saʿadyah's version implies?

9 יארב . . . בסכה omitted from Pesh.; but Erpenius has ܛܫܐ ܒܛܘܫܝܐ ܐܝܟ ܐܪܝܐ ܒܡܥܘܢܗ 'he hides secretly like a lion in his lair'.

בסכה] בְּסֻכָּה Ewald.

10 ודכה] צַדִּיק יִדְכֶּה (Abbott ibid. 292–3) or צַדִּיק יִדָּכֶה (Brown).

ונפל] וְנֶפְלוּ (Hare w. V).

בעצומיו] בְּעָצְמוֹ (Mowinckel w. S), unless an abstr. plur. עצומים 'prowess' may be assumed (Leveen ibid. 18–19).

12 אל נשא ידך] יִנָּשֵׂא דָךְ (= אַל־(יִנָּשֶׁה) (Gunkel); cp. Jer. xxiii 39 for this form of the verb.

אל־תשכח] אַל־תִּשְׁכַּח אֵל (Leveen ibid. 19).

14 כי־אתה] אִתֹּה (= כִּי־(אִתּוֹ) (Merx ibid. 206).

לתת] לְתֻתּוֹ (Leveen ibid. 19).

יעזב *sc.* שִׁיחוֹ (Leveen; cp. Jb. x 1).

יתום] וְיָתוֹם (Gunkel; cp. P).

עוזר] עֹזְרוֹ (Wellhausen w. P).

15 רשע ורע] רָשָׁע וָרָע (Buhl).

בל־תמצא] כָּלוֹ תִמְצָא (Leveen ibid. 19).

16 מלך] יִמְלֹךְ (Graetz w. SVS[H]).

17 תאות 'lament' (Driver *ap.* Leveen ibid. 19) from Arab. أرى 'lamented' (Driver in 'J.T.S.' XLIII 153 on Ps. xxxviii 10).

תכין] תֹּכֶן (Buhl w. SΣPVS[H]).

The most striking note in this Psalm is its artificiality, which is seen not only in its acrostic arrangement but also in the frequent repetition of or harping on catchwords; this is indeed characteristic of all alphabetic Psalms (as *passim* in Ps. cxix). A consequence of this appears in the unnatural phrasing of many clauses and the frequent displacement of single expressions and even whole verses; whether then the verses beginning with פ and ע are rightly put in that order may be doubted and they are here reversed by way of experiment. There is indeed some gain in this re-arrangement of these two verses, since there is then a *crescendo* from carrying off the afflicted in the ע-verse to slaying the innocent in the פ-verse. The question then arises whether the other three or four places in which פ precedes ע[1] are not similarly due to textual dislocation.

## III

I take the opportunity, in view of the difficulty in תָּוִי 'my mark' or 'signature' (R.V.) in place of 'my desire' (A.V.), to translate and explain

מי יתן־לי שמע לי     אֵצֵא פֶּתַח וְלֹא־אָדוּם<br>
הן־תוי שדי יענני     וספר כתב איש־ריבי<br>
אם־לא על־שכמי אשאנו     אענדנו עֲטָרֹת לי<br>
מספר צעדי אגידנו     כמו־נגיד אקרבנו

'If only I had one to hear me,
  I would go out of doors and not rest!
Lo! (it would be) my desire (that) the Almighty would answer me;
  And the indictment (that) mine adversary had written—
Surely I would carry it on my shoulder,
  I would bind it unto me as a crown;
I would state the number of my steps,
  I would present it (in court) as the statement (of my case).'

(Jb. xxxi 35–7). In l. 1 I insert אצא פתח ולא אדם (thus re-arranged) *rhythmi causa* from the previous verse and take אצא פתח 'I would go out of doors' (cp. xxix 7, where בצאתי שער has the same sense) as meaning 'when I leave my house to appear in court'. In l. 2 I take תָּוִי not from תָּו 'mark' (s. p. 89 n. 3 and p. 162 n. 1) but from an otherwise unknown *תָּו or *תָּוֶה 'desire' (after Vulg.'s *desiderium meum* and Targ.'s ריגוגי) from *תָּוָה=אִוָּה 'inclined, desired' (cp. Syr. ܬܘܐ 'inclined, repented' and Arab. تَوِيَ 'passed away'); this suits the parallel מי יתן, which too expresses a wish (Driver in 'A.J.S.L.'

[1] Lam. ii 16–17, iii 46–51, iv 16–7 (M.T.), Prov. xxxi 25–6 (LXX, which is obviously inferior to the M.T.; cf. J. b. Sir. li 23–5 (where פנו is perhaps an error for סורו).

LII 165–6; s. Chajes in *G.S.A.I.* xx 308). In l. 2 I assume that וספר כתב איש ריבי is a *casus pendens* put before the conditional particle (cp. vi 28, where a prepositional expression precedes אם) and that the last clause of l. 2 belongs in sense to l. 3 (cp. x 20–1 xiv 4–5). In l. 3 I change the plural עֲטָרוֹת into the singular עֲטֶרֶת with two Hebrew manuscripts (Kennicott) and several ancient Versions (LXX, Vulg., Pesh.). In l. 4 I take נָגִיד 'set forth' in the sense not of a 'person set in front' = 'prince' (A.V., R.V.) but of a 'thing set forth' = 'statement' put forward as a defence or proof, thus bringing it into connexion with אַגִּידֶנּוּ 'I set it forth' in the preceding clause; and I accordingly take the Hebr. קֵרֵב 'brought near' as a technical term for putting in or producing a document in court, used like the Syr. ܩܰܪܶܒ 'brought near' when applied to presenting a petition to a high officer of state, as in ܟܕ ܫܡܥ ܦܘܠܐ ܕܡܝܬ ܐܣܩܠܦܝܘܣ ܐܬܬܘܝ ܘܩܪܒ ܒܥܘܬܐ ܠܡܪܝ ܝܘܣܛܝܢܝܢܐ ܦܛܪܝܩܝܘܣ 'when Paul heard that Asclepius was dead, he repented and presented a petition to my lord Justinian the patrician' (Hallier *Edessenische Chronik* 130–1 = 155 § 92 [93])*.

In other words, Job was so confident of his innocence that he prayed that he might have a judge to hear him, when he would go into court and speak out, and was even willing to be answered by the Almighty, that he might have the charge in written form put into his hands to carry it prominently for all men to see its absurdity, when he told the whole story of his life (cp. xxxi 4) and entered that as his defence.

## IV

A few words may not be out of place on the attempts which have been made to discover acrostic devices purporting to convey the name of the author or to throw light on the subject-matter of various Hebrew Psalms; for, if correct, they cannot but be of the highest historical and literary importance, whereas, if incorrect, they may be discarded as monuments of misplaced ingenuity.

Ps. ii 1–10: ליניא ואשתו 'for Jannaeus and his wife' (Bickell in 'Academy' [1892] 1040 351 + Baethgen in *Z.D.M.G.* LVII 372) i.e. Alexander Jannaeus (103–76 B.C.); but the last two verses are disregarded and the proper name is unusually spelt (יניא for ינאי or יניי).[1] while no reason is suggested why so undesirable a person is honoured with a Psalm (unless its author is supposed to be some sycophantic ecclesiastical or political admirer).

Ps. iv 1–9: בנר זרובבל 'with the lamp of Zerubbabel' (Slonin *ap.* Pfeiffer 'I.O.T.' 630[11]); but this result is only obtained by reading the initial letters from the end to the beginning of the Psalm, i.e. in inverse order to that in which the Psalm itself is read, and including the title, while no explanation of the phrase thus revealed is offered.

[1] Unless the final א is an abbreviation of אלכסנדרוס (Baethgen).

Ps. xiv 1–6 (cp. liii 1–7): איה השם 'where is the Name, i.e. God?'[1] (Bickell, *Conspect. R. Syr. Liter.* 19–20[18]), which is supposed to be the question to which the fool answers אין אלהים; but the sentence requires the alteration of כלה into הכל in the parallel Psalm and the disregard of vv. 6–7, while שם in v. 5 must almost certainly be altered to שמו and be transferred to v. 4, where קראו has no object (Gunkel; cp. Targ.); this destroys the acrostic arrangement!

Ps. xxvi 1–12: לב כל שאלי אאור 'I will shine (in) the hearts of all that ask for Me' (ibid.), which is obtained again by including the title and also by straining Hebrew grammar.

Ps. xxviii 1–9: אשא תך בי יה 'I bear oppression within me, O Yahweh' (ibid.), where the title is left out of account.

Ps. lxxxvii 1–4+6: ינאי 'Jannaeus' (Gaster in 'Academy' [1892] 1045 424–5), i.e. the same Alexander Jannaeus, although the name is differently spelt; but it is only extracted from the initial letters of the verses by leaving the title and also v. 5 and v. 7 out of account, while the verses are almost certainly out of order (Gunkel).

Ps. xcvi 11: יהוה יהו 'Yahweh, Yahu' (Bickell *ap.* Baethgen in *Z.D.M.G.* LVII 372), which consists of the initial letters of the seven words making up this verse.

Ps. cx 1–7: שמען אים 'Simeon . . .' (Margoliouth ibid. 1033 182–3 and Bickell ibid. 1040 351), i.e. Simon the Maccabee (143–135 B.C.), whose title of אים is unintelligible to the scholars who have revealed it but may *faute de mieux* be translated 'awe-inspiring'*; but this information can only be elicited by disregarding the title and putting שב לימיני before נאם יהוה in v. 1,[2] and also by negating the fact, whatever it may be worth, that שמען is misspelt, since it is apparently always, with the exception of a single Maccabaean coin, written שמעון in Biblical as in extra-Biblical texts.[3]

Finally, in Ps. xxv 22, which is superfluous as it stands outside the alphabetic arrangement of the Psalms, Lagarde (ibid. [1872] 39 12) takes פדה אלהים as a cryptogram for פדהאל and in Ps. xxxiv 23, which is a similarly superfluous verse, he takes פודה יהוה as a cryptogram for פדיה; then, identifying this פדיה with Pedaiah the contemporary of Ezra[4] and supposing that 'Phadaias might have been a brother of Phadael', he claims these two brothers as the authors,

[1] Cp. Lev. xxiv 11, where, however, הַשֵּׁם is probably a scribe's substitution for יהוה, made at an unknown date.

[2] This transference is possibly if not probably correct; for the *pāsēq* or 'note-line' after יהוה may indicate textual disarrangement and נאם יהוה, out of over 350 occurrences, in all but two (Is. lvi 8, Zech. xii 1) is put after the introductory words of the direct oration (Chance in 'Academy' [1892] 1045 424).

[3] Gaster in 'Academy' [1892] 1035 232; s. Margoliouth ibid. 1036 255 and Gaster ibid. 1037 278.

[4] Nehem. viii 4.

פדהאל of the first and פדיה of the second, of the two Psalms under discussion. So too Nah. ii 3 is said to reveal the name of the author of the acrostic poem as שַׁבַּי or שֹׁבִי,[1] while Ecclesiasticus li 30 has been thought to show that of the author of the similar poem to be עֶבֶד;[2] but these speculations, even if not disproved, are unconvincing.[3]

Apart from the particular objections raised against these acrostic devices, two of a general nature may be mentioned: first, the arbitrary treatment of the text that may be required to obtain them, e.g. by omitting verses or by including the titles to Psalms, which can hardly be original; and, second, the fact that, when the names of persons are thus indicated by the acrostic arrangement of the lines or verses, e.g. in Samaritan and Syriac poems, they are those always of the authors, never of the subjects, of the works in which they are found.[4] This last objection is, however, in itself of little force; for early Hebrew practice may have differed.[5]

Some of these attempts to discover acrostic devices may be rejected out of hand, if only because they make little sense; all are not therefore erroneous. Other results, like יהוה יהו, may be ascribed to the accidents of language, comparable with the frequent assonances caused by the pronominal suffixes, which cannot be classed as true rhyme[6] and therefore have no essential value.[7] Bickell indeed so regarded those acrostics which he had noted, while Margoliouth considered them genuine methods of handing down information to posterity. That such devices have been found in cuneiform texts of the Neo-Assyrian empire[8] and in Greek texts of the Seleucid period is indeed an argument in favour of finding them also in any Hebrew psalms which may *ex hypothesi* be of that period or thereabouts; and the difficulty of ascribing intelligible phrases of several words, such as ליניא ואשתו or בנר זרובבל, both in Messianic Psalms, to chance is very great, however strange truth may at times be,[9] whatever may be the case when a single word of only a few letters is in question.

[1] By dropping כי and taking שב י[הוה] as the key-letters.

[2] By retranslating the Gk. ἐργάζεσθε τὸ ἔργον into a supposed original Hebr. עבדו עבדתכם (cp. Pesh.'s ܥܒܕܘ ܥܒܕܝܟܘܢ); but the true form has been found to be מעשיכם עשו (Lévi *L'Ecclésiastique* II 232)!

[3] Gunkel in *Z.At.W.* XIII 244.

[4] Cp. Grimme *Psalmenprobleme* 102–3.

[5] In medieval Hebrew poems acrostic arrangements refer to many other things besides authors' names (s. Zunz *Gottesd. Vortr.* 371–94).

[6] Cp. Zunz op. cit. 379a and Gray 'Forms of Hebrew Poetry' 8, 63, 236–7.

[7] Acrostic words have also been detected in other Psalms (Baethgen in *Z.D.M.G.* LVII 372 and Ps. xxxi 2–12 and Ps. xxxix 2–14) and in the prose books of the Old Testament (cp. Baethgen ibid. on Gen. ii 3 and König *Einl. in d. Alt. Test.* 293 on Esth. i 20).

[8] Zimmern in *Z.A.* x 3–24 and Jensen in *K.B.* VI/ii 108–17 (Ashurbanipal).

[9] S. pp. 179–81.

# ABBREVIATIONS

A.A.S.O.R. Annual of the American Schools of Oriental Research (New Haven).

*Act. Or.* *Acta Orientalia* (Leiden).

*A.H.D.O.* *Archives d'Histoire du Droit oriental* (Wetteren; Paris).

A.J.A. American Journal of Archaeology (Concord).

A.J.S.L. American Journal of Semitic Languages and Literature (Chicago).

*Altor. Bibl.* *Altorientalische Bibliothek* (Leipzig).

*Anal. Or.* *Analecta Orientalia* (Rome).

*A.O.* *Archiv Orientální* (Prague).

*A.Of.* *Archiv für Orientforschung* (Berlin, Graz).

*A.S.A.É.* *Annales du Service des Antiquités de l'Égypte* (Cairo).

*A.S.Bw.* *Archiv für Schreib- und Buchwesen* (Leipzig).

Ass. St. The Oriental Institute of the University of Chicago: Assyriological Studies (Chicago).

B.A. Biblical Archaeologist (New Haven).

*Bab.* *Babyloniaca. Études de philologie assyro-babylonienne* (Paris).

B.A.S.O.R. Bulletin of the American Schools of Oriental Research (New Haven).

*B.A.S.S.* *Beiträge zur Assyriologie und semitischen Sprachwissenschaft* (Leipzig).

*B.B.Kf.* *Berliner Beiträge zur Keilschriftforschung* (Berlin).

*B.D.Bh.* *Börsenblatt für den deutschen Buchhandel* (Frankfurt).

*Berlin* *Sitzungsberichte der Preussischen Akademie der Wissenschaften, Philosophisch-historische Klasse* (Berlin).

B.E.U.P. Babylonian Expedition of the University of Pennsylvania (Philadelphia).

*B.I.C.* *Bulletin de l'Institut du Caire* (Cairo).

*B.I.F.A.O.* *Bulletin de l'Institut français d'Archéologie orientale* (Cairo).

B.I.N. Babylonian Inscriptions in the Collection of J. B. Nies (New Haven).

B.J.P.E.S. Bulletin of the Jewish Palestine Exploration Society (Jerusalem).

*B.M.B.* *Bulletin du Musée de Beyrouth* (Paris).

*B.O.* *Bibliotheca Orientalis* (Leiden).

B.R.M. Babylonian Records in the Library of J. Pierpont Morgan (New Haven).

B.S.O.A.S. Bulletin of the School of Oriental and African Studies (London).

C.B.Q. Catholic Biblical Quarterly (Washington).

*C.I.C.* *Corpus Inscriptionum Chaldicarum* (Berlin, Leipzig).

*C.I.S.* *Corpus Inscriptionum Semiticarum* (Paris).

*C.R.A.I.B.-L.* *Comptes-rendus de l'Académie des Inscriptions et Belles-Lettres* (Paris).

C.T. Cuneiform Texts from Babylonian Tablets in the British Museum (London).

C.T.C.T. Cuneiform Texts from Cappadocian Tablets in the British Museum (London).

D.J.D. Discoveries in the Judaean Desert (Oxford).

*D.P., Mém.* *Délégation en Perse, Mémoires* (Paris).

E.N. Excavations at Nuzi (Harvard).

E.T. Expository Times (Edinburgh).

*G.G.A.* *Göttingische Gelehrte Anzeigen* (Berlin).
*Göttingen.* *Nachrichten von der Königlichen Gesellschaft der Wissenschaften zu Göttingen: Philologisch-historische Klasse* (Göttingen).
*G.S.A.I.* *Giornale della Società Asiatica Italiana* (Florence).
H.T.R. Harvard Theological Review (Cambridge, Mass.).
H.U.C.A. Hebrew Union College, Annual (Cincinnati).
J.A.N.E.S. Columbia Univ. Journal of the Ancient Near Eastern Society of Columbia University (New York).
J.A.O.S. Journal of the American Oriental Society (New Haven).
*J.As.* *Journal Asiatique* (Paris).
J.B.L. Journal of Biblical Literature (Philadelphia).
J.C.S. Journal of Cuneiform Studies (New Haven).
J.E.A. Journal of Egyptian Archaeology (London).
J.E.N. Joint Expedition . . . at Nuzi (Paris and Philadelphia).
J.H.S. Journal of Hellenic Studies (London).
J.J.S. Journal of Jewish Studies (London).
J.N.E.S. Journal of Near Eastern Studies (Chicago).
J.P.O.S. Journal of the Palestine Oriental Society (Jerusalem).
J.Q.R. Jewish Quarterly Review (Philadelphia).
J.R.A.S. Journal of the Royal Asiatic Society (London).
J.T.S. Journal of Theological Studies (Oxford).
*Kedem* Kedem. Studies in Jewish Archaeology (Jerusalem).
*M.Ao.G.* *Mitteilungen der Altorientalischen Gesellschaft* (Leipzig).
*M.A.I.B.-L.* *Mémoires présentés . . . à l'Académie des Inscriptions et Belles-Lettres* (Paris).
*M.I.É.* *Mémoires présentés à l'Institut d'Égypte* (Cairo).
*M.I.F.A.O.C.* *Mémoires . . . de l'Institut français archéologique orientale du Caire* (Cairo).
*M.D.O.G.* *Mitteilungen der Deutschen Orient-Gesellschaft* (Berlin).
*M.M.A.F.C.* *Mémoires de la Mission archéologique française au Caire* (Cairo).
*M.O.* *Monde Oriental* (Uppsala).
*M.S.L.* *Materialien zum Sumerischen Lexikon* (Rome).
*M.U.B.* *Mélanges de l'Université de Beyrouth* (Beirut).
*Muséon.* *Muséon. Revue d'Études orientales* (Louvain).
*M.Va.(Ae).G.* *Mitteilungen der Vorderasiatischen/Vorderasiatisch-Aegyptischen Gesellschaft* (Leipzig).
*O.Lz.* *Orientalistische Literaturzeitung* (Leipzig).
*Orient., N.S.* *Orientalia* (Rome).
*Oudt.Stud.* *Oudtestamentische Studiën* (Leiden).
P.A.O.S. Publications of the American Oriental Society (New Haven).
P.E.Q. Palestine Exploration Quarterly (London).
P.Q.S. Palestine Exploration Fund: Quarterly Statement (London).
P.S.B.A. Proceedings of the Society of Biblical Archaeology (London).
*R.A.* *Revue d'Assyriologie et d'Archéologie orientale* (Paris).
*R.B.* *Revue biblique* (Paris).
*R.d.Tr.* *Recueil de Travaux relatifs à la Philologie et à l'Archéologie égyptiennes et assyriennes* (Paris).
*R.É.S.B.* *Revue des Études sémitiques et bibliques* (Paris).
*R.H.P.R.* *Revue d'Histoire et de Philosophie religieuses* (Strasbourg).
*R.S.O.* *Rivista degli Studi orientali* (Rome).

*S.B.A.W.* *Sitzungsberichte der Bayerischen Akademie der Wissenschaften: Philosophisch-historische Abteilung* (Munich).

*Scr. Hieros.* *Scripta Hierosolymitana* (Jerusalem).

S.D. Studies and Documents (London).

*St.T.* *Studi e Testi* (Rome).

*Syria* *Syria. Revue d'Art oriental et d'Archéologie* (Paris).

*T.Lz.* *Theologische Literaturzeitung* (Leipzig).

*Va.Sd.* *Vorderasiatische Schriftdenkmäler der Königlichen Museen zu Berlin* (Leipzig).

*V.T.* *Vetus Testamentum* (Leiden).

*W.O.* *Die Welt des Orients* (Göttingen).

*Y.B.T.* Yale Oriental Series. Babylonian Texts (New Haven).

*Z.A.* *Zeitschrift für Assyriologie und verwandte Gebiete* (Berlin and Leipzig).

*Z.Ä.S.* *Zeitschrift für Ägyptische Sprache* (Leipzig).

*Z.At.W.* *Zeitschrift für die alttestamentliche Wissenschaft* (Berlin).

*Z.D.M.G.* *Zeitschrift der Deutschen morgenländischen Gesellschaft* (Leipzig).

*Z.D.P.-V.* *Zeitschrift der Deutschen Palästina-Vereins* (Leipzig).

# INDEXES

## I. WORDS AND PHRASES

### *Sumerian*



### *Accadian (Babylonian and Assyrian)*

## Hebrew

## *Aramaic and Syriac*



## *Arabic*

## *Ethiopic*



## *Egyptian*



## *Coptic*



## *Greek*

Σεμεχωνῖτις λίμνη 166
Τάαυτος 128
ταῦ 160
Φοινικήιος 128
φοῖνιξ 195
χάρτης 80, 86
χαρτίον 82

## *Latin*

*calamus* 85
*ductuli cuneiformes, pyramidales* 19
*papyrus* 82
*sti/ylus* 28, 85
*Thoth* 129
*vertere stilum* 28

## 2. GEOGRAPHICAL NAMES

## 3. PERSONAL NAMES

# ADDITIONS AND CORRECTIONS

**P. 1.** Sumerian proverb on Sm.61 r.19 in the British Museum (Langdon in 'A.J.S.L.' XXVIII 242; s. Lambert 'Bab. Wisd.' 258–9, 19).

**P. 1 n. 2.** The form of writing found at Jamdat Nasr is now dated some 200–300 years before the first dynasty of Ur. (Moortgat in *Historia Mundi* II (Bern 1953) 234 f. 239.)

**P. 4.** The Walters-tablet is now in the Walters Art-Gallery at Baltimore, Maryland, U.S.A.

**P. 7.** Writing from the Indus Valley may be dated *c.* 2500–2300 B.C.

**P. 8 n. 2.** The Acc. *immû* 'clay-tablet' (Von Soden *Akk. Hwb.* I 378) is a Sumerian loan-word, and the Acc. *ṭupšinnu* 'tablet of ivory' (Jensen in Schrader's *K.B.* VI i 296–7 iv 8, *si vera lectio*) is a secondary compound noun; but the Acc. *ⁱˢd/ṭupninnu* 'chest, trunk' is one used for clothes and not part of a scribe's professional outfit (Salonen *Möbel* 211–2). The S.-Arab. *ṭf(n)* 'votive tablet' (Rossini *Chrestom. Arab. Merid. Epigr.* 159) is an Accadian loan-word, as the Hebr. טפסר 'marshal' also is (s. p. 71 n. 8).

A considerable number of Sumerian and Accadian terms connected with the work of the scribe are known; but the equations in lexical lists (e.g. Deimel *A.-S.G.* 390) are apt to be inexact if not actually incorrect (Falkenstein in *W.O.* I 176–7; cp. Von Soden in *Orient., N.S.* XX 164–5).

**P. 9 n. 4.** Another word is *šebru* 'broken' in Neo-Babylonian texts (San Nicolò in *Aegyptus* XXVII 137[2];) but *mu'ātum* 'to die' as used in reference to tablets in Old-Assyrian texts (Driver in *Anal. Or.* VI 22 38, Lewy & Eisser *Aa. Ru. K.* 322, 7–8) means 'to be obsolete, invalid' (Contenau *Tabl. Cappad.* 89[3]); cp. Engl. 'dead letter'.

**Pp. 9–10.** Cp. *ᵃᵇᵃⁿkunukki sarti* 'sealed tablet of falsehood' i.e. 'forged tablet' (Landsberger *M.S.L.* I 87 vi iv 15, 18). Old-Babylonian deeds often contain a clause to the effect that, if a previous or different tablet is subsequently produced, this is *s/ṣ/zar iḫibi* or *ḫibi* 'false; it shall' or 'must be destroyed' (Schorr *U.ab.Z.-Pr.* 238 10 258 19 293 28). What *ṭuppum s/ṣ/ziḫtum,* found here and occasionally elsewhere, means is not clear. The precise force, too, of *šiṭirti ṭuppiya mamman lâ ilappat* 'let no one touch the text of my tablet' (Ebeling *Ab.B.* 106 10–11) is also not quite clear, but the context suggests some form of tampering with the text; otherwise, it means 'to make an entry' in a text (s. Von Soden *Akk. Hwb.* I 535).

**P. 10.** A 'baked tablet' is called also *imgiddû ṣarpu* (Lambert 'Bab. Wisd.' 208 R.b. 18).

**P. 10 n. 5.** That *liginnu* means a 'baking oven' is an error; it seems originally to have designated a tablet carrying a single column of writing and to have come to mean one carrying a legal notice and also one carrying texts excerpted for use in schools (Von Soden *Akk. Hwb.* I 552). Hence such expressions occur as *liginnāte ša ṣâte* 'collections of word-lists' (s. p. 67 n. 2), *liginna qabû* or *qit(a)bû* 'to speak, i.e. read, a tablet' (Thompson 'C.T.' XVI 18. 6) and *liginna šuqbû* 'to teach the reading of a tablet' (Moldenke 'Cuneiform Texts in the Metropolitan Museum' 27–30 21 5–6; s. Ungnad in *A. Of.* XVI 62[39a]).

**P. 11 n. 3.** That *IM.GÍDᴰᴬ* = *imgiddû* 'oblong i.e. one-columned tablet' (Von Soden *Akk. Hwb.* 376) may be read also as *u'iltu* 'bond' (Landsberger op. cit. v–vi) is not confirmed by syllabaries (s. p. 16 n. 4).

A *ᴷᵁŠgiṭṭu* 'deed on leather' is mentioned in several late Neo-Babylonian texts (Von Soden op. cit. 294; s. San Nicolò in *Orient., N.S.* XVII 63[3]).

**P. 11 n. 4.** Cp. *kārum ṭuppam lulabiš* 'let the chamber of commerce put the tablet in a case' (Lewy & Eisser *Aa.Ru.K.* III–IV 74–9 R. 37–8) and *šarrum ṭuppam lipte* 'let the king open the tablet' (Dossin *A.R.M.* IV 10 R. 19).

**P. 11 n. 5.** Neither *imgurru* nor *erimtu* means 'tablet' but rather 'case, envelope' (Von Soden op. cit. 241, 376). That *sûtu* means 'envelope' is not certain (David in *R.H.D.* XIV 14[1]). Most probably *širmu* is a 'basket of cut reeds' for holding tablets, as *šarāmu* 'to cut' and *šurrumu* 'to protect with wicker-work' or the like suggest (s. Dossin in *R.A.* XXX 97–102).

**P. 12 n. 3.** So *ana* ${}^{is}$*lê'i šunnû* (Ebeling *Nb. B.U.* 106 34–8). Contrariwise *šutablakkutu* 'to transfer' a text from one tablet to another (Weidner in *A.Of.* XIX 109); cp. Hebr. העתיק 'transcribed' Prov. XXV 1).

**P. 13 n. 3 and p. 14 n. 5.** The Bab. *asumittu*, *us(u)mittu* may be a 'barrel-cylinder' (Ungnad in *O.Lz.* XXV 7) or any inscribed stela of stone or metal (Von Soden *Akk. Hwb.* I 76–77).

**P. 14 n. 4.** So a curse is pronounced on anyone who *nārâ annâ . . . ana mê inaddû ina epiri iṭammiru ina abni ubbatu ina išati iqalû* 'casts this inscription into water, buries (it) under the earth, destroys (it) with a stone, burns (it) with fire' (Belser in *B.A.S.S.* II 120–1 i 32–4). These curses go back to the earliest times, being found already on inscriptions of Narâm-Sin and Šulgi (Thureau-Dangin *Sum. u. Akk. Königsinschr.* 166–7 f iii 5–iv 4, 198–200 d ii 1–11).

The Phoen. אבד is similarly used in invoking a curse on 'anyone who destroys this [inscription]' יאבד ה[ספר.] זא (*K.A.I.* no. 30 line 3).

**Pp. 14–15.** Some Babylonian and Assyrian royal inscriptions, being inscribed behind or underneath, were intended presumably not for mortal eyes but only for those of the gods (Gadd 'Divine Rule' 60–61).

**P. 15.** The dates proposed for Hammurabi range from 2067–2025 B.C. to 1711–1669 B.C. (s. Driver & Miles 'Babyl. Laws' I [1956] xxiv–xxv).

**Pp. 15–16.** Mention is made of a tablet of copper in the time of the third dynasty of Ur (Thureau-Dangin in *R.A.* XI 1–4), others of copper and gold in that of Aššur-nāṣir-apli II (Wiseman in *Iraq* XIV 34 ii 70 and Bottéro in *Sem.* I 25–32), and of yet others of silver and iron in Hittite texts (McCarthy 'Treaty and Covenant' 38); but usually only important public acts would be recorded in such costly form. Occasionally, too, the text leaves it uncertain whether tablets or other objects of the relevant metal are meant (e.g. Messerschmidt *K.A.H.I.* I 13 iv 20–22; s. Luckenbill 'Ancient Records' 141–2 §120 and Weidner *Altor. Bibl.* I 122–3).

A *lê'u ša ḫurāṣi* 'tablet of gold', stolen from a temple and found in the hands of a sculptor, is the subject of a letter to king Esarhaddon (Harper 'A.B.L.' IV 429 O. 6–R. 16).

A scribe who wrote on metal was called *kab/pšarru* (Von Soden *Akk. Hwb.* I 418).

A Carthaginian text on lead (Cooke 'N.-S.I.' 50) and a Himyaritic one on bronze (Winnett in 'B.A.S.O.R.' CX 23–25) are also known.

**P. 16.** Excavations in the wing of the palace of Sargon II (721–705 B.C.) and adjacent buildings at Kalaḫ (Nimrud) in 1952 by Mallowan have recovered an immense number of tablets of various kinds, mostly more or less damaged. Very many were of clay, containing chiefly private records of little importance. Others, however, were of cedar, cypress, or walnut wood, while lapis lazuli, silver, or gold was used for others, all reserved for important documents, e.g. royal edicts, astronomical or religious works. The surface of such tablets was smeared with bees' wax, treated with orpiment or sulphide of arsenic to slow down the hardening of the wax which would have hindered or perhaps even checked the work of the scribe writing out the text. Frames of metal were provided to hold each tablet and the scribe was said to 'fill' (*mullû*) them, i.e. to fix the tablets in place to prevent chipping or breaking them; and the margins of these frames had grooves to hold the hinge-pins by which each might be tied to the next, so that any number of tablets might thus be joined to the next to make up a book. Unfortunately none of the cords used to tie the tablets together have been recovered, presumably as consisting of leather or other perishable stuff. Thus two or more tablets might be joined together to make up a 'diptych' or even a 'polyptych'. These differed, however, from the modern book in yet another important point: that they were not regularly opened from the right but from alternate sides, as the hinges connecting the tablets were so arranged. In other words, they were not opened like a book but like a Japanese fan. The first tablet of such a polyptych carried on the obverse side the title of the work and other necessary information such as the owner's name and the library to which it belonged, as shown in the following inscription on one coming from the collection of Sargon II (pl. 26): *ekal* (*É.GAL*) $^{I}$*Šar*$_4$*-kēn* (*GI.NA*) *šar*$_4$ *kiš-šá-ti*/*šar*$_4$ *māt* (*KUR*) *Aš-šur*$^{ki}$: *Enūma* (*UD*) *Anu* $^{d}$*Enlil* ($^{d}$*EN.LÍL.LÁ*) *iškara* (*ÉŠ.GÀR*)/*ina lê'i* ($^{giš}$*LE.U*$_5$*.UM*) *šinni* (*ZÚ*) *pīri* (*AM.SI*) *ú-šá-áš-ṭir-ma*/*ina qé-reb ekalli* (*É.GAL*)*-šú ina* $^{uru}$*Dūr* (*BÀD*)*-šar*$_4$*-ken*$_7$ *ú-kin*. 'Palace of Sargon, king of the world (and) king of Assyria: he had the serial text (beginning) 'When Anu Enlil . . .' written on a tablet of ivory and deposited (it) in his palace at Dūr-Sargon.' The reverse side seems to be blank. Inversely, the last tablet carried the conclusion of the text while its reverse side was uninscribed. The text itself may have occupied as many as 30 surfaces available for script, each carrying 2 columns together containing *c.* 250 lines, thus being capable of having *c.* 7500 lines.

Indeed, during the reigns of Sargon II and of his successor Sennacherib (705–681 B.C.) Kalaḫ apparently had a flourishing *bît ṭuppāti* 'house of tablets' or 'writing school' (s. pp. 64–6 and additions to pp. 65–6 and p. 74 notes 10 and 11). The *ummânu* 'director' was archivist as well as librarian (s. p. 65–6 n. 10) and three successive members of the same family seem to have held this office about the time here discussed. Writing may therefore not infrequently have been a hereditary skill. This use of the writing board flourished from the time of Tiglath-Pileser I (1115–1077 B.C.), and after the refounding of the library at Kalaḫ in 879 B.C. down to the Neo-Babylonian age (Mallowan in *Iraq* XVI [1954] 98–108, 121–41, Wiseman op. cit. XVII [1955] 3–13 and Howard ibid. 14–20. Cp. for tablets, writing sheets and books in general, Galling in 'Near Eastern studies in honor of W. F. Albright' ed. Goedicke [1971] 207–23).

Such tablets of wood and ivory, which were probably used for taking down immediate notes (Kugler *Sternkunde u. Sternkunst* I 85), were waxed as at Rome, and the writing was scratched on the wax (San Nicolò in *Orient.*, *N.S.* XVII 59–70; s. Wiseman ibid. 5–6). They were folded, requiring to be opened before and closed after use, to protect the writing; this procedure is implied in $^{giš}$*lê'a ša* $^{d}$*Šamaš pitâ* 'open the (wooden) tablet of (the god) Shamash' (Ebeling *Nb.B.* 126 8–9).

Writing tablets were similarly known to the Greeks from an early age. So Homer (*Il.* vi 169) speaks of writing *ἐν πίνακι πτυκτῷ*, and *ἐν πτυχαῖς βίβλων* (Aesch. *Suppl.* 947) as well as *δέλτος* alone and *δελτίον δίπτυχον* (Herod. *Hist.* viii 135, vii 239) are early witnesses to single and double tablets; but *δέλτοι πολύπτυχοι* do not seem to be mentioned before the 2nd century A.D. (Lucian *Amor.* 44).

The Hittites, too, appear to have known the use of boards, probably waxed; and the Ugar. *lwḥ*, *lḥ* (Gordon 'Ugar. Textb. [1965] Gloss. p. 427) and the Hebr. לוּחַ (Is. xxx 8) may reasonably be taken of their use in the west. In fact a folding tablet seems to be meant when God says to the prophet 'Take thee one (piece of) wood and write upon it *for Judah* and *for the children of Israel*, its (one) leaf; and take one/another (piece of) wood and write upon it *for Joseph and all the house of Israel*, its (other) leaf. Then bring them together, one to another, into one (piece of) wood, and they shall be a pair in thy hands' (Ezek. xxxvii 16–17). Thus sense is made of the passage by taking עֵץ '(piece of) wood' as 'wooden tablet', with which the Targum's לוחא 'tablet' agrees, and חָבֵר 'companion' as one of the 'pair' of leaves forming such a folding tablet (Gordon in *Sefer Segal* 6*–7*).

What appear to have been the remnants of a folding tablet of metal have been found at Zinjîrlū (Andrae *ap.* Von Luschan *Sendschirli* v 109–10); whether they may have been such or something like the object which the scribe carries on

*Br-rkb*'s monument and whether they may have been waxed to provide a writing surface or whether the writing may have been painted on to the metal has been disputed (s. Andrae in *A.Of.* XIV 177).

The apocryphal δέλτοι χαλκαί, being intended as unique and lasting records of a friendly alliance between Jews and Romans agreed in the 2nd century B.C. (1 Macc. viii 22; xiv 18, 27, 48) and the Scroll of Copper from Qumrân of the late Herodian period or soon after it containing a long list of treasures, do not come into the same category as the tablets here examined and do not require discussion here. For the latter s. Milik in 'D.J.D.' III [1962] 284–99.

**P. 16 n. 2.** Also $^{GIŠ}$*ZU.U*$_5$ and *GÁL* and *U* (Deimel *S.L.* II 18, 6/30; 190, 80/8; 813, 411/71) as well as $^{GIŠ}$*DA* (San Nicolò in *Orient. N.S.* XVII 59–70) = *lê'u* (*m*) tablet'

**P. 16 n. 4.** Also *kuššu* 'parchment' (San Nicolò in *Orient. N.S.* XVII 70). According to the latest suggestion πάπυρος is derived from an Eg. **pꜣ-pr-ʿꜣ* 'the (stuff) of Pharaoh', being so called as a royal monopoly (Černý); cp. Ass. *ki-ir-ki ni-a-ri* 'papyrus-roll' (Harper 'A.B.L.' VI 568 R. 19).

$^{(im)}$*GÍD.DA* = Acc. *giṭṭu* 'clay tablet' is an old word of Sumerian origin which the N.-Acc. $^{(im)}$*nibzu* representing the Aram. נבז 'document, account, receipt' gradually displaced (Johns in 'P.S.B.A.' XXVII [1905] 187–8; Cowley 'Aram. Pap.' XI 6 and s. p. 34; Von Soden *Akk. Hwb.* II 786). This is the late Aram. ניבזין (Jastrow 'Dict. Targ. Talm. Midr.' II 902) and Samar. נבז = Hebr. גורל (Sam. Targ. Lev. XVI 8–10). The root may appear in the Arab. *nabaḏa* I 'threw from his hand before or behind himself', III 'threw to one another (as though casting a lot)' (Freytag *Lex. Arab.-Lat.* IV 230); but the verb may be derived from the noun.

**P. 16 n. 6.** Both *giṭṭu* and *šipirtu* are written with the determinative signs for clay or for leather (San Nicolò in *Orient., N.S.* XVII 63[2, 3]).

**P. 16/7 n. 7.** Cp. Oppenheim in 'B.A.S.O.R.' XCIII 15[6]. Albright's inference that, because the *sipīru* was someone ranking between a free man and a slave, i.e. only half-free, the word does not mean 'scribe' has no validity. What evidence can be adduced to show that all scribes were free men? No such rule prevailed at Rome. He makes, too, no attempt to prove his assertion that *sipīru* denotes a slave as 'marked' with his owner's mark or name on his body.

Cp. Schroeder in *O.Lz.* XX 204 ($^{LÚ}$*kuššarû* or *kuššaru*) and Lewy in 'H.U.C.A.' XXV 188–202 (*sepīru, sepirru*).

The Neo-Ass. and Neo-Bab. *sepīru* was a specialized term for a clerk able to read and write foreign (i.e. other than Assyro-Babylonian, especially Aramaic) documents. Such persons, when in royal employment, are called $^{LÚ}$*A.BA* $^{KUR}$*Aššur-a-a* and $^{LÚ}$*A.BA* $^{KUR}$*Ar-ma-a-a* and also $^{LÚ}$*A.BA.* $^{LÚ}$*Mu-ṣu-ra-a-a* (Johns 'A.D.D.' **36** 11–12) according to the language in which they are expert, but their duties will have extended far beyond those of mere translators or interpreters (Wiseman in *Iraq* XVII 13); the curious *A.BA.* in these two titles is apparently a pseudo-ideogram formed from the Aram. *'abbâ* 'father', used as the Hebr. אָב 'father' is applied to the master craftsman Huram (II Chron. ii 12, iv 16). Terms of similar import are (*awēl*)*A.BAL* (cp. Sum. *BAL* 'to interpret'), with which (*awēl*)*sepīru* alternates and which *LÚ-KUŠ.SAR* in course of time displaced, and *turgamannu* (cp. Aram. *targēm* 'interpreted'), to which *pašāru* 'to interpret' (cp. Hebr. *pēšer* 'explanation' and *pišrāh* 'diagnosis') and *iṣurtu* 'record in a foreign language and script' may be added (Dougherty in 'J.A.O.S.' XLVIII 109–35 and Lewy in 'H.U.C.A.' XXV 188–202).

The O.-M.-Pers. *dpywr* = M.-Pers. (Pahl.) *dipīr* 'scribe' must be kept distinct; for this is derived from an original *dipi-bara* composed of *dipi-*'writing' (with which the Sum. *DUB* = Acc. *ṭuppu* 'clay-tablet' may be connected) and *bara-* 'bearing, possessing, using', which indicates one who is charged with the performance of a function (Henning).

**Pp. 16–17.** A letter from Sin-idinnam to king Sargon has recently been published in which he says 'if it is acceptable to the king, I will write on parchment (*ina šipri*) and have (it) conveyed to the king', who replies 'why wilt thou not write Accadian (*akkadattu*) in the letter? . . . In this wise may agreement be settled'. Clearly Sin-idinnam as an Aramaean is unwilling to use the Assyrian language, which is written in the cuneiform script on clay-tablets but wishes to use the Aramaic language, which requires parchment, while the king refuses to depart from diplomatic usage; for clay-tablets are durable while parchment easily perishes (Dietrich in *W.O.* iv 89–90).

The *ni'āru/niyāru* 'paper' will probably have been used not for the cuneiform but for the Aram. script; the (*mašak*) *šipirtu* '(leather) document', first found in the Achaemenid age, and the (*mašak*) *magallatu* '(leather) roll' (cp. Hebr. מגלה and Aram. מגלתא 'roll, scroll'), mentioned only on a couple of Neo-Bab. colophons, could serve only for documents written in such a script (Wiseman in *Iraq* XVII [1955] 12–13).

**P. 18.** Assyrian sculptors engraved monuments when already erected *in situ* (Layard 'Nineveh and its Remains' II 255).

**Pp. 18–19.** So *ina ṭuppi u qan-ṭuppi* 'on a tablet and with a reed-pen' (Zimmern in *B.K.B.B.* 8–9 ii 113). The zeugma recalls that in בעט ברזל ועפרת 'with a pen of iron (s. pp. 85–86) and on lead' (Jb. xix 24) in the Old Testament, if rightly so translated; and parallel examples occur in the New Testament (s. p. 86 n. 1).

**P. 20.** Cp. Contenau *Man. d'Archéol. Orient.* IV 2213–6/1244.

**P. 22 fig. 4.** Cp. Gadd 'Stones of Assyria' pl. 13, where two scribes seem to be depicted at the right end of the lower register.

For the illustration given here s. Thureau-Dangin & Dunand *Til Barsib* [1931] 54–6. Papyrus is the material held by scribe A and a clay tablet by scribe B (s. Galling in 'Near Eastern studies in honor of W. F. Albright' ed. Goedicke [1971] pp. 211–13).

**P. 22 n. 2.** Cp. Deimel *Keilschrift-Paläographie* 2 and Unger *Keilschrift-Symbolik* 11.

**P. 27 n. 2.** The Sum. *SAG* 'head' and *DÙ* or *DÀ* (*GAG*) 'peg, stake' have been combined into *SAG.DÙ* or *SAG.DÀ* 'triangle' (Deimel *S.L.* II 304, 115/167), from which the Acc. *santakku* 'cuneiform sign' (Muss-Arnolt 'C.D.A.L.' 787) has been derived (s. Von Soden in *Z.D.M.G.* XCI 193–4 and Thureau-Dangin *T.M.B.* xvii[4]).

**P. 29.** Cp. Meissner *Bab. u. Ass.* I *Abb.* 154 (plan of house) and II *Abb.* 54 (map of Nippur). Such a 'plan' was called *mudasû* (Von Soden in *Orient., N.S.* XX 164–5).

**P. 31 n. 3.** Both *šiṭir šamê* 'writing of heaven' and *šiṭir burum(m)ê* 'writing of variegated pattern' occur, meaning the configuration of the constellations and coloured figures on a blue background (Gadd 'Divine Rule' 93–95). The superficially similar Hebr. מִשְׁטָר refers neither to the zodiacal signs (Cheyne in 'J.B.L.' XVII 104) nor to this Accadian expression (Van der Ploeg in *Oudt. Stud.* X 189), as the parallel clause shows, but to the laws of nature under God's control (Jb. xxxviii 33; cp. Pesh.'s *nāmôsâ* 'law').

**Pp. 33–4.** Definitely wedge-shaped signs begin to appear at Lagash on clay in the time of Entemena *c.* 3100 B.C. and on stone in that of Ur-Bau *c.* 2700 B.C. (Unger op. cit. 9).

**P. 36.** The direction of the script in which the scribes drew the signs was changed apparently *c.* 2700 B.C. (ibid.).

The legends beside figures facing leftwards ran in vertical columns from left to right so as to meet, as it were, the faces of the figures coming towards them. Otherwise, vertical columns running leftwards remained the rule on stone and metal till the end of the first dynasty of Babylon (ibid.). The direction of the script, however, might vary according to the special needs, for example, of maps and plans. So it might occasionally run from right to left instead of left to right on Jewish coins (e.g. de Vaux 'Discoveries in the Judaean Desert' II 46 Mur. 267).

**Pp. 41–2.** The earliest Sumerian scribes wrote from right to left, and the Semites who invented and used the *Καδμήια* or *Φοινικήια γράμματα* continued this practice; the Babylonians, however, although they adopted the Sumerian cuneiform script, reversed the order and wrote from left to right and the Greeks, using the 'Phoenician' alphabet, began by writing *βουστροφηδόν* but soon came to write from left to right. A few Assyrian tablets with reversed script have been found (s. Weidner in *Altor. Bibl.* I [1925] 4).

The origin of the practice of writing from right to left has been held to be religious for the following reasons. The seat of the gods was thought to be in the furthest N., near the pole-star which appeared to be the one fixed and immovable point in the heavens, or on some mountain supposed to lie immediately beneath it. If then a person faced N., looking towards the gods, the right was E. and the left W., whither the dead were supposed to go and which was therefore held to be unlucky; and again, if a person faced N., the sun rose from the right and set towards the left (cp. Plutarch *de placitis philosophorum* 888b ii 101). So too the Hebrews located God's seat in the N. (Ezek. i 4, 28); and the Jews slaughtered the morning sacrifice at the N-W. corner of the altar so that the rays of the morning sun, unimpeded by the E. wall of the court, might fall full on it, and they similarly killed the evening sacrifice at the N-E. corner of the altar that the sun's rays might not be prevented by the W. wall from falling on it (B. Talmud *Yômâ* 62b).

Further, writing was in origin, as it still often was in the Middle Ages, a priestly craft. The writer, who was presumably a priest, would therefore sit facing the pole-star in the N. in order to obtain a divine blessing on his work, as his chief task was to write the record of the divine will revealed in the stars as the *šiṭir* or *šiṭirti šamê* 'writing of heaven' (s. Jeremias *Handb. d. Altor. Geistesk.*[2] 41–43); thus, facing N., he followed the course of the stars as he wrote from right to left (Miese; s. Ettisch in *R.A.* LVI 133–7 and in *Grapholog. Schriftenr.* V 171–5).

These reasons for writing from right to left can hardly be accepted; they run counter to known facts and flout an important technical requirement.

First, the earliest known examples of writing are not religious but economic; and this objection cannot be met by the assumption, which is nothing but an *argumentum e silentio*, that these may or even must have been preceded by other *ex hypothesi* religious texts, because the forms of the signs on those from Uruk are already highly developed (Ettisch in *R.A.* LVI 136[2]). Such texts may have existed but they will not necessarily have been religious texts; the earliest Egyptian texts do not seem to have been necessarily religious, indeed, the earliest Sumerian and Elamite tablets contain nothing but lists of objects with the numbers (s. pp. 2–3), and the earliest Hittite texts are said to have been written for the purpose of recording royal pronouncements (Gurney 'Hittites' 170–7). Whatever may be said of the signs, the mode of expression is crudely archaic, e.g. in their arrangement on the tablet (s. pp. 39–41); and religious works could hardly have been written down at a time when the order of signs and words in a sentence was still unregulated and haphazard. The argument backwards from the Middle Ages, too, does not prove the earliest writing to have been the work of priests, even if such people may have developed and exploited the invention; possibly the earliest Phoenician and certainly the earliest Greek writing was not sacred in origin, and much writing in the Middle Ages was done by merchants and lawyers, while only religious, literary and historical, writing was the business of the cloister.

Second, most men are right-handed, so that the left hand is relatively clumsy and unskilled. The ordinary scribe, therefore, would use his left hand for the simple operation of holding the tablet in position but his right hand for the highly skilled task of imprinting the pictograph, often quite complicated, in the clay. The angle at which the left hand held the tablet (s. pp. 34–36) was such that the stylus as grasped in the right hand would have its point resting on the upper right corner of the tablet; and, as drawing the hand towards is easier than pushing it away from oneself, the writer would tend to make the signs down the right side of the tablet, i.e. in a column running towards himself; he would then start the next column immediately to the left of the uppermost sign in the previous column and so proceed leftwards across the tablet column by column from top to bottom.

Third, a person reading the cuneiform script as impressed on a clay-tablet, if the text ran from left to right, needed to have the light shining on it from the right side or, if running from left to right, from his left side; and the writer would presumably have felt the same need. He would therefore, if writing from right to left, have sat facing N. with the light of the sun coming from his right side in the morning and facing S. with it coming from his left side in the evening; contrariwise, writing from left to right, he would have faced S. in the morning and N. in the evening, when the light would be least helpful to him. In other words, his position would have been dictated not by the rotation of the heavenly bodies *per se* but by the need to have the sun, wherever it might be in the heavens, throwing its light at the proper angle on to the tablet.

The reason for changing the direction of the script from one running from right to left to one running from left to right is also said to have been religious: when a people changed their religion, they changed also their customs either to distinguish themselves from their former fellows or neighbours or else to indicate their new beliefs. For example, the Numidians in the 2nd century B.C. wrote the text on ordinary monuments in horizontal lines in which the writing began at the upper right corner and ran to the left but that in epitaphs in vertical columns in which the writing ran upwards from bottom to top, starting now at the lower left and now at the lower right corner, so that the columns ran either from left to right or from right to left; the reason for thus writing the text upwards was apparently due to a desire to represent the hope that the deceased might rise upwards, i.e. from darkness into light. Or again, the Nestorians, when they separated themselves from their Jacobite fellow-Christians, altered the direction of the Syriac script which they used and wrote it in vertical columns instead of horizontal lines; and for a similar reason some early Christians made an attempt to turn the Greek script 20° round in their inscriptions. No such reasons, however, will account for the difference in the direction of the earliest Sumerian and the Babylonian writing, the former from right to left and the latter from left to right; for no essential differences distinguish the religious beliefs of these two races.

The reason was undoubtedly the danger, inherent in writing with the right hand running from right to left on moist clay, that the writer, as he wrote the second column immediately to the left of the first column, would obliterate the signs there imprinted in the moist and therefore soft clay as he proceeded down and across the tablet; and so each column of writing in turn would be effaced as the next was written (s. pp. 41–42).

The earliest Sumerian scribe began writing the text, for one or other of the reasons given above, at the upper right corner; in short inscriptions the text ran in a horizontal line leftwards (s. fig. 98*a*), but in long texts it ran down the right side of the tablet and the columns then advanced leftwards (s. fig. 98*b*). These methods persisted on stone and metal for some 1,500 years. So soon, however, as clay came into use, writing from right to left, especially in vertical columns advancing in that way, became impossible for the reasons given above. Then, when the tablet was turned round 90° against the clock in the writer's hand, the pictures which the signs originally represented came to lie on their backs (s. pp. 34–36). In this position, the first sign came to be at the left end and the last sign at the right end of the line (s. fig. 98*c*) and at the same time writing in vertical columns gave way to that in horizontal lines, so that only one style was followed. Why, however,

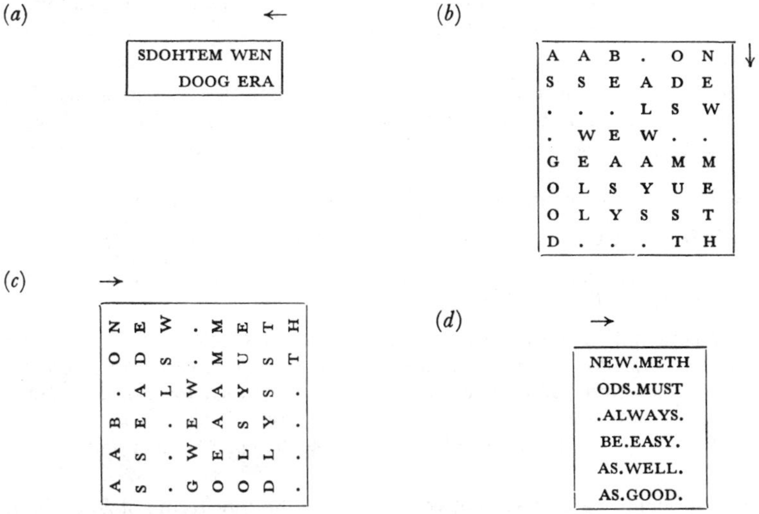


FIG. 98. Writing in various directions.

were the signs themselves turned back so as to lie on their backs and not simply kept standing upright but realigned so as to be read from left to right, being then written in the reverse order (s. fig. 98*d*)?

The reason seems to be this. When introducing novelties, men commonly tend or try to make them as little revolutionary, as like the old, as possible. The method whereby the script, revolved 90°, lies on its back, allows it to be read as before except that the reader's eye runs not from top to bottom but from the left to the right side of the tablet since only the direction of the letters is changed (*c*); it therefore does not require him to learn also to read the individual letters standing in new positions relatively to one another (*d*). The unity of the script therefore was maintained; and the true reason for the new direction was not so much religious conservatism, which had already been breached, as practical convenience (Ettisch in *R.A.* LVI 139–44).

The language itself occasionally is witness to this turning round of the tablets; for example, the left side is called 'upper width (*SAG-AN.TA*)' and the right side 'lower width' '(*SAG-KI.TA*)' (Neugebauer 'Mathematical Cuneiform Texts' 42, 48–49).

**Pp. 42–43.** Other aids to reading were  or  to separate text from commentary and  or  *KIMIN* for *ditto*; and  marked something that was rejected (Labat *Épigr. Akkad.* 30–31).

Few Assyro-Babylonian musical or poetical technical terms are known; one such is *kitmu* perhaps meaning some kind of musical instrument, e.g. a 'flute' (Von Soden *Akk. Hwb.* I 493; s. Galpin 'Music of the Sumerians' 17–18), or a 'song in the second mode' (Wulstan; cp. Kilmer and Duchesne-Guillemin in 'Studies in honour of B. Landsberger' 266–8, 272), which may be compared with the Hebr. מִכְתָּם, an equally obscure word for some kind of 'psalm', (Ps. xvi 1). Other terms are קו 'chord, note; notation' (Ps. xix 5; cp. Ecclus. xliv 5, Masada) and מדה 'measure, metre' (Thanksgiving Hymns i 28–29; s. Dupont-Sommer *Écrits Esséniens* 219[2]).

**Pp. 44–45.** One tablet which seems to have been turned over from front to back, like a page in a book, vertically instead of horizontally over its lower edge is known (Finkelstein in 'J.C.S.' XVII 40–41).

**Pp. 47, 49, and 54.** What *GUD* represents is perhaps not so much an 'ox' as a 'bison' (Hilzheimer *Wildrinder im alten Mesopotamien* [*M.Ao.G.* II 2] 13; Lat. *bos* [*bison*] *bonasus*).

**P. 51.** The earliest archaic texts seem to show some 891 signs (Falkenstein *Uruk* 1–201), but the basic number is estimated at 249 or 250 signs (Unger *Keilschrift-Symbolik* 23–57); the classical syllabary contains 563 (Howardy) or 602 (Deimel) signs.

A practice which came into use in the late period was the conflation of common combinations into a single sign, for example of  *i-na* into  *ina* 'in'; this and other modifications were due to the fact that cuneiform was mainly a cursive script (Labat *Épigr. Akkad.* 11–13).

**P. 53.** The augmentation of a sign by additional strokes was called *GUN*(*U*) 'weight' by late scribes (Langdon 'Sumer. Gramm.' 21–3, Labat *Épigr. Akkad.* 12). More or less definite rules were followed in thus augmenting signs: for example, three or four crossed strokes for fulness, three or four vertical strokes in two rows for darkness, and so on (Unger *Keilschrift-Symbolik* 14–16; cp. Meissner *Bab.u.Ass.* II 338–9).

**Pp. 58–59.** Although *o* and *ô* are not represented in the cuneiform syllabary, both Sumerian and Accadian speakers seem to have produced these sounds, if late Greek transliterations may be trusted: for example, Sum. *DUMU* = Gr. δομ and Sum. *BUR* = Gr. βωρ, while Acc. *îpuš* = Gr. ιφος (Pinches in 'P.S.B.A.' XXIV 109–13; cp. Delitzsch *Sum. Gramm.* 155). Two methods seem to have been tried to make good this deficiency. First, the alternative use of signs like *par* for *pur*, *ṭar* for *ṭur*, and *ṣar* for *ṣur* suggest *por*, *ṭor*, and *ṣor*, as the probable pronunciation (Von Soden *Grundr. d. Akk. Gr.* 12 §9 f.): for example, *ilṭor* is intended when the usual *il-ṭur* (Harper 'A.B.L.' VII 718 R. 6 *alq.*) is written *il-ṭar* (Ebeling *Nb.B.* $63_{18}$). Second, the scribes of Nippur apparently mean *ô* when they use < (*u*) or  ($u_4$) where *a*+*u*> *au* > *ô* is required, while reserving  (*ú*) for *û* (Poebel 'S.A.G.' 117[1]).

The Ugaritic alphabet, too, lacks a sign for *o* or *ô* in regular use but represents it once by <, the normal sign for *ʿayin*, in *ṣpʿn* = *ṣāfôn* 'north' (Gordon 'Ugar. Handb'. [1947] 147 62 16 = B I i 16) and once by the same sign surrounded by a circle, namely , in *pr*©©, which is unfortunately an unknown word (Gordon ibid. 146 60 30, 36, 37). This early use of a form of *ʿayin* for *o* is of considerable interest, since the sign for *ʿayin* was that taken long afterwards for *o* by the Greeks (s. Bauer *Ursprung d. Alphabets* 41); the reason may have been partly that the sign for a pharyngal sound was thought suitable for a back-vowel and partly that it was the last sign available for the purpose (s. pp. 178–9).

The cuneiform syllabary was also inadequate for the representation of half-vowels (cp. Lewy in *Orient.*, *N.S.* XXI 8[4]), for which signs containing full vowels came to be used in the Neo-Babylonian period: for example, *taq-qa-ba-'* for *taq-ba-'* suggests *taq*$^{e}$*bâ* 'thou didst say' (Ebeling *Nb.B.* 189 9, 191 4) and *ta-ḫal-liq* similarly suggests *taḫ*$^{a}$*liq* 'she fled' (ibid. 183 6).

**P. 59.** The relative paucity of sounds in Sumerian as compared with Accadian speech was responsible for much ambiguity in the writing of Babylonian and Assyrian texts; many Sumerian signs could be employed for the same Accadian sound and a single Sumerian sign might have to do duty for several Accadian sounds. Further, as the Accadian speech developed, new sounds for which the old syllabary made no provision came into use.

Various orthographic devices were invented to indicate sounds not normally represented in the cuneiform syllabary, notably *'alif*, *hē'* and *ḥē'*, *ʿayin* and *ġayin*, which were original Semitic sounds: for example, in *te-ri-ḫu-u*, *te-ri-wa-a* and *te-ri-'-a* for respectively *tere'û* and *tere'â* 'you tend' (Ungnad *Bab. Br.* 83 10 85 9 86 9). Such difficulties were commonly evaded in purely Accadian words, while devices intended to meet them were most frequent in the transliteration of non-Accadian Semitic proper names.

Another sound for which the cuneiform syllabary made no provision was aspiration or spirantization, although it was clearly recognized in pronunciation, if only sporadically or in dialect. For example, the variant *ḫiššātum* = *kiššātum* (Boyer, *Histoire Juridique* 65 122 11 15) in the Old-Babylonian period as well as *šamḫatu* = *šamkatu* and *tamāḫu* = *tamāku* (Muss-Arnolt 'C.D.A.L.' 1058, 1167–9; cp. Lewy in *Orient.* XVII, *N.S.* 155–9) in subsequent periods clearly prove a spirant *k*-sound (cp. Hebr. *tāmaḵ* 'seized'; s. n. on p. 155). Whether or how soon a spirant *ḇ*-sound arose is not clear. The common O.-Bab. *babālu*$^{m}$ = *wabālu*$^{m}$ and the rare *bašābu*$^{m}$ = *wašābu*$^{m}$ (Ungnad *Bab.Br.* 130 17), the equally rare *wa-al-gu-ú-a* = *palgûa* (Alexander 'B.I.N.' VII 40 2) and *da-wi-du-ú-um* = *dapdû(m)* 'defeat' (Dossin *A.R.M.* I 69 R. 6+) and similar forms may be called in evidence for it, and comparable spellings in Old-Assyrian texts have been cited to show that it may have been a West-Semitic phenomenon (Lewy in *Z.A.* XXXVIII 248; cp. Stamm in *V.T.*, *Suppl.* VI 171[6]); but all these forms have also been explained as purely orthographic, at any rate in early texts (Von Soden *Akk. Syll.* 102 against Labat *Épigr. Akk.* 15). Yet equations like Acc. *Kaptāru* = Hebr. *Kaptōr* = Eg. *Kfty* give a hint that *p* may have represented a spirant sound, if only in foreign words, at quite an early date. That *pal-gu* is transliterated *φαλαγ* in the Greek period (Pinches in 'P.S.B.A.' XXIV 111–12) may be accepted as evidence of spirantization then; for *φ*, though it continued for some centuries afterwards to be pronounced as aspirate *p-h*, would have had to do duty also for spirant *ph* = *f*, for which the Greeks had no other sign. Again, orthographic freaks like *lidqi* for *lišqi* and *muteraššu* for *muš(š)eraššu* (Ebeling *Nb.B.* 54 16 252 17) in late Babylonian texts reflect fricative *đ* and *ŧ* respectively. Spirantization, therefore, was heard in speech now and then or here and there, even though little attempt was made to indicate it in the written language (cp. Streck in *Z.A.* XIX 235–6, Ungnad in *M.Ao.G.* IV 220–1, Seidmann ibid. IX/iii 12[7]).

Other equations such as *bi-i-bu* = *bi-'u-u* 'conduit, culvert' suggest that *b* may at times serve as a mere glide (Von Soden *Grundr. d. akk. Gramm.* 25 §24*b*; cp. Milik in 'D.J.D.' III 243/60 and 256/193 on the Aram. ביאה and ביבא which are in origin the same word).

Lastly, the spelling of *inádin* or *inaddin* now as *inamdin* and now as *inandin* seems intended for *inańdin* with nasal *ń* (Von Soden op. cit. 33 §32*b*; cp. Landsberger *M.S.L.* II 26–28).

**P. 59 n. 1.** The Accadian order of the vowels as given here is interesting, being obviously based on a phonetic principle. The vowels fall into two groups, the

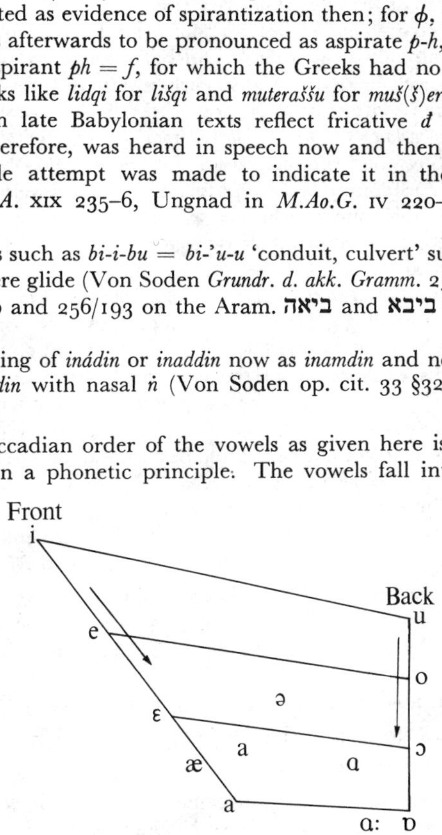


FIG. 99. Changing positions of the tongue in producing Arabic vowels.

first of back-vowels (*u*, *a*) and the second of front-vowels (*i*, *e*); and those in each group follow the movement of the tongue as it proceeds from the upper to the lower position in pronouncing them, i.e. along the lines respectively of the cardinal front-vowels (*i*, *e*, *ε*, *a*) and the cardinal back-vowels (u, o, ɔ, ɑ) as shown in the accompanying diagram (s. Gairdner 'Phonetics of Arabic' 33–44). As the exact sound of the Accadian vowels is unknown and as the four must include numerous modifications of the basic sound which each represents, precision cannot be attained in defining them; but the point may be made that the same principle underlies the order of the Accadian vowels and that of the consonants of the West-Semitic alphabet, that both proceed from back-sounds to front-sounds (s. pp. 182–5).

**P. 59 n. 2.** Or rather, the adjectives *ḫamṭu*/*ḫanṭu* 'swift' and *marû* 'fat' are used to describe respectively light or short and heavy or long grammatical forms: for example, *GA* and *E.DA* are *ḫamṭu* while *GA.GA* and *E.DA.A* are *marû*, and *qalālu* is *ḫamṭu* and *qullulu* is *marû* (Zimmern *Busspsalmen* 84[1], Delitzsch *Sum. Gramm.* 21[2]: cp. Langdon in *R.A.* XIII 92, and Dossin in *A.H.D.O.* III 151); such definitions however are hardly adequate (s. Landsberger in *M.S.L.* IV 3*–32*).

A grammatical form was called *šusḫurtu* (Thureau-Dangin in *R.A.* XXXII 101).

The pronominal *šû* 'same' indicates that the words in the right and left columns of a lexical tablet have the same form and meaning, i.e. that the Accadian word is a Sumerian loan-word, commonly marked by having the final vowel lengthened (Muss-Arnolt 'C.D.A.L.' 993*b*).

**P. 61.** Such spellings as *ma-ru-aṣ* (Dossin *T.C.L.* XVII 29 27) and *ma-ru-iṣ* (Ungnad *Bab.Br.* 227 5) = *ma-ru-(a)ṣ* and *ma-ru-(i)ṣ* for *maruṣ* have been thought to show the beginnings of an alphabetic writing in Old-Babylonian texts (Labat *Épigr. Akkad.* 25); but this may well be doubted at so early a date, whatever the explanation of such forms may be in late texts (Von Soden *Akk. Syll.* 9, 102). In the late period such forms as *a-pa-ta-laḫ* = *a-p(a)-ta-laḫ* for *aptalaḫ* and *ap-ti-qi-di* = *ap-ti-qi-d(i)* for *aptiqid* certainly show the beginning of an alphabet script (Poebel 'S.A.G.' 61–62); for the failure to pronounce at any rate final short vowels is then abundantly attested. For example, such variations as *kàs-pu*, *kàs-pa*, *kàs-pi*, *ka-sap ul ma-ḫir* 'the money has not been received' show that the old case-endings had lost their force, while the need to repeat the vowel or add an orthographic ' when requiring pronunciation, as in *maḫ-ru-ú* or *maḫ-ru-'* for *maḫrū* 'they have received' (cp. Hyatt 'Final Vowels' 28–30, 41–42), or to repeat the last consonant, as in *ša . . . iš-pur-ru* (Ebeling *Nb.B.* 36 $_{10, 18, 24}$) for *ša . . . iš-pu-ru* (Ebeling ibid. 59$_{11, 17}$) is in harmony with this explanation of the erratic case-endings. In other words, a syllabic sign in such a position has the value of a consonant alone. This conclusion is confirmed by the transcription of Aramaic words into the cuneiform script and of Babylonian words into the Greek alphabet: for example, both *-an* and *-ni* have the value of *n* in *li-iš-ša-an* and *li-iš-ša-ni* = לִשָּׁן?, while *ṭu* stands for *-ṭ* and *-tu(m)* for *-t* respectively in *ra-a-ṭu* = ρατ and *mi-ṭer-tu(m)* = μιτερθ (Hyatt ibid. 3–7). The experiment, however, was not carried through to its logical end by the Babylonians, who therefore failed to develop an alphabet (cp. Ungnad *M.Ao.G.* IV 222–4).

**P. 62 n. 2.** The latest dated tablets are now said to be two (apparently still unpublished) astronomical texts, one of A.D. 49/50 and another of A.D. 75 (Schaumberger in *Orient.*, *N.S.* XXII 113 and Parker & Dubberstein 'Chronology'[3] 5; s. Gelb in *B.O.* XV 37).

The 'date' on a tablet was called *uddazallû* (Landsberger in 'J.N.E.S.' VIII 254[31]).

**P. 62 n. 6.** Also *ṭibû* 'to seal' (Langdon in *R.A.* XVIII 42 R. i 45); cp. Hebr. טָבַע 'sank' and טַבַּעַת 'signet-ring'.

**Pp. 62–63.** Tablets sealed with the finger-nail cease to appear towards 670 B.C., when the use of the seal appears to have become universal; they are common in Babylonian deeds of the Cassite period but are found neither on tablets from Nuzi nor on those of the Middle-Assyrian period (Boyer in *Symbolae . . . Paulo*

*Koschaker Dedicatae* 208–19).

Judah gave his 'signet (*ḥôṯām*)' and 'cord (*pᵉṯîl*)' as a pledge to Tamar; and when the question of his identity arose she asked him to see whose were 'the engraving on the seal (*ḥôtemeṯ*)' and 'the strands of the cord (*pᵉṯîlîm*)', which would provide the answer (Gen. xxxviii 18, 25). The different forms of the two nouns are clearly intentional, and the text must not be altered to assimilate the second to the first passage in conformity with the Versions; for the ancient translators are only too likely to have missed or disregarded such fine distinctions. Here then is the only known case in the West in which the strands of the cord carrying the seal serve the same purpose as the fringe of the garment in the East.

**P. 64.** Berosus knew a tradition that Oannes, i.e. the god Ea, transmitted letters to mankind (Müller *F.H.G.* II 496–7 i 3).

**P. 64 n. 5.** Hence (*awīl*)*rab-qanû* 'chief scribe' (Perry *Sin* 4 1 R. 46).

**Pp. 64–65.** Cp. Hyslop in the 'Educational Supplement' XLIII 1957/882 (31.x.1952). What seem to be tablets with students' writing exercises (s. pl. 23, 1) have been found (Hilprecht 'Explorations in Bible Lands' 405; cp. Eilers in *Anal.Or.* XII 74–81).

**P. 65 n. 1.** Cp. Meissner *Bab. u. Ass.* I 387–8 for letters written by women. That Jezebel or even Jehu wrote the letters which they were said to have sent with their own hands (I Ki. xxi 8 and II Ki. x 1) may be doubted.

**Pp. 65–66.** Another scholastic dialogue is to the following effect: 'Come hither'—'I come'—'Whither did you go?'—'I did not go anywhere.'—'If you did not go anywhere, why are you late? Go to school, stand before your teacher. Read your assignment, open your school-bag (?), write your tablet, let your big brother (i.e. teacher's assistant) write your new tablet for you. After you have done your assignment, after you have reported to your overseer, come, pray, to me . . .; do not wander about in the street, return to me. . . . Do you know what I said to you?'—'I know, I will tell it to you.'—'Come, repeat it to me.'—'I will repeat it to you.'—'Tell it to me.'—'I will tell it to you.'—'Come, tell it to me.'—'You told me to go to school, to read my assignments, to open my school-bag (?), to write my tablet; after I have done my assignment, to proceed to my job and, after I have reported to my overseer (?), to come to you, you told me.'—'Come now, indeed, be a man. Do not stand about in the public square, do not wander about in the boulevard; when walking in the city, do not look all around, be humble, show fear before your overseer (?); when you show terror, your overseer (?) will like you. . . .' (Kramer in 'J.A.O.S.' LXIX 207–10; cp. 201–7 where another text of similar import is published).

Several other Sumerian texts, some still unpublished but some published, describing instruction in schools are known. In these the teacher is called *UM.MI.A* (= *ummân*) *É-DUB^BA.A* 'master of the tablet-house', *AD^DA É-DUB^BA* 'father of the tablet-house' or simply *BA.BA* 'papa' (?), while the pupil is *DUMU É.-DUB^BA.A* 'son of the tablet-house'; and one tablet says that the pupil who arrives late at school may be beaten and another that a father, gratified by his son's progress, gives the teacher a gift in addition to his proper fee (Falkenstein in *W.O.* I 172–86 and Kramer in 'J.A.O.S.' LXIX 3–19, 199–215).

Another scholastic expression is *ina É* (= *bît*) *ṭuppi* [*man*]*zalta nazālu* 'to take a teaching position in a house of tablet(s), i.e. a school' if the expression is rightly so explained (Ebeling *Nb.B.* 315 3–5). The master's 'asking questions' was called *maš'altu* (Gadd 'C.T.' XLI 39 R. 11, 41 O. 24).

The Hebr. ישב 'sat' similarly means 'studied' under a teacher II Ki. iv 38; cp. Acts xxii 3); but in the Rabb. חכם שישב בישיבה 'a scholar who sat in the school' it refers to the master who presided over the class (Levy *Neuh. u. Chald. Wb.* II 270–1).

The Hebr. לשכת הספר (Jer. xxxvi 12) seems to have been not a school but a kind of secretary's office (s. Muilenberg in 'Studies presented to G. Henton Davies' 228–30).

**P. 66 n. 1.** Cp. Ebeling *K.A.R.I.* II 367 1–8 (s. *M.D.-O.G.* LVIII [1917] 38–39).

**Pp. 66–67.** Cp. Gadd in 'B.S.O.A.S.' XX 255–65 and Lambert in *R.A.* LVI 83–84 and 'J.C.S.' XVI 59–77 for scholastic literature.

**P. 67 n. 2.** Cp. Ungnad in *A.Of.* XIV 273 (*ṣâtu* and *šût pî*) and Meier in *Z.A.* XLVII 244–5 R. 12 (where *ša pî ummâni* is translated 'oral explanation of a scholar').

**P. 67 n. 2.** Also *muttabiltum* 'long commentary'.

In form *mukallimtu* 'exposition' is a subject-commentary in which the explanation projects beyond the left end of the text being explained (Meier in *A.Of.* XII 299–40; s. Meier in *Z.A.* XLVII 244–5 R. 17 and Kraus *M.Va.-Ae.G.* XL ii 334). The *rikis girri* is a 'tablet of excerpts arranged in the order of the archetype' (Oppenheim 'Ass. Dict.' v 93).

**P. 68 n. 2.** Cp. Von Soden *Akk. Hwb.* I 72, where *arû* is given as meaning (i) 'result of multiplication' (ii) 'multiplier', (iii) 'mathematical' and especially 'astronomical tables'.

**P. 69 n. 2.** Such notes are *ṭuppu ûl šalimtu* 'tablet imperfect' (Scheil in *Z.A.* x 199 O. ii. 14) and *ina ṭuppi ûl šalim ûl alsêš* 'it was not perfect on the tablet; I did (= could) not read (it)' (Gadd 'C.T.' XLI 29 O. 3–4; s. Scheil in *R.A.* XV 143–4 and Offner ibid. XLIV 135–43), added by copyists when the archetypes before them are defective.

**P. 69 n. 3.** Both *meḫru* and *gab(a)rû* mean also 'answer', as in *meḫir ṭuppiya* 'an answer to my tablet i.e. letter' (Ungnad *B.B.* 109 25 124 15 178 18 206 21) and *gabrî šipirti* 'an answer to my message' (Ebeling *Nb.B.* 155 23 283 21).

**P. 69 n. 4.** Other expressions are *ša pî* and *ina pût labīrišu* (Meier in *A.Of.* XII 245).

**P. 69 n. 5.** Cp. Lutz 'P.B.S.' I ii 106, colophon. S. note to p. 67 n. 2.

**Pp. 69–70.** Occasionally a scribe notes that a tablet has been written *šurreš* 'hastily' or *zamar* 'hurriedly' (Clay 'B.R.M.' IV 18 28 and Laessøe *bît rimki* 72–73). Not only are signs miscopied or confused or written out of order, but also obverse and reverse sides of a tablet may be interchanged by careless copyists (Holt in 'A.J.S.L.' XXVII 209–10) and occasionally a copyist may let himself run out of space on the tablet to finish what he is copying (Nougayrol in *R.A.* XLV 69).

A careful scribe may add at the end of his copy *a-a-am-ma ul iḫ-ṭi e-du šu-mu ul ú-rad-di ina muḫ-ḫi* 'He did not leave out one line, nor did he put one in addition.' (Lambert 'B.W.L.' [1960] 337).

**P. 70.** A scribe may also add *šî lû kî'am* 'so be it!' as a pious hope or wish at the end of the text; such a note must be distinguished from the simple *kî'am* 'so, as above' (Landsberger in *W.O.* I 364[1]).

**P. 70 n. 3.** Hence also *nisḫu* (s. p. 70 n. 11) 'paragraph, section, extract; copy, exemplar' (Cardascia *Murašû* 57[6]), with which the Aram. *nusḥâ* and Arab. *nusḫatu(n)* 'exemplar, copy' are connected.

**P. 70 n. 8, n. 9.** The Accadian words for teaching are *kullumu* (Falkenstein in *W.O.* I 184) and *šûḫuzu* (Landsberger *M.S.L.* I 101 iii 19) as well as *lummudu*, those for learning are *lamādu* (Von Soden *Akk. Hwb.* I 531–2) and *aḫāzu* (Von Soden ibid. 18–19). The Acc. *iḫzu* 'receiving' for learning, derived from the last verb, recalls the Heb. לֶקַח 'taking' for 'learning' (Is. xxix 24, Prov. i 5 ix 9). The subjects taught are not only *ṭupšarrūtu* 'clerkly skill' (s. p. 66 n. 1) and *miḫiltu* 'forming signs' (s. p. 73 n. 6) but also *šandabak(k)u* 'secretarial knowledge (?)', and *minûtu* 'counting' and *nikkasu* 'accounts' as well as music (Falkenstein op. cit. 179[28], 185–6).

**P. 70 n. 10.** Also *tâmartu* 'seeing' for perusing a tablet (s. Thureau-Dangin in *R.A.* XXXII 113–4), as in *ana tâmartišu* 'for his perusing' and *ana tâmarti (u) šitas(s)iya* 'for my seeing (and) speaking aloud', i.e. 'reading' (Muss-Arnolt 'C.D.A.L.' 1078, 1172).

That *šasû* 'to speak out loud, proclaim' like קרא 'proclaimed' was used for 'reading' (cp. Lachish iii 9, 12 [?] vi 5, 13) not only to others (Harper 'A.B.L.' IV 391 O. 13–5) but also to oneself (Streck *Assurbanipal* II 356–9 c 9, d 7, *alq.*) is explained by the ancient practice of usually reading aloud whether to others or to oneself. Euripides and Antiphanes perhaps afford the earliest examples of silent reading (Turner in 'Classical Quarterly' XLIII 14[4]); so Caesar was able γραμματίδιον μικρὸν . . . ἀναγινώσκειν σιωπῇ (Plutarch *Brutus* v 2) and Ambrose surprised his friends because *cum legebat, oculi ducebantur per paginas et cor intellectum rimabatur, vox autem et lingua quiescebant. Saepe, cum adessemus . . ., sic eum legentem vidimus tacite et aliter numquam* (Augustine *Confessiones* vi 3).

Does 'this book of the law shall not depart out of thy mouth' (Josh. i 8) reflect reading aloud?

**P. 70 n. 11.** Verbs for 'to write' seem always to have meant originally 'to scratch, incise, cut' or the like. Thus, even if *šaṭāru* 'to write' and *šarāṭu* 'to scratch' are not connected *per metathesim*, the analogy of the Syr. *sraṭ* 'pricked, wrote' illustrates the probable semantic development; so too the Hebr. בֵּאֵר 'engraved' on stone (Deut. xxvii 8) and 'inscribed' on tablets (Hab. ii 2) is cognate with the Arab. *baʾara* 'dug' (Zorell *Lex. Hebr. et Aram.* 93), and the Bab. *ṣiʾpu* 'letter' (Ungnad *B.B.* 364) and the Arab. *ṣaḥîfatu(n)* 'written page' are similarly derived from the √*ṢḤP* as seen in the Arab. *ṣaḥafa* 'dug'. Further, the √*KT* 'to beat', whence the Acc. *katātu* 'to destroy' and the Hebr. *kāṯaṯ* 'hammered' are derived, combined with *B* is the source of the Hebr. *kāṯaḇ* 'wrote' and the Arab. *kataba* 'sewed, wrote', inasmuch as sewing and writing are both forms of pricking; cp. Gr. γράφειν 'to scratch', 'to write' and σκαριφᾶσθαι 'to scratch, sketch in outline' and Lat. *scribere* 'to write', which comes from this word (s. Gelb 'Study of Writing' 6–7).

A general term is *šiṭirtam šakānum* 'to draw up a document' (Ebeling *Ab.B., Louvre* 68–69 94 21).

**Pp. 70–72.** Cp. Meissner *Bab. u. Ass.* II 325–9 for an account of Babylonian schools. The names of many scribes are known and the careers of a few can be traced, if only in outline (Ungnad in *A.Of.* XIV 62–63; s. Huffmon 'Amorite Personal Names' 279, where the names of the scribes at Mâri are listed); the profession seems to have run in families (Lambert in 'J.C.S.' XI 1–14, 112), as the Hebr. בְּנֵי־הַסֹּפֶרֶת as the name of a family of returned exiles perhaps indicates (Ezr. ii 55).

**Pp. 71–72.** Other specialist scribes are *DUB.SAR-ZAG*[GA] = *zazakku, zazazakku* 'geometer', a high administrative officer in Old-Babylonian times (Meissner *Ass. Stud.* I 81 and II 103, Eilers in *Z.D.M.G.* XC 187–8, San Nicolò in *S.B.A.W., Ph.-h.Kl.* 1941 ii/2, 47[1]) and *DUB.SAR-A.ŠÀ* 'field-clerk', who must have been someone of the same sort in Neo-Babylonian times (Ebeling *Nb.B.U.* 191 31); the *ṭupšar piqitti* 'clerk of inspection, surveyor' may have had similar duties (Meissner *M.Va.G.* XXI 155 and in *O.Lz.* XXV 243–4).

**P. 71 n. 2.** The use of *ana . . . qibî-ma umma . . .* 'speak unto B: Thus says A . . .' at the beginning of Old-Babylonian letters implies a runner who knows the contents and on reaching his destination announces them aloud to the addressee (s. Widengren 'Hebrew Prophets' 60–1). This is proved by an Old-Babylonian tablet to the following effect:[1] *ana Kinpi-(il) Marduk qibe-ma*[3] *umma Amat-(il) Mera . . .*[10] *ana Bamatim*[11] *qibe-ma umma Amat-(il) Mera-ma . . .*[15] *ana(il) Mera-nāṣir qibe-ma*[16] *umma (il) Nannar-intuḫ-ma . . .*[1] Say to K.:[3] Thus says A.: . . . .[10], Say to B: Thus says A.: . . .[15] Say to M.:[16] Thus says N.: . . .' (Schroeder *Va. Sd.* XVI 7 1–21). The unnamed addressee in l. 1 is the messenger carrying the tablet, which contains three messages, two from Amat-Mer to two different persons, namely Kinpi-Marduk and Bamatum, in ll. 2–14 and one from Nannar-intuḫ to Mer-nāṣir in ll. 15–20. Neither the messenger nor the recipients can read the tablet; he has received the contents by word of mouth and will repeat them in the same way to them by memory, and thus they will receive it, while the tablet will serve to authenticate the message, if the need arises, and to preserve a record of it (s. Schroeder in *O.Lz.* XXI 5–6).

This is what is meant when the Lord in a vision bids Habakkuk

'write down the vision and inscribe it on tablets
that a reader may run quickly with it'

(Hab. ii 2), *sc.* carry it quickly to those to whom it is addressed. The 'reader' is not the addressee but a messenger described as a 'proclaimer' because, on reaching his destination, he announces the message aloud; the tablet which he carries with him is not necessarily read out but serves to authenticate the message which is written down on it and which he has delivered by word of mouth. Here then רוץ ב׳ 'to run with' is used idiomatically to mean 'to convey quickly', as בוא ב׳ 'to come with' and הלך ב׳ 'went with' connote respectively 'to bring' (e.g. Lev. xvi 3 Ps. lxvi 13) and 'took' (e.g. Exod. x 9, Hos. v 6, and especially II Chron. xxx 6), while the masc. sing. pronoun in בו 'with it' refers back loosely to the vision inscribed on the לוחות 'tablets'. These are probably not 'clay-tablets' but rather 'double waxed writing boards', which will explain the plur. form of the noun (s. n. on p. 16); was then דלת 'leaf (of a door)' a 'leaf' of such a folding tablet as also a 'column' of writing on one side of a sherd (s. p. 80 n. 9)? The messenger must run to deliver the message because 'the vision is yet for the appointed time, and it hasteth towards the end' (R.V.). What 'that he may run that readeth it' (A.V.) is supposed to mean is not clear.

**P. 71 n. 3.** Cp. Meier in *Z.A.* XLVII 244–5 R. 12–16.

**P. 71 n. 8.** The scribe who writes Neo-Babylonian documents often signs himself *šāṭir* *ZAKIŠIB* (= *kunukki*) 'writer of the sealed tablet' (s. San Nicolò & Ungnad *Neobab. Urk.*, Gl. 159–60).

**P. 71 n. 9.** Also (*awēl*) *rêš ṭupšarrī* 'chief of the scribes' (San Nicolò in *Orient.*, *N.S.* XIX 227).

**P. 71 n. 10.** Cp. Keiser 'B.I.N.' I 17 2, *alq.*

**P. 71 n. 12.** Cp. Meissner *M.Va.*(*Ae*).*G.* XXI 155 and in *O.Lz.* XXV 243–4.

**P. 71 n. 13.** Also *ṭupšar minûti* 'scribe of counting' = 'mathematician' (Langdon *Nb.Ki.* 256–7 6 i 32).

**Pp. 72–73.** Both the Sumerian Šulgi king of Ur (*c.* 2048–2001 B.C.) and the Accadian Lipit-Ištar king of Isin (*c.* 1875–1865 B.C.) claimed the title of *DUB.SAR* (Falkenstein in *W.O.* I 172–3).

The king accused of not knowing how to read and write may have been not Cyrus but Nabonidus (Lewy in *A.O.* XVII 68).

**P. 73 n. 2.** The word is the Sum. *KÀM* = Acc. *kammu* 'tablet, text' (Jensen in *K.B.* VI i 385–6) and also 'plate, plaque' of gold or iron serving as an ornament and a 'block' of iron or wood for smoothing the surface of bricks (Von Soden *Akk. Hwb.* 433). Hence *qāṣir kammi* means 'compiler of the text' rather than 'author of the poem' (Gössmann *Era-Epos* 36–37 v 42); Deimel *Šum. Lex.* II iii 655 354 78.

**P. 73 n. 6.** Possibly also *maḫāṣu ša iṣi* (s. p. 19 n. 4) 'to make a stroke, of the stick (i.e. pen)' (Deimel *Š.L.* II 540, 314/14) and *miḫiltu* (= *miḫiṣtu*) 'stroke' (Falkenstein in *W.O.* I 179); but *miḫiṣtu* may perhaps mean also 'section' (Landsberger in *Z.A.* XLIII 76).

**Pp. 73–77.** Cp. Weidner in *A.Of.* XVI 197–215 on royal libraries, especially those of Tiglath-Pileser I (*c.* 1115–1093 B.C.) and Ashurbanipal (668–626 B.C.), whose collection may have amounted to some 5,000 tablets; and cp. Weitmeyer *Babylonske og Assyriske Arkiver og Biblioteker* (Copenhagen, 1955) for an account of archives and libraries.

**P. 74 notes 10 and 11.** The Sum. *GÁ-DUB*$^{BA}$ (s. Kraus *Altbab. Br.* I 10 and II 13, 139) is now given as the Acc. *bît ṭuppi* 'house of tablet(s)' i.e. 'school' (Von Soden *Akk. Hwb.* I 134) and 'archive(s)', whence *DUMU GÁ.DUB.*$^{BA(.A)}$ = *mār bît ṭuppi* 'archivist' (Alexander 'B.I.N.' VII 50 13) and *mārū bît ṭuppi ummênū* 'skilled archivists' (Dossin *T.C.L.* XXII 7 37) come. A *mâr bît ṭuppi ša êkallim* 'archivist of the palace' is also found (Schroeder Va. Sd. XVI 118 20–21; cp. Dossin *T.C.L.* XVIII 149 8).

**P. 74 n. 12.** The Sum. *IM-GÚ-LÁ-GIŠ-TUK* means 'tablet to be read aloud' but the Acc. *girginakku,* with which it is equated, has come to mean 'library', possibly originally one attached to a temple, while the Sum. *GÌR.GIN.NA,* from which it is immediately derived, is a 'serial tablet'; for such were used especially for teaching purposes (Oppenheim 'Ass. Dict.' v 86–87).

**P. 75 n. 11.** Catalogues have been found of liturgies at Asshur (Langdon in 'A.J.S.L.' XLII 110–27) and of Hittite texts at Boğaz-Köy (Laroche in *A.O.* XVII 14–22) as well as of miscellaneous texts from Ashurbanipal's library (Lambert in 'J.C.S.' XVI 59–77).

**Pp. 75–76.** Also at Ur (Nies 'Ur Dynasty' 44 35–36).

**Pp. 76–77.** A tablet not infrequently has a note at the end warning a borrower to replace it in its chest or return it to its owner's house, not to injure it or erase anything on it or put it out of use, not to lend it to anyone else, not to keep it or purloin it by theft, fraud or force ((Scheil in *R.A.* XV 143–4 and Offner ibid. XLIV 135–43). Such a note is *āmeru ai itpil* 'let the reader not misuse' (Meissner in *M.Ao.G.* XII i/ii 46–47) or 'profane' (Lambert 'Bab. Wisd.' 307) the tablet.

**Pp. 78–79.** Cp. Albright in 'B.A.S.O.R.' CLXXIII 52 for the Ugaritic tablet from Beth-Shemesh.

**P. 79.** References to writing can be found also in the works of the prophets of the 8th century B.C. (Is. viii 1 and Hos. viii 12).

**P. 79 n. 8.** The accounts of the writing down of the Law are divergent, some ascribing it to God (Exod. xxxi 18, xxxii 16, xxxiv 1; Deut. v 22, ix 10, x 1–5) and others to Moses (Exod. xxiv 4, xxxiv 28; Deut. xxxi 19); and, as the sources vary, little if any use can be made of them. Further, even if the ancient Israelites could read and write by the 12th century B.C., archaeology has as yet produced no long written Hebrew documents but only scraps of written stuff which can be securely dated before *c.* 1000–8000 B.C. (s. pp. 108 ff. and cp. Millard in *Bibl. Arch.* XXXV [1972] 98–111).

**P. 79 n. 10.** The Eg. *mdꜣ.t* and *sš nṯr* 'writing of a god' mean the hieroglyphic script of ancient Egypt. All scripts were originally pictographic, and God would naturally be expected to use such a script when writing the 'tables of stone' with His own finger (Exod. xxxi 18, E; Deut. ix 10); this would give them sanctity and venerable antiquity (S. R. Driver *Exodus* 346). Contrariwise, Isaiah's 'pen of a man' (Is. viii 1) would be one used for ordinary mortal i.e. cursive script (s. pp. 84–85).

**P. 80.** What exactly גִּלָּיוֹן means is not certain. It is variously translated in the ancient Versions τόμος καινοῦ χάρτου 'piece of new papyrus' (LXX$^{A}$), διφθέρωμα 'scroll of leather' (Theod.), κεφαλίς 'scroll' (Aq.), *liber* 'book' (Jer.), *gelāyûnâ* 'volume' (Pesh.), *lûaḥ* 'tablet' (Targ.), and *ṣafîḥatu(n)* 'plate/sheet of metal or stone' (Saʿad.). Jewish lexicographers have *ṣaḥîfatu(n)* 'leaf, sheet' (alFâsî) and אגרת 'letter' (Qimḥî); their modern successors have *tabula e ligno, lapide aut metallo facta* (Gesenius), *glatte Tafel, Schrifttafel* (Siegfried & Stade), and *tabula cerata* or *pergamentum* (Zorell). Recent suggestions are 'sheet of parchment' (Ginsberg *Marx* 361), 'tablet of polished metal' like those recently found at Gebal (Widengren op. cit. 69[1]) and 'board of wood or metal' (G. R. Driver in Hastings 'D.B.' [1963] 1048). Certainly parchment can be ruled out, since it cannot have been known in the 8th century B.C. and a sheet of metal is unlikely for taking down something resembling a lecture or a sermon; further, the use of the Hebr. גָּלָה 'uncovered' does not suggest anything which can be so called *a detergundo et poliendo* (Gesenius). Rather, like the Syr. ܓܠܐ *denudavit; manifestum fecit; declaravit;* (*librum*) *in lucem edidit*, it suggests simply any unspecified means of recording or publication (cp. Esth. iii 14 viii 13). It may have been a waxed tablet, if this may not have been too small, or a strip of leather (s. G. R. Driver 'Aramaic Documents' 1–2) or perhaps papyrus (s. p. 82), as the Greek versions suggest, even though the actual idea of a roll or scroll may be due to confusion with מְגִלָּה 'roll, scroll' from גָּלַל 'rolled' (s. p. 84 n. 1).

That חֶרֶט 'stylus' used with it superficially suggests something hard (*e.g.* a tablet), not anything soft (*e.g.* leather or papyrus), for which עֵט 'pen' is the proper instrument (s. pp. 84–85), proves little or nothing; for these words may have changed their connotation with the passage of time.

The first letter mentioned in the Old Testament, that of David to Joab, was perhaps written on a sherd, like the *ostraca* found at Lachish; and the story implies Uriah's inability to read it (II Sam. xi 14).

**P. 80.** Cp. Ugar. *dlt* 'note, memorandum' inscribed alone on the back of an alphabetic tablet (Virolleaud in *Syr.* XXVIII [1951] 24 ii rev.) which is intended to warn the teacher that it has a scholastic text on the obverse side. Cp. the Hebr. דלת 'tablet' in כתבתי על הדלת ככל אשר שלח [אדני אל]י 'I have written on the notebook according to all (the instructions) that my lord has sent me' (Torczyner 'Lachish' I iv 3–4 = *K.A.I.* no. 194), i.e. the officer acting for the chief officer has left him a written record of all the duties carried out by him while left alone in charge of the outpost (s. Reider in 'J.Q.R.' *N.S.* XXIX [1938–9] 236). The Biblical דלת 'scroll' is perhaps a column of writing on a manuscript (Jer. xxxvi 23).

**P. 81.** A *papyrus* of the 8th century B.C. has now been found at Murabbaʿât (Benoit, Milik & De Vaux 'D.J.D.' II 93–100). Cp. Galling in 'Near Eastern studies . . . W. F. Albright' ed. Goedicke [1971] 218.

**Pp. 81–83.** Among the earliest examples of writing on skins are the Scroll of Isaiah and a somewhat thinner one of the Commentary on Habbakuk from Qumrân (Trever and Brownlee *ap.* Burrows 'Dead Sea Scrolls' I [1950] xiv–xv, xx–xxi). Rabbinic literature refers here and there to the use of the skins of fishes; for the writing of scriptural passages 'on the surface of the skin of ritually clean fish' s. Neufeld in 'J.A.N.E.S. Columbia Univ.' v [1973] (T. H. Gaster Festschrift) 309–22. For writing on leather s. Driver 'Aramaic documents' 1–3.

**P. 82.** Papyrus was employed very early in the West, where clay was rare; for example, the Byblian prince *Zkr-bʿl* in the 12th–11th centuries B.C. kept his accounts on it (Wilson *ap.* Pritchard 'A.N.E.T.' 27; s. Macalister 'Philistines' 127).

**Pp. 82–83.** Two passages in which leather or papyrus seems to be intended in the Old Testament are the following. In the first Hosea says

> 'the iniquity of Ephraim is bound up,
> his sin is laid up in store'

(Hos. xiii 12, R.V.) where the reference is to rolling up the scroll on which the score of Ephraim's iniquity or sin is written down and tying it up with a cord, after which it is stored away in a jar or other receptacle suitable for the preservation of records (s. pp. 74–76) against the day of reckoning when it will be brought out of storage to be consulted. In the second Isaiah says

> 'bind thou up the testimony, seal it among my disciples'

(Is. viii 16), where 'bind up' similarly means 'roll and tie up' the scroll on which the testimony is recorded. Possibly בלמדי 'among my disciples', which is a curious expression and seems to have little point in the context, ought to be read לָמֹד or בַּל־לָמְדָה (cp. Ps. xxxii 9 for the construction) or מְלַמֵּד (Kittel) 'so that it cannot be studied' after the LXX's τοῦ μὴ μαθεῖν (cp. Targ.'s לא צבן דיילפון בה).

**P. 83.** For the Nash papyrus s. N. Avigad in *Scripta Hierosolymitana* IV [1958] 65–9 and the literature cited there.

**P. 83 n. 10.** Cp. Job xix 23 where the sense is obscured by various dubious translations of בַּסֵּפֶר which are all improbable if not actually wrong, all being more or less inconsistent with יֵחָקוּ 'may they be cut, inscribed'. Further, the Hebr. סֵפֶר, unlike the cognate Phoen. ספר = Aram. ספרא, very rarely designates an 'inscription' (N.E.B.) incised in stone or rock. If, however, it is vocalized סְפָר, which the Akk. *siparru* 'bronze, copper' (s. Von Soden *A.Hwb.* 1048 and Thompson 'Dict. of Ass. Chem. and Geol. [1936] 63–7) suggests, the clause may be translated 'may they (*sc.* my words) be engraved on bronze/copper' and so be imperishable (s. Friedländer in 'J.Q.R.' XV [1903] 102–3). Such a word may probably be rightly recognized in a few other passages (Exod. xvii 14; Jud. v 14), but not in the law of the adulterous woman (Num. v 23). Cp. Perles *Anal. z. Textkr. d. Alt. Test.* [1922] 70.

**P. 84 n. 1.** A Neo-Bab. (*mašak*) *magallatu* 'scroll (of leather)' has been found on two as yet unpublished tablets (Wiseman in *Iraq* XVII 12[118]).

**P. 84 n. 9.** If עֵט is rightly translated σχοῖνος by the Septuagint (Jer. viii 8), which reflects ܥܘܛܐ *gramen, herba* (Wutz *Transkriptionen* 152), a rare word found only in a native Syriac glossary (Payne-Smith), it must originally have denoted a reed-pen, even though it comes to be used also for one of metal. The Acc. *qanû* 'reed' and also 'stylus' shows the same semantic development; cp. Is. xlii 3, where the Hebr. קָנֶה 'reed' has been taken as 'stylus' (s. Koenig in *V.T.* xviii 152–72 on Lambert in *Iraq* xxvii 5/8 ii 23–25).

The ostraca from Lachish and the papyri from Egypt were written with a brush, not a pen (Turner in 'Classical Quarterly' XLIII 11).

**P. 84 n. 11.** In Job xix 24 'with an iron pen and lead' (R.S.V.) for בעט ברזל ועפרת will not stand; for no alloy of iron and lead is known, and lead alone is too weak for cutting stone or rock. Iron alone could serve this purpose. The absence, too, of בְּ 'with' before בַּרְזֶל marks this out as the instrument used for the cutting, while the additional וְעֹפֶרֶת 'and lead' shows this to be something concomitant with the iron, like ink with a pen, showing up the strokes; so Sargon II (721–705 B.C.) speaks of *A.BǍR* (*abāru*) *mu-nam-mir a-ru-uš*(?)-*ti-šú-nu* 'lead which makes their dirt shine', i.e. shows it up by the contrast of colours (Winckler *Keilschrifttexte Sargons* I [1889] $34_{201}$). Here, then, the stylus of iron makes the incisions in the rock representing the required cuneiform signs which the lead makes stand out visibly to the reader against the background of the rock in which they are incised (s. Thompson Dict. of Ass. Chem. and Geol. [1936] 118–19). Thus ועפרת 'and lead', which is not *eiusdem generis* with בעט ברזל 'with a stylus of iron', is added with a *waw copulativum* or *explicativum* (s. Gesenius–Kautzsch–Cowley 484 n. 1 b) to mean 'of course with lead' hammered into the signs already cut in the rock to make them stand out as the Vulg. *stylo ferreo et plumbi lamina* suggests. It remains now only to reveal M.T.'s לעד 'for ever' as לְעֵד 'for a witness' (cp. Theod. εἰς μαρτύριον) as the whole purpose of the process.

Finally, in no case so far as archaeologists have discovered was molten lead ever poured, but only hard lead hammered into symbols incised in rock to ensure perpetuity, as at Nahr-älKälb near Beirut; and so Darius I (522–486 B.C.) had the strokes of the cuneiform signs in the small inscriptions above his head at Bisutûn filled with lead, hammered into them to draw attention to them and to make them, as still now, easily legible (Cameron *ap.* Galling in *W.O.* II [1954–9] 3–6).

**P. 86 n. 4.** The ink used by Jewish scribes was till the end of the 2nd century A.D. non-metallic, being made of soot mixed with oil and gum of balsam, and so was easily washed off with a sponge. When R. Meir tried some time after A.D. 100 to introduce a metallic ink, which was more durable and could be erased only with a pen-knife, R. Ishmael forbade the practice; it was clearly regarded as a pagan innovation (Blau *Studien z. althebr. Buchwesen* 151–7).

**Pp. 86–87.** An Aramaean writing outfit has been found in Egypt (Aimé-Giron in *B.I.F.A.O.* XXXVIII 47–57); and several pots of bronze and of earthenware, which are proved by the traces of ink left in them to have been Jewish inkpots (s. pl. 63), have been found at Qumrân (De Vaux in *R.B.*, *N.S.* LXI 211–2, 229).

**P. 87 n. 6.** On the practice of writing in early Israel cp. Millard in 'Bibl. Arch.' xxxv [1972] 98–111.

**P. 88 n. 8.** That any ordinary boy, met by chance on a journey, can have been able to write at so early a date is improbable; that he can have had the necessary tools with him and that Gideon can have had time to wait while he slowly painted on a sherd or engraved on a piece of stone, already prepared for the purpose, a list of 77 names is equally improbable. Why will he have needed to write and not recite them (Jud. viii 14)? What, too, can have been written down in listing trees so few 'that a child may write them' (Is. x 19)? Surely כתב 'wrote' must in such contexts have had its primitive sense of 'pricked, scratched, i.e. ticked off' e.g. the numbers on a piece of wood or stone to check them as he counted them (s. note to p. 70 n. 11); cp. נכתב 'was tattooed' as a mark of disgrace (Jer. xvii 13, Dillmann).

**P. 88 n. 15.** Apparently Hezekiah, although he kept an officer called a סופר at his court, was able to read (II Ki. xviii 37, xix 14); for קרא 'proclaimed' means here as elsewhere 'read' (s. n. on p. 70 n. 10).

**Pp. 88–89.** Cp. Nielsen 'Oral Tradition' 40–60, who examines all the references to writing in the Old Testament and concludes that, while used to a considerable extent for administrative purposes before the Exile, it can have played only an insignificant part in the transmission of literature till after it.

**Pp. 89–90.** Surely צו לצו קו לקו cannot mean 'it is *ṣāw* for *ṣ* and *qāw* for *q*', meaning that *ṣāw* is the name of *ṣ* and *qāw* that of *q* (Hallo in 'J.B.L.' LXXVI 337–8)? S. n. on p. 90 n. 1 (*infra*).

**P. 90.** The O.T. is said to contain 429 references to writing and written documents (Diringer in Camb. Hist. of Bible I [1970] 13).

**P. 90 n. 1.** Any alphabetic explanation of these words which goes back to the 8th century (Houbigant *Bibl. Hebr.* IV 73–74; cp. Montgomery in 'J.B.L.' XXXI 141–2), however, is open to several objections. First, the context suggests nothing so coherent as a master's repetition of the alphabet to his pupils but rather the fuddled ramblings of a party of drunken revellers; and no master is likely to be teaching it to 'them that are weaned from the milk and drawn from the breasts' (Is. xxviii 9, R.V.). Second, how can learning the alphabet have resulted in the drunkards' downfall? Third, something like אלף בית (לגמל) (cp. Syr. *'ālef bait* or *baitâ*, *'alpâ baitâ* and Gr. ἀλφάβητος 'alphabet') or even מאלף לתו (cp. Engl. 'from A to Z') rather than '*ṣ* to *q*', two letters arbitrarily drawn from the middle of the alphabet, would be expected if the actual 'alphabet' were meant.

Something suitable to drunkards, however, can easily be won for both words without supposing that they actually mean 'vomit' and 'excrement' (Schmidt *ap.* Gunkel *Psalmen* 77); for neither of these meanings makes sense. The note about אשר הלכו אחרי צו הצו הוא מטיף 'those who have gone after *ṣāw*: *ṣaw* is the babbler' (Zad. Doc. vii 1; cp. Hos. v 11), though based on the passage here discussed, shows that צו 'babble, chatter' shows knowledge of such a word; and the

Arab. *ḍauḍā* 'clamoured', *ḍauḍ.ᵃⁿ* 'clamour', *ḍawwatu* 'clamour', and *ḍauḍâtu* 'bawling, shouting' (cognate *ṣûwatu* 'echo') confirm it. In the same way the Psalmist's *qaw* 'chord, note, sound' (Ps. xix 5; cp. Ecclus. xliv 5, Disc. x 9 and Th. H. i 28–29) attest the existence of such a word; and the Talm. Aram. *qawqaw* 'croaking of frogs' and the Syr. *qauqî* = Arab. *qâqa, qauqa'a, qauqā* '(a hen) cackled, clucked' are evidence for the use of a musical term like קו 'chord, note' in a pejorative sense, *e.g.* 'cackle, prattle' or the like. Both words are obviously onomatopoeic; but here they are chosen partly as reproducing the 'shouts and cries of a party of drunkards', but partly also as echoing the קיא 'vomiting' and צאה 'excrement' of v. 8. Similar onomatopoeic sounds are found in other languages, for example the German *A! tara lara da!* in Auerbach's cellar (Goethe) and the English 'with a Hey and a Ho, | Tirra-ley Tirra-low' (Skelton). Finally זעיר שם זעיר שם 'a little there, a little there' is what they say, namely 'another drop (of wine) there, another over there', *i.e.* 'drinks all round', being the Hebrew equivalent of the Greek φέρ' ὕδωρ, φέρ' οἶνον (Anacreon) or the Engl. 'another little drink won't do us any harm!' (Robey); for all the ancient translators take זעיר not as masc. 'boy' but as neut. 'a little' (LXX ἔτι μικρόν, Vulg. *modicum ibi* and Pesh. *qallîl ləṭammān*). All this, says the prophet in God's name, can only result in falling down, being broken and snared and carried off (s. G. R. Driver in Ackroyd & Lindars 'Words and Meanings' [1968] 53–57).

This explanation of צו and קו here does not mean that ץ, צ and ק may not originally have been called respectively *ṣaw* and *qaw*, but only that such names cannot be proved from the present passage.

**P. 91/2 n. 4.** The story of Wenamon shows that papyrus was imported from Egypt to Gebal *c.* 1100 B.C. so that it was used there, but the Phoenician climate is such that little if any would be likely to survive; and in the same story the existence of writing is presupposed in the notice of Zakar-ba'al having the records of his dynasty read out before him (Breasted 'Ancient Records: Egypt' IV 282 § 576, 284 § 582).

The place which the Phoenicians called *Gbl* (Acc. *Gublu*, Can. *Gubla*, Hebr. *Gᵉbal*), meaning 'hill', from its position on a height between Tripoli and Beirut, was called *Βύβλος* by the Greeks as the mart through which *βύβλος* 'papyrus', used for making ropes and paper, was transported from Egypt to Greece. The two words cannot be phonetically connected; the place would therefore have been called *Βύβλος* by the Greeks from the plant of which they knew through the port of Gebal, helped by the superficial resemblance of the two names. The origin of the Greek word, whether Egyptian or Mediterranean, is still a matter of conjecture; so, for example, a √ *bulb-/pulb-* 'to grow', to which both *βύβλαξ* 'oleander' and *βύβλος* 'papyrus' may be referred, has been postulated, although nothing is in fact known of such a root (s. Masson *Recherches sur les plus anciens emprunts sémitiques en grec* 101–7). [Cp., however, Rosén in *V.T.* I [1951] 306].

**P. 92 n. 2.** This decipherment of the proto-Byblian inscriptions has now been published (Dhorme in *Syria* XXV 1–35; cp. Jirku in *Z.D.M.G.* CII 201–14 and Martin in *Orient., N.S.* XXXI 250–71, 339–63).

**P. 93 n. 1.** Also Albright in 'B.A.S.O.R.' CX 6–22 and CXVI 12–14.

**Pp. 90–94.** Cp. Milik in 'D.J.D.' II [1961] 98 for primitive unidentified symbols denoting measures of capacity.

**Pp. 95–96.** The inscriptions from Sarâbîṭ-alḪâdim have been described as written in 'vulgar Canaanite' (Albright in 'B.A.S.O.R.' CX [1948] 22) and alternatively in 'good Canaanite' (Albright 'Archaeology of Palestine' [1949] 188–9); as they can hardly be read, both judgements are premature!

**Pp. 96–97.** Also Bauer *Zur Entzifferung der Sinaiinschriften* [1918] and most recently

Albright in 'B.A.S.O.R.' cx [1948] 15–22; cp. Gardiner 'My Working Years' 213–7 and Albright 'The Proto-Sinaitic Inscriptions and their Decipherment' (Harvard, 1966) 16–30 for a fresh attempt to decipher these inscriptions.

**P. 97 n. 1.** Also in the 'Legacy of Egypt' 55–58.

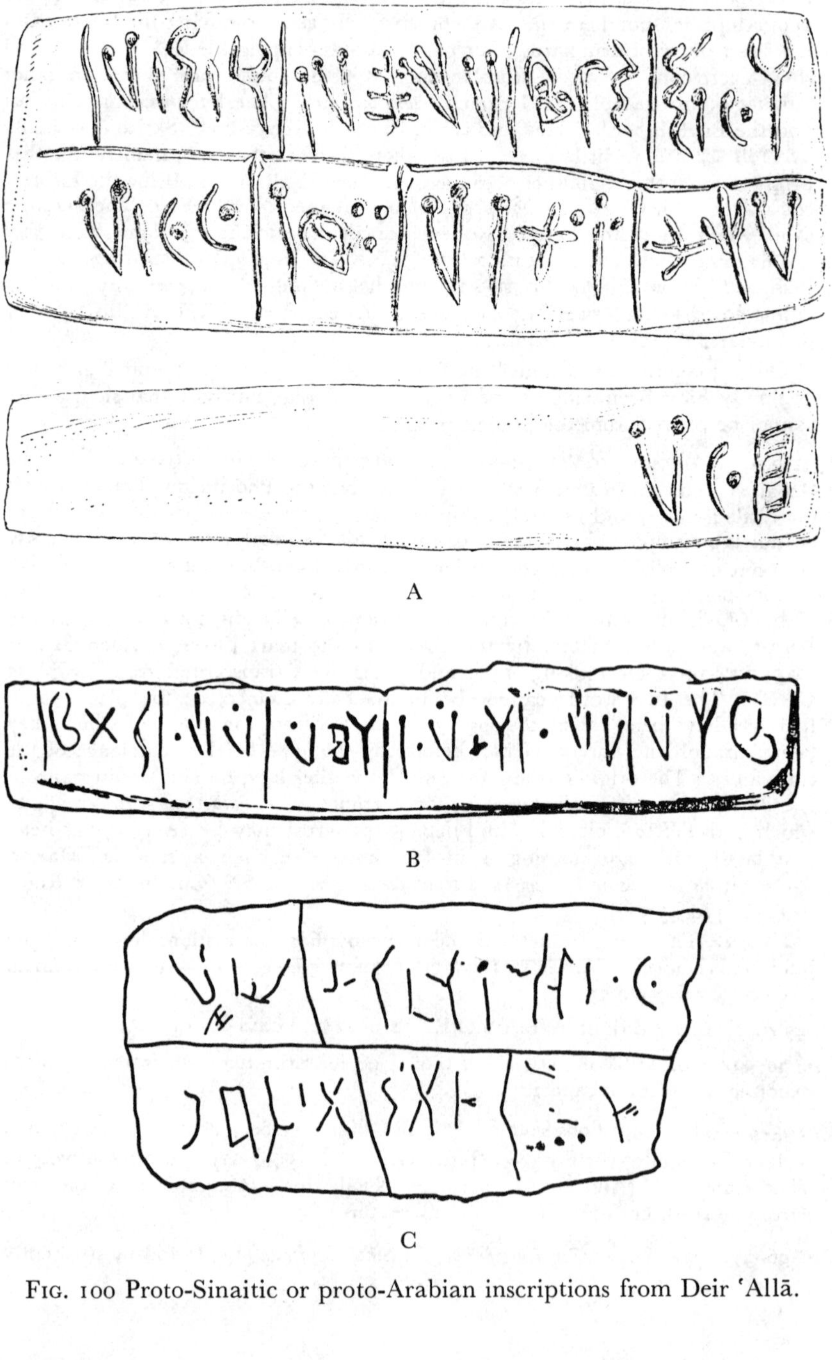

A

B

C

FIG. 100 Proto-Sinaitic or proto-Arabian inscriptions from Deir ʿAllā.

**Pp. 98–106.** The following approximate dates have been suggested for these early inscribed objects: plaque from Shechem (p. 98 fig. 42), 18th–17th century B.C.; potsherd from Gezer (p. 98 fig. 41), 17th century B.C.; dagger from Lachish (p. 99 fig. 43), 17th–16th century B.C.; potsherd from Tell-elḤesy (p. 99 fig. 47), 15th–14th century B.C.; plaque from a Byblian tomb, 14th century B.C.; potsherd from Tell-elʿAjjûl (p. 99 fig. 46), 14th century B.C.; wine-jar and bowl and lid from Lachish (p. 100 fig. 49), 13th century B.C.; sherd from Beth-Shemesh, 13th–12th century B.C.; sarcophagus of Aḥiram (p. 105 fig. 54 and pls. 51–52), 12th century B.C.; inscription of Yeḥimilk (p. 105) and sherd from Tell Bêt Mirsim, 12th–11th century B.C.; and calendar from Gezer *c.* 1000 B.C. (Maisler in 'J.P.O.S.' XVIII [1938] 281–2). Such dates, however, must not be pressed too closely; for palaeography depends on comparable dated texts, which are here unobtainable; only archaeological evidence is available (s. n. on pp. 104–6).

**P. 102.** Excavations at Deir ʿAllā in Transjordan, a site dubiously identified with the Biblical Succoth overlooking the Jabbok from the north (Merrill *ap.* G. A. Smith 'Historical Geog.' [1931] 612[2]) have yielded many relics of the late Bronze (*c.* 1500–1200 B.C.) and early Iron (*c.* 1200–900 B.C.) Ages. The latter, including much damaged pottery, has yielded fragments with traces of writing on them and especially one large piece with some twelve lines of an uncertain Aramaic script in black and red colours (Franken in *V.T.* XVII [1967] 480–1 and pl. IV). The former has produced several old pieces of considerable interest, namely six small oblong pieces of stone marked with approximately 6–13 dots clearly arranged in a definite but uncertain pattern (s. pl. 50.1), an inscription of two lines and a separate piece, apparently complete of only three signs (fig. 100 A and pl. 49, 1 and 2), and two others, the first (fig. 100 B) with one and the second (fig. 100 C and pl. 49, 3) with two lines of text.

All these tablets carry a complete text, written in a script regarded as proto-Sinaitic or perhaps rather proto-Arabian. A proposed decipherment of these texts is that the names of two known South-Arabian (Thamudean) gods, *ʾly* and *Khl*, may be found in them (s. Ryckmans *Noms propres sud-sém.* I [1934] 2, 16) and that A is a lament for a dead child, B a monument in memory of a dead child, and C a thanksgiving to *Khlʾl* for curing an infirmity of a hand (Van den Branden in *V.T.* XV [1965] 129–49 and cp. 532–5).

**P. 103 n. 4.** Another suggestion is that *ḫrṣn* is not a common noun meaning 'axe' but the name of the *rb khnm* 'chief of the priests' (De Langhe *Ras Shamra* I 207, II 297–8; cp. Gordon 'Ugaritic Textbook' [1965] 405/1016). Such names as the O.-Ass. (Cappad.) *Ḫu-ra-ṣa-nu-um* (Stephens 'Personal Names . . . of Cappadocia' 41) and Ass. (Ugar.) *Ḫu-ra-ṣa-na* (Nougayrol *Palais Royal d'Ugarit* III 245) support this suggestion.

**Pp. 104–6.** The approximate dates B.C. most recently assigned to the earliest Phoenician inscriptions are the following (s. n. on pp. 98–106):

| | | |
|---|---|---|
| arrow-heads of *ʿbdlb(ʾ)t* | 1200–1100 (C) | |
| tomb of *ʾḥrm* | 1100 (Y) or 1000 (C) | |
| arrow-head of *ʾdy bn ʿky* [s. below] | 11th cent. (C) | |
| arrow-head of *Zkrbʿl* | 1100–1050 (Y) | |
| spatula of *ʿzrbʿl* | 1100–1050 (C, Y) | |
| arrow-head of *ʾdy bn ʿky* [s. above] | 10th cent. (Y) | |
| building of *Yḥmlk* | 950 (C) | |
| statue inscribed *ʾbbʿl* | 935–914 (C) | 10th cent. (Y) |
| statue inscribed *ʾlbʿl* | 914–885 (C) | |
| *Špṭbʿl* and *ʿbdʾ* | soon after 900 (C) | |

C = Cross in 'B.A.S.O.R.' CXXXIV 9–15.
Y = Yeivin in *RB.*, *N.S.* LXV 588.

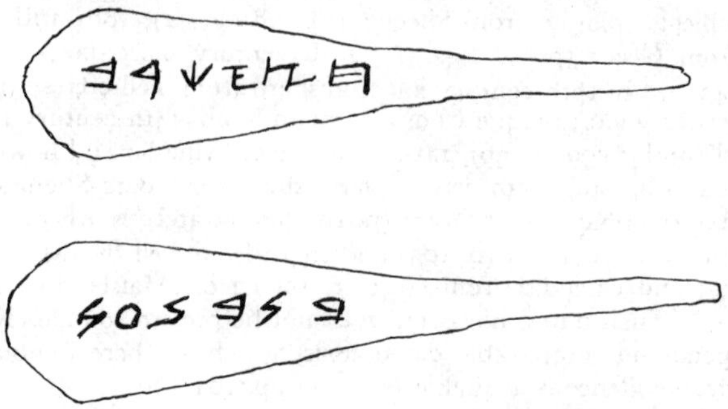

FIG. 101. Inscribed arrow-head from älBiqʿah in the Lebanon (reading of inscription uncertain).

The arrow-head of *Zkrbʿl* (s. fig. 101) comes from älBiqʿah in the Lebanon (s. Milik in 'B.A.S.O.R.' CXLIII 3–6 and Yeivin ibid. 585–7). The inscription on it has been read חץ זכר | בן בנען 'arrow of Zakkur son of Bin-ʿAn' (Milik in 'B.A.S.O.R.' CLXIII 3–6), or חץ זכרבעל | בן בנענת 'arrow of Zakar-baʿal son of Bin-ʿAnat' (Yeivin in loc. cit. 586–7). s. *K.A.I.* no. 22.

Other dates assigned to such early Phoenician inscriptions are the following: ʿAzarbaʿal *c.* 1000 B.C.; 'Aḥiram, early 10th century B.C.; 'Abibaʿal, *c.* 925 B.C.; 'Elibaʿal, *c.* 915 B.C., Shipiṭbaʿal, end of 10th century B.C.; ʿAbdâ, *c.* 900 B.C. (Albright in 'J.A.O.S.' LXVII [1947] 153–60; s. Albright *ap.* Wright 'The Bible and the ancient Near East' 339–40). A date *c.* 1000 B.C. for 'Aḥiram is said to be supported by the evidence of the pottery found by the tomb (Albright 'Archaeology of Palestine' 190); but how exact is such evidence?

Details of these inscriptions can be found in Donner & Röllig *K.A.I.*

**P. 105 fig. 54.** The text reads לדעת הן יפד לך תחת זן meaning 'to know (i.e. for information, namely 'take heed')! For disaster (is) for (i.e. awaits) thee under this stone', namely a warning to the reader not to enter and thereby violate '*ḥrm*'s grave; cp. Hebr. פיד 'disaster, ruin' and Arab. *fâda* (*y*) 'disappeared, died'. The text is given in *K.A.I.* no. 2.

**P. 105 n. 5.** Cp. Ronzevalle in *M.U.B.* XII 3–40, arguing that the script on 'Aḥiram's tomb is already passing from the lapidary to a cursive style.

**P. 106.** The earliest Canaanite inscriptions were written in vertical or horizontal lines with the signs facing in either direction. Vertical writing perhaps predominated in the early period, as on the oldest Sumerian and Egyptian inscriptions; and, when horizontal writing came into fashion, the direction of the script determined that in which the individual signs faced.

In the change-over from vertical to horizontal lines, a tendency to swing the signs round 90°, i.e. to give them a quarter-turn, manifested itself, as it already had in the old Sumerian writing (s. pp. 34–36). If then the script in a horizontal line ran from left to right, the symbols rotated 90° against the clock; if it ran from right to left, the rotation was 90° with the clock, as the evolution of the sign for Y (י) shows.

In the same way the development of the symbol for B can be traced from the original Egyptian hieroglyphic sign to the corresponding Greek letter, showing clearly that all the forms, from the Egyptian to the Greek (with which the Ugaritic may perhaps be included, although the stylization of the cuneiform signs obscures its conformity to the general pattern), of any given letter are in some way or other

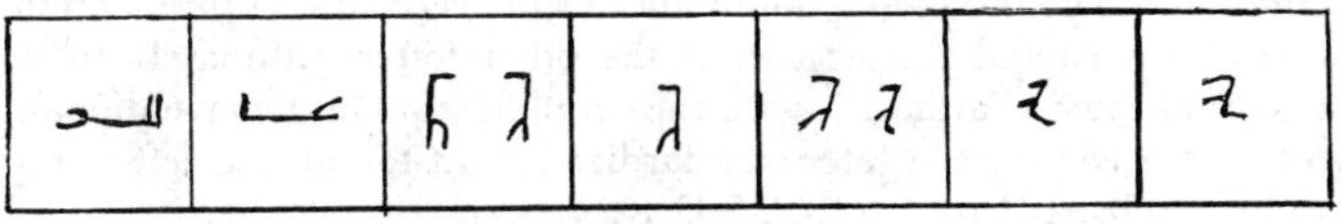

1 2 3 4 5 6 7

FIG. 102. Various forms of the *Y*-sign.

1. Egyptian hieroglyph depicting forearm and hand (s. p. 135 fig. 80). 2. Hypothetical proto-Sinaitic form *c.* 15th century B.C. 3. Hypothetical transitional forms. 4. Form on the ewer from Lachish (s. p. 100 fig. 49 C). 5. Hypothetical semi-cursive form. 6. Form on the arrow-head from Ruwaisah (s. p. 106 fig. 55). 7. Earliest Byblian form, late in the 11th century B.C. (s. p. 192 fig. 96).

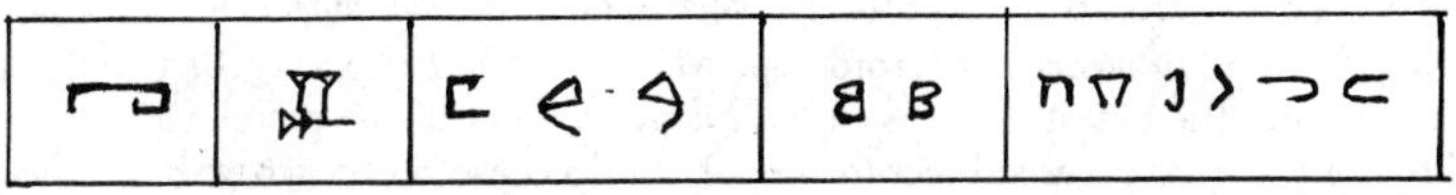

1 2 3 4 5

FIG. 103. Various forms of the *B*-sign.

1. Egyptian sign for a courtyard (s. p. 169 fig. 92). 2. Ugaritic sign (s. p. 149 fig. 83). 3. Proto-Phoenician signs (s. p. 192 fig. 96). 4. Early Greek signs (s. p. 174 fig. 93). 5. South-Arabian signs (s. p. 145 fig. 82 and p. 150 fig. 84).

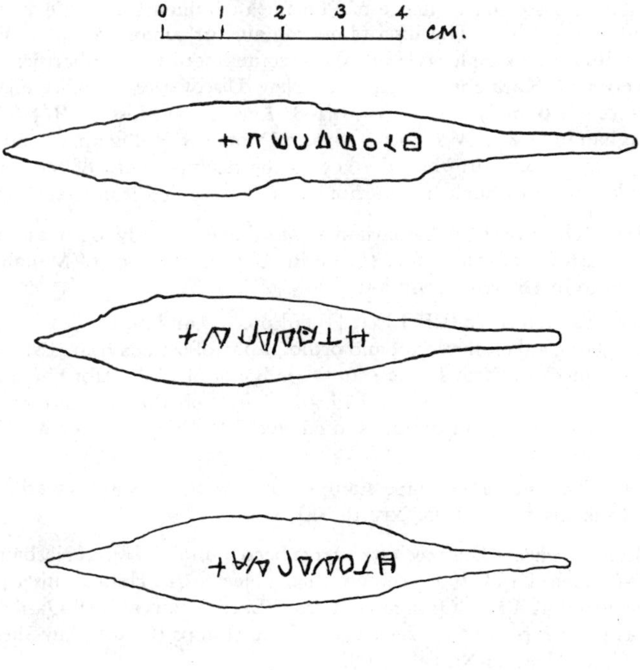


1 2 3

FIG. 104. Inscribed arrow-heads from älḪaḍr: 1, 3 חץ עבדלבאת (*ḥṣ 'bd-lb't*).
2. חץ עבדלבת (*ḥṣ 'bd-lbt*).

interconnected. The increasing dominance of the right-to-left direction in Phoenician inscriptions caused the stances of the other letters ultimately to produce a general shift clockwise, although with the simplification and conventionalization of the symbols the earlier and later standardized right-to-left and left-to-right forms came to be confused (Cross in 'B.A.S.O.R.' CXXXIV 18–19).

The only known example of vertical writing after *c.* 1500 B.C. seems to be that found on three arrow-heads from älḪaḍr, a village situated about 4 km. to the W. of Bethlehem, and dated *c.* 1200–1100 B.C. s. fig. 104. These are inscribed *ḥṣ ʿbdlb(')t* 'arrow of ʿAbdi-laba'ōt' in letters which run from top to bottom, facing on two of them from left to right (2, 3) and on one from right to left (1), as on the dagger from Lachish (p. 99 fig. 43) and as regularly on all subsequent Phoenician inscriptions (Milik and Cross ibid. 5–15). s. *K.A.I* no. 21.

S. further Martin in *R.S.O.* XXXVII [1962] 175–98.

Such arrow-heads served for casting lots and divination and were used by both Hebrews (Ezek. xxi 26; II Ki. xiii 15–18) and Greeks: *hanc autem Graeci βελομαντίαν sive ῥαβδομαντίαν nominant* (Jerome *ap.* Migne *Patrol. Lat.* XXV [1845] 206/249). In Mesopotamia the eldest son was called *bêl zitti* 'owner of the prime share' while the residue of the estate was subject to the lot; in this case blunt arrow-heads inscribed with their respective owners' names were cast *ina* (*libbi*) *išpati* 'from (within) a quiver' and the winner became *bêl pûri* 'owner of an allocation' (cp. Hebr. פור 'lot') or share of the residual property (s. Speiser in 'J.A.O.S.' LV [1935] 439–40).

**P. 107 n. 1.** Cp. Donner & Röllig op. cit. nos. 24, 25 for Kilamuwa's inscriptions.

**P. 108.** The bilingual inscription of *'ZTWD* from Karatepe, dated *c.* 800 B.C., describes the king's extension of his power, his treatment of his subjects, and the building of a citadel; the places named in it are *Mpš* (Mopsuestia) and the plain of *'dn* (Adana), so that evidence of Phoenician influence in Cilician territory at this time is provided. The inscription contains 91 almost complete lines of text and is written in a simple style but shows some linguistic peculiarities (Obermann 'Discoveries at Karatepe', 1948, and 'New Discoveries at Karatepe', 1949; s. Marcus & Gelb in 'J.N.E.S.' VII 194–8, Leveen & Moss in 'J.J.A.' I 189–93, O'Callaghan in *Orient.*, *N.S.* VII 194–8, and Donner & Röllig op. cit. no. 26). Incidentally, these texts furnished the key to the decipherment of the Hittite pictographic language through the inscription accompanying it in that script.

**Pp. 109–11.** The inscribed Samaritan *ostraca* have recently been assigned to the reign of Joash *c.* 798–782/1 B.C. (Milik in 'D.J.D.' II 98) or of Menahem *c.* 752–742/1 (Yadin in *Scr. Hieros.* VIII 9–17).

**Pp. 111–12.** S. Aharoni in 'I.E.J.' XVI [1966] pp. 1–7 and pl. I and Freedman in op. cit. XIX [1969] 52–6 on the script and orthography of ostraca from Täll ʿArad in the Negeb; s. Glueck in 'Near Eastern studies in honor of W. F. Albright' ed. Goedicke [1971] 225–234 for objects from Täll älḪulaifah on the N. shore of the gulf of ʿAqabah carrying brief inscriptions in cursive Edomitic, Aramaic and Phoenician forms of script.

**Pp. 113–4.** The legends on these stamps are now read as abbreviations for יהוד 'Judah' (Sukenik in 'J.P.O.S.' XIV 182–4).

**P. 114.** Stamps bearing Hebrew letters have been found at Täll-änNaṣbäh (McCown 'Tell-en-Naṣbeh' I 158, 169–72), and other objects with Hebrew inscriptions have been recovered at Täll-älQuṣailäh (Maisler 'Excavations at Tell Qasîle' 22–5).

Engravers' errors are found even on official stamps (Grant 'Ain Shems' V 82/6 and McCown 'Tell-en-Naṣbeh' I 158/2).

**P. 115.** Other early Hebrew inscriptions have been found on pots from Hazor dated *c.* 850–723 B.C. (Yadin *Hazor* II 70–75), on a seal from Megiddo (Yeivin in 'J.N.E.S.' XIX 205–12), on two or three tombs in the neighbourhood of Silwân assigned to the reign of Hezekiah (Reifenberg in 'J.P.O.S.' xxi 134–7 and Avigad in 'I.E.J.' iii 137–52, 163), on sherds of the 8th century B.C. from Täll-älQuṣailäh (Maisler in 'J.N.E.S.' x 265–7, who draws attention to the earliest known mention of 'gold of Ophir' there), and on ivories from Nimrûd of the same age (Millard in *Iraq* xxiv 45–50).

**Pp. 117–8.** Cp. Macalister in 'P.Q.S.' xxxiv [1902] 335–6 for non-alphabetic potters' marks, made with the index-finger or punched or scratched with a nail or stick, from Gezer.

**P. 119.** The inscription from Buraij may perhaps be dated *c.* 900 B.C. (Albright in 'B.A.S.O.R.' lxxxvii 25–6). For these three texts s. *K.A.I.* nos. 201, 231–2.

**Pp. 120–1.** Other dates proposed for the inscription of *Zkr* are *c.* 850 B.C. (Albright op. cit. lxxxvii 23–29) or 805 B.C. (Dupont-Sommer *Araméens* 47–48) or 773 B.C. (Black *ap.* Thomas 'Documents from Old Testament Times' 243–4).

The inscriptions from Sûjîn are now published by J. A. Fitzmyer (The Aramaic inscriptions of Sefîre [Rome 1967]).

Other early but brief or fragmentary Aramaic inscriptions are on various objects from Zinjîrlû dated in the last part of the 9th century B.C. (Von Luschan *Ausgrabungen* v 73, 102, 119–20; s. Galling in 'B.A.S.O.R.' cxix 15–18), on an ivory of Ḥaza'el from Arslan Tash (Thureau-Dangin *Arslan Tash* 135–8) and on ivories from Nimrûd of the 8th century B.C. (Barnett 'Catalogue of Nimrud Ivories' 50–51, 161, 213 and Millard in *Iraq* xxiv 41–44), as well as on polished red bricks (one with painted, the others with engraved names or words) from Ḥamath dated *c.* 720 B.C. (Ingholt *Fouilles à Hama* 115–17); most of these inscriptions can be conveniently read in Donner & Röllig op. cit.

**P. 121 n. 5.** S. Donner & Röllig *K.A.I.* ii [$^{2}$1968] 229 ff. on the date and parentage of Bar-Rakub (or rather Bar-Rākib) of Sam'al (*c.* 730 B.C.).

**P. 121 n. 7.** S. further *K.A.I.* no. 27.

**Pp. 123–4.** A South-Arabian inscription with the text running from left to right has been found at Ma'rib (Jamme in 'B.A.S.O.R.' cxxxiv 25–26). The text is written βουστροφηδόν in not a few of these inscriptions (s. Höfner *Altsüdarabische Grammatik* 13 § 6).

The inscription of Aḥiram argues a long period of gestation for the Semitic alphabet before the development of its perfected form; and the peculiarities of the Aramaic and especially of the South-Arabian varieties of the script prove that it cannot have owed its existence to a single initial effort. So the South-Arabian alphabet (s. p. 145 fig. 82), which can be clearly traced back to a West-Semitic prototype, contains some forms clearly older than any in the Phoenician or Aramaean script: for example, the South-Arabic ◇, ○ *f*, which is the Egyptian 𓂋 *r* meaning 'mouth' (s. p. 134), rotated 90° like the other signs (s. p. 150 fig. 84), is older than the Phoenico-Aramaic 𐤐, 𐡐 *p*, also meaning 'mouth (s. p. 157), which has clearly undergone considerable development to facilitate quick writing (s. Cowley in 'J.E.A.' iii 7). Consequently, the Phoenicians cannot be held responsible for the instantaneous invention of a world-wide system, only improved by the Greeks by the addition of signs not required for the Semitic languages, until fresh discoveries have proved it (s. Ronzevalle in *M.U.B.* xii 3–40).

**P. 124 fig. 78.** The text in the lower register of fig. 78A has been tentatively read *DNL YZBL K/DR LŚN* 'Dnl carried the basket for (the god) Sin', i.e. assisted in some building operation or generally performed his due service for the god (s. Albright in 'B.A.S.O.R.' cxxviii 39–41). The Ass. *kudurra zabālu* 'to carry the basket, i.e. to perform servile tasks or feudal duties' (Oppenheim 'Ass. Dict.' xxi 8) justifies the expression here assumed; but *Dnl* for *Dn'l* (cp. Ugar. *Dnẻl* and Hebr.

*Dānī'ēl* 'Daniel') is difficult. The text on fig. 78B may be read *Krs nph̲* '*Krs* the smith' (Driver in 'B.A.S.O.R.' CXXVIII 40).

Another S.-Arabian seal, bearing a legible inscription and assigned to the 8th–7th centuries B.C., may be added to the texts here listed (Albright ibid. 42–43).

**P. 125/6 n. 4.** Similarly, the raised ע in רשׁעים wicked ones' (Job xxxviii 13, 15) suggests that not men but stars, such as the Dog-stars, are meant, being so called because their heliacal rising heralds the dangerous hot season of fever and pestilence; in the same way, though for a different reason, Orion's Hound is described as an evil omen by Homer (*Il.* xxii 29–30), thus illustrating the application of such an epithet to a star (s. Driver in 'J.T.S.' *N.S.* IV [1953] 210). Contrariwise, the raised ע in יער 'thicket' (Ps. lxxx 14) does not import a different reading, e.g. יְאֹר 'Nile' as pointing to the devouring enemy (Grätz *ap.* Delitzsch *Psalmen*[5] [1894] 538 n. 3) if only because the 'vine' has sprung from Egypt, but rather a scribal correction of a variant Hebr. יר corresponding to the Phoen. יר (Levy *Phön. Wb.* [1864] 22) and transliterated *iar* 'wood' by Augustine (Migne *Patrol. Lat.* XXXVII 1644 § 8).

**P. 126 n. 2.** The Palestinian vocalization is found in fragmentary texts dated *c.* A.D. 700–50; the Tiberian vocalization was developed at the beginning of the 9th century A.D. (Kahle 'Cairo Geniza'[2] 72–75).

**P. 128.** Whether the reference in

*πόρεν δ' ὅ γε σήματα λυγρά,*
*γράψας ἐν πίνακι πτυκτῷ θυμοφθόρα πολλά*

(Homer *Il.* vi 168–9) is to magic signs or to alphabetic letters as mysterious and dangerous is not clear; both may have seemed baleful to an illiterate people.

The use of the Phoen. *ethot* (Schroeder *Phön. Spr.* 132[2]) and the Hebr. אוֹתִיּוֹת (Levy *Neuh. u. Chald. Wörterb.* I 48–9 and Jastrow 'Dictionary' I 36) 'signs' for 'letters' may possibly reflect their pictorial origin (Perles *Analekten* 10–11); but all letters, however developed or degenerate, are *σήματα* in some sense.

**P. 128 n. 3.** What the Greeks called *Ἀσσύρια γράμματα* were not necessarily Babylonian or Assyrian cuneiform signs. The inscription which Darius (Herodotus *Hist.* IV lxxxvii 1) erected on reaching the Bosphorus might have been written in the Persian cuneiform script, although this would not have been readily understood there. Elsewhere they were almost certainly the Aramaic cursive form of the so-called 'Phoenician' letters (Thucydides *Hist.* IV l 2 and *Epistologr. Graec.* 21), which the Jews long afterwards called כתב אשורי 'Assyrian writing' (Lewy in 'H.U.C.A.' XXV 184–8).

This כתב אשורי or simply אשרית 'Assyrian script' was so called because it was the originally Aramaean form of the 'Phoenician' script which had been coming into use in Assyrian and Babylonian commercial houses since the 8th century B.C. and which was brought back by Jews returning from the Exile. The 'square script' (כתב מרבע) was derived from this form of the alphabet.

**Pp. 128–9.** Another explanation is that *Τάαυτος* is a Semitic name based on a Phoen. תאות* = Hebr. תַּאֲוָה 'mark, sign, cipher' (Eissfeldt *Taautos und Sanchunjaton* 20–2); this word, which is a by-form of the Hebr. תָּו 'mark' perhaps occurs in קברות התאוה 'the graves of marking' = 'marked graves' (Numb. xi 34, 35 xxxiii 16, 17 and Deut. ix 22), which will then have come to be interpreted as meaning 'graves of desire' by popular but incorrect etymology (Noth *Ueberlieferungsgeschichte d. Pentateuch* 129).

The Egyptian god Osiris, Graecized as Dionysus, was also credited with the invention of the alphabet (Diodorus Siculus *Bibl. Hist.* I xvi 1 i).

**Pp. 129–30.** Cp. Peiser in *M.Va.G.* V ii 3 1–15 (supposed Accadian origin of the Phoenician alphabet), Dussaud in *Syria* XXV 36–52 (proto-Byblian origin of the

Phoenician alphabet) and Jirku in *Z.D.M.G.* C 515–20 (Egyptian and Babylonian influence on Palestinian scripts).

Possibly not every factor points to a connexion between the Egyptian and the Phoenician signs, and objections have been taken to such a connexion on the score that Phoenician scribes agree with the technique of Babylonian and Ugaritic, as distinct from Egyptian, scribes (i) in making all their symbols (except that for *l*) face in the direction of the writing, (ii) in allowing each symbol to occupy its own peculiar space, and (iii) in giving only one single space to each symbol. These points, however, are each in themselves very small; they are therefore not strong enough to outweigh the solid arguments on the other side.

An attempt has recently been made to derive the West-Semitic alphabetic signs and their names from Egyptian prototypes quite different from those here set out, as shown in the following table (Weidmüller in *B.D.Bh* XXXIX [17 May 1960] 1–7 and XLVI [10 June 1960] 1–7).

Many of the identifications put forward in this list are either dubious or impossible for various reasons.

Six of these equations cannot be accepted (s. n. on pp. 179–185), being either dubious or irregular (s. Calice *Grundlagen d. ägyptisch-semitischen Wortvergleichung* 228–35). Five Egyptian signs are misread, namely *dꜣr.t* (4) for *ḏr.t*, *ḏꜣ.t* 'hand', *ḫnw* (16) for *ẖnw* 'spring' (although this error does not affect the argument),

| | | | | | | | | | | | |
|---|---|---|---|---|---|---|---|---|---|---|---|
| 1 | א |  | hand to mouth meaning 'he says' | *i͗ꜣn.f* | *'ālef* | ל |  | lion, panther | *rw.ꜣbw* | *lāmeḏ* | 12 |
| 2 | ב |  | 'house' | *bi͗ꜣyt* | *bêṯ* | מ, ם |  | eagle-owl | *m* | *mēm* | 13 |
| 3 | ג |  | basket made of reeds | *qmꜣ* | *gîmel* | נ, ן |  | water | *nw* | *nûn* | 14 |
| 4 | ד |  | man's hand | *dꜣr.t* | *dāleṯ* | ס |  | back-bone, spine | *sꜣm'kti͗*<br>*sꜣm'k* | *sāmeḵ* | 15 |
| 5 | ה |  | glowing heat | *hh* | *hê* | ע |  | source, spring | *ḫn(w)* | *'ayin* | 16 |
| 6 | ו |  | horned viper | *ḥfꜣ.w* | *wāw* | פ, ף |  | base | *p* | *pēh* | 17 |
| 7 | ז |  | head-rest | *ṯꜣy* | *zayin* | צ, ץ |  | seat, throne | *št* | *ṣādê* | 18 |
| 8 | ח |  | lake, pool | *ẖ(ꜣ).t* | *ḥêṯ* | ק |  | body | *qpꜣ* | *qôf* | 19 |
| 9 | ט | <br> | tears (s. n. 22)<br>source, spring (s. n. 16) | *tꜣw*<br>*ẖnw* | *tāw*<br>*'ayin* | ר<br>ש | <br> | mouth<br>marsh-land | *rꜣ*<br>*šꜣ* | *rêš*<br>*šîn* | 20<br>21 |
| 10 | י |  | desert-hare | *wnw.t* | *yôḏ* | ת |  | tears | *tꜣw* | *tāw* | 22 |
| 11 | כ, ך |  | ship | *kp(n.t)* | *kaf* | | | | | | |

FIG. 105. Suggested comparison of Egyptian and West-Semitic names of the letters.

*qpꜣ* (19) for *ẖ* 'body', *ṯꜣy* (7) of which the meaning is not known for *wrs*, *wrš* 'head-rest', and *sꜣm'kti͗* (15) or rather *smk.t* 'beam, log of wood' for *i͗ꜣ.t* 'backbone'. Two words are mistranslated, namely *qmꜣ* (3) 'basket of reeds' (whose phonetic value is *k* for some unknown reason) for 'reeds', and *tꜣw* (9, 22) 'tears' for 'feather under a hawk's eye'. That *wnw.t* (10) means 'female desert-hare' is a mere conjecture; and, although *wn* is its phonetic value, it is otherwise recorded only as the sign for the snake-goddess at Hermopolis. The explanation of *m* (13) as the 'eagle-owl' is equally uncertain; and that this bird is not certainly found on the Syro-Palestinian coast-land makes its presence in a mnemonic list improbable. The sign rendered *ḥfꜣ.w* (6) means 'reptile, snake', and a different sign serves for *fy* 'horned viper'. The disregard of the final *n* in *kp* (11) for *kpn.t* 'Byblian ship' is impossible, as it is a radical letter. Worst of all, no such word as *bỉꜣyt* (2) 'house' occurs; it is created by combining the two elements in the Eg. *p(r)-ỉyt*, the name of a sanctuary at Letopolis in the Delta, into a fictitious word resembling the Sem. *bêṯ* 'house'. The Eg. *rw.ꜣbw* (12) 'lion, panther' = Copt. ⲗⲁⲃⲟⲓ 'lion' cannot be identified with the W.-Sem. *lāmeḏ* 'goad' (?), being the Phoen. *lb'* (used only as a personal name) = Hebr. *lāḇî'* 'lioness'; for the same word cannot be equated at one and the same time with two such totally diverse words. Lastly, the notion that the sign for *ṭ* is a combination of those for ʿ and *t* (9) is open to phonetic objection (s. note to pp. 166–7 n. 6).

Briefly, only 5 of the 22 equations can stand up to serious examination; consequently, even if some of the errors are not such as to affect the argument, the series taken as a whole is not soundly enough based to afford a reasonable explanation of the origin of the forms and names of the alphabet. If too the difficulty of seeing how the Semites can have used Egyptian words, some of them quite rare words, in framing a mnemonic device for remembering the names of the Semitic letters is taken into consideration, the objections to it must be regarded as fatal.

**Pp. 134 and 135.** The Eg. *ỉd* is an assumed primitive form of the normal *d* and/or *ḏꜣt* 'hand' (s. Erman & Grapow *Wtb. d. aeg. Spr.* v 414, 516; Calice *Grundl. der Ägypt.-Sem. Wortvergleichung* [1936] 25 11).

**Pp. 148–52.** Cp. Rin in *Leshonenu* XXVI 56–61 for the possible connexion of the Ugaritic and Canaanite alphabets and Février in *R.É.S.* 1 1 xiii–xvi for that of the Ugaritic and South-Semitic inscriptions.

**P. 148 n. 2.** Cp. Pirenne in *M.A.I.B.-L.* xv [1955] 114–76, who puts the beginning of the Sabaean inscriptions in the 5th century largely in view of the noticeable Greek influence on the Sabaean script.

**Pp. 150–1.** Cp. Albright 'Archaeology of Palestine' 187–8.

**P. 151 n. 1.** Cp. Virolleaud in *Syria* x 309–10.

**Pp. 151–2.** The order of the Ugaritic alphabet (s. n. on p. 181 and pp. 182–5) shows that it must be dated after the invention of the Phoenician alphabet and the determination of the order of the letters in it; for, while it puts *ả* in the same place as א, namely at the beginning, it puts *ẻ* or *ỉ* and *ủ*, which are mere variations of this letter, at the end as additions. If the author or authors of the Ugaritic alphabet had been arranging a completely new alphabet and not following one in which the order of the letters had already been fixed, all varieties of א would surely have been grouped together.

**P. 152 n. 1.** Another Ugaritic inscription has been found near Mt. Tabor in Northern Palestine (Herdner in *Syr.* XXV 165–8). The writing on both these inscriptions is from right to left, as in Phoenician, not from left to right, as in other Ugaritic texts (s. Grant in 'B.A.S.O.R.' LII [1933] 4, Barton *op. cit.* 5–6 and Albright *op. cit.* LIII [1934] 18–19, Beth-Shemesh; also Hillers in 'B.A.S.O.R.' CLXXIII [1964] 45–50, Taanach).

**Pp. 153–4.** If the signs had preceded the names, there would be no reason why the letters should take any particular form; their forms therefore were based on their names (s. pp. 156–61).

**Pp. 154–5.** Neither *w* nor *y* appear as vowel-signs in Phoenician inscriptions of the 9th century B.C. (Cross & Freedman 'Early Hebrew Orthography' 11–20); but both are found on the Moabite Stone to represent diphthongs, as in *Ḥwrnn* for *Ḥórōnēn* (חֹרֹנַיִם) and *Dybn* for *Dîbōn* (*Δαιβων*). In the 8th century B.C. they occur on the Aramaic inscription of Panammû II as mere *matres lectionis* marking any long vowel, as in *'šwr* for *Aššūr* (אַשּׁוּר), *qyrt* for *qīrāt* (Moab. *qrn* = *qīrān*) 'cities' and perhaps in *'yḥ* (Ugar. *'ḫ*) 'brother'. The earliest Hebrew examples are found at the beginning of the 6th century B.C. in letters from Lachish, which have איש 'man' and מאומה 'anything'; and the Aramaic papyri written by Jews in Egypt and dated from 495 B.C. onwards have them, especially in accented syllables, as in לבוש 'clothing', כתיב 'written', and מהיר 'skilled' as well as מדינא and מדינתא (beside מדנתא) 'province'. Finally, the scribes at Qumrân frequently used these letters simply to indicate what the vowel was without regard to its length or the accent (cp. Philippi *ap.* Kautzsch & Cowley 'Hebr. Gr.'[2] 26[1]).

Discussion has recently been reopened over the question whether the West-Semitic (Phoenician, Aramaic, Hebrew) alphabet ought to be regarded rather as a syllabary (Gelb 'Study of Writing' 122–53, 166–76, 190–205 and in *B.O.* XV 2–7; cp. Février *Histoire de l'Ecriture* 210–12) than as an alphabet (Segert in *A.O.* XXVI 243–7, 657–9).

The first step away from pictography was taken by the Sumerian scribes when they began using phonetic semantic signs representing words as phonetic non-semantic signs representing syllables: for example, the sign for *GI* 'reed' for *gi* as a mere syllable within a word (s. pp. 56–62). That the Egyptians, when they devised a method of adapting their hieroglyphs to an alphabetic system, like the Hittites and other Anatolian peoples when they adapted the cuneiform signs to the needs of their own languages, as well as many others, followed the same course, is seen as an argument for supposing that this was a necessary stage in the transition from an ideographic to an alphabetic system of writing. So the Cypriot syllabary, consisting of 56 signs, all but one of which stand for syllables consisting of a vowel or generally consonant + vowel (*a*; *ta, te, ti, to, ka, ko, ku*, and so on), is taken as a perfect example of this stage, at which it remains fossilized, in the development of the alphabet. If then this is a necessary and unavoidable stage in the process, the Phoenician signs must be considered to represent not bare consonants but syllables consisting of consonant + vowel so that, for example, ת must represent not *t* but *ta, te, ti, to, tu* according to the requirement of the word of which it is a component element; this conclusion is thought to agree with their position in line of development between the Egyptian hieroglyphs and the Greek letters (Gelb). Nothing, however, is known of the origin of the Cypriot syllabary and it never became an alphabet; it is therefore useless as evidence that a syllabary is a necessary stage in the development of the alphabet.

The absolute validity of this argument from a supposed general principle may be doubted on several grounds. The device whereby the Sumerians invented syllabic writing enabled them at the same time to find signs for four of the five vowels (for example, the sign for *A* 'water' served also for *a* and that for *E* 'trench' for *e*, as bare vowels); and this brought them some way towards a pure alphabet, although they themselves never completed the process (s. pp. 58–59). The Egyptian 'alphabet' was employed incompletely and sporadically (except for a brief period at a very late date), and little or nothing is known of its development; and, since it was used almost solely as an alphabet for spelling out foreign words, it affords but slight support for the theory of a universal syllabic stage. Further, the alphabetic use of a restricted number of Egyptian hieroglyphs, even if it is regarded as syllabic, cannot be compared with the elaborate Babylonian syllabary: for example, the

Egyptians used the pictographic sign for *rꜣ* or *rî* 'mouth' (by dropping the final 'weak' sound) for every possible combination of *r* with vowels (*rā*, *ra*, *ār*, *ar*, *rē*, *re*, *ēr*, *er*, and so on), whereas the Babylonians required different signs for each combination of consonant+vowel (*ra*, *ri* or *re*, *ru*) or vowel+consonant (*ar*, *ir* or *er*, *ur*); and these combinations were normally restricted to a single value (e.g. the sign for *ra* could stand only for *ra* and not for *ar* or any other combination). Accordingly, the Babylonians treated almost every sign as representing a distinct syllable; the Egyptians looked to the only stable element in the combination, i.e. the consonantal value of the sign, without regard to the accompanying vowel, which was a variable factor having no necessary connexion with the consonant which it accompanied; in other words, the sign for *r* represented not vowel+consonant or consonant+vowel but only the consonantal element, namely the consonant *r*, without regard to the accompanying vowel.

This line of reasoning may be reinforced by another argument. Egyptian signs representing two consonants could stand for several syllables: for example, that for *pr* 'house' might stand for *par*, *epr*, or *epra* and so on. Here again only the consonants, namely *pr*, are stable, and the sign can hardly be regarded as representing also any variety of syllables or combinations of syllables. Contrariwise, Babylonian signs of this type represented only the consonants with a medial vowel, for example, *bar* or *par*, and values such as *bar*(*a*) and *par*(*a*) or *ama* were nothing but relics of the Sumerian system which had accidentally survived and might occasionally be used, almost as freaks, in spelling out Babylonian words as in *Ti-amat* for *Ti-a-mat* (Segert).

The cuneiform syllabic system indeed contained the seeds of its own decay in itself. So, for example, the Babylonians came almost to regard the single sign for *wa*, *we*, *wi*, *wu* as standing for the consonant *w*, adding another sign to indicate with which vowel it was to be read in any given case (for example, *wa-a* for *wa*, *we-e*, for *we*, and so on); and the Hittites regularly used that for *ya*, *ye*, *yi*, *yu* as representing the consonantal *y*, similarly adding the necessary vowel to indicate which reading was intended. Further, in neo-Babylonian texts the inherent vowel came to be disregarded, so that *a-ra-ku* might be written instead of *a-ra-ak* for *arāk*; contrariwise, if the final vowel had to be pronounced, a different sign was used or another was added to indicate the pronunciation, as in *i-man-gur-u'* for *i-man-gu-ru* 'they agree' and *i-na-di-nu-u'* for *i-na-di-nu* 'they give' (where the final *-ū*, being the plural termination, had to be pronounced). In the same way *aptalaḫ* 'I fear' might be written either *ap-ta-laḫ* in accordance with classical norms or *a-pa-ta-laḫ* (n. on p. 61), in which the intrusive *a* is probably not an anaptyctic vowel but rather an unavoidable element which must be disregarded. So too *pa* ought to be taken as standing for the consonant *p* in such a case (s. Von Soden *G.A.G.* §18*d*). Such forms, then, are not so much instances of abnormal cuneiform writing reflecting a supposed Aramaic syllabic system (Gelb) as the reflection of a tendency to reduce the Babylonian syllabary to the uses of the Aramaic alphabet, when the quality of the superfluous vowel is simply disregarded. In the same way, when *qûm* 'to arise' is written *qu-ú-um* instead of *qu-um*, the inserted *ú* represents the Aramaic *w* which serves as *mater lectionis* indicating a long vowel (due not to the accent but to contraction) in reproducing such a word (Segert).

Further, the syllabic character of the West-Semitic script is thought to be confirmed by the use of the Hebrew *šᵉwâ* (a word of unknown origin and meaning; for the notion that it means 'nothingness' explains only its rarest use), a sign which amongst other functions marks a consonant as vowelless. This fact has then been thought to show that Jewish scholars regarded Hebrew letters as normally representing consonant+vowel; for, if they already represented only the consonant, no sign to show that they were vowelless would be needed (Gelb). The argument, however, has no force, for three reasons. First, although this sign was put on all consonants in the middle of the word which had no following vowel, it was not put on such consonants at the end of the word (except on *k*, where it served a different purpose), where it would be most often expected. Second, the Arabs put the corresponding sign (called *sukûn*) on every consonant which was not followed by a vowel; but the Syrians, who were the earliest to introduce vowel-signs, left vowel-less consonants unmarked. The use of such signs, therefore, was quite arbitrary and in no way suggested that the signs represented consonant+vowel and not consonant alone. Third, the practice, which was extremely late, was introduced by grammarians with no scientific knowledge of the history of the alphabet and so could have no significance of any value for an enquiry into the original force of the alphabetic symbols (Segert).

Further, that these Hebrew and Arabic signs were called respectively *ḥiṭpâ* 'nipping off' and *jazmatu* 'cutting off' does not mean that an unwanted vowel inherent in the symbol representing consonant+vowel has been nipped or cut off (Gelb); for medieval Jewish and Arab scholars, working as much as 2,000 years after the invention of the alphabet, had no conceivable scientific knowledge of the original values of the symbols which they were using or of the development of a possible syllabary, of which they had never heard and could not conceive, into the alphabet with which they were acquainted (Segert). They indicate merely the end of the syllable which is thus 'cut off', i.e. terminated.

The supposed evidence of the Ethiopic syllabary is equally valueless, although it too has been invoked to support the syllabic theory. The Ethiopians had 7 different signs for each consonant according to the vowel which accompanied it: for example, *ba*, *bū*, *bī*, *bā*, *bē*, *bə* (and *b*), *bō*; of these the sign for *ba* was basic and all the others were formed by small modifications of it. The basic forms, however, were derived from the South-Arabian consonantal script, and the earliest inscriptions in the Ethiopic script were written with signs which were not differentiated according to the accompanying vowels (Dillmann & Bezold 'Ethiopic Grammar' §12). The Ethiopians, therefore, so far from using a syllabary (Gelb), realized that their system was consonantal and deliberately modified it in order to turn it into a syllabary, although it remained only a partial syllabary (for only 2 short and 5 long vowels were indicated in it); and, as they seem to have done this under Indian influence, the syllabary thus formed can throw no light on the nature of the primitive West-Semitic system (Segert). In fact, in so far as it has any value as evidence, it tells against the theory of its syllabic origin; for it shows that the Ethiopians must have recognized the true nature and the defects of the South-Arabian (and therewith of every West-Semitic) script as representing only consonants without vowels.

In any case, no late evidence can be put in the scales against that afforded by the earliest scripts. Already *c.* 1400 B.C. the scribes of Ugarit had devised a twofold system in which 3 signs represented consonant+vowel or vowel+consonant (*'a*, *'i*, *'u* and *a'*, *i'*, *u'*) and 26 other signs which can properly be regarded as representing only consonants; these seem to be derived by simplification from corresponding Babylonian syllabic signs whose inherent vowels have been disregarded (for example: that from *za* for *z*, from *ṭi* for *ṭ*, from *se* for *s*, from *lu* for *l*). Clearly the former, representing syllables, differ *toto caelo* from the latter, which must therefore be regarded as purely consonantal (Segert). This mixed system was no exception to the general rule of development (Gelb) but a middle stage between a purely or almost purely syllabic and a purely alphabetic system (Segert). The Etruscan system was apparently similarly mixed; but, if it was not really syllabic, neither was the Ugaritic a syllabary.

What is regarded as a convincing argument for the syllabic nature of the 'Phoenician' alphabet has been found in a cuneiform tablet in which Assyro-Babylonian syllabic signs are used to explain the Ugaritic symbols (s. n. to pp. 161–171).

Two arguments designed to prove that the Ugaritic (and therefore also the West-Semitic or Phoenician) signs must be regarded as representing syllables have been sought in this list. First, each Ugaritic sign is equated with a Babylonian sign representing not a consonant alone but consonant+vowel, namely by a syllabic sign; therefore the corresponding Ugaritic sign is supposed to have represented not the bare consonant but the same combination of consonant+vowel. Second, if the Ugaritic signs had had purely consonantal values, the Babylonian scribe would have used signs expressing the required consonant followed by *a* and none followed by *i* or *e* or *u* throughout the list (namely *ba, da, ṭa, pa, qa, ta, za*; not *be, di, ṭi, pu, qu, tu, zu*), for the Ethiopic syllabary shows that signs representing the consonant followed by *a* must be held to be basic, as all the other signs representing the consonant *plus* any other vowels (*ū, ī, ā, ē, ə, ō*) are formed by modifications of the *a*-signs. The only exception would perhaps be the use of *ú* for *h* (for which the Babylonians had no sign), which is difficult to explain; and, further, no other reason can be found for the Babylonian signs with other vowels (*e, i, u*) being taken to represent the corresponding Ugaritic signs (Gelb).

These arguments are totally, indeed obviously, invalid. First, all Accadian signs, except for the four vowels (*a, u, i, e*), represented syllables (whether open, which here alone come into the question, or closed), and none represented consonants alone; consequently the Babylonian scribe had no other means of representing consonants than by syllabic signs. At the same time he did not restrict himself to signs representing consonants followed by *a* but freely used others compounded of the relevant consonant+a different vowel (*e, i, u*), for which perfectly good reasons can be found (s. pp. 56–62).

In conclusion, then, the nature of the Babylonian signs compelled representation by such as represented syllables and not merely consonants, and these vowels had no connexion with the values of the corresponding Ugaritic signs; also the indifference of the Babylonian scribe to the accompanying vowel was due to his regarding the consonant and not the vowel as the important element in his representation of the Ugaritic signs. These therefore may be held to represent consonants alone, not consonants+vowels.

The theory that the West-Semitic system must be regarded not as alphabetic but as syllabic is also thought to be supported not only by the Egyptian pseudo-alphabet (Brown in 'J.N.E.S.' XIX 46–48) but also by the Etruscan and Iberian systems of writing (Gelb in *B.O.* XV 2–7).

In the Etruscan system, which is found in an archaic form in inscriptions dated *c.* 7th–5th centuries B.C., such spellings as *Mnrva/Menrva/Menerva* and *Flznal/Felznal/Felśnal* suggest that certain signs may have had syllabic rather than alphabetic values; these are the continuant sonants (*l, m, n, r*) and the spirants (*s, ś, z, f*). In course of time these signs came to be written with an accompanying vowel (*el, em, en, er, es, ix, ef*) like the stops, which had always been so written (*be, ce, de,* and so on). Therefore, the Etruscans would have once treated continuants and stops differently, whatever their subsequent practice was. Again, that *C* stands before *i* and *e* while *K* is used before *a* and *Q* before *o* and *u*, suggests that these signs too must have been syllabic (*ci, ce, ka, qo, qu*). Further, Etruscan syllabaries listing syllabic signs (e.g. *CI, CA, CU, CE, VI, VA, VU, VE,* and so on) have been found both separately and also in conjunction with abecedaries listing individual consonants without accompanying vowels (*A, B, C, D, E,* and so on). The Etruscan is thought therefore to have been originally a syllabic system from which an alphabet will have been evolved. This conclusion is supposed to be confirmed by the marks of punctuation found in some dialects, which provide certain signs representing word-initial vowels and syllable-final sounds with dots, as in *i·tan·* and so on; these have been taken as an indication of the syllabic nature of the script (Gelb). All this is very doubtful; and indeed the variations in the use of the signs for *c/k/q* seem rather to show that the Etruscan script must originally have been alphabetic (Segert).

The Iberian script, devised in the 6th–5th centuries B.C. for the Celtiberian languages in Spain, was partly alphabetic and partly syllabic; it had distinct signs for the 5 vowels (*a*, *e*, *i*, *o*, *u*), eight to represent sonant (*l*, *r*, *ṙ*, *m*, *ṁ*, *n*) and sibilant (*s*, *ṡ*) sounds, without any indication of vowels, and 15 signs for the 3 stops (*b*/*p*, *d*/*t*, *g*/*k*), each modified in 5 ways to indicate vowels. Clearly the vowel-signs were alphabetic and those for the stops were syllabic; the others lay between these two groups. The system therefore was mixed (Gelb).

The phonological reason why the signs indicating continuants, both sonants and spirants, have syllabic values is simple: all are syllable-forming consonants and can therefore be pronounced only with some vocalic element (Gelb). So, for example, the modern Serb writes *Srb* for 'Serb'. This, however, does not mean that *r* has syllabic value, representing consonant+vowel; for, when it is accompanied by any other vowel than the colourless sound without which it cannot be pronounced, it must be followed by a special symbol or letter indicating the nature of this vowel. Basically therefore the sign representing *r* has in most positions an alphabetic, even though it may in certain circumstances have what appears to be a semi-syllabic, value. What is written then is an alphabetic symbol although it may occasionally be treated as representing a syllable.

The origin of the Etruscan system of writing is obscure but is commonly supposed to be Chalcidian or Aegaean, and any direct link with the Phoenician or Etruscan systems is far from being generally admitted (s. Diringer 'Alphabet' 493–6); and the Iberian system almost certainly comes from the Aegaean field. Here both the Cypriot and Linear B syllabic systems were in use and would readily explain the presence of syllabic beside alphabetic signs in the Etruscan and Iberian systems without going further afield, e.g. into the Syro-Phoenician coast-land, to account for them. Indeed, by the time that the Etruscan and Iberian systems were in use, the West-Semitic alphabet had long come to be regarded, whatever its origin might have been, as purely consonantal; otherwise the use of the 'weak' letters (א, ה, ו, י) to indicate the vowels would not have been introduced. The argument, however, has been put forward that, as no Aegaean influence can be traced in Spain whereas Phoenician or Punic influence was very strong there, the Iberian system must have owed its syllabic elements to that influence, on the supposition that the Phoenico-Punic script was syllabic (Gelb). The whole argument, however, from the Phoenician system comes very near to being an *argumentum in circulo*: Phoenician as the source of the syllabic element in the Iberian system was syllabic and Iberian was partly syllabic in consequence of its connexion with the Phoenician system! Lastly, Punic was steadily extending the use of vowel-signs, showing that the letters were being increasingly recognized as purely consonantal symbols.

Another argument to support the theory of the syllabic nature of the West-Semitic alphabet has been sought in the vestigial use of ἦτα for 'hē', of which the Phoen. *hê* is obviously the source, in early Greek inscriptions (s. Jeffery 'Local Scripts of Archaic Greece' 28[1]). This survival, however, proves nothing; for the consonant could not be pronounced alone and the speaker was therefore forced to supply a vowel to enable him to pronounce the letter or else to use its name. So an Englishman must say *be*, *ce*, *de*, *ge* or *ef*, *el*, *em*, *en* because he cannot otherwise indicate the bare consonants (*b*, *c*, *d*, *g* or *f*, *l*, *m*, *n*). Such letters are therefore called 'consonants' because they cannot be spoken without an accompanying sound, i.e. a vowel; but this peculiarity does not mean that they are syllabic, representing consonant+vowel or vowel+consonant; that the nature and position of the accompanying vowel is variable (as in *qu* and *ar*) proves that it is something accidental and inessential.

The final argument, that only linguists and all linguists accept the syllabic explanation of the West-Semitic symbols (Gelb in 'Language' XXXVIII 212–3), has no force; all magicians and the vast majority of lay mankind once believed magical practices to be valid, but they were wrong! The truth of a belief does not depend on the number of the believers.

The use of vowel-signs begins with the introduction of the signs for the 'weak' letters (s. pp. 154–5) to indicate the pronunciation of proper names and diphthongs on the Moabite Stone and to show ordinary long vowels and 'weak' letters belonging to the roots as in the Old-Aramaic inscriptions from Zinjîrlû *c.* 850–800 B.C., exactly when the Greeks were adapting the West-Semitic alphabet to their own language.

The obvious conclusion, then, would seem to be that the West-Semitic system, apart from the three discarded (Ugaritic) signs for *'ālef*, was, in origin, a purely consonantal alphabet; so, for example, ג stood not for *ag, eg, ig, og, ug; ga, ge, gi, go, gu* but simply for *g* unaccompanied by any vowel. This conclusion is proved by the nature of the original vowel-signs; for, if *w* and *y* (like the corresponding Accadian and Hittite signs) were read respectively as *wa, we, wi, wo, wu; aw, ew, iw, ow, uw* and *ya, ye, yi, yo, yu; ay, ey, iy, oy, uy*, they would have been useless as indicators of the pronunciation. So too, while *qm* and *qr* could each be read in 5 different ways (*qam, qem, qim, qom, qum; qar, qer, qir, qor, qur*), clearly *qwm* and *qyr* could each be read (if possible final vowels are disregarded) in 25 ways (*qawam, qawim, qiwam; qayar, qiyir, qiyâr*, and so on) instead of simply as *qûm* or *qôm, qîr* or *qêr*, as intended. Here is the *reductio ad absurdum* of the syllabic theory as applied to the West-Semitic alphabet; such a helping sign only increases the confusion!

Thus the Phoenicians and Aramaeans were in exactly the same position as the Greeks. The West-Semites invented a purely consonantal alphabet which the Greeks took over for their own use, and each found it inconvenient without any signs for the vowels. The Moabites and Aramaeans were already experimenting in the 9th–8th centuries B.C. with weak letters to make good this defect when the Greeks adapted the Aramaean consonantal system; but, whereas the Semites had only (at any rate originally) two or three signs which they could adapt for use as vowel-signs (s. Cross & Freedman 'Early Hebrew Orthography' 58–60), the Greeks found 6 signs ready to hand and so, although they were not the originators of the system whereby both consonants and vowels were represented by their respective signs, they perfected it by finding signs for necessary use in indicating every one of the vowels. The argument, therefore, that the Phoenician alphabet is not an alphabet in the true sense because the Phoenicians failed to analyse every word into its constituent elements, both consonants and vowels, as the Greeks at once did (Février), is hardly fair; the Moabites and Aramaeans had discovered the need and had made a beginning of indicating vowels by separate signs but did not fully exploit the discovery; the Greeks, having learnt it from them, only perfected it.

The reason for this failure on the part of the West-Semites fully to exploit the possibilities of the alphabet is not far to seek. Neither the Egyptians, whose language though partly Hamitic was also partly Semitic, nor the West-Semites felt much or perhaps any need to indicate the vowels in their respective alphabets, not so much because vowels were not as important in their languages as in those of the Indo-Aryan peoples (even though a Semitic word consisting only of vowels is inconceivable, while many such Indo-Aryan words can be found) but rather because morphological and semantic differences were originally and usually indicated by external additions, for example, terminations, in the latter and relatively rarely by internal modification of the vowels as in the former (as in *qatala* 'he killed' but *qutila* 'he was killed') group. Thus in the Egyptian and Semitic languages the vowels were relatively unstable while the consonants remained unaltered; and their scripts were naturally based on and designed for the representation of the stable rather than the variable elements in the word (Gelb). Briefly, the Semites had a language which when written could be read without vowel-signs, whereas the Greeks had one which could be neither written nor read without them.

In conclusion, then, the claim that a syllabic system was a possible stage between the logographic and alphabetic system in the development of writing can be conceded; but the three stages are not necessarily all found within any given language. It was not therefore a necessary stage in the development of an alphabet. So, on the one side, it was the Sumerians who invented writing by means of pictographs but soon came to use a few of their signs to represent syllables and even vowels, the Babylonians and Assyrians who developed so elaborate a syllabary that the system began to break down and who eventually went a stage further when they came near to using some few of their syllabic signs almost to indicate the consonant alone, and the Hittites who further developed this system, as the Persians also did (s. pp. 131–2); on the other side, the Egyptians adapted their hieroglyphs to the purposes of a purely consonantal alphabet. The scribes of Ugarit drew inspiration from both sides; the idea of 3 separate signs for *'ālef*, differentiated according to the accompanying vowel, was derived from the cuneiform system, while that of the remaining 26 consonantal signs was obviously due to Egyptian influence. The Phoenicians in designing their alphabet were clearly influenced by the purely consonantal Egyptian and the predominantly consonantal Ugaritic scripts; and their attempts to indicate the vowels, coming long after the disappearance of the Ugaritic alphabet, must be ascribed to the pressure of their own need to facilitate reading what they had written, even if Greek inventiveness was not also a contributory factor in giving an impulse to this development.

**P. 155.** How soon the בגדכפת may have been aspirated (i.e. pronounced with an *h*-sound added to them) is not certain. Greek equations such as *κύπρος* = כֹּפֶר do not show aspiration, while others such as *χιτών* (Homer) and *κιθών* (Herodotus) = כְּתֹנֶת suggest it; and the Greek names of the letters fluctuate similarly, most being unaspirated (*βῆτα, δέλτα, ἦτα, ἰῶτα, κάππα, κόππα*) and few aspirated (*ἄλφα, φῖ, χῖ*). Aspiration, therefore, was beginning by the 9th century B.C. and was fully established by the 3rd–2nd century B.C., having affected first *k-p-t* and afterwards *b-g-d*; for the Septuagint has abundant examples of it. So, too, Plautus commonly shows it in his transliteration of Phoenician words, for example, in *chi* = כ (Hebr. כִּי) and *yth* = אית (Hebr. אֶת). These Greek and Latin transliterations, however, must not be taken as evidence of spirantization (i.e. pronunciation with an accompanying emission of breath); for the Greeks pronounced *θ*, *φ*, and *χ* as double consonants (e.g. *θ* as *t-h* in 'ant-hill' and not as *th* in 'anthem' and so *ἄλφα* as *alp-ha* rather than as *alfa*) till the 2nd–3rd century A.D. (Goodwin 'Greek Grammar' [1894] §28, 3; s. Lejeune *Phonétique Grecque* [1935] 49–51), as the Romans also did. Spirantization, however, began early amongst the Semites. It can be traced in the time of the first dynasty at Babylon, and the Babylonian transliteration of *meleḵ/malkâ* as *milḫ(i)* in Aramaeo-Hebrew names proves it in the 5th century B.C., e.g. in *Ab-di-mil-ḫi* = עבדמלך (Clay 'P.B.S.' II/i 226 19, L.E.; cp. Hilprecht & Clay 'B.E.U.P.' IX 77 and X 71), which seems to militate against Sievers' suggestion that spirantization arose through the influence of a preceding vowel on a consonant; the Samaritans, too, seem to have had it from a very early date. Possibly, then, the Samaritans and the Hebrews derived it from a common source, namely the Aramaeans, before the schism. It can, however, be directly proved in the Hebrew language hardly before the Exile, as in פַּרְוָר (II Ki. xxiii 11) for פַּרְבָּר (I Chron. xxvi 18) and בַּת שׁוּעַ (I Chron. iii 5) for בַּת־שֶׁבַע (II Sam. xi 3), unless these are simply instances of the interchange of labial sounds, especially when they occur in attempts to represent foreign words; so too the pre-exilic language has only אַרְגָּמָן while post-exilic literature has both this form and אַרְגְּוָן (II Chron. ii 6), which is of Aramaic origin and alone is found in the Aramaic portions of the Old Testament. Again, just as Plautus has *rufe* = רוֹפֵא 'physician' (Schröder *Phön. Spr.* 113–15) and *v(e)*- for *we*- 'and', so the Septuagint has *Ρααυ* for רְחֹב (Josh. xix 30, B), which is clear evidence of spirantization, and the translator called ὁ *'Εβραῖος* has [ι]εσχαυ for יִשְׁכַּב (Gen. xxxiv 2); further, one of the Scrolls apparently has יכתיו *yikkāṯêv* corrected to יכתב *yikkāṯēḇ* (*Disc.* viii 19). Origen and Jerome show it everywhere, even in positions where the Massoretes do not recognize it. Spirantization, then, was perhaps brought back from the Exile or in any case began soon afterwards and was fully developed by the 2nd or 3rd century A.D.

The pronunciation of *yôḏ* is confirmed by its being written *plene* as יוד in a Jewish-Aramaic letter of 411 B.C. (Cowley 'Aramaic Papyri' 28 4–5).

**P. 156 n. 2.** The final *-a* added to the Greek names of some letters of the alphabet was not derived from the Aram. *-â* added to nouns in the 'emphatic state', i.e. when determined, if the letters and their names were taken from the Phoenicians, who did not employ this termination; possibly the analogy of their own language (cp. γράμμα 'picture; letter') suggested the termination to the Greeks (Nöldeke *Beitr. z. sem. Sprachwiss.* 134–5; cp. Lewy in *Orient., N.S.* XIX 29[6]).

S. also Walters 'Text of the Septuagint' [1973] 166–9.

**P. 159 n. 2.** If the Aram. זְיָנָא 'weapon' is a Persian loan-word, it must be disregarded in explaining the Hebr. *zayin* (Tur-Sinai [Torczyner] in 'J.Q.R.' N.S. XLI 92).

The O.-Eg. *zwn, zin* is generally replaced by M.-Eg. *swn, sin* 'arrow' (Erman & Grapow *Wb. äg. Spr.* III 426–7) in texts from *c.* 2200 onwards (Barns).

**Pp. 160–1.** The acrophonic explanation of the names of the letters has recently been called in question on the grounds that these originally consisted simply of the bare consonant *plus* a following vowel to enable them to be pronounced and that the traditional names were not primary but secondary, indeed relatively late, inventions (Hallo in 'J.B.L.' LXXVII 324–38; s. Gelb 'Writing' 140 ff.).

These propositions are held to be supported by the following facts. I. In the list in which Accadian signs are used to explain Ugaritic signs (e.g. *be* for *b*, *ga* for *g*, *di* for *d*, *qu* for *q*, and so on; s. n. on pp. 161–171), the former are syllabic, each representing not a simple consonant but consonant+vowel; the latter therefore must have had similar values (namely, not *b, g, d, q* but *be, ga, di, qu*, and so on). II. This is not only the earliest but also the simplest method of naming the signs; and, as it can be shown to have been used for some of the West-Semitic signs (e.g. *h, w, p, ṣ, t*) and is known to have been used partly or wholly by other nations (e.g. Arabs, Greeks, and Romans), it may be assumed to have been a universal principle and therefore to have been that followed in naming the rest of the West-Semitic signs. III. Names for alphabetic signs do not seem to have been an original need, if only because several of the West-Semitic names consisting of the consonant+vowel (e.g. *wāw* and *tāw*) have apparently no conceivable Semitic etymology. So such nouns as *wāw* 'hook, peg' and *tāw* 'mark' were derived respectively from **wa* 'w' as represented by a hook and **ta* 't' as represented by a cross, and not *vice versa* (Torczyner). That many nations have entirely dispensed with distinct proper names for the letters of the alphabet confirms the view that they are not necessary and are probably therefore not original. IV. Few of the West-Semitic names of the letters refer to the objects represented by the corresponding Egyptian symbols, and many of them hardly call to mind the objects which their names denote; for example, the sign for *'ālef* does not call an 'ox' to mind. V. Lastly, the traditional names of the letters of the Hebrew alphabet are not attested before the 2nd century B.C. although the Greek names can be traced back to the 5th century B.C. (s. p. 152); these presumably, since they are demonstrably Semitic in origin, were coined in the 9th century B.C., when the Greeks adapted the West-Semitic alphabet to their own needs (s. pp. 176–8). No evidence has been found for their existence before such a date.

All these arguments are fallacious.

I. The Accadian syllabary had no signs for simple letters (except the four vowels), so that the Ugaritic signs, whether syllabic or alphabetic, could be represented only by syllabic signs in such a table. II. The Babylonians gave some of their signs names based on their syllabic values with the addition of a nominal termination, but others names which were quite distinct from these values (s. Meissner *Bab.u.*

*Ass.* II 345–8). III. This explanation of such forms as *wāw* and *tāw* begs the question. No evidence is produced to show that *wāw* 'hook' and *tāw* 'mark' may not have been early words; and, as they are not likely to have occurred frequently in religious works, which are all that has survived of old Hebrew literature, no one can say how old they may have been. In fact *wāw* may be of gestural and *tāw* of deictic origin, so that both of them may have been primitive biconsonantal terms. Also, if *wāw* 'peg' and *tāw* 'mark' were so called after the names of the two letters, how did the letters come to be represented by the symbols for respectively a peg and a mark (cross)? The suggestion, too, that *gaw* 'back', formed from the original **ga* 'g', may have been the earliest name of this letter is devoid of proof and conflicts with the Egyptian evidence (s. pp. 163–4). IV. The claim that the West-Semitic signs do not recall the objects which they are supposed to represent is strained; it overlooks the effects of the long period of gestation during which the forms were developed and of the inevitable deterioration due to constant use and increasing speed in drawing or writing them; and the disparity between form and name can easily be exaggerated, as it is in the case cited as a typical example of non-resemblance (s. pp. 152–3). V. The argument from the date at which the names make their first appearance is an argument from silence and proves nothing. The Bab.–Ugar. list proves nothing; for its author's purpose is not known. Possibly he wished only to indicate the consonantal value of the Ugaritic signs and had no interest in their names; and, if he had wished to indicate their supposed biconsonantal names, such equations as *ú* for *hê* or *wa*/*i*/*u* for *wāw* or *ḫa* for *ḫ* and *ǵ* would not have served his purpose. If, too, the traditional names had already been in existence and he had wanted to give them, he could easily have written them out in the cuneiform script.

What has been overlooked is that the two methods of nomenclature serve different purposes. The one method, that of the Ugaritic list, indicates the spoken sound which the symbol represents; the other, for example, that of the Hebrew alphabet, gives the name of the object which the written symbol reproduces or is thought to reproduce. If this made a known word (e.g., *wāw*, *pēh*, *tāw*) it remained in use unchanged for spoken sound and written symbol; otherwise it commonly gave place to the name of the object depicted (e.g. *'ālef*, *bêṯ*; *ṣāḏê* replacing *ṣāw*, *qôf* replacing *qāw*; *rêš*, *šîn*). Some alphabets were unitary, clinging to the name of the sound in every case (e.g. Ugaritic, so far as the names are known, Arabic, and Mandaean) or to that of the object depicted (e.g. Hebrew, with one or two possible exceptions), while others preferred a mixed system of nomenclature (e.g. Greek). The principle underlying both methods was acrophonic; and this may therefore still be accepted as offering the best explanation of the connexion between the sound-values represented by the letters and the developed forms represented by their names.

The stages in the development of the alphabet now become clear. Pictography or ideography, however useful for representing concrete objects by signs, is cumbersome; and it runs into almost insuperable difficulties so soon as abstract ideas require to be communicated in written form. The writer must then devise a different method of representing what he wishes to write down. He begins by isolating the various sounds which make up a word, breaking it down into syllables, and reducing these to their simplest forms, i.e. to sounds consisting of consonant and/or vowel. The consonants predominate but cannot be pronounced without vowels. The writer therefore isolates each individual consonantal sound, pronouncing it by means of a helping vowel. This vowel depends naturally on the nature of the consonant to which it is attached: *a* with guttural, *u* with labial, *i* with sibilant, and back-vowel with 'emphatic' sounds. The process yields, for example, *ḫa* for *ḫ*, *pu* for *p*, *ši* for *š*, and *qu*(*qô*) for *q*. Some of these 'names', if they can be so called, at once suggest words in common use: for example, *pu*, the 'name' for *p*, suggests **puw* 'mouth', and so that letter comes to be represented by a sign depicting the human mouth; this sign is then called *pêh* in the Hebrew form in which it has been transmitted (Acc. *pû* = Hebr. פֶּה 'mouth'). Such monosyllabic words, however, do not make provision for the whole alphabet. An obvious alternative course, then, is on the same principle to choose words similarly designating common objects but ending with the same sound as that with which they begin, what may be called echoing words; so *mu* suggests **muw* 'water' (preserved in the Gr. μῦ; cp. Acc. *mû* 'water') and so the sign is called *mîm*, *mêm*, being thus assimilated to the Hebr. *mayim* 'water', and somewhat similarly *na*, the 'name' for *n*, is displaced by the echoing Hebr. *nûn* 'fish'. Echoing words, however, are also rare, and the inventor has recourse to any words depicting a common object, especially any easily depicted part of the body, for the remaining letters: for example, *š* which is called *š(i)* suggests **šinn* 'tooth' and so comes to be represented by a symbol depicting a tooth or the teeth, and *r* called *r(a)* suggests **ra'š* 'head', and these receive respectively *šîn* and *rêš* as their names by adaptation to the current forms of the names by which they are called. Finally, the inventor is driven to use any terms designating well-known objects for the purpose: so *'(a)* is represented by **'alf* (Acc. *alpu* = Hebr. *'elef*) 'ox' and *d(a)* by **dāleṯ* (Acc. *daltu* = Hebr. *deleṯ*) 'door' and so on. Both stages in the process are natural, being suggested by previous inventions: the representation of the sound by the consonant with a helping vowel suitable to its nature goes back to the method of the Ugaritic scribe, while the representation of the letter by the object which when spoken it recalls, and the naming of it after the word which designates it, is based on the Egyptian hieroglyphic system. Thus the Semitic alphabet is the result of the fusion of the Ugaritic and Egyptian scribal traditions.

**P. 162.** The existence of וָו 'peg' has been needlessly called in question (Tur-Sinai [Torczyner] in 'J.Q.R.' *N.S.* XLI 171–4); s. preceding note.

**Pp. 162–3.** Cp. Six in *Act. Or.* III 134–7, where the earliest forms of א, ך/כ and ם/מ are examined.

**P. 163 n. 4.** Cp. Peiser in *M.Va.G.* v ii 3 14 and Thureau-Dangin in *R.A.* x 225.

**Pp. 163–4.** The Acc. *gamlu* 'throw-stick, boomerang' (as a curved weapon) and the Syr. *gmālâ* 'hook-nosed' have suggested that *gīmel* may originally have meant 'hook'; this idea has the advantage that a hook, unlike a boomerang, is an object in common use, and no objection to it can be raised on the ground that *wāw* means to all intents and purposes the same thing, since *yôḏ* and *kaf* as commonly explained are near synonyms (Lewy in *Orient.*, *N.S.* XIX 28–30). No direct evidence, however, has yet been found to prove that any term derived from the √*GML* actually denoted a 'hook', other than a hooked weapon such as a boomerang or the like. The same idea may equally well be suggested by the shape of the head and neck of a camel (Acc. *gammalu*, Hebr. *gāmāl*, Aram. *gamlâ*, Arab. *jamalu*, Eth. *gamal*).

**P. 166 n. 1.** This explanation of the Aram. סמכו in ימא דסמכו has been disputed (s. Neubauer *Géogr. du Talm.* 26[2]).

**Pp. 166/7 n. 6.** The explanation of the signs for ט and ק given here raises the whole question of the 'emphatic' consonants, whether they were velarized variants of the simple corresponding sounds, as the Arabic are, or ejectives like the Ethiopic. If these signs were composed respectively of *t* and *k* in combination with *'ayin*, they would be ejectives. Another explanation, however, is possible: if the sign for *'ayin* did duty also for *ġayin*, the sign for *t* combined with that for *'ayin/ġayin* might suggest a *t*-sound *plus* a velar sound, namely a velarized *t* (Prof. J. A. Emerton in a private communication). The evidence of the origin of the symbols for these letters, therefore, must be regarded as ambiguous.

**Pp. 161–71.** In examining the names of the letters care must be taken to distinguish those which merely reproduce the sound of the phoneme and those which represent what the sign depicts. One, namely *hē'*, hardly goes beyond reproducing the sound, while most are the names of the objects depicted. Yet in other cases, such as that of *ṣaw*/*ṣāḏê* and *qaw*/*qôf*, both have been thought to be preserved in an Isaianic oracle, although both may be otherwise explained (s. n. on p. 90 n. 1).

That ץ, צ is named in the LXX τιαδη var. σαδη, τσαδη (Lam. i 18, ii 18, iii 52, iv 18) and also σαδην (s. Nöldeke *Beiträge* 127–9) seems to support צָדֵי 'cricket, grasshopper' although this does not suit all the earliest forms of the sign or symbol for this letter. These are found on five arrow-heads, now in the Museum at Beirut (numbered B 1–5), on one from Ruwaisah (numbered R), and on three javelin-heads from älḪaḍr (numbered H 1–3) dated *c.* 12th–11th cent. B.C. s. fig. 104. All bear legends beginning with *ḥṣ* 'arrow' followed by the name of the owner and his father. When allowance is made for the turning round of the signs by 90° in the gradual change-over from writing in a vertical to that in a horizontal direction, so that the signs seem to lie on their backs, those on B 2–5 and R seem clearly to depict a cricket or grasshopper; equally clearly those on B 1 and H 1–3 represent something quite different. The plausible suggestion has therefore been made, by comparing these with corresponding Egyptian hieroglyphic, proto-Sinaitic, and proto-Byblian signs, that they represent a blossom; but whether the original name of the sign was צִיץ *ṣîṣ* 'flower' (Cross in 'B.A.S.O.R.' CXXXIV 24[32]) must remain doubtful (Martin in *R.S.O.* XXXVII 180–91). Such a name indeed agrees well enough with the acrophonic principle and with the tendency to call the letters by names beginning and ending with the same letter (*mêm*, *nûn*); but this name is not found anywhere in extant literature and must remain conjectural, however plausible it may be.

The existence of these two signs for the single historical ץ/צ suggests that, since the *ṣ* in חץ (*ḥēṣ*) 'arrow' is not *ḍ* (ض) but *ḏ̣* (ظ), the sign for a blossom may originally have been designed as a separate symbol for this last sign. These three or four centuries, however, were just those when it was coming to be regarded as otiose to have distinct signs for *ṣ*, *ḍ* and *ḏ̣*, because the Phoenicians (like the Hebrews and Aramaeans but unlike the Arabs) were beginning to confuse them in pronunciation and therefore ceased to feel the need to represent them each by its own peculiar sign; the process was helped, presumably, by the fact that *ḏ̣* was probably, as it was also in the Arabic language, not used so much as the other two sounds. Ultimately, the sign depicting the cricket or grasshopper came to serve for all three sounds.

That *ṣāḏê* is a name peculiar to the Aramaic and Ethiopic languages (Martin ibid. 188[4]) is immaterial; the Hebr. *ṣāḏāh* 'laid waste' (Zeph. iii 6) attests the

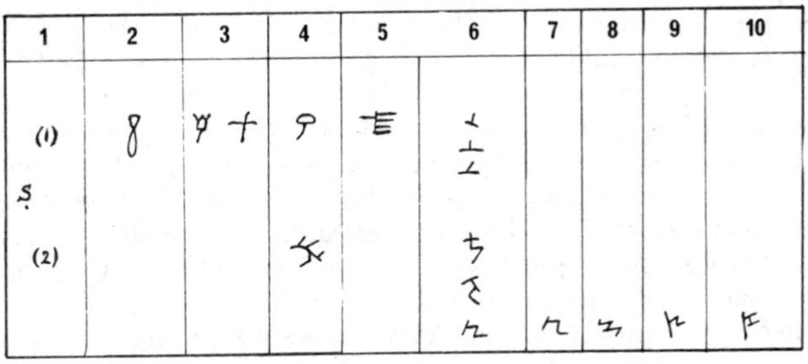

FIG. 106. Development of the *ṣ*-sign.
1. Phonetic value. 2. Egyptian hieroglyph. 3. Proto-Sinaitic signs, *c.* 18th century B.C. 4. Proto-Byblian signs, *c.* 17th–15th century B.C. 5–6. Linear Canaanite signs, (*a*) *c.* 15th century B.C., (*b*) *c.* 12th–11th century B.C. 7. Moabite signs of Meša', 9th century B.C. 8. Signs at Siloam, 8th century B.C. 9. Signs at Sidon, 6th century B.C. 10. Signs at Carthage, 4th century B.C.

antiquity of the root, and the absence of the word from extant Hebrew literature may be purely a matter of chance. Otherwise, it may have been a late name given to the letter by Aramaean scribes who saw a grasshopper in the form of the sign known to them (s. pp. 167–8).

The identification of the Ugaritic signs and the order of the signs in the Ugaritic alphabet, together with that of the letters in the Phoenico-Hebrew alphabet, have been recently confirmed by the discovery and publication of a bilingual tablet, nearly perfect, on which the Ugaritic signs are given in the left column and their values are given in Babylonian signs in the right column (Virolleaud *Palais Royal d'Ugarit* II 201–3; s. Hallo in 'J.B.L.' LXXVII 335–8 and Cross & Lambdin in 'B.A.S.O.R.' CLX 21–26); s. pls. 47–48 and fig. 107.

A purely consonantal value could not be given to the Ugaritic signs in such a list by the Babylonian signs, since these normally represented only consonant+vowel or vowel+consonant and never the consonant alone. In this list the Babylonian scribe represents *'ālef*+vowel by the corresponding vowel-sign (*a*, *i*, *u*), as the Babylonian syllabary allows him to do. When giving the value of the consonantal sign, he gives the Babylonian sign for the corresponding consonant+*a* in 7 cases, the consonant+*e* in 1 case, the consonant+*i* in 3 cases, and the consonant+*u* in 5 or 6 cases.

This procedure raises the question, why does he not use the form with *a* all down the list? The answer is simple: he uses *be* instead of *ba* for *b* because that for *ba* can be read also as *pá*, and *pu* for *pa* because this can be read also as *bá*, both variant equivalents occurring in the texts from Täll-äl-ʿAmârnah; he uses *di* for *d* and *ṭi* for *ṭ* as also *tu* for *t* because the signs for *da*/*ṭa*/*ta* are readily confused; he uses *zi* for *z* and *zu* for *ẓ̌* because *za*/*ṣa* has already been used for *ṣ*; and he uses *qu* for *q* because this sign serves also for $qa_5$ at Ugarit.

The next question which immediately arises in this: why does the scribe, when not using an *a*-sign, choose an *e*-sign or *i*-sign or even an *u*-sign in preference to one with any other vowel? The answer to this question is similar. The sign for *bi* can be read also as *pí* and that for *pi* as *bí*, so that he must take an *i*-sign for one and and an *u*-sign for the other of the two signs (*b*, *p*) to indicate exactly which consonantal value he intends; contrariwise *zi* and *zu* cannot exchange values, so that he is free to choose which he likes for each letter (*z*, *ẓ̌*), so long as he does not choose the same equivalent for both letters.

This answer, however, poses yet another question: why, for example, does he take *be* instead of *bi* or *bu* for *b* and *pu* instead of *pe* or *pi* for *p* or *ṭu* for *ṭ* and *ti* for *tu*, as he can obviously do? The answer would perhaps be that, knowing what the symbols represented and inferring or knowing their names, for example, that the symbol for *b* represented a house, he chose *be* (rather than *ba* or *bu*) as echoing *bêṯ* 'house'; so also he would choose *di* for *d* as echoing a primitive **dilt*<**delt*<**dalt* (cp. Eth. *dənt*, *dant*) 'mouth, door', *pu* for *p* as echoing **puw* (Acc. *pû* = Arab. *fû*), *qu* for *q* as echoing **quf* (Acc. *uqupu* = Hebr. *qôf*) 'ape', *tu* for *t* as echoing **tuw*> *tāw* (cp. Eth. *taw*) 'mark'. This principle may have been a contributory element in many other cases: for example, proto-Sem. **ra'š* 'head' influencing the vowel in *ra*, proto-Sem. **šann*>*šinn* (Hebr. *šēn* and Arab. *sinnu*) 'tooth' influencing that in *ša*, and perhaps a proto-Sem. **gaml* (Acc. *gamlu*) 'boomerang' (s. pp. 155–6) or Hebr. *gaw* 'back' being responsible for that in *ga* for *g*, and so on. At the same time phonetic principles, sometimes acting alone but at other times co-operating with one or other of the factors here mentioned, may have played a part in the choice of a vowel: so the vowel in *ḫa* = *h* and *ḫa* = *ġ* (which is lost in the Accadian language and is therefore represented by no cuneiform sign) may be due to the guttural nature of these two sounds, *pu* may owe its vowel to the labial nature of *p*, and *qu* may take *u* because a back-consonant tends to require a back-vowel. Finally, if *hē'* is rightly explained as exclamatory in origin and so connected with the Hebr. *hē'* 'lo!' (s. p. 162), the explanation of the Ugar. *h* by the

Obverse

| | | |
|---|---|---|
| . . . | . . . | |
| ả | a | |
| b | be | |
| g | ga | . . . |
| ḫ | ḫa | . . . |
| d | di | |
| h | ú | |
| w | wa | |
| z | zi | |
| ḥ | ku | |
| ṭ | ṭi | |
| . . . | . . . | |

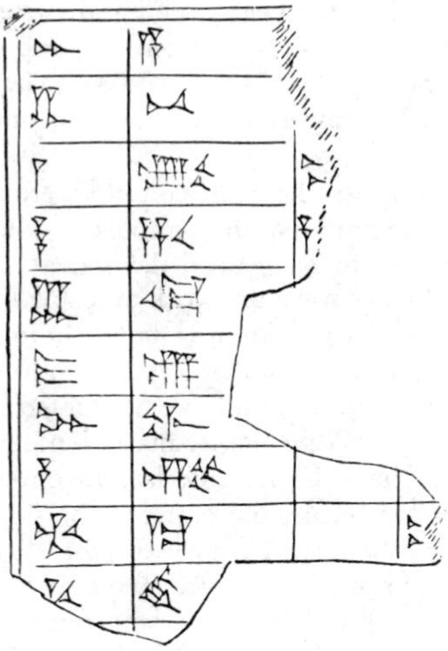

Reverse

| | |
|---|---|
| . . . | . . . |
| [p] | pu |
| [ṣ] | ṣa |
| q | qu |
| r | ra |
| š | ša |
| ǵ | ḫa |
| t | tu |
| [ỉ] | i |
| ủ | u |
| ź | zu |
| . . | . . . |

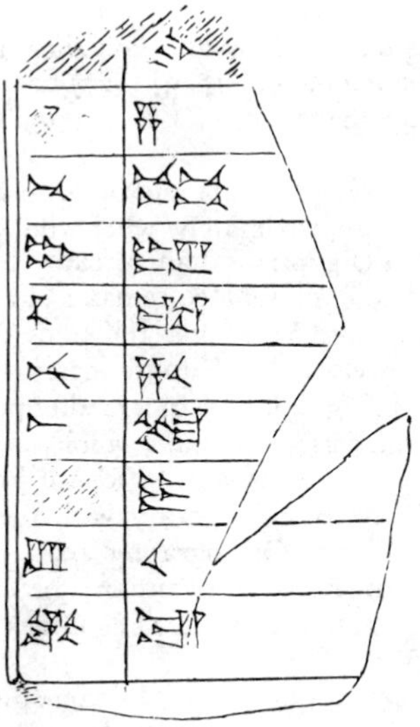

Fig. 107. Names of signs in the Ugaritic alphabet (s. pls. 47, 48).

Acc. *ú* may reflect a proto-Semitic **haw*>**hū* = Hebr. *hôy*, *hô hô* 'ah!, woe!'; the loss of *h* will then be due to the absence of any sign for this letter in the Accadian syllabary.

A final difficulty remains in *ku* for *ḥ*, since the equation of *k* with *ḥ* is phonetically incorrect, and the Acc. *ku* has no other suitable value. The most probable solution is that *ku* is an error for *ṭe* in l. 9 and that this line has been accidentally transposed with l. 10, so that in *ḥ* = *ḫe* l. 9 and *ṭ* = *ṭe* in l. 10 will have been the true reading (Albright in Wright 'The Bible and the Ancient Near East' 358/64). The vowels then correspond to those of *ḥêṯ* and *ṭêṯ*, the Phoenico-Hebrew names of these two letters.

If then the vowels in the names of the sounds in the right column were in some cases or to some extent affected by those in the names of the symbols or signs in the left column, both series of names would seem to have been devised at approximately the same time; indeed, that both schemes were the work of a single scribal school, possibly spread over a number of years, would seem to be likely in view of a certain unity appearing to lie behind them both. Both the vocalization of the names of the sounds and the names of the letters may well have fluctuated and not been finally stabilized for quite a long time, alternative names may even have been current for a while, and some names may have been quite late inventions (cp. Albright in 'B.A.S.O.R.' CXVIII 13–14). For example, the name of the sign for *ga* might as well have been *gaw* 'back' as *gaml* 'boomerang' (s. Albright *ap.* Wright op. cit. 358/64) until the latter ousted the former; or again *ṣa* might have had originally a different name, now lost, which was displaced in Aramaean centres by *ṣāḏê* 'grasshopper', when the picture in course of time came to resemble that creature. The explanation of *qôf* may be similar; for *qôf* 'ape' seems not to have been originally a Semitic, but an Egyptian word.

The tablet then will have presented in one column the sound of the phone as spoken and in the other the name of the symbol (letter) representing it in written form. The alphabet then could be recited in two ways: either by the names of the signs (as in the English *a-b-c* and so on) or by the names of the letters (as in the Greek *alpha-bêta-gamma* and so on). One person, whether teacher or scribe, might prefer one method, another the other in reciting it or in naming what he wished to see written down.

**Pp. 171 ff.** The old theory of an Aramaic (as distinct from the Phoenician) origin of the Greek alphabet (Taylor 'History of the Alphabet' [1883] II 27) has recently been revived in the light of modern knowledge (Segert in *A.O.* XXVI [1958] 572–8) and must be briefly considered.

The Greeks took over the alphabet, as here argued, in the middle or in any case well before the end of the 9th century B.C., approximately when the Aramaic inscriptions at Zinjîrlû were composed. The Egyptians had already begun to indicate vowels by means of signs intended to represent consonants during the New Kingdom (*c.* 1575–1087 B.C.). The Moabite Stone has the signs for half-vowels and weak consonants both for long vowels and for diphthongs (namely *-h* for *-ā*/*-ē*/*-ō* and *-w* for *-ū* in final positions, as well as *-w* for *-au* in a medial position); and the inscriptions from Zinjîrlû have a similar usage (namely *-h* for *-ā*/*-ê*, *-w* for *-ū*, and *-y* for *-ī* in final positions, as well as *-w* for *-au* and *-y* for *-ai* in medial positions). No Phoenician inscriptions, however, contemporary with these have any vowel-signs (Cross & Freedman 'Early Hebrew Orthography' 19, 31, 43–44). Other signs for vowels were apparently an inner-Greek invention; for example, that for *ḥêṯ*, which became (*h*)*ēta*, was used for both *h* and *ē* in some Greek dialects (Jeffery 'Local Scripts of Archaic Greece' 28–29).

The names of the letters may perhaps be taken as pointing in the same direction. While the forms of a few are clearly Phoenician (for example ἰῶτα from *yôḏ*, possibly πεῖ, πῖ (from *pēh*, and perhaps ῥῶ(ς) from *rôš* (cp. Harris 'Gramm. of the Phoen. lang.')), those of others seem to be equally clearly Aramaic (for example, ἄλφα from *'ālef* and βῆτα from *bêṯ*); others cannot be definitely assigned to either language. Further, the final -α may be at any rate partly due to the analogy of the Aram. *-â*, a termination attached to nouns in the so-called 'emphatic state' (although it is not found with the names as usually quoted in their Semitic forms), even if it can equally be explained as an ordinary Greek termination (s. p. 156 n. 2 and note thereto). That the Aram. *-â* is accented but the Gr. -α unaccented is no objection; for the names, while originally furnished with an Aramaic termination, may easily have been assimilated to Greek nouns and treated as such (as are γέεννα and πάσχα). That *'ālef* 'ox' is a Phoenician but not an Aramaic word is no longer a valid objection, as אלפא has now been found in an Aramaic text (Jean & Hoftijzer *Dict. d. Inscr. Sém.* 15). The argument from the names of the letters, then, while it does not prove the Aramaic origin of the Greek alphabet, also does not disprove it.

The Greeks then called their alphabet Φοινικήια γράμματα not because they had consciously got it from the Phoenicians but because they did not ordinarily distinguish them from the Aramaeans, of whom they apparently knew little; for, although a people called Ἄριμοι are mentioned twice in early poetry (Homer *Iliad* ii 783 and Hesiod *Theogony* 304), whether they are in fact the historic Aramaeans or some mythical people is quite unknown. The earliest Phoenician inscription that is known in the West is probably the bowl of Hiram king of Sidon, which was found at Limasol, although its precise date is uncertain (s. p. 107 n. 3); but a number of inscribed potsherds are evidence of a considerable trade advancing westwards, and this may well have brought increasing knowledge of the alphabet to the Greeks and so apprised them of the possibility of turning such an invention to their own use.

The argument, therefore, would seem to show that the Greeks derived the alphabet rather from the Aramaeans than from the Phoenicians and that they did not invent the vowel-system but extended its use to both long and short vowels, having learnt it from the Aramaeans at a time when it had not yet been introduced into the Phoenician alphabet. The scales seem then to be weighted in favour of the Aramaic as against the Phoenician origin of the alphabet, but definitive proof has not yet been found.

**P. 176.** Cp. Albright *ap.* Wright 'The Bible and the Ancient Near East' 350, where the invention of the Greek alphabet is dated in the late 9th or early 8th century B.C.

The early Greek *E*, *Z*, *H*, and *N* resemble most closely the Byblian forms of the corresponding Phoenician letters. The Greek *A* always has the open or looped top first found on a Byblian inscription (Byblos B III) and *M* reflects a form which begins at Zinjîrlû, not being vertical throughout its length but having the top running out to the left side.

The father-in-law of Odysseus is said to have been called both Ἰκάδιος and Ἰκάριος (Aristotle *Poetica* 61b §25); is this difference due to δ having a tail and so being easily confused with ρ in the Cephallenian alphabet (Mr. H. M. J. Loewe in a private communication)? How long archaic forms may have lingered in the backwoods of civilization cannot be said; so, for example, tailless ך, כ persisted into and perhaps after the 8th century B.C. away from the Syrian mainland (Barnett 'Catalogue of Nimrud Ivories' 51–52).

S. on the Greek alphabet further M. Falkner in *Frühgeschichte und Sprachwissenschaft* ed. W. Brandenstein [1948] 110–33 and the literature given in Gelb 'Study of Writing' 267, 294 n. 32.

**P. 178.** The Phoenician centre from which the Semitic alphabet reached Greece was perhaps Poseideion, now älMînâ, on the Syrian coast; and the date, as now generally accepted, was *c.* 750 B.C. (Jeffery op. cit. 5–21); such a date approximates closely enough to that which is here suggested. However, until later examples of the relevant forms of the Phoenician letters are found, any gap can be bridged only by the assumption that experiments in devising a Greek alphabet, which can hardly have been suddenly invented, took a longer time than hitherto supposed and might well have been in progress during a whole century in some bilingual community on the coastal plain.

The dissemination of the alphabet seems to have followed the commercial relations of the principal trading centres in the 7th century B.C. (Drerup *ap.* Carpenter in 'A.J.A.' XXXVII 21); but there is no valid reason for supposing the loss of writings of the 9th–8th centuries B.C. to be very improbable (Carpenter ibid. 26–27). All possible sites are far from having been even sounded or excavated, especially along the Syro-Phoenician coast, where some Greek colony may have used the alphabet long before its passage to the islands or mainland of Greece (s. Jeffery op. cit. 10–12).

**Pp. 178–9.** The adaptation of the symbols for the 'weak letters' to serve as vowel-signs seems to have coincided with the conversion of the Phoenician to the Greek alphabet, which must have been useless without them (Nillson *ap.* Carpenter ibid. 20–21). If this practice grew up *c.* 850 B.C. and was fairly well established *c.* 750 B.C., the Greeks, who derived their own from the 'Phoenician' alphabet at some time between these dates, could not have invented this method of indicating the vowels; it was already in use, so that their contribution, due to the very different nature of their language, was simply to extend the employment of these signs to enable the vowels to be represented independently of the consonants. In any case, their adaptation to this purpose must have coincided immediately with the conversion of the Phoenician to the Greek alphabet, which can have been of no use without them (Nilsson *ap.* Carpenter in 'A.J.A.' XXXVII 20–1).

**P. 179.** The relation of the Phoenician to the Greek names for the sibilant sounds is a difficult problem, of which the following is perhaps a not implausible solution. The Greeks took over the Phoenician letters arranged visually, i.e. to be read, in the original or correct order but did not learn them orally, i.e. in reciting the

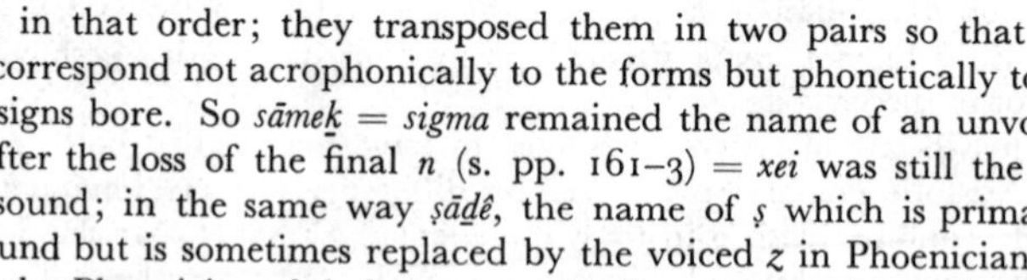

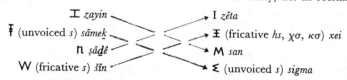

FIG. 108. Phoenician and Greek signs and names for sibilant sounds.

alphabet, in that order; they transposed them in two pairs so that the names came to correspond not acrophonically to the forms but phonetically to the values that the signs bore. So *sāmek̲* = *sigma* remained the name of an unvoiced sound and *šîn* after the loss of the final *n* (s. pp. 161–3) = *xei* was still the name of a fricative sound; in the same way *ṣād̲ê*, the name of *ṣ* which is primarily an unvoiced sound but is sometimes replaced by the voiced *z* in Phoenician words and which in the Phoenician alphabet serves also for two voiced sounds for which the Arabic alphabet has distinct signs, was converted into *zēta* as the name of the voiced Greek *z*, and *zayin* the name of the voiced Phoenician *z* was corrupted into *san* as the name for a sibilant sound of which the nature is unknown but which may at any rate in some dialects have been voiced (Jeffery op. cit. 25–28). That Codex B of the Septuagint represents שׂ (*ś*) once by χς in ρηχς for *rêš* (Ps. cxix [cxviii] 153) and once by σχ in σχεν for *šîn* (Ps. cxix [cxviii] 161) is a curious fact (Nöldeke *Beitr. z. Sem. Sprachw.* 127[2]) which to some extent supports the explanation here given of one of these equations.

The Greek contributions to the alphabet were said to be τὰ δασέα (θ, φ, χ) and τὰ διπλᾶ (ζ, ξ, ψ) and τὰ μακρὰ (η, ω), according to ancient tradition (Irenaeus *Contra Haereses* I XV 4); but in fact ζ was not a Greek invention.

The form of *Φ* may have been based on ק, that of *X* on ח, and that of *Ψ* on ש (Lidzbarski *E.S.E.* II 119–21); alternatively one form of *Φ* has been thought to be based on ט and another on ק (Carpenter loc. cit. 21).

**Pp. 179–85.** A new explanation of the order of the letters is that they are grouped in pairs, each pair representing a biliteral Egyptian word denoting a part of, or an organ in, the human body, as shown in the following table:

| | | | | | | | |
|---|---|---|---|---|---|---|---|
| (1) | אב | *ꜣb* | 'heart, soul' | כל | *qn* | 'bosom, breast' | (6) |
| (2) | גד | *qd* | 'human figure' | מן | *mn* | 'upper thigh' | (7) |
| (3) | הו | *hv* | 'muscle, sinew' | סע | *ś*ʿ | 'gall-bladder' | (8) |
| (4) | זח | *zẖ* | 'blood' | פץ | *pꜣd* | 'knee' | (9) |
| (5) | טי | *tẖy* | 'tongue' | קר | *qr* | 'testicles' | (10) |
| | | | (11) שת *šꜣ.t* internal organ | | | | |

(Weidmüller in *B.D.Bh.* xciv, 24 November 1959, 1–5).

This ingenious scheme is open to serious objections on several scores. First, that the inventor or inventors of the West-Semitic alphabet should have chosen Egyptian words in constructing a mnemonic device for the use of Semitic scribes would seem in the highest degree improbable; it would have been or would soon have become useless for the very purpose for which it was designed. Second, nine pairs are vitiated by dubious or impossible equations; these are *q* = *g* (2) and *k* (6), and *ẖ* (10), *f* = *v* (3), *t* = *ṭ* (5), and *ḏ* = *ṣ* (9). That *q* is equated with *g* (2) and *k* (6) and *ẖ* (10) is enough to show how unscientific the list is. Third, several of the Egyptian words have been misread or misunderstood. So *śẖ*, not *ś*ʿ (8), means 'gall-bladder' and *ẖrwy*, not *qr* (10), means 'testicles'; and the supposed alternative Egyptian forms do not exist and cannot be postulated. Or again *tẖ*, not *tẖy* (5), is the 'tongue' of a balance and is never used for that of a living creature (as the Germ. *Zunge* and the Engl. 'tongue' are used), and *zẖ* is a misreading of *dšr* which is read *dš* in the Graeco-Roman period and means 'red(ness)', only coming to stand for 'blood' in the same late period, long after the naming of the letters of the alphabet. Finally, no such word as *hf* (dubiously written also *ḥv*) 'muscle' is recorded in the dictionaries; is it perhaps a faulty echo of *ḥꜣ* 'mussel' (a kind of shell-fish)?

Only three words (namely *ỉb* 'heart', *mn.t* 'upper thigh', *šꜣ.t* 'internal organ' of some sort) are free from serious objection. So ill-founded a system, therefore, cannot be accepted as a valid explanation of the order of the letters of the alphabet.

Two other explanations of the order of the letters in the Semitic alphabet may here be noted. The first is that the letters represent a didactic poem (Tur-Sinai [Torczyner] in 'J.Q.R.' *N.S.* xli 288–96); but the language and style of the supposed poem are enough to condemn the suggestion. The second is that it is based on the notation of the Sumerian musical scale (Heichelheim in *Epigraphica* xii 111–15; s. Galpin 'Music of the Sumerians' 43–48); but how the West-Semitic inventors of the alphabet can have obtained any knowledge of this scale is not explained.

**P. 181.** The traditional order of the alphabet is confirmed by a number of abecedaries, Ugaritic (s. n. to pp. 182–5), Hebrew (s. p. 116 fig. 70), and Aramaic (Dupont-Sommer in *R.A.* xli 105–6), as well as Greek (s. Hallo in 'J.B.L.' lxxvii 325–37). The Greek, dated *c.* 700 B.C., is so old as to retain *san* in its original place, while the numerical values given to the Greek letters further attest their order. The Aramaic from the Wâdī Ḥamâmât in Egypt, dated in the 5th century B.C., is obscured by the author's attempt to make an intelligible sentence of the letters as alphabetically arranged (Hallo loc. cit. 334). The South-Arabic of the 4th–3rd century B.C. from Timnaʿ reflects the order of the first seven letters of the Ethiopic alphabet but otherwise goes its own way (s. n. to p. 182 n. 1). The Hebrew abecedaries from Murabbaʿât on the NW. side of the Dead Sea represent the traditional order of the alphabet, while they include the final forms of the five letters beside their initial/medial forms (Benoit, Milik and De Vaux 'D.J.D.' ii

[1961] 91–2, 175, 178–9; s. p. 91 for references to literature).

The fact that ע precedes ף/פ in one but follows it in three acrostic poems (Lam. i 16–17, before; ii 16–17 iii 46–51 iv 16–17, after) has been taken as a mark of different authorship (Bentzen 'Introduction to the Old Testament' II 187). The unusual order of the letters in these poems may well be original, although it is contradicted by the Syriac version and is reversed in a number of Hebrew manuscripts (De Rossi); for these may have been altered to conform to the usual order. Further, שׂ seems originally to have preceded שׁ (s. p. 184 n. 3).

The order of the alphabet is further confirmed by the numerical use of the Hebrew letters. The Phoenicians and Aramaeans used ciphers for numbers; one Hebrew weight may have || for '2', but its interpretation is uncertain since no measure is named. Further, the name of the number is commonly spelled out (Diringer *Iscrizioni* 263–90). The Hebrews, however, seem to have employed the letters of the alphabet sometimes as abbreviations for the names of the numbers and sometimes as having numerical value, based on their position in the order of the alphabet already before the time of the Septuagint (s. Driver in *Textus* I 112–131 and IV 76–94 and Aharoni in 'B.A.S.O.R.' CLXXXIV 13–19). For example, its translation of בשנה החמשית by ἐν τῷ ἔτει τῷ ὀγδόῳ (Jer. xxxvi 9, B) rests on an archetype having בשנה הח׳, where ח has been taken as the symbol for 'eight' by the Septuagint but as an abbreviation for חמשית 'fifth' by the Massoretes, and that of בחדש העשירי by ἐν μηνὶ τῷ ἐνάτῳ (Jer. lii 4, B) goes back to one having בחדש ט׳ in which ט׳ = טבת (the 10th month) has been taken as ט׳ = 9 (Zuckerbram in *Melilah* III–IV 6).

So, too, archaic South-Arabian (Sabaean) inscriptions (*c.* 5th century B.C.) have the numbers indicated sometimes by strokes suitably arranged and sometimes by the initial letter of the word designating the required number: for example, *ḫ* for *ḫms* 'five', ʿ for *ʿśr* 'ten', *m* for *m't* 'hundred', and ʾ for *ʾlf* 'thousand' (Höfner *Alt-südar. Gramm.* 14 § 9).

The earliest external evidence for the use of letters as numbers is afforded by coins of the two Jewish revolts (141–136 B.C. and A.D. 66–70), which are dated by years numbered א, ב, ג, ד, ה for '1, 2, 3, 4, 5' according to the years in which they were issued (Madden 'Coins of the Jews' 66–9 and Reifenberg 'Ancient Jewish Coins' 11).

The practice known as 'gematria', however, which is clearly pre-Septuagintal, affords evidence for the use of letters as numbers according to the order of the alphabet in the Old Testament, where several examples of it have been detected (Nestle in 'E. T.' XVII 44–45, Beer *Exodus* [1939] 68–69, and Bertholet *Hesekiel* [1897] 26; cp. Driver in 'Studies presented to S. H. Hooke' 83–84, 86–87 and 'Judaean Scrolls' vii 339, 357–8). This device is found also in the New Testament (Matth. i 17, Rev. xiii 18) and is common in Rabbinic literature; cp. Cornill *Die siebzig Jahrwochen Daniels* [1889] and s. Driver in S. Wagner (ed.) *Bibel und Qumran* [1968] 75–81 (where the printers' transliteration of the Hebrew letters has obscured the sense).

Abbreviations are occasionally found in late Assyrian or Babylonian texts, where, for example, *Siluku* (Seleucus) may be written as *si* and *tašpiltu* as *taš* (Gelb in *B.O.* xv 37); but they are nowhere common except perhaps in texts dealing with technical subjects, in which, for example, *mi* = *minû* 'what?' and *ta* = *taraḫḫu* 'side' (Neugebauer & Sachs 'M.C.T.' 168, 172–3) and *zi-iq* or *zi* = *ziqpu* 'altitude' (Neugebauer *Math. Kt.* I 122 ii 16, 22) occur.

Early Phoenician and Aramaic texts have a small number of abbreviations, chiefly for weights and measures, and for some common articles and commodities; they are also used for names and titles on coins and seals, where the limited space available makes them necessary. In the Old Testament they seem to have been used for words of frequent occurrence, especially those recurring in the same context, for proper names and numbers, for pronouns and particles, and occasionally also for headings and even for quotations; they can generally be recognized from translations deriving from the Massoretic text, especially those of the Septuagint, and may often be invoked to explain words and phrases where the text is corrupt (s. Driver in *Textus* I 112–31 and iv 76–94). One example suffices to illustrate this practice. When Saul is described as בן שנה 'a year old' when he must have been in middle age, an abbreviation may be suspected. The Septuagint's υἱὸς τριάκοντα ἐτῶν suggests בן ש׳ שנה = בן שלשים שנה 'thirty years old' which is found in two Greek manuscripts of the Septuagint (Holmes and Parsons); such a solution of the problem of Saul's age, however, whatever the LXX may have guessed or thought, is not free from chronological difficulties (s. Noth *Geschichte Israels²* [1954] 163). Alternatively בן חמשים שנה = ב׳ נ׳ שנה 'fifty years old' may have been intended (I Sam. xiii 1); the abbreviation here postulated may then be illustrated by בן עש for בן ע(שרין) ש(נה) 'twenty years old' in a Scroll from Qumrân (Milik 'D.J.D.' I 109–10 28A i 27).

**P. 181 n. 6.** E. Hommel *Untersuchungen zur hebräischen Lautlehre* (= *Beiträge zur Wissenschaft vom Alten Testament* XXIII [1917]) 32–3 n. 3, 116; A. Jeremias *Das Alte Testament im Lichte des Alten Orients⁴* (1930) 773–4; H. E. Ettisch *Hebräisch: ein uraltes Hieroglyphen System* (1951) and *Astrologie im hebräischen Alphabet* (1952). S. Gesenius–Kautzsch–Cowley 'Hebr. Gr.' 29.

**P. 182 n. 1.** The South-Arabic list, which is not a true abecedary but a series of stones in a guttering inscribed each with a letter of the alphabet to ensure their arrangement in the proper order, is the following:

| ↾ | Ψ | ⅃ | ? | ⟩ | ⟩ | ⍍ | ⍑ | Ⴤ | ⎮ | ⍑ | ↳ | Ч | ? | Ⴟ | ◊ | ⍑ | ○ |
|---|---|---|---|---|---|---|---|---|---|---|---|---|---|---|---|---|---|
| l | ḥ | m | ? | š | r | ġ | s | h | b | k | n | ḫ | ? | ś | f | ʾ | ʿ |

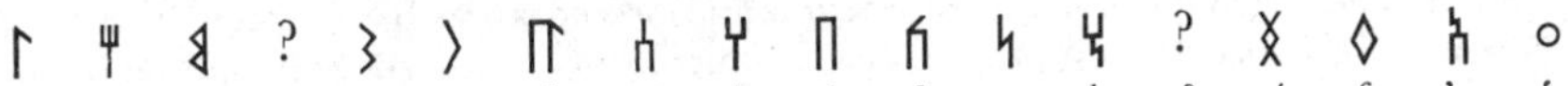

(Hallo in 'J.B.L.' LXXVII 332–4). Obviously the order of the letters here is not dictated by phonetic principles; rather, the signs seem to be arranged, with occasional exceptions, according to their forms. The first sign is the simplest, being little else than a vertical stroke, and the last is a circle, so that an initial tendency to start from strokes and terminate with box-shaped or circular signs may be detected; then they seem to be arranged in groups according to their shapes (namely, m-r, ġ-k, n-ḫ, s-ʿ). Only ḥ seems to be misplaced between l and m and not beside ḫ, which closely resembles it in form.

**Pp. 182–5.** The reason for beginning the alphabet with א is that it is the first letter of the phonetic alphabet, starting from the bottom of the throat instead of the lips.

A tablet recently recovered from Râs-ăšŠamrah gives a complete list of the Ugaritic signs arranged by the copyist in three lines (s. fig. 109).

This list is confirmed by several other abecedaries from Ugarit (Gordon 'Ugar. Handb.' II 172/320 and Virolleaud *Pal. Roy. d'Ugar.* II 199–203; cp. Virolleaud *ap.* Gordon in *Orient.*, N.S. XIX 375⁶ and in *R.A.* XXXVII 34).

These abecedaries show that the traditional order of the letters in the West-Semitic alphabet, which in its Ugaritic form is clearly not acrophonic (Albright in 'B.A.S.O.R.' CXVIII 13–14), is almost if not actually as old as the invention itself of the alphabet (Hallo in 'J.B.L.' LXXVII 335); but it raises interesting questions about the additional sounds not recognized in the Phoenician alphabet and the places which they occupy in the Ugaritic alphabet (ḫ, ẓ, ṣ, ṯ, ġ, ẹ, i, ủ) and why certain other letters occupy places different from those of the corresponding letters in the Phoenician alphabet (š and perhaps ś).

The order of the letters in the Phoenician alphabet is based not on any single, for example the phonetic, principle (Albright in 'B.A.S.O.R.' CXVIII 13–14, where the explanation suggested in the present work is misrepresented) but on three principles, namely the nature of the sound, the form of the sign and the meaning of the name; and the position of the variant or additional letters in the Ugaritic alphabet agrees with one or other of these principles, with a few easily explained exceptions. First, one of these owes its position to the nature of the sound which it represents: the velar *ḫ* is put immediately after the velar *g* which it follows in the phonetic order of the alphabet, and *ẓ̌* follows *n* as consisting of three strokes

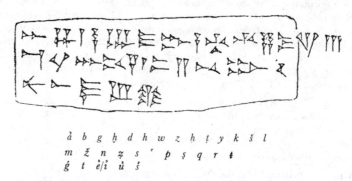

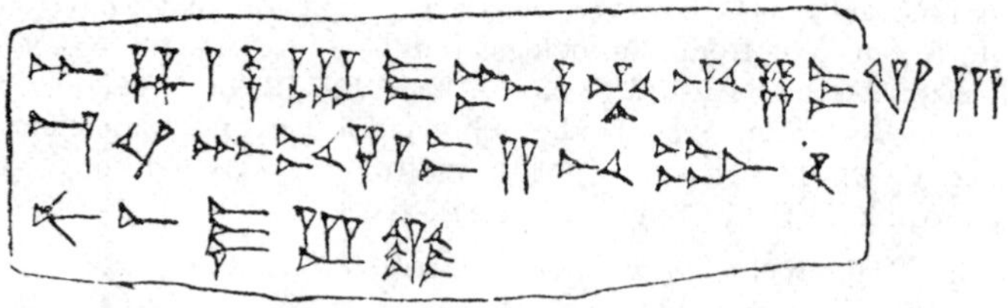

*ả b g ḫ d h w z ḥ ṭ y k š l*
*m ž n ẓ̌ s ʿ p ṣ q r ŧ*
*ǵ t ẻ/ỉ ủ ś*

Fig. 109. Order of signs in the Ugaritic alphabet (s. pl. 46, 2).

more or less facing in the same direction and precedes *s* as both represent sibilant sounds. Others owe their position solely to the form of the signs representing them: thus *š* comes between *k* and *l* since all consist of three strokes hardly differing except in the angles at which they stand; and *ŧ* and *ǵ* are put immediately before *t* as consisting of the same horizontal stroke, though diversified by cross-wedges at different angles. This explanation leaves the places only of '*i/i*' and '*u/u*' and of *ś* unexplained. The first two seem to have been introduced into the alphabet by way of experiment and are therefore not original letters but subsequent additions to the alphabet; they therefore naturally find their place at the very end of the list. Similarly *ś* is superficially a mere variant form of *s*, found in a very few foreign and native words; it may have been intended originally to represent a non-Semitic sound and have been used only accidentally or erroneously in native words (Gordon in *Orient., N.S.* xix 376) and soon discarded as otiose.

There has been some divergence of opinion on the nature of *ả*, *ẻ/ỉ* and *ủ*, whether all three are consonants (Bauer *Alphabet von Ras Schamra* 27–28) or vowels (Friedrich in *Orient., N.S.* xii 14–15), or whether *ả* is consonantal while *ẻ/ỉ* and *ủ* are vocalic (Speiser in 'B.A.S.O.R.' cxxi 17[4]; cp. Gordon in *Orient., N.S.* xix 375). [See now J. Blau and S. E. Loewenstamm in *Ugarit-Forschungen* ii [1970] 19–25.] The only plausible view is that the sign for '*a/a*' originally represented nothing but the glottal stop and that this ' like א then contained no inherent vowel and that it acquired the value of *ả* only when distinct signs for *ẻ/ỉ* and *ủ* were invented, possibly to serve as vowel-signs in Hurrian words consisting solely of vowels (Gordon ibid. 376); if so, the signs for *ẻ/ỉ* and *ủ* were perhaps originally vowel-signs standing respectively for *e* or *i* and *u*, and they carried with them the originally consonantal ' to serve also as a vowel-sign, namely for *a*, in foreign words. This usage, however, was rarely if ever applied in Semitic words; the only possible instance is *nblảt* 'flames' (B ii vi 23, 25, 28, 30), and this can be explained as a strengthened plural form like those with inserted *h* or *w* in various Aramaic dialects. Otherwise, wherever these three signs occur in Semitic words, the corresponding words in the most closely related languages have a consonantal א, whatever the vowel may be.

The need to represent vowels by special signs, however, was not strongly felt and the experiment was not repeated even in the transcription of foreign words by contemporary Semites.

Another question is whether the longer (Ugaritic) or the shorter (Phoenician) alphabet is the original alphabet. Two arguments have been adduced in favour of the longer Ugaritic alphabet. The first is that the additional letters are more likely to have been dropped than inserted, especially as their places would be hard to explain if they were late insertions (Gordon ibid. 374–6); but their peculiar positions would be equally difficult, if not in some cases impossible, to explain if they had been assigned to them in the original alphabet. The second is that, as the Sinaitic alphabet had 27, not 22, phones, the original Semitic alphabet had that number and that the Ugaritic was therefore nearer than the Phoenician to the original alphabet (Albright in 'B.A.S.O.R.' CXVIII 12–13); but this is virtually a *petitio principii*, since no one knows whether the Sinaitic is the original alphabet and in any case the interpretation of the Sinaitic texts is in the highest degree precarious. The question, however, is improper; for the Hebrews recognized in speech but did not write some of the additional sounds, while the speakers of various Aramaic dialects continued to write letters which they had long confused with others in use. There is, therefore, no priority in time of one alphabet over the other, since the same people never use both longer and shorter alphabets; some (Ugaritians, Arabs) felt, others (Phoenicians and Hebrews, Aramaeans and Syrians) did not feel the need to distinguish certain sounds in writing as in speech.

No light is thrown on the order of the alphabet by the device known as א"תב"ש (*'aṯbaš*), whereby names are supposed to have been disguised by substituting the last letter for the first, the next last for the second, and so on; for this is a fiction originally invented to explain two names in the Old Testament which must have remained unintelligible to those ignorant of the Babylonian language till its recovery and decipherment in the 19th century. The first is ששך *Šēšaḵ* (Jer. xxv 26 li 41), which is not such an inversion of the Hebrew בבל *Bāḇel* but the Babylonian *Šišku* or *Šešku*, a neo-Babylonian name of that city (Lauth in *P.S.B.A.* II [1881] 47–8). The second is לב קמי *lēḇ qāmāy* (Jer. li 1) which is supposed to mean 'the heart of them that rise up against me' (R.V., marg.) and as such to stand by a similar inversion for כשדים *Kaśdîm* 'Chaldaeans', as the LXX took it; this has, however, been plausibly explained as an erroneous attempt to make sense of קמבלי *G/Qambulāy*, the name of a powerful Aramaean tribe following a nomadic existence on the Babylonian frontier (Sarowsky in *Z.At.W.* XXXII [1912] 150–1). Ingenious Rabbis have discovered other examples of this mythical figure, equally implausible, in the Old Testament (Buxtorf & Fischer *Lex. Chald. Talm. et Rabb.* [1859] 131).

**P. 183.** Cp. Walters 'Text of the Septuagint' [1973] 172–3 on *dāleṯ* = δέλτος 'door'.

**P. 184 n. 3.** The signs for שׁ and שׂ are not separately represented in the acrostic poems of the Old Testament.

**P. 185.** Also የ ደ (*y-d*). The Ethiopians use *yaman* 'right hand' as the name for *y*, since *'ed* 'hand' begins with the wrong letter (Ullendorff in *Africa* XXI 211).

The Ethiopic method of indicating the vowels by modifying the signs for the consonants is said to be due to Indian influence (Friedrich in *A.S.Bw.*, *N.F.* II 17–18).

The Qatabanian order of the letters, as restored from masons' marks made *c.* 300 B.C., seems to have closely resembled that of the Ethiopic alphabet (Honeyman in *Africa* XXII 136–47).

**P. 186 n. 2.** On the tablets from Ugarit a small wedge separates words, and on the inscription from Karatepe spaces are left between words for the same purpose.

**P. 186 n. 5.** The West-Semitic alphabet not improbably had 27 letters before the 12th century, but whether the letters additional to those of the traditional Hebrew alphabet were *ḫ-ś-ẓ-ṭ-ǵ* is another matter (Albright in 'B.A.S.O.R.' CXVIII 12–13;

cp. Martin in *R.S.O.* xxxvii 175–6); and the Hebrews and presumably the Phoenicians originally distinguished the same or a similar number of phones in speech if not in writing, if the evidence of Greek transliterations of Phoenician and Hebrew letters may be cited. The Septuagint clearly distinguishes *ḥ* (as in *ααθ* = אַחַת) from *ḫ* (as in *Αχαζ* = אָחָז) and ʿ (as in *Αμαλεκ* = עֲמָלֵק) from *ǵ* (as in *Γάζα* = עַזָּה), thus adding two sounds to those represented in the alphabet. They seem also to have tried here and there to distinguish three other sounds, namely *ṣ* (as in *Σιδών* = צִידֹן) and *ḍ* (as in *τσαδη* = צָדֵי) and *ḏ̣* (as in *Ιεσσααρ* = יִצְהָר or *Τύρος* = צֹר), thus adding another two sounds. They may thus have recognized 26 sounds as against the 22 letters of the alphabet. Their transliterations, however, are so unscientific and erratic, and they must have laboured under such difficulties with the deficiencies of the Greek alphabet for such a purpose, that they cannot be trusted as exact guides to the pronunciation which they are trying to reproduce; but these transliterations do seem to show that they must have recognized more sounds than those represented in the Phoenico-Hebrew alphabet. The suggestion has also been made that one of the arrow-heads at Beirut (B 5) may perhaps show an attempt to distinguish *ḏ* (ذ) from *z* (ז) in writing *Yḏr-bʿl*, the name of the owner's grandfather, with a peculiar sign ⵜ); for the name seems to mean 'Baal has dedicated' from *yḏr* = نذر *naḏara* 'devoted' (Martin in *R.S.O.* xxxvii 182–3). Further, the Gr. *θωρ* = Hebr. *šôr* and Arab. *ṯauru*(*n*) 'ox' also suggests that *ṯ* may have been distinguished, as spoken if not as written, at some period or in some districts in the Phoenician dialect from *š* on the one side and from *t* on the other side; but the evidence for this is late. The distinction between שׂ (*ś*) and שׁ (*š*) does not seem to have been original; if it represents a sound-shift between ס (*s*) and שׁ (*š*), it cannot have been original or primitive. Consequently 27 (if not 28) distinct sounds may very well have been recognized in the earliest West-Semitic forms of speech.

**P. 188 n. 5.** S. n. to pp. 134 and 135.

**Pp. 192–3.** Cp. Friedrich *Phön.-Pun. Gramm.* [1951], *Taf.* 1–2 for tables of the Phoenician and Punic alphabets and Rosenthal *Aramaistische Forschung* [1939], *Taf.* 2–4 for the early Aramaic alphabet. Cp. further Naveh 'Development of the Aramaic script' [1970] with twelve tables of symbols; Cross & Freedman 'Early Hebrew orthography' [1952] 45–57; Milik in 'D.J.D.' ii [1961] p. 94 fig. 25 for the old Hebrew alphabet and pp. 72–3 figs. 23–4 for literary and legal as well as cursive scripts; Cross in 'D.J.D.' iii [1962] p. 218 fig. 12 for a table of Herodian and post-Herodian scripts.

**Pp. 194–5.** The suggestion that the Hyksos may have been a Byblian people and that Byblian scribes invented the alphabet (Dussaud in *Syria* xxv 36–52) is chronologically unlikely, if the Semitic interpretation of the Sinaitic inscriptions is correct (s. pp. 96–97), whether the script in these is regarded as standing in the direct line of development from it or as an offshoot from it.

**P. 198.** Another interpretation of the potsherd from Gezer (p. 98 fig. 41), according to the direction in which it is read, is *m* (or *š*) *yd* or *dym* (or *š*), which is supposed to mean 'of . . .' (Obermann in 'A.J.A.' xliv 99–104). This form of the Aramaic particle, namely *d* for *z*, is justified at any rate as far back as *c.* 1400–1350 B.C. by Ugaritic usage; but the suggestion does not carry the interpretation of the text very far!

Another interpretation of the potsherd from Tell-elḤesy (p. 99 fig. 47) is *wld*, namely *wālid* 'father', which is then explained as referring to a deity in a theophorous proper name (Obermann ibid. 93–9); but this usage of the verb is late (s. Tallqvist *Götterepitheta* 87; cp. Deut. xxxii 18, Ps. ii 7), and the proposed reading is almost equally uninformative.

**P. 199.** Another interpretation of the text on the ewer from Lachish (p. 100 fig. 49*c*) is *mtn ṭy* or *ṡy l*[*rb*]*ty* *'lt* 'a gift of tribute to my [lady] 'Elat' (Cross in 'B.A.S.O.R.' CXXXIV 19–21), which makes good sense; cp. Ugar. *mtn tm nkbd. ảlp.š.lỉl* 'a gift, perfect (and) noble, (namely) an ox (and) a sheep for 'El' (Gordon 'Ugar. Hb.' 129 l 2).

**Pp. 200–6.** Ps. ix 7–8. The LXX's *μετ' ἤχοῦς* and Vulg.'s *cum sonitu* for the senseless הֵמָּה 'those' suggest הֹמֶה 'growling' (Kraus after Buhl) or rather הָמָה 'he has growled', a post-Biblical name from al-'Ulā dated in the 2nd century A.D. (Jaussen

הָמָה יהוה (ו)לעולם יָשַׁב כונן למשפט כסאו

as the text may now be read, will mean 'Jehovah has thundered (and) from ages past taken his seat, he has set up his throne (i.e. his court)' *sc.* to try the wicked enemies of his people. Elsewhere the Lord expresses his wrath by roaring (Am. i 2, Joel iv 16, Jer. xxv 30) i.e. by the thunder, but nowhere by growling in the Old Testament; but a similar use of המה 'growled' is found in המהדד 'Hadad-has-growled', a post-Biblical name from al-'Ulā dated in the 2nd century A.D. (Jaussen & Savignac *Miss. Archéol. en Arab.* II *Texte* 642/3, 643/5). Clearly ו before יהוה must be shifted to precede לעולם (unless it is dropped with one Hebr. MS., Kenn.), and the impf. יֵשֵׁב must be corrected to the pf. יָשַׁב (Gunkel; cp. Ps. xxix 10) in parallelism with the other verbs; then והוא in v. 9 marks the change in the subject's attitude (cp. Is. liii 7) from the action of setting up the court to the intention of judging the world. Finally לעולם 'to eternity' must here be translated 'from eternity, long ago'; for, like the Ugar. *l-* (Driver 'Canaanite Myths and Legends' 158), the Hebr. 'ל 'in respect to' can mean either 'to' (*passim*) or 'from', as in כבר היה לעלמים אשר היה מלפנ(י)נו 'that has happened long ago, which has happened before our time' (Eccl. i 10, where the Pesh. has *men ʿālmîn*; cp. Ps. cxi 5, also Pss. xxix 10 cvi 31 and Lachish 3, 10 where לנצח seems to mean 'ever before').

That the Lord takes his seat before setting up his throne reverses the natural order of his actions (cp. Is. xvi 5); but such a *hysteron proteron* is not unexampled in Hebrew poetry (cp. Ps. ix 8 xliii 1).

Ps. ix 18. That 'the wicked shall return to Sheol', where they have not yet been, makes no sense; the verb must be read יָשִׁיבוּ 'they shall rush headlong', from Hebr. שיב = Arab. *sâba* (*y*) 'flowed; went quickly, rushed madly hither and thither'. This verb may be recognized in such other passages as כלה שׁב במרצותם 'every one running wild in headlong career' (Jer. viii 6; s. Driver in 'H.T.R.', N.S. XXVII 105; cp. Aq.) and ישיבו < ישובו לערב 'they run wild towards evening' (Ps. lix 7, 15; s. Thomas 'Revised Psalter' 22). The same idea is found in a similarly misunderstood passage, namely in כצאן לשאול שָׁתוּ < שַׁתּוּ 'like sheep they plunge headlong into Sheol' (Ps. xlix 15), where the verb is an otherwise unknown Hebr. שָׁתָה = Arab. سَتَا (*satâ*)' 'hurried', with which the Arab. سَدَى (*sadā*) 'went headlong with long strides, bolted' is perhaps cognate.

Ps. ix 10; x 1. Not 'in times of trouble' (R.V.); s. Meek in 'J.B.L.' LXVII 236–8.

Ps. x 3. The position of מְהַלֵּל or מְהֹלָל and בֹּצֵעַ as two parallel circumstantial participles describing the רָשָׁע of the preceding verse and anticipating the finite verb which follows is not unparalleled (cp. Gen. xlix 11).

The force of the suffix with תאות נפשו can be carried through to do duty also with רֶשַׁע in the following stich (s. 'J.R.A.S.' N.S. LXXV [1948] 164–5).

Ps. x 6–7. Clearly אֲשֻׁרוֹ לא־ברע אלה 'his course does not falter in any misdoing' or 'for any misfortune' constitutes a half-verse. If then it is rightly put after יחילו דרכו בכל־עת in v. 5, clearly לא . . . אלה must mean something similar to יחילו; consequently the Hebr. אלה may here perhaps be equated with the Arab. أَلَا *defuit minus faciens quam oportuit, officium non implevit, impar fuit* (Freytag).

(Cp. also أَلَّى *tardus fuit, cunctatus fuit, desiit, cessavit* (Freytag)). This verb has long been recognized as occurring in the O.T. (1 Sam. xvii 39; s. 'J.T.S.' xxxiv 33), but its rarity has caused it to be overlooked here and to be confused with אָלָה 'adjuration' and transferred to the following verse through incorrect association with מרמות 'deceitful thoughts' and תך 'oppression'. The position of the negative phrase, though rare, is found occasionally elsewhere (e.g. Deut. viii 9 Ps. xlix 18 Jb. xxxiv 23).

Ps. x 7–11. Cp. Lam. ii 16–17 iii 46–51 iv 16–17 and Prov. xxxi 25–6 (LXX), where too the positions of ע and פ in the alphabet are reversed; but the reason for the variation in the order is unknown (s. Kautzsch & Cowley, 'Hebr. Gr.' 29[3]).

**P. 207.** The use of קֵרַב 'presented (a plea)' and הִגִּיד 'stated (a case)' in court elsewhere in the Old Testament (Is. xli 21–22) supports the suggestion that כמו־נגיד אקרבנו means 'as a statement (of my case) I would present it (in court)' (Jb. xxxi 37); cp. לכל־נגיד 'on every point set forth for discussion' (1 Chron. xiii 1).

**P. 208** on Ps. cx 1–7. Presumably אים 'terrible' may have had a colloquial sense, like the Engl. 'terrific' (cp. Ct. vi 4, 10; s. Goitein in 'J.S.S.' x 220–1); but the suggestion is as much a counsel of despair as is Ἀρχιερεὺς Μέγας, in which A–I–M may be thought to reflect the Hebr. '–*Y*–*M* (cp. 1 Macc. xiii 42, where the title of 'great high-priest' is given to Simon). The whole idea is at bottom highly improbable (s. Driver in *Sefer Segal* 30*–31*).

# PLATES

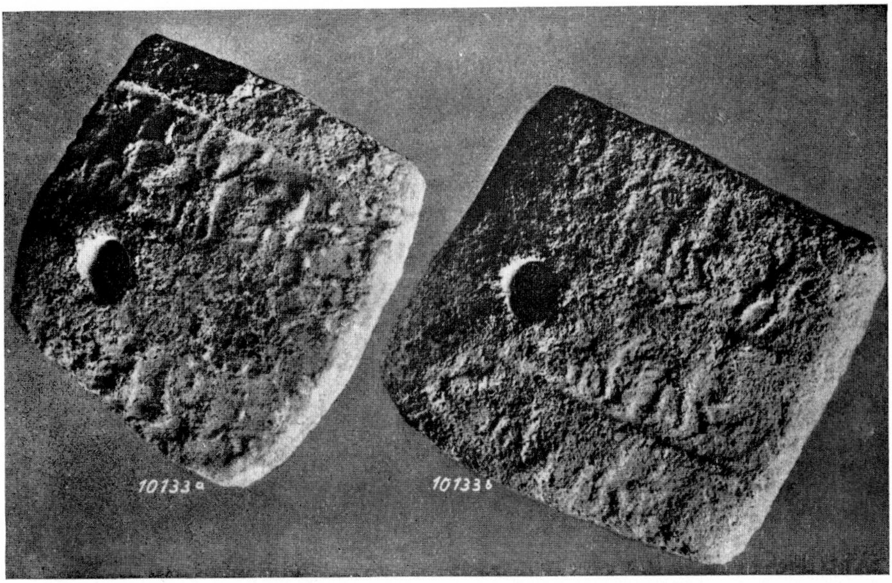


1. Primitive tablet with impression of seal and numerical marks from Uruk

2. Earliest pictographic tablet from Kish

3. Tablets from Uruk IV

Obverse

Edge

Reverse

Tablets from Uruk IV

1. Tablet from Uruk III

2. Hoffmann tablet

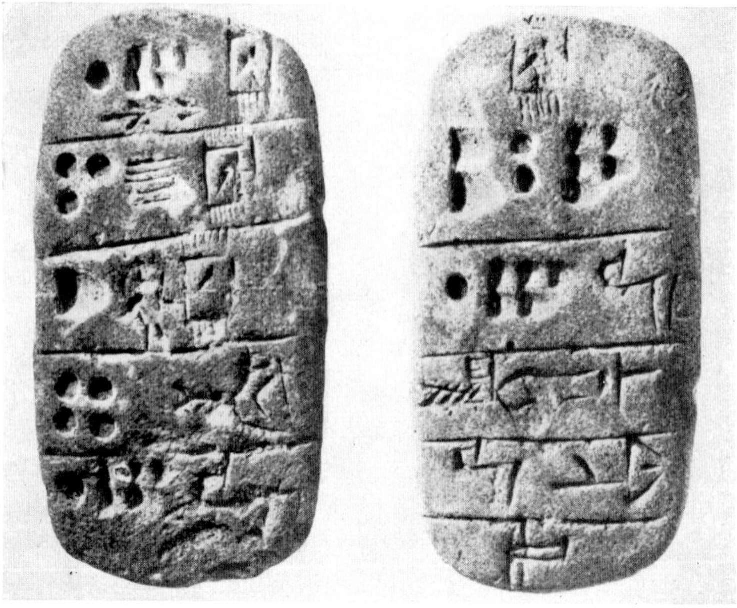

Obverse Reverse

Edge Obverse Reverse

Tablets from Jamdat Nasr

Tablets from Ur

Obverse

Reverse

1. Economic text from Shuruppak

Obverse

Reverse

Obverse

Reverse

2. Scholastic texts from Shuruppak

1. Archaic tablet of stone

Obverse

Reverse

2. Tablet of stone from Uruk

1.Sumerian statue with vertical inscription

2. Assyrian relief with horizontal inscription

A. Accadian seal

B. Neo-Assyrian seal

C. Middle-Assyrian seals with horizontal legends

Seals with vertical and horizontal legends

Tags with Sumerian legends, imprints of seals and marks of thumb-nails

1. Amulets of stone

2. Amulet of clay

3. Hepatoscopical text on liver-shaped tablet

4. Inscribed bracket

Obverse Reverse

1. Tablet (above) with case (below) showing impressions of seals

2. Tablet in case

1. Scribe's finger-marks on the edge of an Old-Babylonian tablet

Obverse

Reverse

Left edge

Lower edge

Upper edge

2. Impressions of seals running over the duplicate text on an unopened Old-Babylonian case-tablet or envelope

Obverse

Reverse

Edges

1. Neo-Babylonian deed of sale with conventionalized marks of thumb-nails on the edges

2. Imprint of the fringe of a garment on the edge of a tablet

Obverse

Reverse

1. Neo-Babylonian lease of land written lengthwise across the tablet

2. Golden disks of Shalmaneser III with circular cuneiform legend

1. Astronomical tablet

2. Map of the known world

3. Drawing on a clay-tablet

1. Babylonian tablets with Aramaic endorsements

2. Babylonian inscription on stone with Aramaic summary

1. Clay-tablet with Greek transliteration of Babylonian words

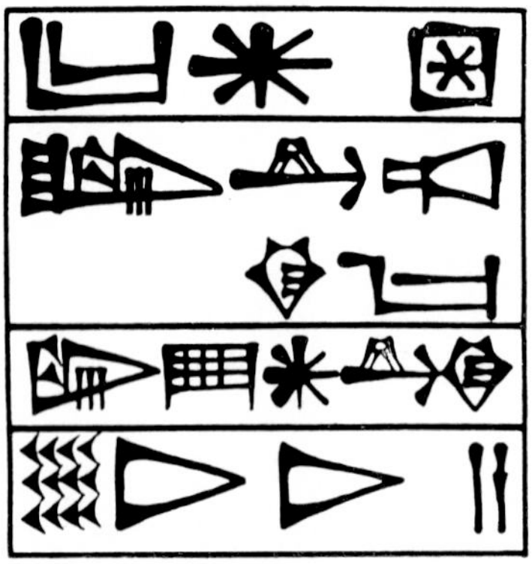

A. Original text

3. Neo-Babylonian squeeze of Old-Accadian tablet

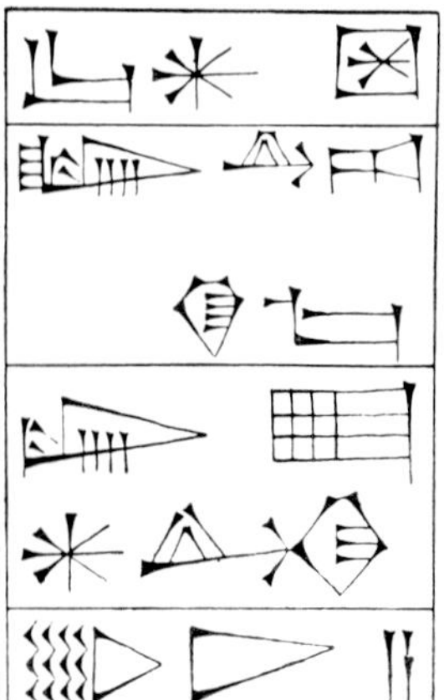

B. Late copy

2. Archaic Sumerian inscription

4. Cancelled tablet

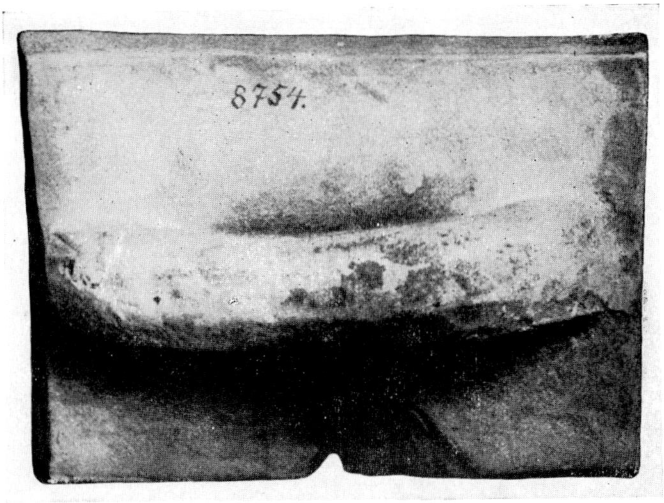


1. Handle of stamp for multiplying copies of inscriptions on bricks

2. Stamp with inverted text for reproduction by impression on clay-bricks

1. Clay showing pattern of cloth

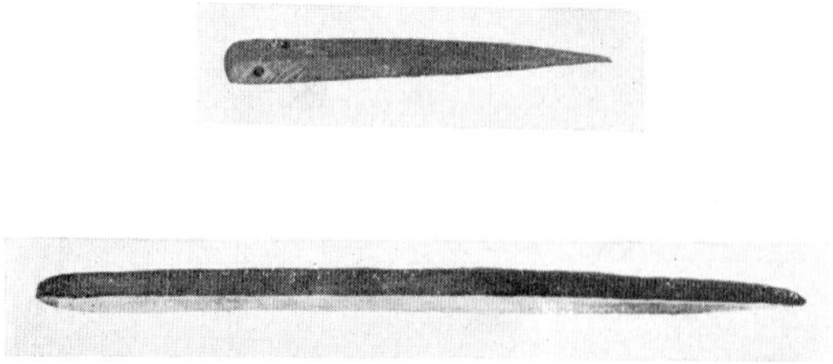

2. Suggested tracer (above) and stylus (below) from Kish

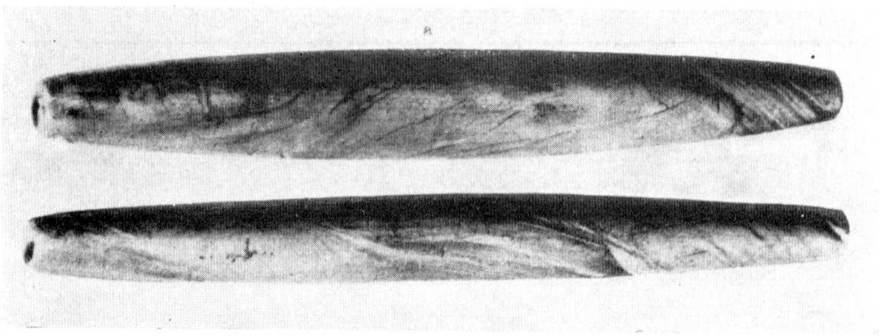

3. Suggested stylus-holders from Uruk

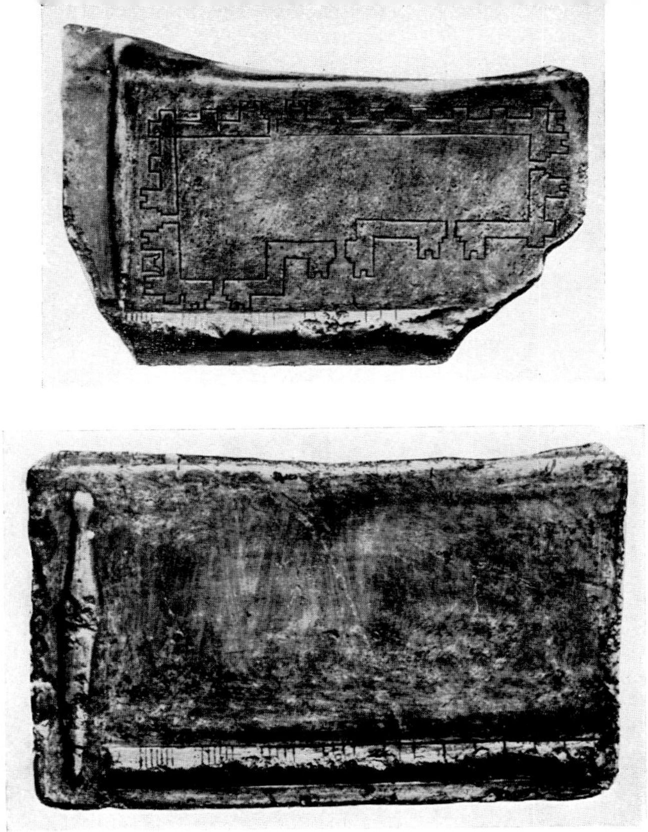

1. Babylonian plan (above) with surveyor's tracer and measuring rod (below) carved on stone

2. Stylus in natural form on a Middle-Babylonian boundary-stone

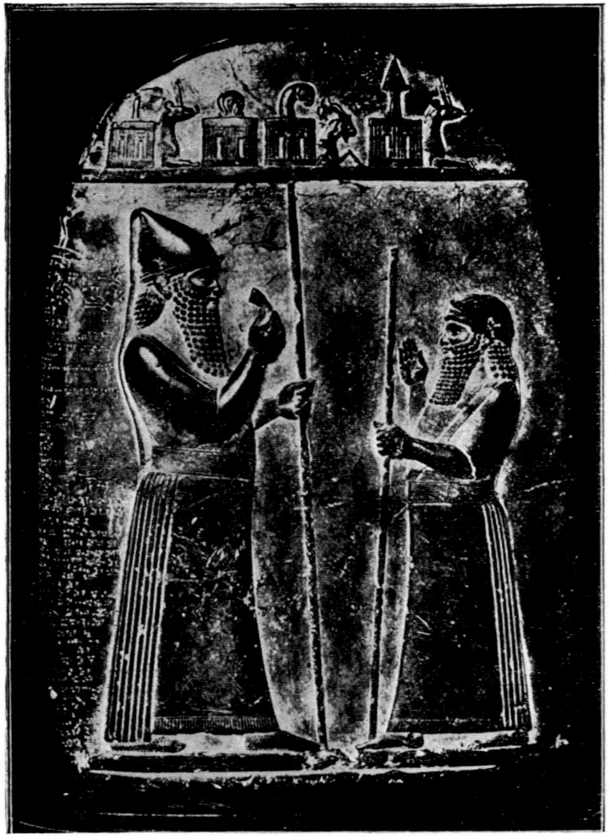

1. Conventionalized single stylus on a base or throne

2. Conventionalized double stylus on a base or throne

1. Learner's exercise in making cuneiform signs

2. Assyrian scribes of Tiglath-Pileser III writing out lists of prisoners

Assyrian scribes of Sennacherib writing out lists of prisoners

Assyrian writing-boards of ivory, reconstructed

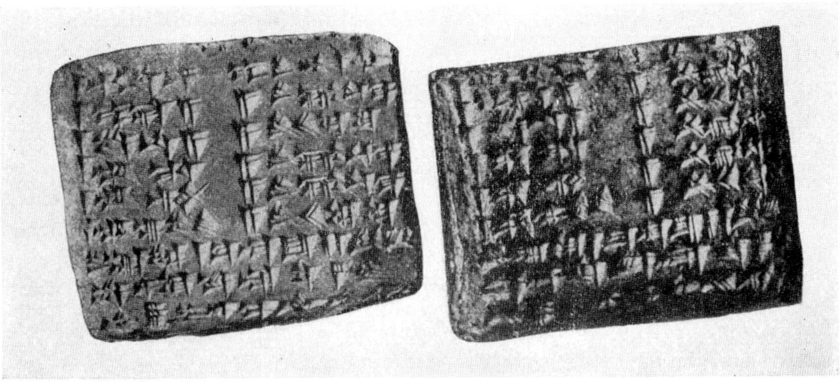

A B

1. Modern copy (A) of ancient tablet (B) made by Messerschmidt

A

B

C

D

E

2. Modern copies of ancient tablet (A) made with instruments of Zehnpfund (B) and De Morgan (C) and with Clay's square-ended (D) and bevel-ended (E) instruments

1. Ruined temple-library at Nippur

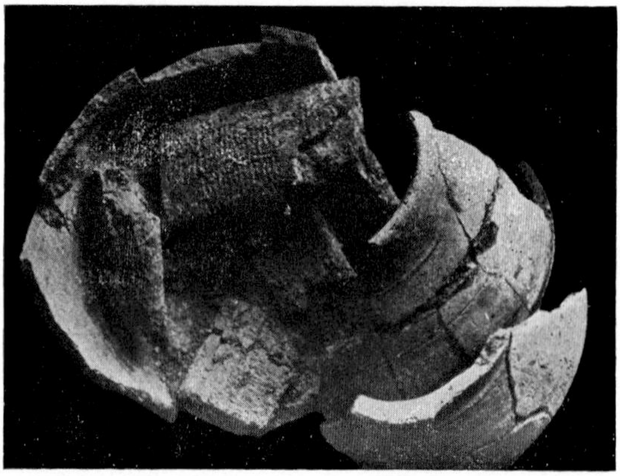

2. Jar containing tablets

3. Chest for tablets

1. Scholars' benches in a temple-school

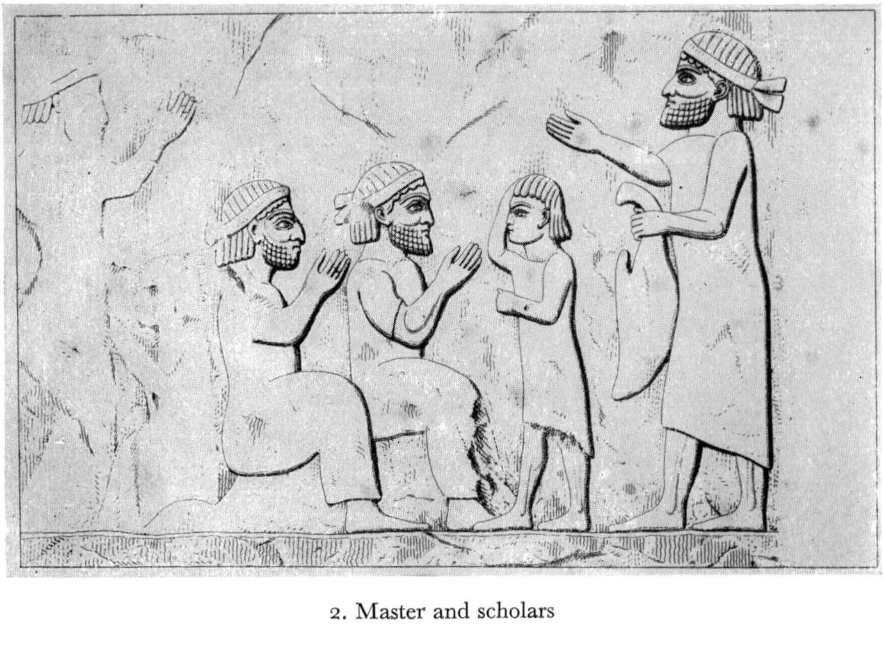

2. Master and scholars

Papyrus pulled and stripped by ancient Egyptians

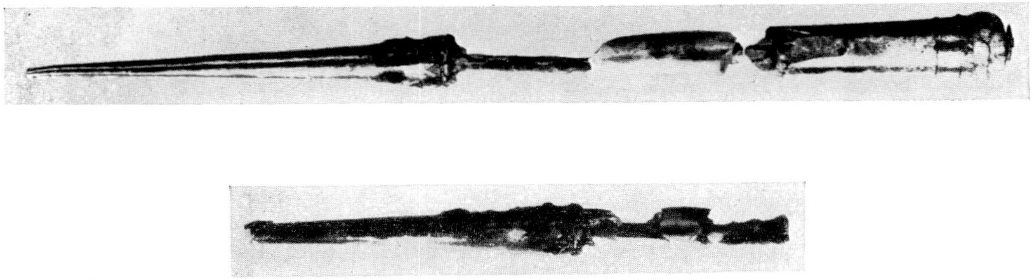

A. From a Syrian grave

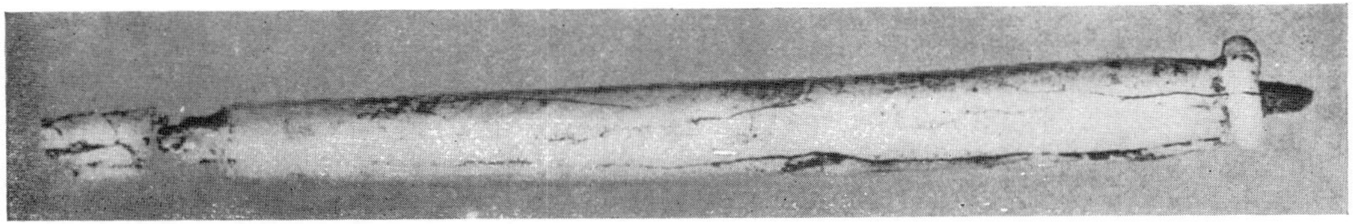

B. From a grave at Megiddo (enclosed in glass-paste)

Supposed writing implements of bronze

Back Front

A B

Egyptian writing outfits of (A) alabaster and (B) ivory

1. Aramaean scribe holding Egyptian writing outfit

2. Supposed ink-pot with pens or pen-rack over an Aramaic inscription

1. Marked objects from Moab

2. Scored pebbles from Sidon

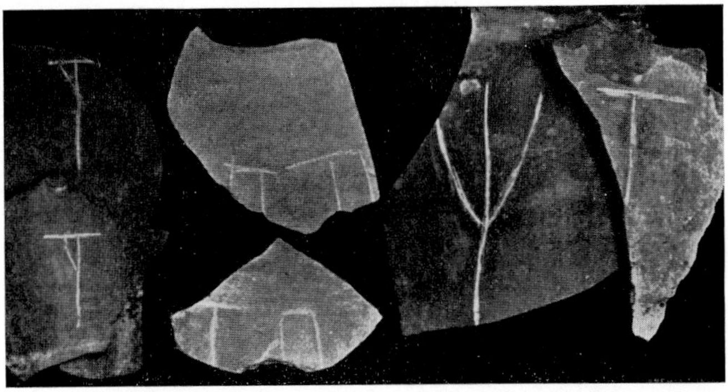

1. Prehistoric Egyptian pottery with foreign marks

2. Egyptian pottery of the XIIth–XVIIIth dynasties with foreign marks

1. Stele from Gebal

2. Plaque from Gebal

Two inscriptions in unknown languages

1. Slab of stone

2. Spatula of bronze

3. Stele of stone

Fragments of pseudo-hieroglyphic inscriptions

Pseudo-hieroglyphic inscription from Gebal

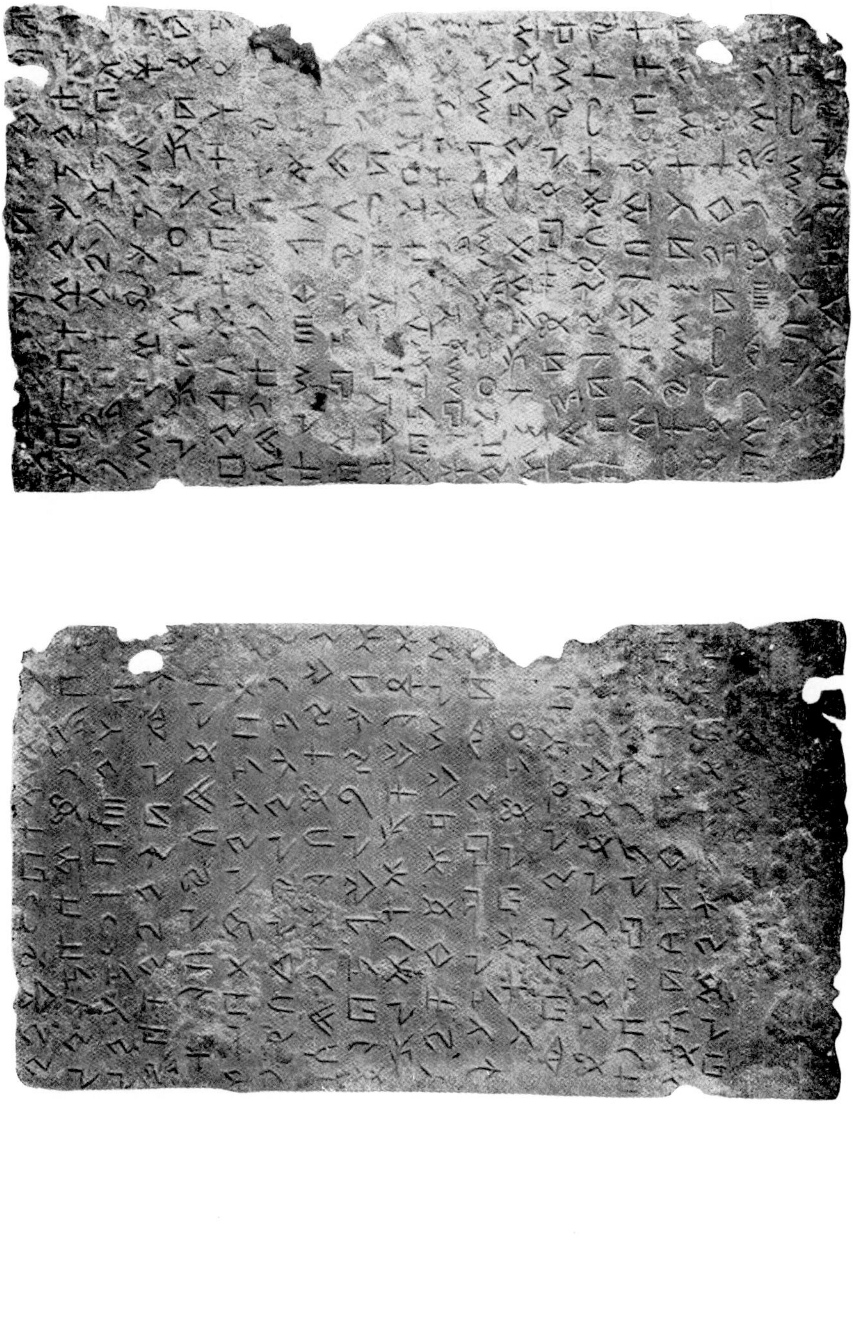

Pseudo-hieroglyphic inscription from Gebal

1. Inscribed [*t*]*nt l–b'lt* 'gift for Baalat'

2. Inscribed *tnt* 'gift'

Sinaitic inscriptions

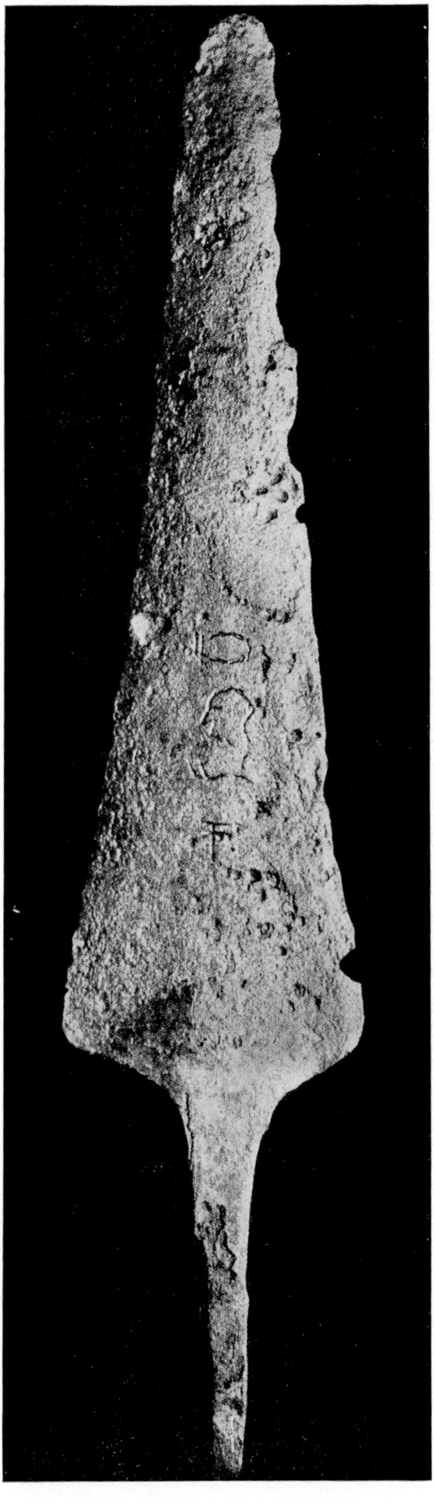

Inscribed dagger from Lachish

Early potsherd from Beth-Shemesh

1. Bowl from Lachish

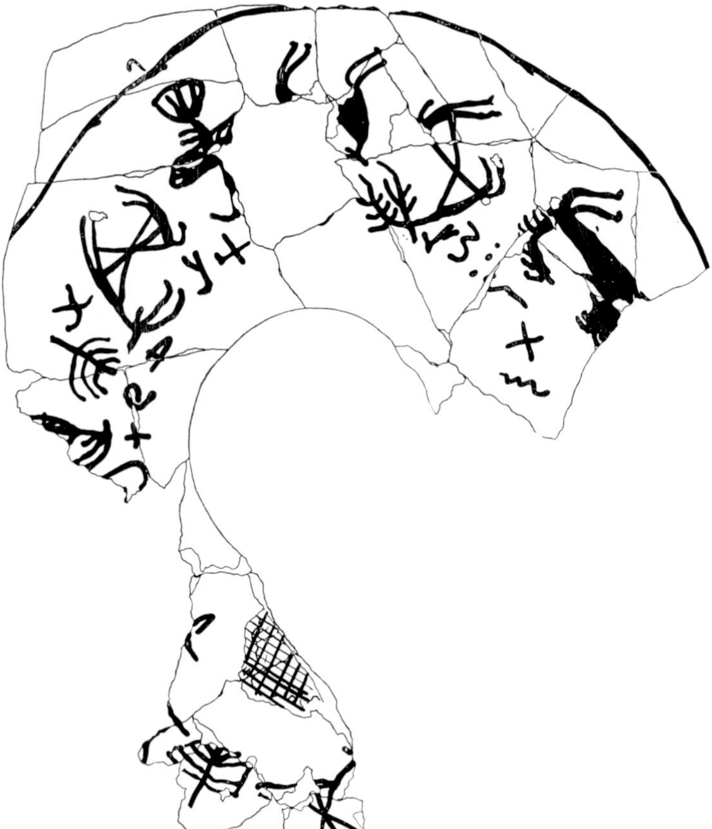

2. Fragments of ewer from Lachish

1. Babylonian letter from the governor of Ashkelon to the king of Egypt

2. Neo-Babylonian tablet from Gezer

1. Tablets *in situ* at Ugarit

2. Tablet from Ugarit

1. Inscribed axe-heads from Ugarit

2. Cuneiform alphabet from Ugarit

1. Fragmentary Ugaritic-Accadian alphabet (obverse side)

2. Fragmentary Ugaritic-Accadian alphabet (reverse side)

1.

2.

3.

Proto-Sinaitic or proto-Arabian inscriptions from Deir-ʿAllā in Transjordan

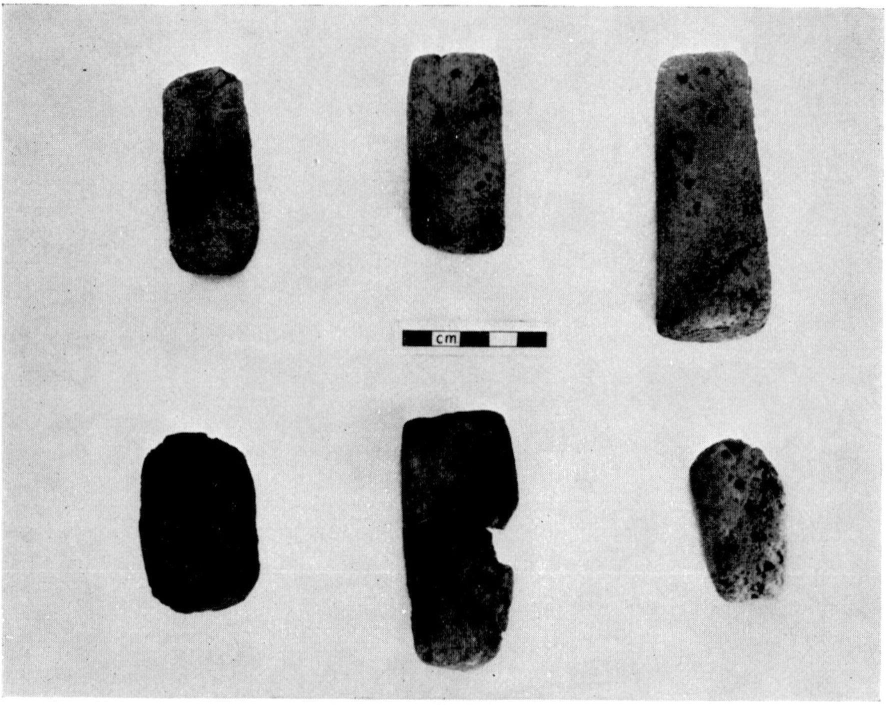

1. Uninscribed but dotted clay-tablets from Deir-'Allā

2. Inscription of Shaphaṭbaʿal

Earliest Phoenician inscriptions

1. Inscription of 'Abdâ

2. Inscription of Aḥiram

Inscription of Aḥiram

1. Inscription of Yeḥimilk

2. Spatula of ʿAzarbaʿal

1. Hebrew calendar from Gezer

2. Hebrew inscription from the Pool of Siloam

1. Jar of a royal standard of capacity with Hebrew text

2. Potsherd with marks or letters, possibly scribbled by a child

1. Royal stamps on jars

2. Private stamps on jars

Hebrew stamps

Imprints of Israelite seals with Hebrew legends

1. Hebrew seal and its imprint in clay, enlarged

2. Imprint of a Hebrew seal on the front and marks of the papyrus on the back of a clay-sealing

3. Hebrew letter on a potsherd from Lachish

1. Aramaic monument with the text running across the relief

2. Aramaic inscription above a relief

Aramaic inscriptions

1. Aramaic political letter on a potsherd from Asshur

Obverse

Reverse

2. Aramaic notes on a clay-tablet

1. Assyrian seals with Aramaic legends

2. Papyrus with Judaeo-Aramaean letter from Egypt

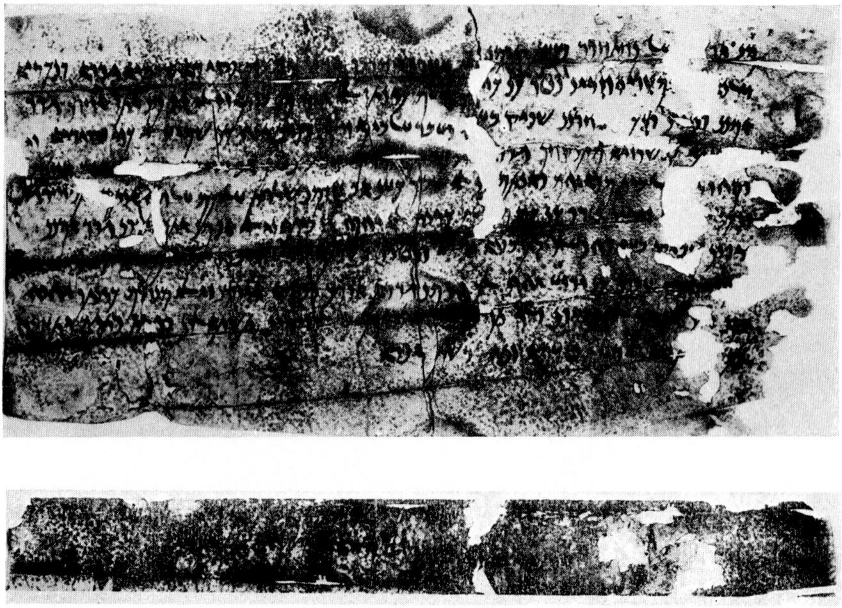

1. Aramaic letter on leather

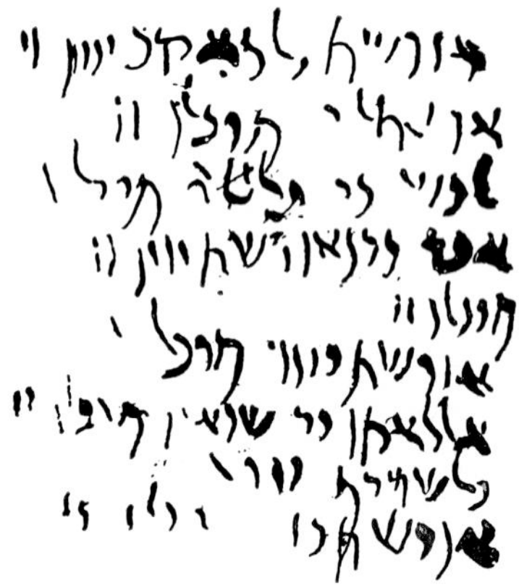

אנושת בלסאקב זוזן ||

אנושתלי מובלן ||

׳בש בר בלטי מובל |

אב- נדנאנושת זוזן ||

מובלן ||

אנושתוצר מובל |

אללאתן בר שוארדן מובלן ⁝

בלשמדן זוז |

אנושתבנ ____ מובלן ||

2. Aramaic text on a potsherd from Nippur: original text with transcription into Modern Hebrew letters

1. Inkwells from Qumrân

2. Jars for storing documents from Qumrân

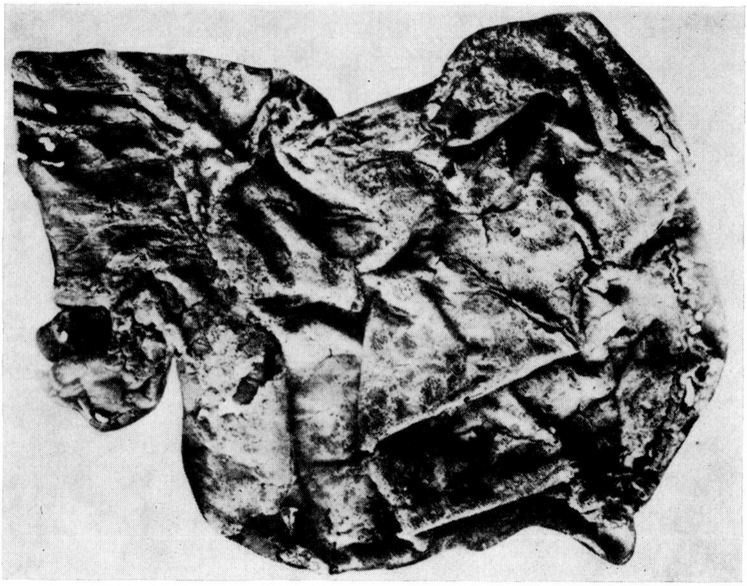

A

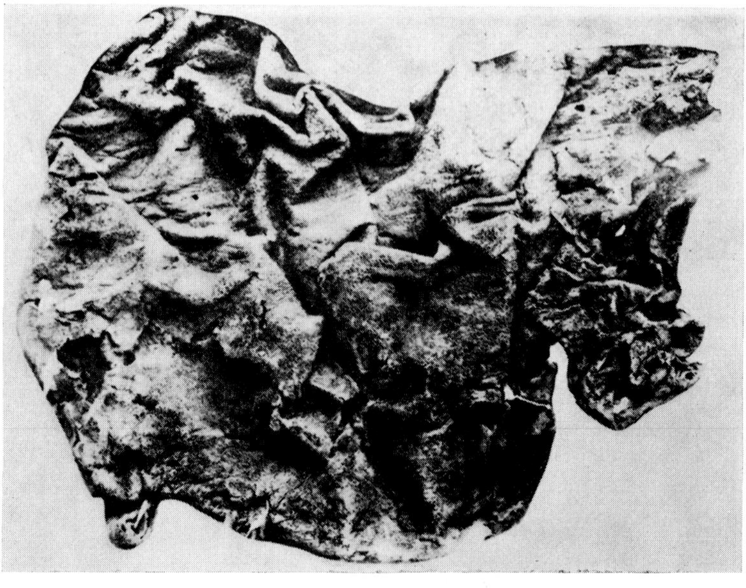

B

Achaemenid post-bag for official mail. A recto; B verso

Supposed writing tables from Qumrân

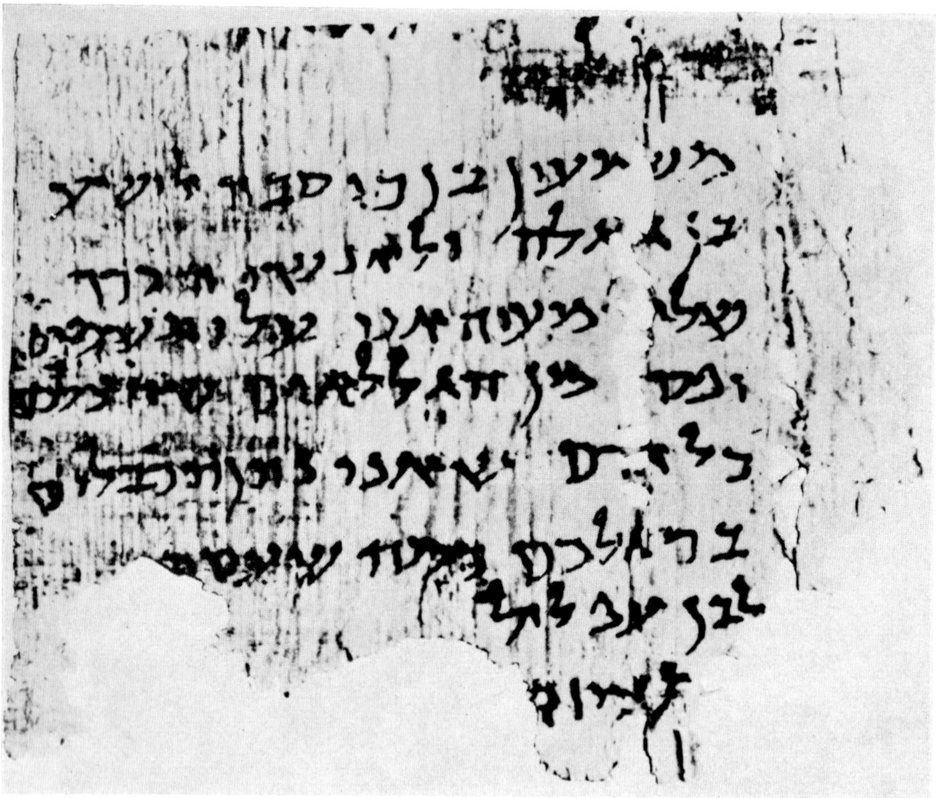

A

משמעון בן כוסבה לישע
בן גלגלה ולאנשי הברך
שלום מעיד אני עלי ת שמים
יפס[ ] מן הגללאים שהצלכם
כל אדם שאני נתן ת כבלים
ברגלכם כמה שעסת[י]
לבן עפלול
[ש]מעון ב[ן כוסבה] על [נפשה]

B

Hebrew letter from Simeon son of Kôsēbāh to Yēšūa' son of Galgulāh: (A) Original text and (B) transcription into modern Hebrew letters